The Time Traveler's Guide to Regency Britain

THE
TIME TRAVELER'S GUIDE TO

Regency Britain

A Handbook for Visitors to 1789–1830

IAN MORTIMER

PEGASUS BOOKS
NEW YORK LONDON

THE TIME TRAVELER'S GUIDE TO REGENCY BRITAIN

Pegasus Books, Ltd.
148 West 37th Street, 13th Floor
New York, NY 10018

Copyright © 2022 by Ian Mortimer

First Pegasus Books cloth edition April 2022

ISBN: 978-1-64313-881-7

10 9 8 7 6 5 4 3 2 1

Printed in the United States of America
Distributed by Simon & Schuster
www.pegasusbooks.com

For my cousin, Stephen Read, and his wife, Edori Fertig,
with much love

Contents

Acknowledgements

Writing a *Time Traveler's Guide* is not an easy undertaking and, of the four now completed, this has been by far the hardest, due to the greater scale and complexity of the society in question. I am therefore enormously grateful to all those who have assisted me over the four years I have been engaged on this project.

I am more indebted than ever to my editor, Jörg Hensgen. His painstaking work on the massive and unwieldy first draft deserves the very highest praise. If ever there is an Editors' Corner in Westminster Abbey, he deserves a prominent place in it.

I would also like to thank Stuart Williams for commissioning this book and for being so patient in waiting for it to be delivered; and Joe Pickering, Tom Drake-Lee, Lauren Howard and all the stalwart staff at The Bodley Head and Vintage who have helped with my books over the years. A similar debt of gratitude is owed to my agent, Georgina Capel, and the staff at her agency, particularly Irene Baldoni and Rachel Conway, without whom I could not do this job of thinking and writing about the past. Thank you too to Mandy Greenfield for copy-editing this book and to Peter McAdie for proofreading it.

Several specialist readers and advisors have also helped. I would particularly like to hear a round of applause for Euan Clarke, who taught me history at Eastbourne College in the early 1980s, little realising that it was to become a job for life. He read through the bulk of the first draft and identified a number of points where improvement was possible. Dr Margaret Pelling helped to tighten up my medical-history chapter, and Professor Jonathan Barry made several valuable suggestions concerning passages in the central portion of the book. Obviously any remaining errors and ambiguities are entirely my fault. I'd like also to thank Gary Calland, who kindly gave me a copy of his book on the debtors' prison in St Thomas, Exeter; Dr

Greg Roberts, for his inspiring and informative Twitter stream and specific advice on a certain fig leaf mentioned in chapter 2; and Sir Eric Anderson, who generously sent me a copy of his edition of Sir Walter Scott's diary and inspired me to think further about Scott and the nature of historical fiction in the Regency period.

My largest debt of gratitude is, of course, to my wife, Sophie. There must have been times when she despaired this book would ever be completed, like an early nineteenth-century reformer wondering whether the Reform Bill was ever going to be passed or slavery was ever going to be abolished. But like Lord Grey and William Wilberforce, she stuck at it and continued to support me until the job was done. I am enormously grateful to her for all her encouragement.

Ian Mortimer
Moretonhampstead, Devon

The most ordinary articles of domestic life are looked on with some interest, if they are brought to light after being long buried; and we feel a natural curiosity to know what was done and said by our forefathers, even though it may be nothing wiser or better than what we are daily doing or saying ourselves. Some of this generation may be little aware how many conveniences, now considered to be necessaries and matters of course, were unknown to their grandfathers and grandmothers.

James Edward Austen-Leigh, *A Memoir of Jane Austen* (1869)

Memory is not a book where things and events are recorded but rather a field where seeds grow, come to maturity and die.

Louis Simond, *Journal of a Tour and Residence in Great Britain* (1815)

Author's Note

This book is about the island of Great Britain – England, Wales and Scotland – between 1789 and 1830. I refer to the whole of this period as 'the Regency', in line with most other historians, literary critics and antiques experts. Readers should be aware, however, that the official Regency lasted only from 1811 to 1820, when Prince George ruled instead of his mentally ill father, King George III. The starting date for this longer Regency is set by two factors. First, the prince's interim rule was initially proposed in Parliament in February 1789, and although on that occasion his father recovered his senses, the prince was thereafter the Regent-in-waiting, in case the king fell ill again. Of course his influence only grew when he succeeded to the throne as George IV in 1820. The second reason to begin in 1789 is that the French Revolution broke out in the summer of that year, raising profound questions about constitutional reform in Britain as well as on the Continent. As for the end of the period, this is also marked by the question of reform. George IV hated the very idea of constitutional change, largely as a result of the fate of the French royal family. He thus did all he could to thwart it. It was only after his death that the government of the day was free to draft the much-needed Reform Bill and set about tackling some of the social issues raised by the French Revolution. Hence the terminal point of the period is set by the king's death, on 26 June 1830.

Introduction

On Thursday 28 January 1790, the Reverend Thomas Puddicombe brushed the dirt from his hands and returned to his vicarage in the village of Branscombe, on the South Devon coast. The ceremony at which he had just officiated was, in many ways, a routine one. The words of the burial service were time-honoured and familiar; the sombre dress of those attending was prescribed by custom, their grief unsurprising. No less ordinary was his final duty that day, which was to record the date and the name of the deceased in the parish register. However, when he sat down at his desk and dipped his quill in the ink, he did not write an ordinary entry. He added the cause of death, as follows:

> White, John, aged 77. This man lost his life by a very trifling accident: paring his toenail with a penknife a little too close, so as just to draw blood: it rankled, and a mortification coming on, carried him off in a few days.

Anyone who is familiar with English parish registers will be surprised at this level of detail. But Mr Puddicombe often wrote something about the manner of his parishioners' deaths. After Joseph Hooke, the thirteen-year-old son of a local farmer, met with an accident in 1803, the vicar felt obliged to record that the lad 'was run away with by a spirited horse, fell at the corner of the lane by Hangman's Stone; was dragged the distance of half a mile and found dead in the lane a little way above Higher Watercombe'. And when Jane Toulmin, a twenty-five-year-old woman, drowned herself in May 1798, he wrote three-quarters of a page about the last two days of her life, ending with a description of how:

Before she quitted her sister's house, she put out what money she had, and left it in her bedroom and, in this state, without a sixpence in her pocket, she wandered about till Tuesday morning, the day on which, it is to be feared, she put an end to her existence. She was seen at Beer walking very fast up Common Lane between three and four o'clock; and about a quarter past 5 o'clock she was discovered in the water by one John Parrett, a carpenter.

When you read such passages, the world they create doesn't quite chime with our picture of the Regency – the fine houses, the costumes and the carriages. But, of course, country churchyards, horse-riding accidents and young women in a state of distress are also part of the period. And every detailed entry in Thomas Puddicombe's burial register raises questions. Was it usual for people to pare their toenails with a penknife in 1790? Were riding accidents like Joseph Hooke's common? As for poor Jane Toulmin, did people in the 1790s have an understanding of mental illness? You won't find the answers in the pages of a Jane Austen novel: yet they are as revealing of the real world in which she lived as the complex interplay of the characters in her books.

Mr Puddicombe's descriptive burial-register entries abruptly come to an end in 1812. From then on, he was officially prevented from composing them. This was not because he had done anything wrong but because in that year the government imposed a printed form for recording the details of a burial. Each page consisted of a series of boxes in which the officiating minister was required to write the deceased's name, age, place of residence and date of burial – and nothing else.

This shift, from effusive individualism to government-imposed standardisation, is indicative of wider changes. For many people in the 1860s the Regency seemed like the last age of true freedom before the regulation of society started in earnest. The Great Reform Act of 1832 signalled the beginning of the end of the political domination of the aristocracy and landed gentry. In 1833, the Factory Act set limits on the number of hours that children could work each day. That same year, slavery was abolished throughout the British colonies. In 1834 the gibbeting of murderers came to an end. The once-common sight of public executions became rare as abolitionists argued against the death penalty with increasing success. Cruel sports such as cock-fighting and bear-baiting were outlawed in 1835. The compulsory state registration of births, marriages and deaths began in 1838. The standardisation of the screw thread by Joseph Whitworth was introduced in 1841, paving the way for mass production. From the mid-1840s, the telegraph enabled messages to be sent instantly over long distances. Trains replaced the regular mail coaches and stagecoaches, rendering highwaymen a thing of the past. Photography started to rival painting as the most common means of recording scenes and portrait images. On top of all these things, a new morality swept across society in the early Victorian period, limiting people's freedom of behaviour. Attitudes to adultery, gambling and unpaid debts especially hardened. You can see why those who looked back from the 1860s saw their Regency forebears as an unfettered and wild bunch, among whom Lord Byron was not the only man who was 'mad, bad and dangerous to know'. It had been a time when gentlemen and ladies, beggars and clergymen, soldiers and tramps, employers and courtesans could all pretty much behave as they saw fit, in a world that gleamed with gold and heroism, drink and sex, excitement and opportunity.

Our own impressions of the years from 1789 to 1830 are not that different. Today, the period is still seen as a time of exuberance and unchecked bad behaviour. Indeed, we consider the conduct of the upper classes to have been particularly immoral, on account of the self-indulgence of the Prince Regent and his companions. The inscription on the Ancient Greek temple of Apollo at Delphi might have instructed the wise to do 'nothing in excess' but the classically educated English upper classes appear to have taken it as a challenge – to do *everything* in excess. Hence you have a royal court of rakes, dandies and hellhounds, all stuffing themselves with rich food, drinking huge amounts of port and gambling away fortunes until the early hours, at which point they would either go to bed with their mistresses or collapse untidily around their mansions – 'snoring in boots on the sofas', as Princess Caroline put it – before waking up to escort their hangovers down to the Houses of Parliament, where they would make speeches about the future of the country. To the ranks of these privileged scoundrels you can add a wide range of other dubious characters: dashing highwaymen, cunning smugglers, gentlemen pugilists and political duellists of all ranks and persuasions. In short, for many of us today the Regency period simply was *the* Age of Excess. Sandwiched between the slightly dull elegance of the eighteenth century and the prim moral superiority of the early Victorians, it all seems licentious, naughty, dazzling, dangerous, shocking, offensive and yet, oh, *so* entertaining and attractive.

Hang on a minute, you might say: was this not also the period in which John Nash laid out Regent Street and Regent's Park in London, with their magnificent houses? Was this not the time when George Stephenson built his pioneering steam engines and Michael Faraday developed the electric motor? And have I forgotten that the early nineteenth century saw the establishment of the National Gallery, the decipherment of hieroglyphs and the installation of the Elgin Marbles in the British Museum? Are not the riotousness of the period and these cultural refinements at odds? They are indeed. And you could go further with this line of argument. With regard to the new houses up and down the country, it was precisely in these stately homes, urban squares and crescents that the most riotous people lived. Think of the landscaped gardens of the great houses laid out by Humphry Repton and Lancelot 'Capability' Brown. Picture their furniture, made from designs by George Hepplewhite and Thomas Sheraton. Remember the rugs, the paintings, the ornaments, the sculptures, the porcelain, the musical instruments. Many still consider Regency design to be the height of good taste and elegance. To think that it was also associated with the rakes, reprobates and riotous members of society is more than a little surprising.

But herein lies our key to understanding the time. It is only when you find the apparent contradictions in a subject that you begin to appreciate it fully. As the wealthy seemed determined to do everything in excess, it is hardly surprising that their exuberance extended also to spending money, as they sought to demonstrate their place in society by building ever more magnificent houses and commissioning ever finer furniture. As for the intellectual and cultural innovations of the period, can you be surprised that artists and manufacturers went to such extraordinary lengths to please their patrons when there were enormous financial rewards on offer? With the upper classes determined to spend as much money as they could, they created an environment in which the most brilliant artists, architects, scientists and innovators were able to flourish, thereby leaving the impression that this was a golden age. Although the labourers who helped create those fortunes saw only modest improvements in their own living standards and rose up in protest on more than one occasion, that is another matter. After two hundred years, the riots are much less obvious to the modern eye than the splendid, well-furnished houses that the wealthy left behind.

The tensions in Regency society were not limited to the contrasts of privilege versus penury, and individualism versus state control. They were also the result of profound social and economic changes. The population of Britain was increasing at a faster rate than it had done at any point in history (and faster than it has done ever since, for that matter). It was also rapidly becoming more urban. Herein we have another contradiction. Did the artists of the time celebrate the growth of the industrial towns? No. They did exactly the opposite: they celebrated the natural world that was being lost. John Constable's most famous painting, *The Hay Wain*, completed in 1821, shows two men chatting leisurely on a cart in the middle of a river. They seem to have all the time in the world, apparently unconcerned about the changes around them. Theirs is an environment shaped by the rhythm of the seasons and a river that will always flow. No columns of smoke cloud the sky; no urban back yards confine their world. John Clare's poetry similarly harks back to a rural idyll, surrounded only by nature and the village life of his childhood. Where artists and poets directly addressed the forces reshaping the landscape, they hardly ever did so in a positive, glorifying way. William Blake's 'dark satanic mills' belched fumes over 'England's green and pleasant land': there was nothing here to delight an artist. The old biblical image of fire coming down from Heaven had been reversed: now the fires reached up to Heaven from Earth. Perhaps the most brilliant artistic evocations of the era are to be found in music, most notably in the universally popular works of Ludwig van Beethoven, but even here we find a cultural conflict. Beethoven's famous Fifth Symphony thundered out like a colossal engine in London for the first time on 15 April 1816. It is difficult to reconcile the majestic, strident, four-note theme with the delicate sensitivities of Jane Austen's *Persuasion*, written that same year.

It is a truism to say that the reality of the past is always more complex and varied than our image of it. In this case the very word 'Regency', with all its grand connotations, is part of the problem: it makes everything sound luxurious. Victorian romantics looking back to what seemed a time of greater individual freedom tended not to see how few opportunities were open to *Regency* labourers and their families in the expanding industrial towns. When we look at the handsome coins and banknotes from the period it is a salutary thought that most working people never handled gold or paper money. Mention Nelson's navy to them and they would have thought of pressgangs and the conditions aboard those heaving wooden ships, the ear-splitting explosions of cannon and shocks of splintered wood during battle, the cold wind whistling through the rigging and the prospect of a watery grave. But say the words 'Nelson's navy' to a late-nineteenth-century Englishman and he would probably have pictured a print showing the dramatic moment of Nelson's death aboard the *Victory*. The lesson to us is obvious. In order to understand this extraordinarily varied and contradictory period we must detach ourselves from past attempts to romanticise it or to celebrate it as the last age of 'true freedom' or Britain in its bucolic bliss. We must do more than simply look at the waters of time passing from the riverbank: we must dive in and immerse ourselves.

'Immersing ourselves' is easier said than done, however. How do we go about it? The answer lies in accessing sufficient evidence and, just as importantly, in understanding its context and relevance. This is not difficult for the Regency: huge numbers of documents, books, images, objects and buildings survive. One particularly useful text in this respect is *Letters from England by Don Manuel Alvarez Espriella*, first published in three volumes in 1807. This is purportedly a travel guide to England in the years 1802–3 by a Spanish gentleman but is actually by the English poet laureate Robert Southey: its conceit is thus not so different from this present book and, being composed by a know-ledgeable contemporary, I have used it as a general guide. However, gathering and assessing evidence only gets us so far. To assume that it is synonymous with reconstructing the past is like thinking that, if you could reconnect all the bones, sinews and muscles of Admiral Nelson's body, he would somehow walk and talk again. While analysing historical information is a science, reconstructing the past in a meaningful way is an art. We need to draw on our own experiences to blow life into the evidence, and the way to do this is to focus not on the documents, paintings and buildings themselves but on the actions, needs and ideas that lie behind them. If, as a historian, you regard a physical document as the limit of the knowable truth, without trying to imagine what it was that made people cry, scream and pray, then you are simply undertaking an academic exercise. Don't get me wrong, academic exercises are hugely valuable: they are essential for a proper understanding of the past. But they have their limitations. Nelson's bones could tell us many things about the man but not necessarily what we most want to know. Indeed, you would never guess just from a skeleton that a human being could smile.

Herein lies the essence of a time traveller's guide. You can see the life that lies behind the evidence, complete with all its contradictions. How should you cut your toenails in 1790 if you want to avoid dying of blood poisoning? How can you get help if a member of your family is suffering from a mental disorder in 1798? How are you going to travel around safely? What are you going to wear; where might you stay; what should you eat; and what might you do for fun? While I cannot predict what Jane Austen might make of you, if you were to knock on the door of number 4 Sydney Place, Bath, in 1803, I can suggest what you would see if you visited the town in that year, and what you might make of the standard of living that she and her family enjoyed, and the spirit with which they and their contemporaries faced the world each day.

Here, then, is a guide to four of the most exciting and culturally important decades in British history. It was an age of elegance and violence, of freedom and protest, of old-style heroism and increasing urbanisation. It was also a time of war: more than half of the period was spent fighting the French, heralding such household names as Lord Nelson, William Pitt and the duke of Wellington. It saw campaigns for liberty, political and social reform, and greater compassion towards the less-fortunate members of society. It was an age of industrialisation, when Britain emerged as the prime economic power in the world. It was also a great age of invention, from the steam locomotive to the electric clock and the earliest photograph. And, of course, it was an age when millions of ordinary people lived ordinary lives – including those named in Mr Puddicombe's burial register and, indeed, the vicar himself, as the sun finally set on his world.

1

The Landscape

My living in Yorkshire was so far out of the way, that it was actually twelve miles from a lemon.

Sydney Smith[1]

As your ship approaches the south coast of England, you'll be looking out for land. If you are sailing from France, the white cliffs of Dover may be in your sights for most of the crossing. If you are travelling from America, you will be staring at the horizon for days, searching in vain for that rising blue ridge of the south-west peninsula, and seeing nothing but the dreary waste of white foam on heaving grey-green water. However, the tedium will not be your main concern. Sailors as well as passengers feel anxious when entering the English Channel, particularly after dark. Often you have no warning before a sudden thud sends you sprawling across the deck, accompanied by ear-splitting creaks as the ship's hull is wrenched apart. At night your eyes scan the blackness for any visible feature, with the wind buffeting the canvas sails and the waves constantly crashing against the bow. Then, at last, you see a pair of lights in the distance. A crew member assures you that they are the twin beacons of the Lizard lighthouse, on the south coast of Cornwall. The next light you'll see, he tells you, will be from the Eddystone, built on a remote rock 13 miles from shore. 'If we were to sail closer in,' he explains, 'you'd see the lights of Falmouth and Looe. To the east of them, there'd be Plymouth. And further up the Channel you'd spy Teignmouth, Dawlish, Exmouth and Sidmouth. It's as if someone's lighting all the lamps to greet you.'

This lighting-up of the coastal towns is something new. In the mid-eighteenth century you'd have seen just occasional pinpricks of light from the few large houses near the coast. Now there are sea-facing town houses with chandeliers burning in their drawing rooms. Even where these are obscured by curtains or shutters, you may see the bright lanterns above the front doors. Carriages wait outside with their mirror-backed glass lamps alight. What's more, by 1800 almost every large town has oil-fuelled street lights. They may only be visible individually from a mile or two away, but a cluster of lights can be seen from a much greater distance.[2] By the mid-1820s, some places on the south coast are even illuminated by gas – Brighton, Portsea and Dover among them. If you could make a time-lapse film of the south coast of England at night between 1789 and 1830 you would see tens of thousands of lights coming on, and growing brighter, as the coast gradually emerges from the darkness.

You may well think about those lights while your ship lies safely at anchor. They have more significance than simply allowing people to find their way around. They mean that men and women are no longer huddling around their fires in their homes after dark but are happy to go out and socialise, drink, gamble and dance, or listen to concerts and attend plays. A way of life that previously could only have been enjoyed in the larger cities is now spreading to many small towns up and down the country. People are no longer beholden to daylight. Many more are working at night too. The drivers of those horse-drawn carriages will be waiting to carry tired concert-goers to their homes. Proprietors and staff at the assembly rooms must be prepared for the carousing to carry on into the early hours. Street vendors selling hot pies and other snacks now have queues of late-night customers. And the once-dangerous streets are safer because there are more people circulating. The country you are about to visit has literally been 'enlightened'.

Brighton and the Coastal Resorts

You can't help but smile as you ride into Brighton on a summer's morning in the mid-1820s. First there are the bright-red jackets of the Grenadier Guards officers coming and going between the town and the barracks on the Lewes Road. Then you'll see the Pleasure Gardens on your right, with their gothic tower, aviary, promenades, bowling greens, grotto, maze, tea gardens and assembly rooms. Next you'll see the cricket pitch, where the king and his friends used to play in their younger days. Adjacent to that is the Hanover Arms, which, unusually for a public house, has an open-air fives court attached. A little further on you'll see a huge building site where the great church of St Peter's is steadily rising from the ground, on schedule for completion in 1828. Already you'll feel that you are entering a modern town characterised by ostentation, entertainment and expansion.

Ride on a little further and, to your left, you'll see Richmond Place: a terrace of elegant four-storey houses. Directly ahead of you is a long public lawn, enclosed by a low wooden railing and overlooked on both sides by tall houses with sash windows and canopied balconies. You can hear your horse's hooves on the gravel-covered road, the excited shouts of children playing with a hoop nearby, and the music from an open window as a young lady perseveres with her piano lesson. There's the distant knocking of hammers from the houses under construction in the side roads, and the occasional call of command as a servant exercising his master's dogs tries to restrain their pulling. Gentlemen in top hats and tailcoats discuss business as they walk by. Ladies in long dresses stroll along the pavement in front of the houses. A mail coach arrives, speeding around the other side of the lawn with rattling wheels. Custom says you should drive on the left but there is no law on the matter. In Brighton there is enough space that people can go whichever way they please, especially in a street as wide as this.

A few hundred yards on, the lines of houses open out even further, embracing another wide public lawn. On your left is the Grand Parade. These four-storey luxury dwellings are all different in design: some are faced with flint; some with stucco or brick; and some with 'mathematical tiles', designed to look like brickwork. Most have bow-fronted windows, each one incorporating a dozen or so panes of glass. Several of these houses are still being built: men are climbing ladders to platforms on wooden scaffolding poles, hauling up buckets of mortar with winches and pulleys. Despite the hotchpotch of designs, there is an elegance to every one of them. They give the impression of so many wealthy onlookers behind the railings at the finish of a race, all eager to see what is going on.

The 'finish line' in this case is the Royal Pavilion, on the other side of the wide lawn. It is an extravagant confection of cream-painted stucco and minarets, tent-like roofs and onion domes, with Indian-inspired parapets, gothic arches and Moorish arcades. From its Mughal gatehouse to its classical pillars, it is quite unlike any other building in the world. It looks like a chaotic mixture of the best and worst styles of three continents – but, at the same time, every part looks exactly as if it was intended to be that way. Nothing about it is slap-dash, utilitarian or complacently traditional. It does not sprawl but confidently dominates its grounds, announcing to everyone who sees it that its owner is rich, powerful, eccentric, extravagant and utterly immoderate in his tastes. At night the exterior is lit up by gas lights, making it feel both modern and outlandish at the same time. It looks out of place in Brighton – it would look out of place anywhere – but that is exactly what George IV wants. Not everyone loves it, of course. The German prince, Hermann Pückler-Muskau, who visits in February 1827, declares that 'it would be no great subject of lamentation' if it were to be demolished.[3] Nevertheless, it is the very epitome of all that is exotic in British architecture.

Unusually for a British town, the heart of Brighton is not the town hall or a castle, marketplace or great church. Rather it is this irregularly shaped patch of flat grass where you are standing now, called the Steine. Just look around you: not only does the Royal Pavilion face it but so do many houses belonging to the nobility and gentry. A wide road runs around the perimeter, where men and women are walking or riding in their best clothes. You can tell from the way everyone looks at the other promenaders that this is *the* place to be seen. Military officers eye up the young demoiselles out with their watchful chap-erones. Well-dressed young rakes catch the attention of ladies, who quietly hope one of them will have the boldness to invite her to a ball. Here you'll also find many of the amenities that cater to the rich and well connected: coffee houses, bathhouses and the best libraries. Then there is the roll call of celebrity mansions. One with a charming balcony and veranda is where Mrs Fitzherbert, the king's unofficial spouse, has lived since 1804. The whole area feels like a village green populated entirely by the rich and famous, with the odd fashionable adventurer and fortune-seeking seductress thrown in.

Two hundred yards further on is the source of Brighton's prosperity: the sea. When you arrive at the seafront, you'll see a carriage drive closed by elaborate iron gates. This is the entry to the Royal Chain Pier, which opens in 1823 and extends out over the waves for more than 1,000 feet.[4] The 30ft-wide deck is suspended from four tall cast-iron towers and ends in a landing stage of stone, from which you may

embark on the steamships that leave daily for Dieppe. Even if you are
not travelling abroad you can visit the pier, for an entrance fee of
tuppence (2d), and I recommend you do so. Walking along its length,
you'll see booths in the towers where you can buy prints of the town,
exotic seashells and a *camera obscura* image of yourself. But when you
reach the end of the pier and turn round to look back at the seafront,
your amusement at this fledgling seaside souvenir industry will give
way to amazement. The lines of houses facing you extend along the
coast for a mile in each direction and they are as architecturally impressive as the finest London squares. To the right of the pier you'll see
Marine Parade, which begins with a series of charming guesthouses
and continues with a row of very impressive residences, including the
Royal Crescent and, further on, Lewes Crescent and Sussex Square.
This is where you will find the Brighton homes of the marquess of
Bristol, the duke of Devonshire and the countess of Molande. To the
left of the pier is another long line of noble houses, including
Brunswick Square and Regency Square and their adjacent magnificent
terraces. Here are the homes of the duchess of St Albans, the countess
of Aldborough, the earl of Munster and a whole string of knights,
ladies, baronets and retired admirals and generals.

It will probably seem perfectly natural to you that most of these
grand houses face the sea – even those that do not tend to have bow-
shaped fronts, so that residents may catch at least a glimpse of the
horizon. However, not that many decades ago this would have been
the very last place where the rich and fashionable wanted to live.
The sea was perceived as a threat, bringing invaders and harsh
weather, and not as a thing of beauty. People only lived on the coast
if they had to. Most ports were home to merchants and dockworkers,
fishermen and net-makers, shipwrights, labourers and their families.
But in the eighteenth century things began to change. Physicians
started to recommend bathing in the sea and even drinking sea water.
The wealthy accordingly packed their bags and headed off to the
coast to cure their ailments, gathering at a few favoured spots where
they could socialise while undergoing a sea-water treatment. The first
such resort, gaining popularity in the 1730s, was Scarborough in
Yorkshire; it was soon followed by Brighton, Hastings, Margate and
Weymouth. In 1750 Dr Richard Russell published a surprise bestseller
entitled *A dissertation on the use of sea water in the diseases of the glands*,
in which he drew particular attention to the health-giving properties

of the sea water at Brighton. Three years later, he built a large house and consulting room near the seafront, and patients began to flock to him. Even now, long after his death, they keep coming. Visit in 1789 and you'll find that Brighton's population has doubled since Dr Russell's time, to about 4,000 people. Come back in 1801 and it will have almost doubled again, being 7,339 in the census of that year. It continues to grow at this rate for another three decades. In fact Brighton is proportionately the fastest-growing town in the whole of Regency Britain. In 1830 it is home to more than 40,000 people, ten times as many as in 1789. We have come a long way from a society in which the upper classes did their best to avoid the sea: now they are desperate to live facing it – to the extent that only the very wealthy can afford to do so.

The Old Town – the original 'Brighthelmstone', as it was known before the wealthy arrived – still stands, boxed in by its original perimeter roads: North, East and West Street. Here the houses are of a very different construction from those noble structures facing the Steine or forming the seafront terraces and squares. Whereas the new parts of the town are all open, light and spacious, the Old Town is narrow, dark and cramped. The lanes are mostly lined with small timber-framed houses with a shop on the ground floor and living accommodation for the family upstairs and a small back yard. Among them are tailors, woollen drapers, boot-makers, cabinet-makers, tea-dealers, coal merchants, chemists, butchers, pie-makers, grocers and many more tradesmen. Some upmarket businesses are located here too – bankers, jewellers and gunsmiths. Put them together with the old fishermen, net-makers and labourers, and about one-third of the population still lives in the Old Town in the 1820s.[5]

As you may have begun to realise, whatever you fancy, it is available in this town. Fancy a Turkish bath? You'll want to pay a visit to Mahomed's Warm, Cold and Vapour Baths by the seafront.[6] Fresh fish? Head down to the beach, where there is a fish market every morning, supplied by about a hundred boats drawn up on the pebble shore. What about a flutter on the horses? At the top of the hill to the east of the town you'll find Brighton Racecourse. If you're feeling energetic, there is a tennis court in town – for real tennis, of course, the traditional, walled-court version of the game. Maybe a swim is more to your fancy? There are plenty of bathing machines for hire. These are wooden cabins on high wheels, which are drawn by horses out into the chest-high water. You change inside the cabin and then, when you are out deep enough and your 'dipper' tells you it is safe to do so, you plunge into the brine in your bathing suit, which will resemble a large dress for women and a pair of drawers for men. If dancing is more your sort of thing, then you may go to a ball at the Old Ship Assembly Rooms at the bottom of Ship Street; they have card tables there too, if you are the gambling type. Those seeking sexual thrills will find women of affordable virtue in the streets around Upper Furlong to the north of the Old Town. As for high culture, a fine new theatre stands between North Street and Church Street, with two tiers of boxes and a large gallery. Plays are put on here from the end of July to the end of October: performances take place on Tuesdays, Wednesdays, Fridays and Saturdays; tickets cost five shillings (5s) for a seat in a box, 3s for the pit and 1s for the gallery.[7]

With its large number of aristocrats and royal patronage, Brighton is not your typical seaside town. However, it sets the pattern for many others. By the 1820s, in addition to the original five resorts, you might choose to visit Ramsgate in Kent, Worthing in Sussex or any one of several 'watering places' on the Devon coast: Sidmouth, Teignmouth, Exmouth and Dawlish, to name just the most prominent. Some of these have been quietly growing for decades. The Reverend John Swete travels through South Devon in 1795 and remarks that 'Sidmouth is the gayest place of resort on the Devon coast, and every elegancy, every luxury, every amusement is here to be met with – iced creams, milliners shops, cards, billiards, plays [and] circulating libraries'. With regard to Dawlish he writes that:

about twenty years ago the price of the best lodging house per week was not more than ... half a guinea, but so fashionable is Dawlish in the present day that, in the height of the season, not a house of the least consequence is to be hired for less than two guineas per week, and many of them rise to so high a sum as four or five.[8]

Despite these early seaside developments, it is the final defeat of Napoleon at the Battle of Waterloo in 1815 that heralds the heyday of the seaside towns. Many of them are developed to accommodate the great influx of wealthy Londoners who come down to the sea each summer. The seventy-four small round forts built along the south coast to protect the country from a French invasion in the first decade of the century – commonly called Martello towers – suddenly seem to belong to a bygone age. People love the sea now, they no longer fear it. And that love grows ever stronger. By 1830, the centre of Brighton has subtly shifted away from the Steine to the seafront itself, the 'New Steine'. When the good people of the town want to celebrate a grand occasion such as a royal birthday, they head to the seafront, where they can see the night sky set ablaze with brilliant fireworks and the Royal Chain Pier lit up with thousands of oil lights, visible from far out at sea.

Large Towns and Cities

When the young German philosopher Karl Philipp Moritz comes to England on a walking holiday in the 1780s, he writes in his journal that 'of all the towns I have seen outside London, Nottingham is the loveliest and the neatest'.[9] This will perhaps come as a surprise to some readers. I suspect that, if you were asked which town you think the 'loveliest and neatest' in the Georgian period, you would say Bath, Brighton or Edinburgh – and only those in the know might suggest Buxton (for its Crescent) or Liverpool (for the area around Abercromby Square and Rodney Street). But you could pick practically any town in Britain and praise its Regency architecture. Quite simply, *every* town is expanding at this time. The seventy-seven largest places in 1801 – those with a population of 7,000 or more – see an average increase of 83 per cent over the next thirty years. Twenty-two of them double in size and all but two grow by at least one-third.

As you can imagine, the expansion of all the major towns and cities has a profound effect on the landscape. Great Britain has always been a relatively rural island but, from the late eighteenth century, massive population growth results in a heavy swing towards urban living. If you include all the small towns – those with at least 2,500 inhabitants – then 44 per cent of the population is urbanised by 1831.[10] A Regency town is thus a work in progress, with a mass of new streets and building sites popping up between and around older properties. Hundreds of thousands of acres of fields are sacrificed to facilitate this growth and the infrastructure needed to support it. Of course all these growing communities now want their assembly rooms, theatre, post office, concert hall, workhouse, infirmary and library. Whereas previously one large church might have served the whole population, that is hardly practical when the town is home to more than 10,000 people. In 1818 the government passes the Church Building Act, granting £1,000,000 to a commission to provide new churches for the expanding towns. At the same time, growing religious tolerance gives an impetus to many nonconformist congregations to build their own places of worship. Bristol in 1830, for example, has its cathedral and twenty-one other Anglican churches and chapels; four Baptist, seven Independent and six Methodist chapels; plus individual chapels for the Countess of Huntingdon's Connexion, the Moravians, Seceders, Unitarians and Whitfieldites; a Welsh chapel, a Roman Catholic chapel, a Friends' meeting house and a synagogue.[11]

Alongside all the new houses, churches and chapels, the urban landscape is changing as a result of many towns obtaining an Improvement Act. This enables a town corporation to appoint local commissioners to improve its sanitation, paving, policing and lighting, and in some cases to pull down houses in order to widen the streets. In Birmingham the commissioners purchase the manorial rights so they can relocate the main market. After all, if you've just bought a handsome new house in the centre of town, the last thing you want is hundreds of grunting, lowing and bleating animals outside your front door, with all the smells, dung and piles of straw that go with them. At the same time, the growing population sustains more specialist shops, such as milliners, opticians, booksellers and jewellers, and these businesses begin to push the traditional market traders out of the town centres. Visitors increasingly expect that a high street will be a wide, straight thoroughfare open to coaches, carriages, horse-riders and pedestrians, where they will find a range of shops selling genteel and manufactured items. They do not want to be confronted with ramshackle stalls and pens of livestock.

Towns that still have their crooked streets, narrow lanes and central markets are considered old and dirty. City fathers thus

The largest towns and cities in Great Britain, 1801–31[12]			
Town or CITY	**1801**	**1831**	**Growth**
1 LONDON	865,845	1,471,069	70%
2 Manchester	84,020	182,812	118%
3 EDINBURGH	82,266	162,156	97%
4 Liverpool	79,722	189,242	137%
5 GLASGOW	77,385	202,426	162%
6 Birmingham	73,670	146,986	100%
7 BRISTOL	63,645	103,886	63%
8 Leeds	53,162	123,393	132%
9 Plymouth	43,194	75,534	75%
10 Newcastle-on-Tyne	36,963	57,937	57%
11 NORWICH	36,832	61,116	66%
12 Portsmouth	32,166	46,282	44%
13 Sheffield	31,314	59,011	88%
14 Paisley	31,179	57,466	84%
15 Nottingham	28,861	50,680	76%
16 BATH	27,686	38,063	37%
17 Hull	27,609	46,426	68%
18 ABERDEEN	27,608	58,019	110%
19 Dundee	26,804	45,355	69%
20 Sunderland	26,511	43,076	62%
21 Bolton	18,574	43,396	134%
22 Greenock	17,458	27,571	58%
23 EXETER	17,398	28,201	62%
24 Leicester	16,953	39,306	132%
25 YORK	16,145	25,359	57%
26 COVENTRY	16,034	27,070	69%
27 CHESTER	15,052	21,363	42%
28 PERTH	14,878	20,016	35%
29 Great Yarmouth	14,845	21,115	42%
30 Stockport	14,830	25,469	72%
31 Shrewsbury	14,739	21,227	44%
32 Rochdale	14,491	26,404	82%

	Town or CITY	1801	1831	Growth
33	Wolverhampton	12,565	24,732	97%
34	Oldham	12,024	32,381	169%
35	Blackburn	11,980	27,091	126%
36	Preston	11,887	33,112	179%
37	OXFORD	11,705	20,434	75%
38	Colchester	11,520	16,167	40%
39	WORCESTER	11,300	18,610	65%
40	Tynemouth	11,136	16,926	52%
41	Wigan	10,989	20,774	89%
42	Derby	10,832	23,607	118%
43	Warrington	10,567	16,018	52%
44	Chatham	10,505	16,485	57%
45	Ipswich	10,402	20,454	97%
46	Walsall	10,399	15,066	45%
47	CARLISLE	10,221	20,006	96%
48	Dudley	10,107	23,043	128%
49	King's Lynn	10,096	13,370	32%
50	Cambridge	10,087	20,917	107%
51	Dunfermline	9,980	17,068	71%
52	CANTERBURY	9,791	14,463	48%
53	Reading	9,742	15,595	60%
54	Lancaster	9,030	12,613	40%
55	Halifax	8,866	15,382	73%
56	Falkirk	8,838	12,743	44%
57	Macclesfield	8,743	23,129	165%
58	Whitehaven	8,742	11,393	30%
59	Inverness	8,732	14,324	64%
60	Wakefield	8,131	12,232	50%
61	South Shields	8,108	9,074	12%
62	Kilmarnock	8,079	18,093	124%
63	Montrose	7,974	12,055	51%
64	Merthyr Tydfil	7,705	22,083	187%

	Town or CITY	1801	1831	Growth
65	Bury St Edmunds	7,655	11,436	49%
66	Southampton	7,629	19,324	153%
67	Durham	7,530	10,125	34%
68	Whitby	7,483	7,765	4%
69	LINCOLN	7,398	11,892	61%
70	Brighton	7,339	40,600	453%
71	Dumfries	7,288	11,606	59%
72	Huddersfield	7,268	19,035	162%
73	GLOUCESTER	7,261	11,933	64%
74	SALISBURY	7,126	9,876	39%
75	Dover	7,084	11,924	68%
76	Bury	7,072	15,086	113%
77	Northampton	7,020	15,351	119%
	Average growth 1801–31			**83%**

embrace modernity by demolishing alleys and building eye-catching grand architecture. All seven of Exeter's medieval city gates are demolished between 1769 and 1825, allowing the widening of the principal roads. The mayor and council also demolish the great conduit in the centre of the city that has supplied water for centuries. They replace the open sluices that run down the middle of the streets with gently cambered surfaces that drain to the sides. They encourage the building of Bedford Circus, Barnfield Crescent, Baring Crescent and the elegant terraces of Southernhay, Northernhay and Pennsylvania. With the exception of its great cathedral, Exeter turns its back on its past and prides itself instead on its modern public buildings: its assembly rooms, ballroom, card room, hotel, libraries, post office, bathhouse, prison, law courts, hospital, public dispensary, eye hospital, lunatic asylum, grammar school, military barracks and theatre.

By 1800, most towns have oil lamps installed at regular intervals along the main roads. The best streets in a fashionable place like Bath have glass globes on iron stands set up at regular intervals, all burning colza or rapeseed oil.[13] Glasgow starts to illuminate its streets in 1780 when nine oil lamps are mounted in the Trongate; by 1815, the total number of lights maintained by the city authorities has risen to 1,274.[14] Thereafter, gas is the key to the spread of street lighting. By 1830, more than half of the largest towns in Britain have at least one gas company to illuminate the streets, public buildings and commercial premises.[15] Those that don't, like Plymouth and Newcastle-on-Tyne, continue to depend on oil lamps suspended from iron frames projecting from street corners until the 1840s.

Look beneath the surfaces of these large towns and you will realise they differ enormously. Consider Liverpool, for example. Like Brighton, it is situated close to the sea, being on the east side of the Mersey estuary. Also like Brighton, it has grown extraordinarily over the last century. In 1700 it had only about 5,000 inhabitants but since then its population has doubled every twenty-five years. The reason is the expansion of trade across the Atlantic, especially in sugar, cotton and tobacco. This has led to considerable investment in the docks, which now command the respect of all who visit them. The town hall in Dale Street in the centre is a magnificent building constructed in the mid-eighteenth century by John Wood – the man responsible for building the Royal Crescent and the Circus in Bath. Behind the town hall is the Exchange: a large court with an arcade running around it for merchants to meet and trade. Here too are the assembly rooms and council chamber. Such is the booming prosperity of the town that the Bank of England opens a branch here in 1827. By this time the fields to the south-east of the centre have been built over with long lines of elegant town houses and squares. Walk along any of the wide avenues here, or through Abercromby Square or Falkner Square, and you will think that Liverpool is as wealthy as Brighton. However, if you stray away from this quarter, you will soon discover that the two towns have very little else in common. For while Brighton is a place of entertainment, health and luxury, reflecting the predilections of the rich, Liverpool is a place of commerce and labour, reflecting the ambitions of businessmen and the mundane struggles of the poor.

Nothing you have seen in Britain at any time in its history is likely to prepare you for the sheer squalor of the poorest parts of Regency Liverpool. Almost half the population here live in cellars and courts or 'back houses'. These are terraces of small dwellings crammed in behind the houses facing the streets. A narrow passage runs from the street through the house at the front into an alley or 'court' between 10 to 12 feet wide. Two rows of brick houses face each other here, one on either side of the court, with communal latrines at the far end. We will see later what it is actually like to live in such places – in chapter 8, 'Where to Stay', although in this case it might better be called 'where *not* to stay' – but for the sake of describing the urban environment, this is what you will hear, see and smell when you walk through Liverpool and enter one of these courts.

The first thing you'll notice is the noise. The extreme density of housing and the almost complete lack of privacy in the courts and streets mean that the air is constantly rent with shrieking and laughing, babies wailing and children crying, with curses, insults and threats shouted through windows and across the streets. What a contrast to the Steine in Brighton, with its piano rehearsals and servants walking their master's dogs! Many of the road surfaces are still unpaved, the mud or gravel strewn with dung from the horses of delivery wagons. They remain in this state until the weekly visit of the street sweepers or 'scavengers' who clear away the muck to a manure depot.

From a pedestrian's viewpoint, the streets of Liverpool are quite wide, even in the poorest areas. It is when you turn off them into the courts that you will plunge into darkness. The tunnels are as long as the front houses facing the street are deep. When you emerge into daylight again, you will feel like you've crept through a cave. And this is where the stench will hit you.

The sea breezes that Liverpool's wealthy classes associate with the healthiness of the town never stir the foetid air here. The courts aren't paved. Nor are they swept by the town scavengers. Drains are rare, because both the developers and the town authorities expect the rain to wash anything noisome down the tunnel and back into the street. However, as one medical investigator, Dr Lyon Playfair, notes:

In numberless instances, courts and alleys have been formed without any declination for the discharge of surface water. Many are laid without channels, and while the solid refuse thrown upon them rots on the surface, the liquid matter is absorbed, and much of it finds its way into the inhabited cellars of the courts. The north end of town is full of pits of stagnant water, which form so many receptacles for the putrid matter that is constantly thrown into them, such as dead animals and the drainage from starch and other manufactories; and in hot weather, the stench from these places is frequently intolerable.[16]

Rain pours into the cesspits too, and after a heavy downpour the levels rise, causing the excrement, rotting offal and other disgusting things to spill out. Normally a court containing sixteen houses will have two privies for the accommodation of eighty people or so, but it is not unknown for twenty to share a single dwelling, so two privies might serve two or three hundred people. Then the single cesspit beneath them ends up containing an enormous amount of filth.[17] Moreover, as Dr Playfair observes:

The privies, frequently without doors, and common to both sexes, must outrage modesty, if they do not lead to licentiousness. It is not uncommon to find necessaries built without doors, the excuse given for this deficiency being that if these were attached, they would be broken up for firewood …

In 1790 there are already 1,608 such court houses in Liverpool, mostly built to house immigrant labourers from Lancashire, Ireland and Wales.[18] That number continues to grow, so that by 1830 there are about eight times as many, accommodating more than 70,000 people in a squalid mass of Stygian dimness and breath-stopping stench. In Crosbie Street in 1790 there are sixty-one front houses and eighty-four court dwellings, with a further forty-two cellars beneath them. The front houses are occupied by 360 people, the court houses by 434 and another 181 live in the cellars. That is a total of 975 people living in 145 houses – which equates to a population density of 777 per acre. That is one of the most densely settled places on earth. Incredibly, it continues to increase, reaching an extreme of 1,300 people per acre.[19]

In general, very little infrastructure is provided in the rapidly growing industrial towns. In Liverpool there are libraries and assembly rooms for the rich, and there are newly built churches for the pious, but there are no public parks. The large communal gardens are privately owned, managed for the benefit of subscribing key-holders. The only public amenity areas are the streets, which are crowded with horse-drawn vehicles. Small wonder, then, that so many working people spend their time in public houses. You won't see any public fountains here; nor is there a public bathhouse. If you wish to bathe, then you must resort to 'the shores of the river at the north and the south ends of town'.[20] The River Mersey might be large but it is where all the sewers empty out and where all the industrial pollution ends up. Talking of sewers, although the authorities levy a rate to pay for sewerage in the town, this is only extended as far as wealthy people's addresses. The same goes for the water companies: almost all the courts are without a piped supply. It is a dreadful state of affairs – and a severe lesson in what happens when town planning is left to profiteers.

What do contemporaries think of Liverpool? Most affluent residents will tell you it is a forward-thinking, progressive, modern town; they have probably never been to Crosbie Street, let alone into the courts there. Opinion among visitors is divided. The Reverend Nathaniel Wheaton, visiting from America in 1823, remarks that Liverpool is a 'city of docks, fat men and fat women, coal smoke, dirty streets, cast iron, mammon and mud'.[21] Robert Southey similarly notes that 'the outskirts of Liverpool have an unsightly appearance: new streets of houses for the poorer classes, which bear no marks either of cleanliness or comfort, fields cut up for the foundations of other buildings, brick yards, and kilns smoking on every side'.[22] Others completely overlook the dirt and poverty. The Frenchman Louis Simond, who comes here in 1810 after spending twenty years in America, compares the town favourably with New York.[23] To him, Liverpool's public buildings are both more numerous and more pleasing in their architecture and he is impressed with the warehouses, some of which are thirteen storeys high. He doesn't remark on the living conditions of the labourers. Likewise the Swiss industrialist Hans Caspar Escher notes only positive things about the 'fairly well-planned' town in 1814.[24] It just goes to show that people's impressions are more often formed by what they want to see than by what is actually there to be found.

Moving away from Liverpool to other industrial towns, you will find the environment increasingly blighted by manufacturing processes during the period. This includes industrial waste. At the smaller end of the scale, there are no limits on what activities can be carried on in the courts of developing towns, so people keep animals there and slaughter them on the same premises. In Birmingham, the engineering capital of Britain, there are 1,600 pigsties.[25] In Bristol the low standards of hygiene are illustrated by a shopkeeper's comment to a medical inspector about the yard behind his house, where his neighbour slaughters pigs imported from Ireland:

Often the pigs, in coming over in the packet [ship], die, and I have seen as many as thirty dead pigs at a time brought into the yard. They are thrown under that shed there, until there is time to cut them up, and by that time, I have seen the maggots fairly dropping out of them. Then they are cut up and, I believe, are made into salt bacon or sold for sausages. The entrails of such pigs are generally too far gone to be of use, and they are thrown into the dunghill. When the dunghill is stirred up to be taken away, oh! Sir, the smell is awful. We are forced to shut our windows and doors, and stuff pieces of cloth into the keyholes, but all this does not keep it out. The entrails of the live pigs killed in the yard are boiled and sold, and give out a very bad smell, but nothing like the others.[26]

At the top end of the scale, industrial pollution can be overwhelming. In 1802, Robert Southey records the following view of Birmingham:

A heavy cloud of smoke hung over the city, above which in many places black columns were sent up with prodigious force from the steam-engines ... Everywhere around us, instead of the village church, whose steeple usually adorns so beautifully the English landscape, the tower of some manufactory was to be seen in the distance, vomiting up flames and smoke, and blasting everything around with its metallic vapours. The vicinity was as thickly peopled as that of London. Instead of cottages we saw streets of brick hovels, blackened with the smoke of coal fires, which burn day and night in these dismal regions. Such swarms of children I never beheld in any other place, nor such wretched ones, in rags, and their skins encrusted with soot and filth. The face of the country as we advanced was more hideous than can be described, uncultivated, black and smoking.[27]

You will find similar scenes in many other industrial towns. The whole area around Swansea is suffering from the 'copper smoke' belched out by the coal-burning furnaces. The locals don't know why it happens – and I don't suggest you try to explain to them that the smelting process gives off sulphur dioxide and hydrogen fluoride, which react with moisture in the air to form sulphuric acid, or 'acid rain' as we know it – but they know the copper works are the cause and it stops anything from growing in their gardens.[28] People who live near gas works say they can't dry their washing out of doors because soot keeps raining down. The sulphurous stench when it 'lets off' is more disgusting than that of putrid carcasses, they say. Then there is the lime-water released by the purifiers. When gas companies allow this to run into the rivers, it kills all the fish.[29]

Mention of smoke brings us face to face with one of the most striking features of the age: the shift to steam power. It is an extraordinarily rapid transformation. In 1789 Manchester has a dozen mills, all of which are powered by water. In 1801 there are still only forty-two large mills, and they are all still water-driven. The first successful steam-powered cotton factory is not built until 1806. But then more than 2,000 steam-driven cotton mills are constructed in just twelve years.[30] In the 1830s, Manchester and Salford are home to 6,000 cotton-spinning and weaving mills, 1,200 bleaching and dyeing mills, 700 foundries and industrial mills, and almost 2,000 other mills of varying descriptions – all of them powered by steam. Picture a tall chimney for every single one of these 10,000 mills, and imagine the smoke rising from them into a great glowering cloud that hangs in the air. Some factories along the Rochdale Canal are immense eight-storey brick buildings, more than 100 feet high and 300 feet long, swarming with workers. More than 1,000 people are employed in the McConnel & Kennedy Mills alone. Artificial lighting – including 1,500 gas lights installed in a single building in 1809 – means that the *thud, thud, thud* of the steam engine keeps going all night. Any romantic idea that these buildings are 'the cathedrals of their age' soon disappears when you experience the noise, the smells and the pollution that attend them. They might be awe-inspiring but the great churches of the Middle Ages were built for the glory of God and the benefit of the souls of the worshippers who entered them: they promised redemption and everlasting peace. These huge edifices have been built for profit, not glory, and although they provide many men, women and children with employment, they certainly don't benefit the bodies of those who labour in them for fourteen hours a day, let alone their souls.

Small Towns and the Countryside

Just as large towns vary according to their levels of elegance and effluence, so too do small towns. Some expand massively and acquire all the amenities of large towns, such as a theatre, assembly rooms and a private library; others hardly alter and remain steadfastly rural in character. Axminster in Devon has 2,154 inhabitants in 1801 and still only 2,719 thirty years later: an increase of just 26 per cent. Its buildings are old and its lanes awkward for coach travel. Ironically, this under-development gives rise to more criticism than is generally levelled at the expanding towns billowing out smoke and pollution. When the London surgeon George Lipscomb passes through on his way to Cornwall in 1798 he declares: 'Axminster is a most miserable town. The houses are extremely mean and many of them covered with thatch ... All the streets are narrow, crooked, and in the highest degree inconvenient and disgusting.'[31] With somewhat greater diplomacy, the compiler of *Pigot's Directory* describes Axminster in 1830 as 'respectable but irregularly built'.[32] The problem is not so much the dirt as the antiquity. The only things that are praised are the inns, the parish church and the carpet factory, established in 1755. But do not be put off by such reports: small towns are essential to the well-being of the people who live in rural areas. Axminster, for example, has:

3 auctioneers	1 bookseller	2 cabinet-makers
5 bakers	6 boot-makers and	4 carpenters and
3 banks	shoemakers	joiners
3 blacksmiths	1 butter seller	3 coopers

4 dressmakers	3 lawyers	1 spirits-dealer
2 druggists	5 linen and woollen	3 stonemasons
5 fire-insurance offices	drapers	2 straw-hat makers
3 gardeners and	2 maltsters	3 surgeons
seedsmen	1 marble mason	3 surveyors
4 grocers and	3 millers of corn	5 tailors
tea-dealers	3 plumbers and	1 tallow chandler
1 hairdresser	glaziers	1 tobacconist
1 hotel	1 post office	2 watch- and
7 inns	3 saddle-makers	clock-makers
1 iron merchant	6 schoolmasters	2 wheelwrights and
2 ironmongers	8 shopkeepers	1 wine merchant.

It also holds an excellent meat market three times a week in the centre of town, and three cattle fairs per year. Coach services depart daily to London, Bath, Bristol and Exeter; those to Portsmouth and Southampton go three times a week. Small it may be, and unfashionable it clearly is, but Axminster is an invaluable, bustling centre for those living in its hinterland.

Much the same can be said for another 1,000 or so market towns in Great Britain.[33] When Louis Simond alights at Falmouth in 1809, his immediate impression is that the town is 'little, old and ugly'. In fact, he dismisses almost every old town he comes to as 'ugly'. Chester has 'a barbarous antiquity', Salisbury is 'very ugly', Carlisle is 'dull and ugly enough' and 'Llangollen is, like all the little old towns of this and all countries, a hideous object'.[34] Nathaniel Wheaton similarly turns his nose up at most small towns. According to him, Wolverhampton is 'old, dirty, with narrow streets and black with coal dust'; Ware is 'old and miserably built with very narrow, crooked and dirty streets'; and the streets of Stamford are 'narrow, irregular and dirty'.[35] But all of these places perform many valuable functions for their citizens and everyone else living in the area.

As you travel further into the countryside you will find that the Industrial Revolution has left its mark on even the most out-of-the-way places. Thousands of miles of canals now link the towns with the major rivers. Coal is transported by local freight railways: by the 1820s you will find several collieries with steam engines taking coal to the nearest port. Most striking of all, factories and mills are built in the countryside too, some of which are nearly as large as those behemoths

in Manchester. Frequently these are accompanied by new villages to
house the workers, especially if they operate around the clock. The
most famous example is New Lanark, a large complex of imposing
four-storey mills in a leafy valley of the River Clyde, 27 miles south-
east of Glasgow. Here the industrialist Robert Owen has not only
expanded his father-in-law's water-powered cotton mills but has built
houses and cottages for more than 2,000 people, together with a
school, nursery block, infirmary and many of the amenities of a small
town. Dozens of entrepreneurs do likewise, although not always to
the same high standards as Owen.

As you can see, the Industrial Revolution is not just about steam-
powered factories and improved transport connections but more
fundamentally about the desire to make money. The evidence is all
around you. If any asset can be made more profitable, its owner will
generally try to exploit it. What do you do with the 200 square miles
of barren land that make up Dartmoor? Some men refuse to accept
that it is unsuitable for farming and lease swathes of it. They bring
in a phalanx of farmers from the Scottish Highlands in the hope of
turning a profit. When the hardy Scotsmen also fail to make money
out of the acid soil and permanently sodden tussocks of marsh grass,
the very remoteness of the moor acquires value. A large prison is
placed in Princetown, on the basis that a desolate wasteland surrounded
by mists, bogs and mires is the ideal place to incarcerate French and
American prisoners of war. In some areas the real riches are underground. Thus steam-powered beam engines appear in the valleys of
Devon and Cornwall – to power the pumps that drain the tin and
copper mines. The same goes for the coal fields across the country.
Where there is china clay, used to produce porcelain from the mid-
eighteenth century, hundreds of acres of moorland are scraped clear
to reveal the bright white matter. From 1820, granite quarried on
Dartmoor is transported by horse-drawn carts running on a railway
made of carved granite blocks down to the Stover Canal, whence it
is shipped to the capital. Here it is used to build the new London
Bridge and parts of the British Museum.

Although the new industries carve deep gashes into the rural landscape, the most painful wounds are caused by something you would
have thought innocuous – farming. How come, you may wonder?
After all, a cow is a cow, and a field of corn is a field of corn. Well,
no. A Regency cow produces more than twice as much milk as its

Elizabethan predecessor, and about three and half times as much as its ancestors in the early fourteenth century.[36] Over the years, farmers have bred their animals to be bigger and bigger. Your average medieval cow would yield about 170lbs of beef but in the early 1800s its descendant is carrying more than 500lbs. Sheep too have trebled in size since the early 1300s; even pigs have doubled in weight. Much the same can be said for the fecundity of the fields. Using new systems of crop rotation and fertilisation, Regency farmers are able to grow more than twice as much wheat per acre as their medieval forebears, and almost three times as much rye, barley, oats and pulses.[37]

Larger animals are not themselves the problem. It is the changes in the landscape that go with the new farming methods that have caused the above-mentioned painful wounds. For centuries now manorial lords have gradually been winding up the system of communal farming that has been employed since medieval times, in which all the men and women of the manor work their strips of land in two or three huge open fields. The fact that the smallholders co-operate means that they can share communal assets such as ploughs and teams of oxen. They can also take advantage of the commons for grazing their animals, gathering firewood and cutting rushes for re-thatching their roofs. It means that even poor families can eke out a living. But it's a very inefficient way of farming if you are the land-owner and your prime concern is profit. Thus lords are keen to enclose the open fields, which can extend to more than 1,000 acres. They obtain an Act of Parliament allowing them to do so, and then divide each field up into small parcels of 4–10 acres to be worked by a single farmer, who is expected to pay a higher rent for his exclusive access to the land. They do the same with the commons. It is not that they are purely selfish; in fact, most of them believe they are improving the land. In some respects they are right, for small enclosures enable livestock to be better maintained and isolated from diseased animals; and ploughing, manuring, sowing and harvesting can all be managed much more efficiently when the land is worked in one block and not spread out in small strips across vast fields. The result is a significant increase in the amount of food produced, and this goes to feed the burgeoning populations of the towns. The richest farmers become richer and the manorial lords do exceedingly well. However, there is a downside. The majority of tenants who previously rented only a few acres are unable to make ends meet, with just one or two enclosed fields. They cannot afford their own plough, let alone the animals to pull it. They no longer have the right to gather firewood or rushes, and their grazing lands have disappeared. Many end up working as labourers for the more prosperous farmers or moving away to find work in the towns and cities.

By the beginning of our period things have come to a head. Whereas in the seventeenth century a great deal of enclosure was brought about by mutual agreement, the fields that remain open now are those where communal farming is still cherished. But Parliament has chosen to come down heavily on the side of the landowners. Almost 400 Enclosure Acts are passed in the 1790s; and by 1800 only 16 per cent of England's agricultural land remains unenclosed.[38] The next twenty years see the passing of almost 1,000 more Enclosure Acts, throwing the cottagers and small-time farmers off the land.[39] 'What is it to the poor man to be told the Houses of Parliament are extremely tender of property, while the father of the family is forced to sell his cow and his land because the one is not competent to the other?' asks the agricultural writer Arthur Young.[40] The reason why so many cottage-dwelling labourers plant their gardens with potatoes in the 1820s is not that they are particularly fond of the crop but because they are desperate: it is a survival strategy.

For travellers who are unaware of these agricultural changes, the landscape simply appears beautiful. Prince Hermann Pückler-Muskau writes to his wife in the 1820s about 'fertile and well-cultivated fields' and 'thousands of comfortable and pretty farmhouses and cottages scattered over every part of the country'.[41] Louis Simond too rhapsodises about the landscape between Stourhead and Bristol, calling it 'the most beautiful country, a continual garden full of gentlemen's houses and grounds'. In Wales he is delighted by the many white-washed cottages, with roses, honeysuckle and vines around the doors.[42] But you will not be able to escape the fact that land ownership in Britain has acquired a more proprietorial character. One day Karl Moritz is walking near Windsor when he notices a perfect, picturesque view. Naturally he decides to climb to the top of a nearby hill to enjoy it but as soon as he steps off the road, he is confronted by a sign that reads: 'Take care! Steel traps and spring-guns are laid here.'[43] The beauty is marred by hidden mantraps than can snap your leg and tripwire-triggered hidden guns that are intended to kill poachers. On a slightly less threatening level, everywhere you will find walls and fences enclosing the new fields, and long lines of newly planted hawthorn hedges dividing up the remaining commons. Huge flocks of sheep inhabit the fields: there are more than twenty million of them in the early 1800s, twice as many as there are people.[44] Thousands of farmhouses have been built by farmers who now own large blocks of land, having benefited from the economies of enclosure.

The increased income from the land has affected the ancient manor houses and mansions too. Most of the formal gardens of the seventeenth century have been torn up and replaced with 'natural' landscapes designed by William Kent, Lancelot 'Capability' Brown and Humphry Repton. These men have introduced temples, follies, grottoes and serpentine lakes into the parks of the gentry and aristocracy. They have planted decorative trees that were previously only found in botanical gardens, such as Norway spruce, Oriental plane, European larch, Italian cypress, cherry laurel, holm oak, Norway maple, lilac and horse chestnut – all of which were brought to Britain in the sixteenth and seventeenth centuries. They have introduced new trees too, such as the red oak, Turkey oak, Corsican pine and Douglas fir. Capability Brown has planted countless cedars of Lebanon and London planes in his 'natural' parks; and he has removed or built entire hills, in his attempt to 'improve' nature. One contemporary worries that, unless he dies and goes to Heaven soon, it will have been 'improved' by Mr Brown by the time he gets there. It all goes to show that the landscape is never static. The more mills, factories and chimneys that are constructed, the more those who profit from them surround themselves with green parks, gardens and wilderness, seemingly yearning for the natural world they are helping to destroy.

You might have thought that the remotest part of Great Britain would be the exception to this trend but it's the Highlands of Scotland where the collision of the modern world of profit and the traditional one of local rights and customs is most violent. This is partly because the relationship between a chief and his clansmen has traditionally been more protective and binding than that between a landowner and his tenants. But many of those chiefs now live in Edinburgh or London and have little or nothing in common with their Gaelic-speaking followers, whom they regard merely as tenants. And most of those tenants still practise subsistence farming, producing only what they themselves need. As the price of livestock has risen significantly in recent years, so the Scottish landlords regard the rents their tenants pay as mere pittances. They are therefore keen to clear the people off the land to make way for vast sheep farms that will yield good profits. One of them, James Ramsay, notes that 'the gentlemen who make self-interest the rule of their conduct get in some cases triple or quadruple of what was formerly paid'.[45] Many farmers are relocated to the coast, where they are expected to take up employment in the kelp industry or in fishing. Others are given a one-way ticket to Canada. This is why on a visit to Scotland you will sometimes pass through empty hamlets and see the ghostly shadows of windows and doorways staring at you – or, rather, staring at nothing, like the eye sockets of a skull.

If you travel to the valley of Strathnaver in the north of Scotland in early 1814 you will still find about forty small settlements, each containing about a dozen Gaelic-speaking farming families whose menfolk make their living from weaving, shoemaking and milling. The houses have low stone walls and are thatched, surrounded by infields planted with oats, and outfields where black cattle and horses are grazing. The total population of the valley stands at about 2,000. The appearance of the place and its way of life have changed little since the Middle Ages. But on Monday 13 June 1814, Patrick Sellar, the estate agent of the countess of Sutherland, arrives to evict the inhabitants. He is particularly keen to remove William Chisholm, who is unpopular with his neighbours. It is late morning when Sellar and his men arrive at Chisholm's house. The agent orders it to be torched. When he is informed that Chisholm's bedridden mother-in-law is still inside and too frail to be moved, being almost 100 years old, he shouts: 'Damn her, the old witch, she has lived too long; let her burn!' Chisholm's friends manage to rescue the old lady from the building as the fire takes hold, burning their hands in the process, but she is traumatised by the event and dies five days later, having not spoken a word since her eviction. Her fate, in many ways, stands for all the communities destroyed by the Highland Clearances. People are moved out and their houses burnt to stop them coming back. They themselves are silenced, their Gaelic language consigned to oblivion, like their ancient farming practices. The blackened walls of their old homes become stark memorials, like so many gravestones among the wind-tugged heather and sheep paths. Between 1807 and 1821 approximately 10,000 people are removed in this way from the countess of Sutherland's estates and are forced to live in windswept crofts by the sea.[46]

2

London

Why, Sir, you find no man, at all intellectual, who is willing to leave London. No, Sir, when a man is tired of London, he is tired of life; for there is in London all that life can afford.

Samuel Johnson[1]

London is the centre of British government, finance and culture. Its position at the heart of an empire that is constantly growing in wealth and influence means it is steadily becoming richer and more powerful, and while the benefits do not trickle down to every citizen, they are distributed widely enough for the increasing prosperity to be noticeable in all but the poorest areas. It is also by far the largest city in Great Britain, with a population of almost 866,000 in 1801 and 1.47 million thirty years later. If you include its suburbs, 1.1 million people live here at the start of the century and 1.9 million in 1831. By the end of our period London has overtaken Peking (modern-day Beijing) as the largest city in the world. So rapid and extraordinary is the change that I suggest you visit at least three times – in 1790, 1810 and 1830 – to make sure you see the various stages of its development.

1790

Picture yourself walking into London from the village of Clapham on a bright morning in April. There are fields on either side of the gravel-and-mud main road, with primroses and cowslips sporadically lightening the verges. A little way on, to your left, you'll see the Oval, which is still a market garden. Sheep graze on Kennington Common to your right, their lambs gambolling in the sun. But you won't have any doubt that you are not in the country, even here. Dozens of carriages and wagons are passing, with their harnesses rattling, hooves clopping and wheels grinding on the gravel. Ahead there are houses – at first in ones and twos but, from the turnpike at Newington Butts, in solid terraces all the way to London Bridge. As you walk on, every junction reveals more streets of houses leading off to the sides, with small-scale industrial buildings, timber yards and tanyards tucked in behind. Handwritten advertising boards abound, telling you the name of a saddler, cabinet-maker, grocer or tea-dealer. If you look to your right as you approach Borough High Street, where the traffic starts to slow with the congestion, you'll see a large new courthouse and the county gaol. A little further on, the old Marshalsea prison still stands. Ahead are the lines of Southwark's red-brick houses: three or four storeys high, many with the names of the shop's proprietor emblazoned in large letters on the front. When they were built, they did not have shop fronts as such. Now every shopkeeper has converted the front of his building to a wide display window composed of dozens of small glazing panels.

When you reach the Thames you'll see that all the houses that used to stand on London Bridge have been demolished, to widen the road for traffic. Now there is just a balustrade on either side, so nothing interrupts your view of the river. You cannot miss the impressive new stone structure on your left, Blackfriars Bridge, built about twenty years ago, with its nine graceful arches. There is another elegant stone bridge around the bend in the river at Westminster, completed in 1750. These two additional permanent crossings have effectively unlocked the land to the south, so that gentlemen and employees in the professions can commute in from their suburban houses in Lambeth, Vauxhall, Clapham and Kennington, their carriages rattling over the flagstones of the bridges every morning until they too grind to a halt in the congestion.

Pause for a moment on London Bridge. If you ever want to gauge the pulse of society, this is the place to do it. London is the heart of England, and the Thames is its major artery. If you look downstream, you'll see a mass of large seagoing vessels moored up in the part of the Thames known as London Pool. There are East Indiamen with three or four masts that have arrived from Bengal, bringing in indigo, muslin and spices. Other ships have come from China, laden with tea. Then there are West Indiamen full of sugar, rum and molasses from Barbados and Jamaica; brigs from the Mediterranean stuffed with coffee, drugs and oils; whalers and trawlers that sail out across the Atlantic; colliers that bring coal down from Newcastle; wine ships that have arrived from France, Portugal and Spain; trawlers heavy with the night's catch; and barges, coasters and lighters involved in domestic trade. There are so many ships that they are stacked four or five deep against the wharves on both banks. Small boats and wherries cross the gap between them. With the forest of masts along each riverbank, you can barely see the Custom House on your left, the Tower of London further on or the warehouses and breweries on your right. Nowhere else in Britain will you find such a crowded waterway.

As the morning light reflects off the crests of the waves and gulls swoop down, calling their harsh cries, you cross to the other side of the bridge and look west. No large ships are to be seen here. Instead there are hundreds of small boats. Watermen ply their trade, rowing or sailing their wherries across from one set of river stairs to another with one or two passengers, or bobbing where they are moored in clutches of threes or fours at the wharves. Just where the river bends, beyond Blackfriars Bridge, there is a stately new edifice rising high above the line of warehouses and wharf buildings. Somerset House is the masterpiece of the architect Sir William Chambers, built recently to house civil servants, the Royal Academy and learned societies. A little way beyond that is the Adelphi, the triumph of Robert Adam, the other great architect of the time. This is a magnificent development of town houses, the finest of them a line of aristocratic residences overlooking the river, raised on a classical colonnade. Behind these buildings on your right the skyline is sprinkled with church towers and spires, all of which are dominated by the great dome of Sir Christopher Wren's cathedral. In the distance you can see the roofs and towers of Westminster Abbey, St Margaret's Church and St Stephen's Chapel, which now serves as the House of Commons. A little further to your left is the south bank, a more industrial environment, as you can tell from the innumerable warehouses and tall chimneys of the dye works, foundries and breweries. One of the most striking buildings is the Albion Mill at the southern end of Blackfriars Bridge, a recently completed six-storey structure. This is where almost all of the city's corn is ground, between twenty pairs of steam-driven millstones.[2] Equally impressive is the Anchor Brewery in Park Street, the largest such establishment in the city. Nearby stands the medieval tower of St Saviour's church, better known to you as Southwark

Cathedral, which still proudly lords it over all the chimneys in the neighbourhood.

Now turn towards the heart of the city. Straight ahead of you, just north of the bridge, stands the impressive column of the Monument, topped with its gilded urn, commemorating the Great Fire of London. This side of it is the tall stone tower of St Magnus the Martyr, with its black clock set on a long metal arm above the roadway, telling all those crossing the bridge exactly how late they are running. On a spring morning such as this, many shop attendants, clerks, traders and businessmen are keeping an eye on it as they hurry along, sometimes stepping into the road and running the risk of being struck by a carriage. Once inside the city, the tall houses make the streets them-selves dark and labyrinthine.[3] The smoke-blackened bricks of the buildings do not help: these were originally a rich red but have turned a filthy dark brown after more than a century of smoke and dust. Indeed, it is only because it is a spring morning that your view of the buildings is not shrouded in smog.

You will soon get lost. It's difficult not to, given the size of the place. Contemporary guidebooks delight in providing mind-twisting statistics to emphasise the capital's scale. The third edition of John Mazzinghi's guide, published in 1793, notes that the city has more than 8,000 lanes, courts and streets, 71 squares and 152,169 houses. In addition, there are almost 500 churches and chapels; 43 law courts; 19 prisons; 23 hospitals; 300 schools; 4,000 private academies; 742 taverns; 580 inns; 822 coffee houses; and almost 8,000 alehouses.[4] Already the city is too large for anyone to know it entirely: even the hackney-cab drivers occasionally get lost.

'Improvement' is just as much a watchword here as it is in the provincial towns. All eight of London's historic gates have long since been removed, the last being demolished in 1767. The street surfaces throughout the city have been improved with Scottish granite slabs, with drainage channels on both sides and raised pavements of Purbeck stone. By 1790 you will find very few cobbled streets in the city centre, and hardly any with gutters running down the middle. The old signs projecting out across the roadways have similarly been taken down and placed flat against the shop fronts, creating a much cleaner street scene. Pairs of street lamps that used to be lit only on moonless nights, and which were extinguished after midnight, are now lit every night and allowed to burn through to daybreak. It is spectacular to look along

Oxford Street after dark and see the whole length lit up.[5] It is not surprising that London is said to be the best-paved and best-lit capital in Europe. When the prince of Monaco visits, he arrives in the evening and thinks that the whole city has been illuminated in his honour.[6]

The quality of domestic housing is also improving. Indeed, you will be able to date the houses around you simply by glancing at them. If the building is wooden and jettied out over the street, it pre-dates the Great Fire of 1666. If it is built of red brick and has sash windows with frames that are flush with the walls, rather than being set back a few inches, it probably pre-dates the Building Act of 1709. If the bricks are dark grey, then the house dates from the eighteenth century. If the wooden sides of the windows are almost invisible – not just set back from the front but recessed into the walls on either side – then the house was built after the Building Act of 1774. This last-mentioned Act also stipulates that bow-shaped shop windows cannot protrude more than 10 inches into the street and that no woodwork should be on display except for shop fronts and doors. Such rules were devised to limit the risk of fire – the impact of the Great Fire is deeply etched on the minds of Londoners – but the result is the distinctive appearance of a London town house.

As we have already seen, 'improvement' makes land a profitable investment, which means that meadows are now turned into streets and squares. A key moment in this respect is the building of the New Road (known to you as Marylebone Road and Euston Road) in the 1750s. This not only provides a fast route between the old city and the West End but extends the capital's northern border and draws people's attention to the many acres that are just waiting for development. The landowners are only too pleased to oblige, with elegant new squares and streets. Manchester Square is built in 1776 and work on Bedford Square starts the same year. Robert Adam switches his attention from the Adelphi to Portland Place at about the same time, aiming to create an avenue of noble palaces that will join up with the New Road near the southern edge of Marylebone Park (known later as Regent's Park). To the west, on the other side of the marsh that will become Belgravia, the architect Henry Holland is constructing the core of Hans Town – Hans Place, Cadogan Place and Sloane Street – by building plain brick terraces of houses for the middle classes.

A city whose fashionable areas are expanding on this scale requires a similar growth of working-class housing. Hence the slums of

St Giles-in-the-Fields are spreading out, populated by Irish immigrants. In Westminster the clearance of the narrow streets has led to the displacement of many working-class families to the other side of the river, where lines of small houses are being squeezed in between the main streets. East of the city, low-value terraces are spreading along the main roads, the areas between them being filled with the 'rookeries', where every room from the cellar to the garret is let out at cheap rates. Often there are several families living in each one. Those in the cellars frequently share their accommodation with their pigs.[7]

Of all the building sites in and around the city, the most prestigious is undoubtedly that of Carlton House. This early-eighteenth-century mansion was once the home of Prince Frederick, father of George III, but is a somewhat rambling monstrosity by 1783, when the king gives it to his twenty-one-year-old son, the future Prince Regent, as his official residence. The prince commissions Henry Holland to remodel the building. Now you'll see a screen of Ionic columns fronting Pall Mall and, in the courtyard behind it, a great portico, which projects far enough to allow carriages to collect and deliver the prince and his entourage without them getting wet in the rain. Elegant shallow wings of stone are symmetrically placed on each side of the north front, with a balustrade across the top of the whole edifice. But it is the interiors that are its chief adornment, especially Holland's great oval staircase and the state apartments. Every visitor who comes to London wishes to see it, in preference to the rambling old St James's Palace, George III's official residence further along Pall Mall, and Buckingham House, where Queen Charlotte spends most of her time.

If you walk east along Pall Mall, you will search in vain for present-day Trafalgar Square. Its site is still occupied by the Royal Mews, which now serve as the royal stables, overlooked by St Martin's Church and the parish workhouse. Down where Cockspur Street meets Whitehall, the statue of Charles I stands in the middle of the road, acting as a roundabout for the traffic of carriages and wagons supplying the city's markets. At the bottom of Whitehall, the Palace of Westminster is still a cluster of medieval buildings around Westminster Hall, albeit with the addition of the New Stone Building, dating from the 1760s. Coffee houses are built right up against the hall itself, obscuring the fine sculptures of the old building. Heading on back to the Strand, the houses and shops seem to jostle each other on both sides of the street. On the north side is the Exeter Exchange, a shopping arcade built in the previous century and still popular for its fashionable tailors, hosiers and milliners. On the upper floors you'll find an auction room and a menagerie. You can sometimes hear big cats roaring and monkeys screeching as you gaze at the wares on display in a shop window. Other than this, it will be the hundreds of large signboards in the Strand that command your attention, emblazoned in large golden characters with the name and trade of every sort of artisan: from cobblers and hatters to tea-dealers and umbrella-makers. The most common designation among them all is 'Dealer in foreign spiritous liquors'.[8]

Turn up Southampton Street to Covent Garden. The piazza, which Inigo Jones laid out 150 years ago, is still home to the second-largest market in London, after Smithfield.[9] Here, between Jones's church and the Covent Garden Theatre, traders are doing business among a dozen ramshackle buildings and sheds, selling flowers, fruit and vegetables. Many of them are women, hauling full baskets from the back of their covered stalls to the front, where they arrange them artfully to catch the eye. Men and women push wheelbarrows through the crowds of shoppers and people gossiping, with dogs running around their heels. Horse-drawn wagons stand around the perimeter, waiting to be unloaded. Listen for a moment and you'll hear the iron-tired wheels grinding on the cobbles and market traders calling out in hard London accents how much their flowers or oranges are. Others are shouting out the prices of hot pies or copies of the latest broadside ballad. Some lads advertise their shoe-cleaning services; girls with pails suspended from a yoke across their shoulders call out in the nearby lanes for anyone who wants to buy milk. Everything is on sale here, it seems, from matches to the morning newspapers.

This is another dimension of London's expansion: its trading activity. John Mazzinghi's guidebook will tell you that there are thirty-four markets in the capital.[10] Some of them are only for wholesale dealing, such as the Corn Exchange in Mark Lane and the Coal Exchange in Thames Street. Others are purely retail establishments, especially the food markets in the newly developed residential areas, like Carnaby Street, Oxford Street and Shepherd's Market. A few are both retail and wholesale, including Covent Garden, Billingsgate Fish Market and Spitalfields. Vegetables and fruit are carted through the city from the market gardens to the west and south. Animals bound for Smithfield are driven there on the hoof: more than 90,000 cattle and almost one million sheep and lambs change hands there every year. This is in addition to the 337,000 pigs sold at various markets in the city. Billingsgate sees seventeen million mackerel sold annually, and thousands of boatloads of other species – 'every fish except the whale and the goldfish', as the market traders will proudly tell you. The guts, scales and blood give the place a powerful aroma: people looking for the fish market are told to head to the Monument and then follow their noses. As for drink, it is said that every year the good people of London and their guests quaff 84 million gallons of beer, 10 million gallons of wine and more than 14 million gallons of spirits.[11] Even including the suburbs and the large number of visitors, that is an awful lot of booze. London produces more than 90 per cent of the nation's supply of gin – but as you can see, a lot of it does not travel very far.[12]

To escape the stench and bustle of the city, you'll want to head to one of the capital's parks. These are all open to the public during daylight hours, as you'd expect, but none of them looks like it does in the modern world. Green Park is a meadow enclosed by a high brick wall; it has a long, oval reservoir at its north-west corner; another artificial pond, Tyburn Pool, in the centre; and a library. It is now a popular venue for gentlemen to fight duels at dawn; so, depending on the time of your visit, you may find it unusually dramatic. St James's Park is also enclosed by a wall and locked at night, but there are so many key-holders that it might as well be open to the public. Coming here on a spring morning, you might consider it rather ordinary: just a semicircle of ground dominated by a large pool called the 'canal' – half a mile long and 100 feet wide – between the queen's residence, Buckingham House, at one end, and the Parade Ground, at Whitehall, at the other. However, if you return in the afternoon you'll see the crowds of well-to-do Londoners who promenade here; and if you come back after dark, you'll encounter a small army of prostitutes who have copies of the keys, like their clients. As for Marylebone Park, it is much more peaceful, being leased out to farmers as fields. You won't see any hot-headed duellists or dusky damsels here – just ruminating cattle.

Hyde Park is the most social of all the London parks. It is a largely treeless, grassy expanse, still surrounded by a 10ft-high brick wall built by Charles II. It owes much of its appearance to Queen Caroline, wife of George II, who created the natural-looking lake, the Serpentine, in the southern part. Each Sunday afternoon in spring and summer a grand display of gentility and fashion takes place here. Thousands of spectators crowd alongside a railing that runs for three-quarters of a mile from Oxford Street to Hyde Park Corner, to watch a parade of two rows of open-top carriages: one moving slowly one way, the other moving equally slowly in the opposite direction. The carriages all sport coats of arms on their black lacquer doors and in them sit the noble and the wealthy, the ambitious and the famous, talking to their companions.[13] Young gentlemen on horseback ride among them, talking to the ladies in the carriages or their mothers and fathers. Every so often a passenger calls to her driver to halt, so she can speak to a friend in a carriage travelling the other way, and the whole gay procession comes to halt. The extraordinary spectacle emphasises the great importance of being seen – and that applies as much to the spectators behind the railings as to the *haut ton*, the people of high fashion riding around the park.

The other delightful green spaces that you should take advantage of on your visit to late-eighteenth-century London are the tea gardens. These are places where refreshments are provided and where customers may wander across the lawns. They can often be found in the grounds of old manor houses a little way out of the city and are particularly popular with middle-class citizens on Sunday afternoons. Mazzinghi lists eighteen of them, including the famous White Conduit House in Islington; Canonbury House, also in Islington; the Cromwell Gardens in Brompton; and Grove House in Camberwell. At the Adam and Eve tea gardens in St Pancras the proprietors keep cows and provide guests with syllabubs made from their cream.[14] Other tea gardens specialise in almond cheesecakes and dainty fruit tarts and pastries. The New Tunbridge Wells garden in Islington prides itself not only on its ornamental sculptures and urns placed picturesquely around the grounds but also on its chalybeate spring, where you can drink the supposedly healing waters. Alternatively, just down the road, you can watch cricket while drinking tea at the White Conduit House.

Pleasure gardens are a much more elaborate affair. In fact there is nothing quite like them in the modern world. They are decorated with fountains and illuminations, and concerts, dinners and dances all take place. Their proprietors try to create a multisensory experience, through the scents of flowers, the sound of music, the taste of food and drink and the visual design of the grounds. If you add the erotic thrill of a secret assignation in a dark corner or a grotto, you could add a few more sensations to that list. The Vauxhall Gardens, south of the river, welcome visitors every day except Sunday from May to the end of September. On paying your 1s entrance fee and entering the gate, you'll see the South Walk: a wide, gravelled path about 300 yards long, with beautifully kept trees on either side interspersed with flower beds, and three classical arches along its length framing a view of the 'Ruins of Palmyra' at the far end. In the trees hang thousands of lamps, which, as the evening draws in, gild the leaves beautifully with different colours. A Chinese pavilion is situated in the middle of the gardens, where an orchestra plays every evening. Here, in what is called the Grove, people dance, prior to taking their seats in the colonnades of porticos where private supper tables are arranged, attended by a mass of waiters. The food is extremely expensive and you don't get much for your money: the ham is cut so thin that it becomes a talking point in itself. But you don't come here for the food. In one corner of the garden there is a great rotunda: a round theatre 'glistening with resplendent chandeliers and large mirrors and adorned all around with paintings and sculptures'.[15] There is also an impressive water feature – an immense cascade that is turned on at nine o'clock each evening for fifteen minutes. As you can see, it all adds up to a great theme park of luxury, novelty and indulgence.

Vauxhall's principal rival, Ranelagh Gardens in Chelsea, is smaller but more fashionable and more expensive. The entrance fee is 2s 6d but refreshments are included – you can have as much tea, coffee or punch as you want. It also has long illuminated avenues of trees and flowers, as well as a famed Chinese pavilion. However, the main attraction is the rotunda, which is even more magnificent than that at Vauxhall. It measures 150 feet in diameter and consists of three storeys of splendid classical architecture. The ground floor has dozens of painted arched chambers facing the centre, with candlelit dinner tables set within them. At the centre of the whole edifice is an enormous fire, set under what looks like a church tower supported on four great columns. The venue is one of the wonders of the capital. Karl Moritz declares that all of fashionable London revolves around this building, adding:

On my entry I mixed with this crowd, and what with the constant changing of the faces around me (most of them strikingly beautiful), the illuminations, the majesty and splendour of the place, and the ever-present strains of music, I felt for a moment as a child would on first looking into a fairy-tale.[16]

1810

In marked contrast to the delights of a pleasure garden in late spring, an extended visit to London in winter twenty years later will be char-acterised by the smell of burning coal, stinging smoke and mist. Even from a distance you can see the great round haze of the smog hanging above the city.[17] As you walk through the streets, particles of soot float down through the air and land on you. As Louis Simond puts it, the air

> is loaded with small flakes of smoke, in sublimation – a sort of flower of soot, so light as to float without falling. This black snow sticks to your clothes and linen or alights on your face. You just feel something on your nose or your cheek – the finger is applied mechanically and fixes it into a black patch![18]

For this reason, the *haut ton* vacate the city in November, often not returning until the spring. For those who remain, the city takes on a different atmosphere. Coaches throng the foggy and damp streets, each one equipped with a pair of bright lamps, their light reflected by the wet flagstones of the pavements. The street lights struggle to cut through the mist, which is made darker by the soot particles it contains. Sometimes the fog and smoke are so thick that shops have to keep their lamps burning all day, even at noon.

If you follow the same route that you took on your previous visit, you'll see that the city has expanded even further to the south, reaching down to Kennington Common and beyond – a full two miles from London Bridge. In the chilly December air, the congestion on the bridge itself is worse than it was twenty years earlier: 90,000 people now cross it every day, as well as 4,000 carts, wagons and carriages.[19] Looking out from your previous viewing point, you'll see that there are many more industrial chimneys too. The German visitor Christian Goede describes the south bank as 'black houses of various forms rising here and there in irregular heaps, crowned with clouds of smoke issuing from numerous furnaces'.[20] Beneath Blackfriars Bridge the river is dark with the effluent of sewers.[21] The Albion Mill has recently been demolished, having been gutted in a great fire in 1791 and left derelict until 1809; houses are currently being built on the site. The Anchor Brewery has grown even larger and has now been renamed the Barclay Perkins Brewery. Production has trebled to 260,000 barrels of porter a year, making it the largest brewery in the world.[22]

Looking eastwards, to London Pool, there aren't as many large vessels here as before. The explanation lies downstream, where new docks have been built. Previously there was only Greenland Dock on the south bank, where whalers and timber ships could unload their cargoes. Other vessels had to come up to the city itself to unload. But the East India Dock has recently been built at Blackwall and a little nearer to the city, at the Isle of Dogs, the West India Dock is now also complete. London Dock is open at Wapping and, on the opposite side of the river, the new East Country Dock, the first of what will become the Commercial Docks, is a mass of masts and merchandise. All of these quays and wharves are abuzz with activity even in winter, with massive cranes for unloading and lading the ships, and labourers hauling huge carts of tobacco, wool, cotton and hides in and out of the brick warehouses.

Your first visit will have left you with the impression that London is really two places in one: the fashionable residential district that is expanding to the west, commonly referred to as the 'West End' or 'town', and old London, or 'the city', which is expanding to the east. The official dividing line between the two lies at Temple Bar: the ceremonial archway over the street at the point where Fleet Street becomes the Strand, marking the extent of the authority of the lord mayor of London. If you start out at Temple Bar and walk east into the city, even before daylight you'll find sweepers clearing up the horse dung in the lamplit streets as the night watchman makes his round, calling out the time and the weather. His shouts are accompanied by wagons clattering over the flagstones, already taking goods to or from the warehouses by the river. At dawn you can smell coal smoke in the air from the morning fires and hear the ringing of a dustman's bell, and his regular shout of 'dust ho!' Before long the businessmen's carriages arrive from their residences in the suburbs. The pavements are now likewise filled with pedestrians making their way to work. As daylight grows, the shops start to open. Every blank wall and building-site hoarding is covered with an advertisement for something or other – the most efficacious medicines, the smartest coats, the most accurate watches, the most resilient umbrellas. Occasionally a lane leading down to the river permits a glimpse of labourers working on the barges beneath the seagulls' cries at the quayside. Even though the new docks have taken much of the physical trade out of the city, London still relies on the quays here for its own supplies. Thus you will see many crates and baskets stacked on the wharves awaiting a cart or a barge to take them away.

Walking further east you'll notice that several new public buildings have been erected, despite there being a war in progress. The Bank of England has been wholly transformed by Sir John Soane's grand classical design of interlocking banking halls and offices, surrounded by an imposing high wall with no external windows. Down on the river you'll see that the buildings around Billingsgate Market have also been replaced. The ground floor of the new block beside Billingsgate Wharf has a large open area, where many stalls are set up from 4 a.m. each morning. In the old market square outside you'll see thousands of fish laid out on tables or in baskets. Those who live in that newly built block must either have a very high tolerance for the smell or pay a very low rent. Further to the east, just beside the Tower, the Royal Mint has been completely rebuilt. Continue walking out this way, along the north bank of the river, and you'll pass merchants' houses and lower classes of residence, before reaching an area of rundown maritime-supplies stores, carpenters' workshops, ship-painters' offices and rope-makers' sheds, all of them scented with the rough salt smell of the sea. Beyond these are the new, vast docks with their flagstone-covered piazzas, tall cranes and large warehouses set around a forest of ships' masts.

If you walk in the opposite direction, west from Temple Bar, the streets of the West End are almost empty before dawn. The shops are still closed and the lamps still burning on their tall metal posts. Only the cries of the night watchman and the clatter of the odd stagecoach coming into the city break the silence. At Exeter Exchange, you may well still hear the roar of a lion: there is now a massive signboard on the front of the building that reads: 'Pidcock's Royal Menagerie'. But there are no crowds of men and women flocking to work. At dawn the watchman's voice gives way to that of the rag-and-bone man slowly leading his cart up and down the street, crying,

'Clothes, clothes!' Then the coal wagons arrive, stopping outside almost every house for the coalman to shovel a load directly into the basement. Along come the milkmen, calling out their wares from their slow-moving carts. The mail coaches arrive at speed, swerving around the slow and stationary vehicles, hammering the recitative of iron tires on flagstones. *Clang* goes a street sweeper's spade on the stone as he removes a pile of dung. There is a rumble of traders' carts coming into Covent Garden, and women calling to each other or singing as they set up their stalls. The pavements away from the marketplace, however, are still almost empty, occupied by only a few servants heading out to fetch provisions, and raggedly dressed carpenters, bricklayers and roofers walking into work from their houses in the poorer parts of the city. Not until about eight o'clock do things get going, when the shopkeepers unlock their doors, draw back the shutters and put their choice goods in their windows. A few shops carry the carved and painted royal coat of arms above their signs, with gilt lettering announcing that the proprietor is honoured to serve the royal family.[23] Hackney carriages with their blinkered horses arrive in the fashionable shopping districts carrying those who have remained in the city for the winter, who are now making their way to the coffee houses to read the papers. Gradually more gigs and carriages appear. But it is nothing compared to midday in summer, when the gentlemen with houses in this part of town finally pull their cravats straight, close their doors and step outside to visit one another or their tailors, hatters or snuffbox-makers, and the fashionable ladies go shopping. Then all the streets are filled with coaches, carriages and sedan chairs carried by liveried porters. That brightly coloured bustle lasts until about 3 p.m., when the rich head to dinner and the traffic subsides briefly before the evening rush. This commences about 6 p.m., when people start to head out to brilliantly lit receptions, illuminated shops, raucous alehouses or the theatre. At 10.30, when all the shops are shut, the streets are left to the carriages of party-goers, swift-marching groups of parish constables, people returning from the theatre and prostitutes looking for inebriated clientele.

If your last visit to London was in 1790, by 1810 you will be walking through the city in a state of amazement. Christian Goede leaves the capital for only a few months in 1807 and is astonished by what he finds on his return. 'The principal streets have undergone great changes so that a map made a few years since would now be of little use to a stranger,' he declares.[24] Near his own residence, in Southampton Row, he says:

> The duke of Bedford is engaged in very extensive buildings, and has some thousands of workmen in his employment ... I paused and asked myself whether I had not previously seen these new streets, new squares, new gardens – in a word, this new city ... The opposite side of Southampton Row, late an open space, was not only built upon but inhabited; a coffeehouse was open and some very handsome shops exposed their merchandise to sale![25]

What Goede is witnessing is similarly to be seen wherever great lords have decided to demolish their grand old mansions and turn the sites and their gardens into squares of elegant town houses, to be leased out at substantial rates. In the case of Bedford House, the duke of Bedford is working with the architect James Burton to develop the site and the fields to the north as a huge urban estate, centred on Russell Square.[26] Other lords are doing the same all around the city, albeit not for the same class of residents. Suddenly there are blocks of houses and shops alongside every road emanating from the capital – along Kingsland Road to the north, Mile End Road to the east and the Old Kent Road to the south-east.

Turning to the open spaces, the tea gardens and pleasure gardens are all closed at this time of year. However, if you peek over the walls of Vauxhall Gardens, you'll see that workmen are busy replacing part of the Grove and the Grand Walk with a colonnade decorated with coloured lanterns. This will be the new attraction when the gardens open again to visitors in the spring. As for Ranelagh, alas, that place of wonders is no more: it shut its gates for ever in 1803 and was entirely demolished two years later. It put on some grand events in its final years, with magnificent outdoor 'afternoon break-fasts' for 2,000 people, complete with balloon flights, music and a magnificent ball. Now the gardens form part of the grounds of the Royal Hospital at Chelsea. But their splendour will be remembered by ladies who'll never forget the dashing officers who paid court to them all night in quiet alcoves in the rotunda, or portly old gentlemen who tell you with a wistful sigh that Ranelagh was the place where the most beautiful women in London 'came swimming by you like swans'.[27]

1830

If you thought that a great deal had changed by 1810, then you are in for a shock when you return in the summer of 1830. Even before you get to London Bridge, you'll notice the extension of the built-up area to the south, the infilling of so many fields, the relocation of Bethlehem Lunatic Asylum to St George's Fields and the rebuilding of the Marshalsea Prison, where Charles Dickens's father has recently spent a few unhappy months. In Southwark you'll see that the shop windows have grown taller and wider as manufacturers work out how to make larger panes of crown glass. But then you'll come to the bridge and will forget about window sizes, for a little to the west of old London Bridge stands the stunning New London Bridge, consisting of five low stone arches, designed by the Scottish engineer John Rennie. The old crossing, which has stood since the twelfth century, is due to be demolished in August next year. Look downstream across London Pool, and you'll see a new quay, St Katharine Docks, just beyond the Tower, and more docks and wharves on the south bank of the river. Paddle steamers with tall funnels and plumes of smoke rising above them now regularly make the trip down to Gravesend and Margate. For fifteen years these vessels have puffed their way through wind and waves to the wharves here, their lights of an evening 'dancing on the ripples like will o' the wisps'.[28]

Turn the other way and you are in for just as great a surprise. Between you and Blackfriars Bridge there is Queen Street Bridge (later known as Southwark Bridge), another of John Rennie's designs, built in 1819. It consists of three iron spans, each 240 feet wide. The waves sparkle bright in the summer sun but if you squint you might see that, on the far side of Blackfriars Bridge, there is another new stone bridge, Waterloo Bridge, again designed by John Rennie and completed in 1817. If you were to sail upstream you'd also float under Vauxhall Bridge, the first iron bridge over the river, finished in 1816, and Hammersmith Bridge, opened in 1817. All these new bridges are having a huge impact on the wherries and watermen. Who wants to disembark from a carriage, step onto an unstable boat and run the risk of getting splashed or soaked, pay for the privilege, and then have to hail a hackney cab on the other side? It's much easier simply to drive across the river in style and safety, paying merely a few pennies for the convenience. Thus there are many fewer small craft on the

river than there were in 1790. Their numbers will continue to decline
too: workmen are currently constructing a tunnel from Wapping to
Rotherhithe – the world's first underwater thoroughfare – under the
direction of Marc Isambard Brunel, ably assisted by his son, Isambard
Kingdom Brunel. They still have another ten years' work ahead of
them but, evidently, the days of the watermen are numbered.

Even a cursory tour of the city will reveal many new public buildings. There are now two universities: London University in Gower
Street (later known as University College London), and King's College,
currently under construction in the Strand. Another major educational
edifice, the London Institution, has been erected in Finsbury Circus,
where it occupies the former site of the Bethlehem Lunatic Asylum.
In addition, dozens of large churches have been built by the Church
Commissioners. The site of what will become Trafalgar Square is
being cleared; the old houses and the Royal Mews have already been
demolished. The College of Physicians building, designed by Robert
Smirke, faces the site. Smirke is also responsible for the impressive
new General Post Office in St Martin's le Grand, as well as an experimental new prison at Millbank, and the main wing of the British
Museum, currently under construction. James Wyatt and John Soane
are two more architects who have been hard at work on public buildings: between them they have completely remodelled the area around
the Houses of Parliament so that Wyatt's neo-gothic House of Lords
now faces the street and Soane's law courts surround Westminster
Hall, where once those coffee houses used to stand. If you drop by
Covent Garden you'll see that the whole area is currently a building
site, as the new granite market building is laid out. If high-class shopping is your thing, then you'll be pleased to hear that Burlington
Arcade has opened its doors on the north side of Piccadilly. Or if
conviviality is more your cup of tea, many lavish new club houses
have been built, including the United Service Club, the Travellers Club
and the Athenaeum, all on Pall Mall.

The biggest surprise to you, however, will be the great development
of Regent's Park and its long, curling tail, Regent Street. Over the last
twenty years the Prince Regent has attempted to realise his dream of
creating an architectural heart to his metropolis to rival Paris. Now,
to the north of the New Road, where before there were only fields
and gardens, there is a town within a town. The prince's chosen
architect, John Nash, first builds Park Crescent at the top of Portland

Place, which looks out north over the New Road. Significantly, he covers the brickwork in stucco: a fine plaster that gives a smooth finish to the walls and which can be used to provide ornamental detail. This sets a pattern for all the magnificent terraces that he goes on to construct around the park. Look out for the fine cast-iron railings and gas lamps as you walk around these streets. Note too how the road surfaces are watered twice each day, to stop the dust rising and choking those riding in open-topped carriages.[29] In the park itself, where the grass is fading in the summer heat, there is a nursery at the centre and a great lake on the west side. The grounds and buildings of the Zoological Society, with aviaries for eagles and pens for lions and wolves, can be found on the north side. On the south-east corner there is a circular building, the Colosseum, modelled on the Pantheon in Rome, where you can queue up to see the enormous 360-degree panorama of London – claimed to be the largest painting ever made – drawn by Thomas Hornor from the top of St Paul's Cathedral and painted by Edmund Parris. In behind the aristocratic terraces, working-class districts have been constructed where Nash has also laid out Cumberland and Clarence Markets, alongside houses where the market traders live. The new Regent's Canal runs along the top of the park, providing a link between the Grand Junction Canal at Paddington and the Thames at Limehouse.

The royal development doesn't end there. Coming south from Regent's Park you will pass through Park Square and Park Crescent into Portland Place and then Regent Street. This is the new wide avenue that connects Regent's Park with Carlton House. The buildings here are an array of private and public structures: three churches, a concert hall for the London Philharmonic Society called the Argyll Rooms, a hotel, a bank, many shops and fine town houses. Anne Lister, a young gentlewoman from Yorkshire, writes that 'surely there is not so fine a street in Europe – so long, so spacious, so consisting entirely of beautiful buildings. Houses like palaces, noble shops ... '[30] All this gives the city a much more European feel. Prince Hermann Pückler-Muskau declares that London is 'much improved in the direction of Regent Street, Portland Place and Regent's Park', adding that, as a result, it 'has the air of a seat of government and not of an immeasurable metropolis of shopkeepers'.[31] This would be music to the king's ears, for it is exactly what George IV has been trying to achieve. But then, three years after the building of Regent Street, the king decides to demolish Carlton House – the very building on which the whole development is centred. Instead, he redevelops his mother's residence, Buckingham House, turning it into a palace, with a white marble arch designed by Nash as the main gate (subsequently relocated to the top of Park Lane). The work proves incredibly costly and is still unfinished at the time of the king's death, in the summer of 1830.

Wandering around the city, you'll see no abatement in the amount of development under way. Many London squares have been newly laid out to accommodate the prosperous classes, among them Torrington, Woburn, Euston, Tavistock, Bryanston, Montagu and Dorset Squares. Some of these are constructed of brown brick with contrasting plaster cornices; some adopt Nash's stucco across their frontage. Most are built around small private gardens, enclosed by iron railings. The smell of mignonette (*reseda*), which the well-to-do like to place in their front windows, wafts across the pavements.[32] Perhaps the most elegant of all the new houses are those currently under construction around Belgrave Square and Eaton Square. Thomas Cubitt is the man behind these: he has drained the marshes and set about building mansions to rival those around Regent's Park designed by Nash. Indeed, the aristocracy hardly know which end of town to live in.

Not all the new building in London consists of town houses for the rich. A vast amount of cheaper accommodation is being constructed too. Much of this is built on the site of the old rookeries. When the radical campaigner Francis Place undertakes a thorough inspection of the East End in 1824 he remarks that:

> Great as is the mass of poverty and misery of places along the shore from the Tower to the Isle of Dogs, still, except in the very worst of these places and among the most wretched of the wretched, there is also considerable improvement. On the leading streets [in Wapping] the improvement in all respects is great. The old wooden houses ... have either been pulled down or burnt down, and others of brick built in their places.[33]

Similar improvements are to be found to the south of the river. As Francis Place observes, 'many of these streets are inhabited by very poor people but neither the streets nor the houses are by any means so dirty as were the narrow streets and lanes which have been destroyed to make way for modern improvements. Nor do they stink as such places used to do.'[34]

If you visit the parish of St Giles, however, you will find that Place's positive remarks are not the whole story. The clearing away of the old courts here has led to more overcrowding, as there are now fewer houses to accommodate a growing number of people. Moreover, not every old house has been rebuilt, and not every new one is properly maintained. In the working-class districts, therefore, you'll still find courts and tenements reminiscent of Liverpool's deprived areas. In his work as a surveyor, Mr Howell comes across buildings that are too repulsive even to enter. On one occasion, when examining some houses in St Giles High Street, he walks through the passage beneath the first house and is met with the following sight:

> The yard [was] covered with night soil from the overflowing of the privy, to the depth of nearly six inches, and bricks were placed to enable the inmates to get across dry shod; in addition to this, there was an accumulation of filth piled up against the walls of the most objection-able nature. The interior of the house partook something of the same character, and discovering upon examination that the other houses were nearly similar, I found a detailed survey impracticable, and was obliged to content myself with making general observations. My duties, as one of the surveyors to a fire office, call me to all parts of the town, and I am constantly shocked almost beyond endurance at the filth and misery in which a large part of our population are permitted to drag on a diseased and miserable existence.[35]

There is another aspect of London life that is arguably even more unpleasant than the overflowing cesspits – overcrowded cemeteries. Cremation is illegal, so the huge increase in the population of the capital has meant that the old churchyards are crammed with decom-posing corpses. As one report notes, the vaults and burial ground of Brunswick Chapel in Limehouse are in a particularly poor state:

> From the accounts of individuals residing in the adjoining houses, it would appear that stench arising therefrom, particularly when a grave happens to be opened during the summer months, is most noxious. In one case it is described to have produced instant nausea and vomiting,

and attacks of illness are frequently imputed to it. Some say they have never had a good day's health since they have resided so near the chapel ground, which, I may remark, is about five feet above the level of the surrounding yards, and very muddy – so much so that pumps are frequently used to expel the water from the vaults into the streets.[36]

After experiencing the stench of ordure and bodily decay, you will no doubt be happy at last to reach the sunlit parks, even though the grass is somewhat faded in the heat. In St James's Park you'll see that the straight 100ft-wide canal, which led from Buckingham House to Horse Guards Parade, has now been redesigned with an undulating bank, to resemble a natural lake. Several massive bronze cannon have been placed near the gates.[37] As you walk towards Hyde Park, you can't fail to notice the new triumphal arch at Hyde Park Corner and the screen entrance to the park itself, both designed by Decimus Burton (son of James Burton). These face each other, thereby creating an impressive link between the park and Buckingham Palace. Walking into the park, you'll see a bridge has been built over the Serpentine, and a statue of Achilles the Defender erected. The funds for this monument were raised by a group of British ladies to honour the achievements of the duke of Wellington and many people snigger at this fact, for the Greek hero's supersized manhood was initially on view for all the patriotic ladies to see – so obviously so that it had to be covered up with a well-positioned fig leaf. Down towards the river, Chelsea is still home to a large number of market gardens, where hundreds of acres are dedicated to producing vegetables for the city. Do not think of trespassing here: on the fences are boards painted with the words, 'Beware of man traps and spring guns.'[38] As for the Vauxhall Gardens, sadly, they are now struggling to attract a clientele. They only open three days a week in summer, and admission has gone up to 4s 6d. Their new owners are doing their best to attract the fashionable set with such initiatives as having 1,000 soldiers re-enact the Battle of Waterloo in the grounds, but the sad truth is that such venues have had their day.

Finally, to appreciate the London of 1830 fully, you need to see it at night. Where once Oxford Street was a two-mile-long stretch of burning oil lamps, now it is a blaze of gas lights outside all the gentlemen's houses and places of entertainment. From London Bridge you can see the ships' lamps flickering on the waves of the Thames, the long lines of street lights along the north bank, the lights in the windows of the private houses of the Adelphi, and the gas lights across the bridges. In the Strand, people are gathering around the gas-lit windows of Ackermann's Repository, viewing the latest caricature prints. In a nearby chemist's shop there are large globes of glass filled with illuminated liquid coloured deep red, blue and green.[39] In the street, kidney-pie vendors underneath a gas street lamp are vying with oyster sellers to attract the custom of the passers-by, who are returning in twos and threes from the theatre. Horse-drawn hackney cabs, each with a pair of headlamps, are making their way towards Drury Lane to collect theatre-goers. You notice a board above a closed shop advertising top hats 'twice as tall as any other'. There are no more lions to be heard roaring in the Strand: Exeter Exchange has been demolished. As you walk past the site, where scaffolding surrounds the future Exeter Hall, you might reflect on the changing times. Twenty-two miles away, at Windsor, King George IV is dying. How much has changed in the four decades since he was first proposed as regent.

3

The People

The extremes of opulence and of want are more remarkable, and more constantly obvious, in this country than in any other I ever saw.

John Quincy Adams (1816)[1]

How many people live in Regency Britain? This is a burning question in the London clubs and coffee houses, for never has the country seen anything like the present levels of growth. In 1791 the population stands at just under 10 million; by 1831 it has reached 16.3 million – an increase of two-thirds in only forty years. Never before has it grown so rapidly, nor will it ever do so again. Wonderful, you might think: surely this is a sign of better health and greater prosperity? In some respects, it is. But that's not the whole story. If your country has limited resources and the population increases by two thirds, you cannot expect everyone to be as well off as before. If all other factors stay the same, the capital assets of the nation will be shared by two-thirds more people and thus real wealth per head will decline in proportion. In reality, of course, all other factors do *not* stay the same. A greater labour force increases production. Imports and exports grow in volume and value. Technology improves and manufacturing processes become more efficient. However, one important factor does stay constant: the ownership of assets. Agricultural land, mines, factories and docks remain in the hands of a relatively small number of rich families. As the population grows still further and demand for food and consumer goods grows even greater, so these families become even wealthier. At the same time, those who have nothing to sell but their labour become comparatively poorer. They are forced to compete for jobs with more and more workers. In the industrial towns, where economic activity attracts incomers by the thousand, the very prosperity of a community can lead to overcrowding, reduced wages and the general impoverishment of working people – which is something of an irony, as I am sure you will agree.

Population of Great Britain (millions)[2]			
	England	**Wales**	**Scotland**
1791	*c.* 7.8	*c.* 0.5	*c.* 1.5
1801	8.30	0.59	1.60
1811	9.49	0.67	1.80
1821	11.19	0.79	2.09
1831	12.99	0.90	2.37

The key to understanding the problem of deprivation in this period is food. Although it is untrue that Marie Antoinette says 'let them eat cake' during the French Revolution (the phrase comes from an earlier French princess), those words are a salutary reminder that the poor do not always have enough to eat and the rich do not always appreciate this – and that goes for Britain as well as France.[3] This is why in 1798 a conscientious clergyman, Thomas Robert Malthus, publishes *An Essay on the Principle of Population*. He is concerned that, while the country as a whole is getting richer, the poor are worse off than before. He disagrees with those who believe that political reform is a silver bullet that will alleviate the suffering of landless labourers and their families. Rather, he sees the fundamental issue as 'natural law', or more specifically, 'the constant tendency in all animated life to increase beyond the nourishment provided for it'.[4] He reckons that the population of Great Britain, if it is unchecked by food shortages and diseases, will double every twenty-five years, as it has done recently in the newly independent United States. Food production on a heavily populated island like Great Britain simply cannot keep pace. Already by 1806 the country is importing £600,000 worth of butter and cheese every year and £2.2 million of corn.[5] Heavy tariffs on imports and transportation keep prices high. Thus the plight of the poor grows worse every year precisely because the population is increasing. When there is a harvest failure, the result is widespread malnutrition and real hardship.

Malthus's *Essay* attracts a great deal of criticism. It is true that it does not give sufficient weight to technology. In addition, he overestimates how much the suffering of the poor is a common concern. Factory owners naturally welcome the lower wages that accompany population growth. Political reformers also dislike Malthus's economic theory because it threatens to invalidate their calls for change: they want to blame the political system for the current levels of deprivation, not 'natural law'. Still others have professional reasons for denigrating Malthus's theory. The statistician John Rickman observes that population growth is partly the result of people living longer. He estimates that the proportion of the British population dying every year has declined from one in forty in 1780 to one in fifty by 1810.[6] But Malthus has his supporters too. Robert Southey is one of them, and he comments on the subject with wry humour:

> It has been discovered that the world is over-peopled, and that it always must be so, from an error in the constitution of nature; that the law which says 'increase and multiply' was given without sufficient consideration; in short, that He who made the world does not know how to manage it properly, and therefore there are serious thoughts of requesting Parliament to take the business out of His hands.[7]

Almost the only point on which everyone agrees is the need for the government to have precise population figures. The Census Act is accordingly passed by Parliament. On Tuesday 10 March 1801, government officers ask how many people live in every single house in the kingdom. They also compile records of how many baptisms and burials take place annually in each parish, thereby allowing them to determine rates of population growth. John Rickman is appointed to oversee the process, which is thereafter repeated every ten years.

The early-nineteenth-century censuses show that Regency society is very different from its twenty-first-century equivalent. Well over one-third of the population is aged under fifteen; in the twenty-first century it is less than one-fifth.[8] At the other end of the age spectrum, only about one in twenty is aged sixty-five or over: an even smaller proportion than in Tudor times, and nowhere near the one in six in the twenty-first century.[9] In short, society is much younger than it is in the modern world.

The small proportion of old people seems to counter John Rickman's assertion that people are living longer. But as always, the truth lies in the detail. Overall, life expectancy at birth in England does increase

Age-related structure of English society (in per cent)[10]					
England	Aged 0–14	15–24	25–44	45–64	Over 65
1801	36.40	17.71	25.37	15.52	5.00
1831	38.76	18.75	24.72	13.49	4.28
2011	17.68	13.08	27.53	25.37	16.34

by about five years between 1780 and 1816, from thirty-five to forty.[11] However, this bald statistic fails to differentiate between rural and urban living. In London, a newborn baby can look forward to almost twenty-seven years of life. In Leeds, life expectancy at birth is twenty-one; in Manchester, twenty; in Bolton, nineteen; and in Liverpool, just seventeen.[12] Large towns are places of sickness and death, and the industrial towns are the worst of all. But this geographical differentiation still doesn't tell the full story. If you are born into a wealthy family in London, you can expect to live to forty-four; if you belong to a tradesman's family, you'll probably be buried at twenty-five; and if you are born into a labourer's family, you will be lucky to see your twenty-third birthday. Still, London labourers are generally better off than those in the industrial towns; the average age at death among the working class in Preston is eighteen and in Liverpool it's sixteen. Living conditions are the primary problem of course, as we saw in chapter 1. The average worker in Bury or Ashton-under-Lyne can expect to live to nineteen, but if you are living in the unsewered slums of one of those towns, then your life expectancy at birth is just thirteen.[13] These figures may be compared with the levels of mortality among enslaved people in Trinidad, where the average age at death is seventeen.[14]

One of the reasons why these average ages are so low is that many deaths occur in infancy. Across Britain's entire population, almost one in three children dies before his or her fifth birthday.[15] As you'd expect, the industrial towns see the sharpest levels of infant mortality. In Liverpool, 53 per cent die before they are five; in Preston, 57 per cent. Again, these figures may be compared with those of enslaved people in the West Indies, among whom 55 per cent of boys and 58 per cent of girls die before their fifth birthday.[16] Although John Rickman claims that the poor too must be experiencing the longer lifespans that he has noticed nationally, you cannot help but feel he should visit Preston and see for himself. Here, the truth of Malthus's message is startlingly clear. As the population of the town dramatically increases, life expectancy shockingly diminishes – from thirty-one in 1783 to eighteen in 1821.[17]

So what counts as 'old age' in Regency Britain? On the strength of the above, you might be forgiven for thinking that you are 'old' if you reach adulthood. Indeed, if you make it to twenty-five in the 1820s you're already older than half the population. 'We live a large portion of our lives between fifteen and twenty-five,' writes Elizabeth Ham, a farmer's daughter, in her autobiography.[18] Lord Byron similarly declares that 'the better part of life is over' by the age of twenty-five.[19] If you think he is exaggerating for effect – which he frequently does – bear in mind that he himself expires at the age of thirty-six, despite all his privileges. But do people really consider themselves 'old' at thirty? No. The concept of 'old age' doesn't quite work that way – and for a very interesting reason. In the modern world, when life expectancy at birth is seventy-nine for men and eighty-three for women, the modal age at death – the most common age at which men and women die after surviving infancy – is eighty-five for men and eighty-eight for women. This close correlation of the mean and the mode is typical in a civilised society with good medical care. In the early nineteenth century, when life expectancy at birth is about forty, the modal age of death is over seventy – more than *thirty* years greater than life expectancy at birth. Thus the biblical 'three score years and ten' is quite achievable, and it is mainly that figure which denotes 'old age'. You just have to be lucky. A few very lucky people live to see their hundredth birthday. Phoebe Hessel dies on 12 December 1821, aged 108, having been baptised in Stepney on 13 April 1713 – and she achieves that age despite receiving a bayonet wound when fighting alongside her lover at the Battle of Fontenoy in 1745.[20] Cases of extreme longevity are regularly reported in *The Times*. On 5 August 1797 the small print carries an obituary of Daniel Bull Macarthy esquire, who has died at the age of 111. The paper attributes his long life to the fact that he used to walk eight miles or more every day with his greyhounds and drink copious amounts of rum and brandy. I suspect that his fifth wife might have had more to do with it. When they married he was eighty-four and she just fourteen. They had twenty children together over the following twenty years.

Social Order

Which is more important to you: status or wealth? You might reply
that they are pretty much the same thing. However, in the Regency
period, status means much more than wealth, and wealth is no guarantee of high status. For instance, the politician Thomas Creevey
moves in the highest social circles even though his personal income
is no more than that of a yeoman farmer: members of the upper
classes never cease to regard him as 'one of us'. Conversely, you might
be a millionaire industrialist but find yourself shunned by the *haut ton*
on account of having made your money through trade. Strange as it
may seem, it is socially acceptable to have inherited your wealth from
knights who slaughtered people in the Middle Ages but not to have
made it yourself by manufacturing useful things that improve people's
lives. That is why people make such a show of their status, parading
their coats of arms at every opportunity – on the doors of their
carriages, on the handles of their cutlery, on their hat boxes, snuffboxes, walking canes, signet rings, bookplates and dinner services – and
commemorating their distinguished ancestors in portraits, books and
church memorials. Evidence of your family history is a status symbol.
Having said all this, even the oldest noble families sometimes fall on
hard times, and when that happens, they quickly learn to swallow
their ancestral pride and embrace the self-made super-rich as if they
were long-lost cousins. Many an ancient family is saved from ruin by
a marriage between the heir and a *nouveau riche* bride.

These points about status and wealth feed into a widespread concern
with social class. Whether or not you will be able to rent a house,
hire a coach or even have credit in a shop will depend on whether
you look as though you come from a prosperous family. When entering
an inn, the landlord will decide which room to offer you based on
the impression you make. If you go to church on a Sunday, you'll see
members of the local gentry take their places in their private boxes:
if you are not with them, you'll sit with their tenants on the common
pews. Whether or not you can vote in a parliamentary election is also
a matter of class: only men who own freehold land worth £2 per year
or copyhold land worth £10, or have attended an English university,
can take part in an election. This only includes about 450,000 voters.[21]
Although modern concerns about class are passionately argued, they
are a pale shadow of the Regency obsession with the subject.

THE MONARCHY

In terms of status, the king is the highest-ranking individual in the United Kingdom of Great Britain (which, from 1801, formally becomes the United Kingdom of Great Britain and Ireland). He has the power to form governments and to dismiss them. He is the head of the Church of England. He can create lords and thus put men directly into Parliament. His spending power is greater than that of any other individual because royal building projects and patronage are undertaken for the benefit of the whole nation and thus may be underwritten by general taxation. He does not rule without curbs on his authority, however. He may neither practise Roman Catholicism nor marry a Catholic; nor may he promote Catholics to positions in the army or at a university. Nor can he dismiss any judge. Although in theory he can veto any Bill passed by Parliament, no monarch has done so since 1708. George III threatens to stop a Bill allowing Catholics to serve as army officers in 1807 but before he can do so, his ministers withdraw it. The king is therefore a constitutional monarch in a kingdom without a formal constitution – and he has to feel his way in exerting his authority, just as his ministers have to in exerting theirs.

Royal authority, however, is steadily giving way to that of the king's ministers. The longer the king does not veto a parliamentary Bill, the more doubtful it is that he can in fact do so. At the same time, the growing power of the press forces the king and his government to listen to the people. Members of the royal family realise that a revolution could break out in Britain as happened in France in 1789, and they have little doubt whose heads are most likely to end up on the block if it does. But the most important reason for the decline of royal power is the increasing complexity of government. By 1800, the king cannot be expected to understand all the duties of the various departments, let alone oversee them. Thus he is forced to choose ministers who themselves understand the science of government; he cannot just appoint his friends. When the nation is at war, a huge amount of professional expertise is required to direct military and diplomatic strategy. Likewise, the growth of British overseas influence means that foreign policy can no longer be left to patriotic amateurs. However, in one of the great ironies that attend the history of the royal family, the more the king cedes actual power to others, the more his own status grows. The greater the wealth of the nation and the further its territorial influence extends, the greater the prestige of the monarch. In 1802, during discussions over whether George III should give up the ancient English claim to the French crown, it is suggested that he might call himself 'Emperor of the British Isles'. Although he declines such a portentous title, it does not appear out of place in the early nineteenth century. The monarch's standing increasingly depends on the power and wealth of his subjects, and less on his own authority.

Having said this, the king's personal influence is still considerable. Thus you should know something about the personalities of the two men who reign over Great Britain in this period: first, George III, and then, from 1811, his son Prince George, who becomes George IV in 1820.

Few monarchs in British history are as misunderstood as George III. In the modern world he is often presumed to be German at heart, on account of his being the hereditary prince-elector of Hanover. However, George is an Englishman through and through, having been born in St James's Square, London, in 1738. He never even visits Hanover. In fact, he barely leaves the south-east of England. When he does, it is normally only to travel to Weymouth in Dorset, where he takes his holidays and bathes in the sea. Another misunderstanding is that he is a tyrant. This is an American myth, having its origins in the American War of Independence. He is by nature a homely man, sober in his behaviour, a good Anglican and devoted to his wife, Charlotte of Mecklenburg-Strelitz, with whom he has fifteen children. Unlike his predecessors, he does not keep a mistress. His nickname among the people is 'Farmer George' on account of his love of rural pursuits. He prefers family dinners, riding and hunting to excessive carousing and gambling. His passions include astronomy, horology, chess, fine art, music, card games, visiting the theatre and collecting books. He amasses the King's Library, one of the greatest private libraries ever assembled, which consists of 65,250 printed volumes and nearly 20,000 tracts, pamphlets, charts and maps. This is his personal contribution to the culture of the nation. All things being considered, it would be hard to find a monarch less disposed to tyranny than George III.

He is, however, an unlucky king. His siblings especially let him down through their numerous affairs, forcing him to introduce the Royal Marriages Act. This forbids any member of the royal family from marrying without his permission. Unfortunately, this does not stop his sons from secretly marrying inappropriate women and openly maintaining mistresses. As you can imagine, such things cause the king enormous stress. Nor is he mentally strong enough to deal with them: from the 1780s he suffers periodic bouts of insanity. Then you have to consider all his political troubles. The progress of the French Revolution naturally gives rise to much anxiety, especially after the French king and queen are guillotined in 1793. On top of everything else, he is steadily going blind. His principal solace lies in his younger children, especially his youngest daughter, Amelia. But here, too, misfortune beckons. Amelia falls seriously ill in the summer of 1810 and dies in November of that year, prompting the king's final mental collapse. The Regency Act is passed on 7 February 1811, which invests royal power in his eldest son. By the time his beloved queen passes away in 1818, George III is not only mad and blind but deaf too, and probably insensible to the news. He himself breathes his last on 29 January 1820.

In marked contrast to his father, George IV is one of the laziest, most vain, spoilt, arrogant, self-indulgent, profligate, uncaring and conceited Englishmen ever to have lived. He is a lecherous, drunken boor; a glutton, a prig and a snob. He does have some positive virtues but they are so heavily outweighed by the negative aspects of his character that to give them priority would be disrespectful to anyone who is forced to put up with him. And everyone, in some way or other, has to do just that – from his exasperated parents to the politicians he bullies, the friends he insults, the people he rules and the women upon whom he lays his increasingly bloated, corpulent frame.

Let's begin with those women. After a plethora of teenage dalliances as prince of Wales, his first serious mistress is an actress, Mary Robinson. Their affair begins in about 1780, when he is eighteen and she twenty-three. Over the next four years, his bed welcomes a steady procession of overnight visitors before he falls in love with Mrs Maria Fitzherbert, a Catholic widow. So great is George's passion for her that, when she tries to leave the country to escape the attention, he stabs himself in a pathetic attempt to try to persuade her to stay. She relents and secretly marries him, in defiance of the Royal Marriages Act. But he soon has more affairs – with Lady Melbourne, the wife of Viscount Melbourne, a prominent politician; the actress Anna Maria Crouch; the countess of Jersey, who is nine years older than him and the mother of ten children; Olga Zherebtsova, the Russian mistress of the English ambassador to Moscow; and Isabella Seymour-Conway, marchioness of Hertford. The last-mentioned affair, which greatly displeases the lady's husband, lasts from 1807 to 1819. The marchioness seems to satisfy the prince's desire for older, ample-bosomed women who will cosset, pamper, dominate and indulge him. His last mistress, Elizabeth, marchioness of Conyngham, is only different from this type in that she is a few years younger than the prince.

The lack of self-control and loyalty in his love life is revealing of George's personality in general. He cannot abide being bored for a moment and hates anything that resembles hard work. He ignores his religious duties. He stuffs himself with large amounts of rich food and becomes exceedingly fat. He gambles heavily, drinks prodigiously and takes huge quantities of laudanum – a tincture of opium in alcohol – sometimes imbibing more than 200 drops in a day. He has no time for the poor. Prince Hermann Pückler-Muskau describes him as 'the chief actor in a pantomime before an audience whom he deems infinitely beneath him'.[22] Unfortunately the 'pantomime' in question is no laughing matter. George congratulates the magistrates responsible for ordering the assault that results in the killing and wounding of many peaceful demonstrators in Manchester on 16 August 1819 – a disaster popularly known as the Peterloo Massacre. On a personal level, his lack of feeling for his wife, Caroline of Brunswick, is appalling. On the night of the wedding he drinks himself into a stupor and falls into the fireplace in the bedroom. By the morning he has recovered enough to clamber into bed with her to consummate the marriage; their ill-fated daughter, Princess Charlotte, is born as a result. They never share a bed again. Instead, he returns to the tender embraces of Mrs Fitzherbert. Shunned and humiliated, Caroline naturally makes friends with her husband's political opponents. George responds by having her investigated for adultery. Although no evidence of impropriety is found, he tries to get a divorce in the House of Lords. He fails. But when he is eventually crowned king, he has his queen barred from the ceremony, to which he invites his mistress at the time, Lady Conyngham. Queen Caroline dies a few weeks later.

One of the most disturbing aspects of the 'pantomime' of the prince's life is his readiness to get into debt. His conscientious father is staggered when Parliament recommends that the decadent prince receive £100,000 per year on his attaining the age of twenty-one. The prince is eventually given half this sum, plus the revenues of the duchy of Cornwall (£12,000 per year), a one-off payment of £60,000 and Carlton House. In no time at all the lump sum has been spent and the prince is writing spiteful letters to his father, full of resentment at not being given more. The money goes on card tables, the turf, his stables and his houses in London and Brighton, as well as satisfying his more carnal appetites. By 1785 he owes almost £270,000. Parliament agrees to pay the major part of this sum but within ten years he has managed to rack up further debts amounting to £630,000. His income falls far short of such obligations. Even as Prince Regent in 1812, he has just £172,000 per year at his disposal.[23] As we have seen earlier, much of this debt is incurred in remodelling Carlton House. But when he finally becomes king, he simply demolishes it. That colossal waste demonstrates to contemporaries that he truly is the king of profligacy.

Everyone despairs of George IV. Whig politicians despise him because he keeps them permanently out of office. His Tory friends do not trust him because he is fickle. The common people see him as a spendthrift glutton who does not give a fig for anyone but the very rich. Catholics hate him because he refuses to grant them the basic rights of ordinary citizens. Radical politicians detest him, not just because he is the titular head of a system they fundamentally oppose but also because he obstinately stands in the way of reform. His obituary in *The Times*, which appears on 16 July 1830, the day after his funeral, describes him as 'an inveterate voluptuary ... of all known beings the most selfish' and declares that 'there never was an individual less regretted by his fellow-creatures than the deceased king ... If George IV ever had a friend – a devoted friend – in any rank of life, we protest that the name of him or her has not yet reached us.' Charles Greville, clerk of the privy council, writes in his diary on 29 January 1829 that 'a more contemptible, cowardly, selfish, unfeeling dog does not exist ... There have been good and wise kings but not many of them ... and this I believe to be one of the worst.' Sir Robert Heron sums up his character in just three words: 'faithless, worthless, heartless'.[24]

To be fair, George does have some redeeming qualities. His contribution to the architecture of London is considerable. You could say that, whereas George III's principal cultural legacy is creating a great library, George IV's is creating a great city. His patronage of visionary architects and developers makes London almost a rival to Paris. He is the man who turns Buckingham House into Buckingham Palace and makes it fit for monarchs for centuries to come. He commissions Jeffry Wyatville to remodel Windsor Castle at enormous expense. His indirect influence on fashion is significant, especially through his friendship with the dandy, Beau Brummell. He spends a great deal of money on supporting the playwright and politician, Richard Brinsley Sheridan, whose cultural influence extends far beyond merely writing for the stage. In giving his father's library to the British Museum, he encourages the construction of the building to house it, which stands thereafter as a monument to the wide cultural horizons of the British. He enhances the royal collection with art of the highest quality and opens it to public view. Despite its later demolition, the vast amounts he spends on decorating Carlton House are not entirely lost as many of the paintings, clocks, sculptures, tapestries and carpets find their homes in other parts of the royal collection. Not since the days of Charles I has Britain had such a great collector and patron of the arts for a king. It's just a pity he is such an insensitive, selfish pig.

THE ARISTOCRACY

The next tier of the social order is the aristocracy – 'the Corinthian capital of polished society', to use the phrase of the political writer Edmund Burke. The royal dukes are the highest rank of all – the philandering younger brothers of George III and George IV – followed, in descending order, by non-royal dukes, marquesses, earls, viscounts and barons. In 1812, the magistrate and statistician Patrick Colquhoun calculates that there are 516 noble families in Great Britain and Ireland, each enjoying an average income of about £10,000 per year.[25] In reality, most noble families have less than this: the least-wealthy 300 have an average of £4,000 per year. Some, however, have far more. The royal dukes each enjoy £18,000. Several lords have incomes of more than £100,000 per year, including the dukes of Northumberland, Devonshire and Newcastle, the marquess of Stafford, Earl Grosvenor and the earls of Egremont and Bridgewater.[26] These colossal incomes are substantially made up from agricultural rents, which double in value over the Regency period.[27] Hence you might come across genuine millionaires, even in the money of the early nineteenth century. The duke of

Queensberry's estate is worth about £1 million, the marquess of Stafford's more than £1.25 million and the duke of Buckingham's £1.8 million. The richest man in the kingdom is probably William Vane, duke of Cleveland, whose estate is worth in the region of £4 million, including £1 million of silverware and jewels.[28] If you should venture into the London showroom of the goldsmiths Rundell & Bridge and see a silver dinner service priced at £50,000 – and wonder who on earth can afford something that costs five times the average lord's annual income – now you know.[29]

On top of their wealth and status, noblemen enjoy certain privileges. They cannot be imprisoned for debt, which is just as well in some cases. However, the most important right is a permanent seat in the House of Lords. This not only gives them political power but also greater security than their elected colleagues in the House of Commons. Of the nine prime ministers to govern England in this period, five of them lead the nation from the House of Lords. Even those leaders who sit in the Commons preside over Cabinets dominated by hereditary peers. When William Pitt becomes prime minister for the second time, in May 1804, he is one of only two members of the Cabinet to have been elected: the others all sit in the House of Lords except for Lord Hawkesbury, who is the son of the earl of Liverpool.

Prime ministers of the United Kingdom

Date	Dominant party of government	Prime minister
1783–1801	Tory	William Pitt
1801–4	Tory	Henry Addington
1804–6	Tory	William Pitt
1806–7	National unity	Lord Grenville
1807–9	Tory	The duke of Portland
1809–12	Tory	Spencer Perceval
1812–27	Tory	The earl of Liverpool
1827	Tory	George Canning
1827–8	Tory	Viscount Goderich
1828–30	Tory	The duke of Wellington

It is easy to regard the political domination of the aristocracy as merely an extension of their wealth and privilege. But many of them display a selfless dedication to duty, in marked contrast to the self-indulgence of other members of their class. As the American ambassador Richard Rush makes clear in his memoir of his time in London between 1817 and 1825:

> In France, before the Revolution, the noble families were computed at thirty thousand. In England they may perhaps be computed at six or eight hundred. This handful does more of the everyday business of the country than the thirty thousand in France. In France they did the work of chivalry; they fought in the army and navy. In England, besides this, you trace them not merely as patrons of the arts but in road companies, canal companies, benevolent and public institutions of all kinds, to say nothing of their share in politics; in the latter, not simply as cabinet ministers but speakers, committee men, and hard workers otherwise.[30]

THE LANDED GENTRY

The landed gentry are upper-class landowning families without peerages. The highest social rank among them is a baronetcy (a hereditary knighthood); next comes an ordinary knighthood; and, last, a plain gentleman or lady. As you are no doubt aware, this is the class that fascinates Jane Austen: she rarely focuses on the aristocracy but pays great attention to the Mr Bingleys and Mr Darcys of the world, with annual incomes of £5,000 and £10,000 respectively. Both are very well-off compared to most of their contemporaries but they are far from being the richest members of their class. At the top of the pile you have a few estate owners with incomes as great as those enjoyed by aristocrats. William Jennens, the 'miser of Acton Place', is reputedly Britain's richest commoner. He has £107,000 deposited in five London banks, plus a rent roll of £8,000 and shares paying him a further £150,000 per year when he dies at the age of ninety-seven in 1798.[31] John Lambton inherits coal fields in County Durham that generate about £80,000 per year. When Thomas Creevey asks Lambton how much money a man needs to be a gentleman, he replies that he 'might jog along' with an income of £40,000. This causes great hilarity – and everyone thereafter knows Lambton as 'Jog along Jack' or 'King Jog'.

Obviously the term 'gentleman' covers a great spectrum of wealth, and while Lambton is entitled to his view, most people would say that you count as landed gentry if your rent roll adds up to £1,500 per year. Patrick Colquhoun reckons in 1812 that there are 861 baronets with an average income of £3,510, and about 11,000 other families who might be classed as landed gentry, whose rents yield an average of £2,000 per year. These families tend to have a house in town as well as in the country and observe certain codes of conduct, such as fighting duels when their honour is affronted. Their younger sons are expected to choose a career in one of the four forms of public service: Parliament, the civil service (abroad as well as at home), the armed forces or the Church. Advancement in each of them is heavily dependent on wealth and status. You'll have to pay a large sum of money for your son to be an army officer, and the amounts increase with the rank and social standing of the regiment. To be a captain in the infantry, for example, costs £1,800 but a captain in the cavalry is £3,225 and a major in the Guards, £8,300. Politics can be almost as expensive. To enter Parliament a young man will need the support of someone who 'owns a borough' where the election can be managed in his favour; this generally incurs expenditure in the order of several thousand pounds.

Another thing you'll need to be aware of when trying to understand the status of a landed-gentry family is that it matters how long they have owned their land. If you simply make a lot of money in business and decide to set yourself up as a country gentleman or lady by buying a country estate, you will find it's not that easy to gain admittance to upper-class social circles. Some say it takes as long as three generations. One reason is simply the upper-class aversion to trade: the taint of having had to work for a living does not wear off easily. A second reason is that it takes a long time to establish your social standing among other landed-gentry families in the locality. They will regularly sit as magistrates and lords lieutenant of the county, and chair committees and societies for the benefit of the public. If you do not make a similar effort, you will be regarded as shirking your duties and you won't be invited to balls, hunts, concerts and other social events. A third reason why it takes such a long time to be accepted is that you have to spend years developing relationships of trust in your community. There will be times when your tenants have to rely on your benevolence and charity to get by. Your attitude to your wealth becomes hugely important when they cannot pay the rent or they trespass on your rights, such as by poaching game or fish. The question is: are you a man like Sir Robert Heron, who in the difficult year of 1814 makes provision for all his poorest tenants?[32] Or are you the sort of landlord who orders his gamekeeper to place mantraps throughout his parkland, so as to break the legs of poachers, with no thought for the hardship his family will endure after their breadwinner has been so cruelly mutilated? Similarly, do you play cricket with your tenants on the village green in summer? If they don't really know you, they won't trust you and word will get back to your neighbouring landowners. Then you will never enjoy high social status, however many acres you may own.

THE SQUIREARCHY

Despite what John Lambton thinks, you don't need to have £40,000 a year to be considered a 'gentleman'. It is enough just to have a relatively high income – as long as you do not have to earn it by following a trade, or by labouring with your own hands. This *not* working for your income is important: no less a figure than the duke of Devonshire declares that his cousin, Henry Cavendish, is not a gentleman because he is employed.[33] But supposing you do have a private income, how much is enough to qualify? Colquhoun reckons £700 per year. Any less and you'll see the trappings of gentlemanly status fall away. In *Sense and Sensibility*, Mrs Dashwood describes all the marks of good living that her kinsfolk cannot hope to enjoy on an income of just £500 a year: 'They will have no carriage, no horses and hardly any servants; they will keep no company, and can have no expenses of any kind!' However, in rural areas you might be regarded as a gentleman with just this sum, especially in Wales or Scotland. If you spend your income sensibly, have the appropriate social connections and are well educated, then the doors of country houses will be open to you. This is especially the case if you are entitled to bear a coat of arms and thus can have the word 'esquire' placed after your surname. You will be called 'Mr' and considered a member of the *local* gentry – or 'squirearchy', to use the phrase coined to describe this class in the 1790s.

The squirearchy is exclusively a rural class. In most parishes you'll find no resident aristocrats and only one or two members of the landed gentry, so those who fill the next tier of respectability are generally expected to take a leadership role in their community. Country gentlemen sit as magistrates and chair the boards of hospitals and other charitable institutions. It doesn't matter that they don't have a house in London: their importance is entirely local. Much the same can be said for the local Anglican clergy. Their status relies heavily on their relationships within the parish and, in their case, it does not particularly matter how much they earn. James Woodforde, the rector of Weston Longville in Norfolk, receives just £400 a year from his living.[34] Nevertheless, he too is a member of the squirearchy.

Colquhoun estimates that there are about 35,000 gentlemen and ladies in this class receiving about £800 per year. Add approximately 12,000 Anglican clergymen and the squirearchy includes about 47,000 families. They form the rural upper middle class. They have enough money to educate their sons at a university, and they may even own the right to present them to their local church when a vacancy arises. But they are not on a par with the landed gentry. They cannot presume, for example, that their son might marry the daughter of a nobleman. Nevertheless, their collective income rivals that of the landed gentry and nobility combined, being in excess of £30 million.

INDUSTRIALISTS AND FINANCIERS

The phenomenon of the self-made man has always been a problem for the established classes described above. There they are, the lords and gentry, all set in their comfortable positions of power – living in their ancestral castles and stately homes, justifying their superiority through their contributions to the public good – when along comes a bunch of upstarts, who seemingly do nothing for society or the nation, yet acquire massive fortunes. Such impudence! It's not just that these industrialists and financiers are wealthier than the old earls and barons: it's that they are changing all the rules. Money is becoming more important than breeding.

Patrick Colquhoun estimates that in 1812 there are about 3,500 eminent merchants and bankers in Britain with an estimated average income of £2,600. There are in addition almost 70,000 lesser merchants, manufacturers, warehouse owners and shipbuilders with an average income of roughly £800, and nearly 9,000 ship owners with an average of £600 per year. As with the upper classes, these modest averages conceal some huge fortunes. Among those with £500,000 or more are Richard Arkwright senior, the inventor of cotton-spinning machinery; Thomas Williams, a Welsh copper entrepreneur; Josiah Wedgwood, the porcelain manufacturer; and John Julius Angerstein, an insurance broker. When the brewer Samuel Whitbread dies in 1796, he is rumoured to be worth £1 million.[35] The London banker Thomas Coutts is worth £1 million on his deathbed in 1822, and so is the economist David Ricardo when he dies the following year – which is remarkable, considering that his father disowned him thirty years earlier. Richard Arkwright junior is worth about £1 million by 1830, as are the financiers Hudson Gurney, Philip Miles and Nathan Mayer Rothschild and the draper James Morrison. In a still wealthier bracket are the Scottish gunpowder-dealer John Farquhar, with about £1.1 million at his death in 1826; and the jeweller Philip Rundell, the principal partner in Rundell & Bridge, who is worth more than £1.4 million when he retires in 1823. Even richer are the Yorkshire ironmaster Richard Crawshay, whose wealth tops £1.5 million in 1810, and John Marshall, the flax-spinner from Leeds, who retires in 1830 with assets of about £2 million. As you can see, a 'rich list' for Regency Britain would feature almost as many industrialists as noblemen.

So, what are your chances of joining the super-rich? Not bad, actually. Many have extremely humble origins. James Morrison, for example, is the orphaned younger son of a Hampshire innkeeper. His great break comes from joining a London haberdashery business at the age of twenty and marrying the senior partner's daughter. He then guides the company to international success and, as his fortune builds, proves himself a sound investor in overseas businesses, especially in America. By the time he dies in 1857 he will be a millionaire six times over. Philip Rundell is the son of a maltster from the small town of Norton St Philip, in Somerset. His career commences at the age of fourteen when he becomes an apprentice to a jeweller in Bath. That these men could rise from such lowly origins to such levels of wealth makes at least some members of the establishment pause for thought. Can these people really be looked down on because they *work* for a living? If a provincial apprentice can become a millionaire, while a gentleman exists on just £700 a year, is it not time that the etiquette book was revised?

THE PROFESSIONS

In the Regency period a 'profession' is not just any occupation, it is one that requires high levels of knowledge and either a degree or equivalent level of education or a commission. As a result, such positions are only open to men. Generally speaking, the law is the most lucrative. According to Colquhoun, there are about 19,000 judges, barristers, solicitors, attorneys and other lawyers and clerks in Britain, earning an average of £400 per year. Some lawyers are paid far more than this, of course: a handful of judges receive more than £10,000. Lloyd Kenyon earns £6,000 in fees each year. When he dies in 1802, as Lord Kenyon, his estate is valued at £260,000. John Scott makes even more money. Born the third son of a moderately successful Newcastle coal merchant, he is raised to a peerage as Lord Eldon and becomes Lord Chancellor in 1801. He regularly receives annual fees in excess of £15,000. Needless to say, most civil servants don't earn anything like this. Senior officers might earn £1,000 but most have to be satisfied with nearer £300.[36]

The popularity of the Church as a profession illustrates that not all middle-class men want to make a fortune. Many are happy to settle for a living of between £200 and £500 and join the local squirearchy. Those who are more ambitious aim for the top jobs of bishop, dean or archdeacon. Their salaries range from £7,000 for the archbishop of Canterbury and £6,000 for the bishop of Durham down to an average of £600 for the higher clergy who support them. Bear in mind that you will have to wait some time to enjoy one of these lucrative appointments: promotion in the Church, as in the civil service, is very much a matter of stepping into dead men's shoes. A curate at the bottom of the pile might be worse off than a rural vicar, having to make do with less than £50 per year. Thus you may well consider the alternative path of a university fellowship, as incomes in excess of £600 can be earnt from teaching at an Oxford or Cambridge college. The only drawback is that you won't be allowed to marry.

If instead you feel drawn to medicine, and can obtain the necessary qualifications and testimonials, you can earn significant fees. The physician Erasmus Darwin makes about £1,000 per year and is worth more than £33,000 when he dies in 1802. John Lettsom, who works around the clock and never takes a holiday, builds an even more valuable medical practice: by 1800 he is earning £12,000 per year. He does not die rich, however, as he gives away most of his wealth to charity and philanthropic causes.[37]

On top of the foregoing traditional professions, new ones are emerging, which rely on specific technical skills practised by men with high levels of expertise. Architects, shipwrights, surveyors, master builders and engineers are all stepping forward to join the ranks of professionals. Being dependent on ability, these positions are much less prone to prejudice than the higher echelons of the older professions and so are open to men from a wide range of backgrounds. Thomas Telford, the great civil engineer, is brought up by his widowed mother in poverty on a sheep farm in Scotland. At first he labours as a stonemason, but by his thirties he has worked his way up to being a clerk of works and an architect. Then he embarks on his life's mission: redesigning harbours, building canals, draining the Fens, engineering railway lines and constructing bridges and thousands of miles of new roads. His most dazzling achievement is the Menai Bridge, a 579ft-long suspension bridge between the Isle of Anglesey and North Wales, which takes seven years to complete and is finished in 1826. Despite his humble start in life, he becomes the first president of the Institution of Civil Engineers in 1820 and his estate is worth more than £20,000 when he dies in 1834.

SHOPKEEPERS AND URBAN ARTISANS

The French revolutionaries refer to Britain as a 'nation of shopkeepers' and they don't mean it as a compliment. However, the first person to employ the phrase, the economist Adam Smith, means no disrespect by it. He uses it to explain the imperial ambitions of the British in *The Wealth of Nations* – that a nation of shopkeepers needs an empire of customers. Having said this, the shopkeepers and urban artisans of Great Britain do not enjoy high status as individuals: it is only as a group that they play an important role. Colquhoun reckons that there are 235,000 shopkeepers and shop assistants in the country, plus 44,000 tailors, milliners and dressmakers; 70,000 silk lace workers, embroiderers, makers of umbrellas and laundresses; and about 87,500 publicans and innkeepers. If you also place the 35,000 schoolteachers in this status bracket, as most of them enjoy similar incomes, then this group numbers almost half a million people in 1812 – a significant proportion of the population. Together they earn more than £62 million, roughly the same as all the nobility, landed gentry and squirearchy put together, which goes some way to justify the 'nation of shopkeepers' comment.

At an individual level, successful shopkeepers might make in excess of £200 per year and their assistants £70. Schoolmasters are also estimated to bring home about £200 per year, and publicans £100. Nevertheless, some tradesmen build significant fortunes. You've already heard about James Morrison. The political reformer Francis Place is another man who raises himself through hard work. The illegitimate son of a London innkeeper, he is apprenticed to a breeches-maker at the age of fourteen. When he is nineteen he marries his sixteen-year-old sweetheart, who is equally penniless. But then the demand for breeches dries up, and Francis and his new wife come close to starvation; they only survive because he pawns his work tools. But he struggles on and in 1800 he opens his own tailoring service. Over the next thirty years, it becomes one of the leading such businesses in London, earning Place in excess of £2,500 a year – certainly more than most of his clients.

THE RURAL LOWER MIDDLE CLASS

Regency farmers make quite a disparate group. Some are wealthy, even though they have to work for a living. Louis Simond remarks that in Norfolk they 'ride about over-seeing their labourers, looking like rich manufacturers, not at all like peasants. Agriculture is evidently not a beggarly trade here.'[38] The Northumberland farmer George Culley – the son of a coal carter – makes a fortune from his innovative stockbreeding, having particular success with sheep. By the 1790s he is leasing seven large farms, paying a total rent of £5,000 per year, yet making as much again in profit, most of which he reinvests in his business. In 1807 he is able to buy a large estate for £45,000, thus elevating himself to the ranks of the landed gentry.

About 280,000 farmers in the country are yeomen, who own their own land; a similar number are husbandmen, who don't. Colquhoun estimates that a quarter of the yeomen have incomes averaging £275 per year, with the rest getting by on about £100. Husbandmen lease their land for a specific number of years or (in the West of England) for the duration of three named 'lives'. When all the named people have died, the land reverts to the landowner. For this reason most people name their youngest child in the lease: then, if your ten-year-old son lives to be seventy, your family will enjoy that low rent for the next sixty years. This explains why husbandmen are often better off than those who have borrowed money to buy their own land: Colquhoun reckons the average husbandman makes £120 per year. But it is noticeable that George Culley builds his fortune by leasing his farms; he only buys his land when the leases and rents start to go up in price.

How do farmers rank in terms of social status? This is a matter of some controversy. On the one hand, the gentry, squirearchy and profes-sions look down on them as uneducated, uncouth country bumpkins. As the wealthy Emma Woodhouse declares in Jane Austen's *Emma*, the yeomanry 'are precisely the order of people with whom I feel I can have nothing to do'. For this reason, both yeomen and husbandmen are increasingly trying to better themselves. They buy books and pictures, educate their children and do up their farmhouses as if they are members of the squirearchy. And this is where the controversy comes in. While *some* people will appreciate these signs of gentility, their social superiors will insist that such marks of grace are preten-tious and shallow. So too will some of their peers. The political jour-nalist William Cobbett is appalled to walk into an old farmhouse leased to a husbandman and see carpets covering the flagstoned hall, decanters and wine glasses instead of beer flagons, and 'some showy chairs and a sofa' in the parlour.[39] Indeed, the very fact that the house has a room called a *parlour* tells Cobbett that the farmer is attempting to pass himself off as a squire. This is why the diarist Elizabeth Ham is so particular when she describes herself as being

> respectably descended from that class of yeomen and small proprietors of which there are now so few specimens left, who kept their own place in society, were in habits of intimacy with the neighbouring clergymen and gentry, dined often at the squire's, and entertained him once a year or so.[40]

Ironically, therefore, those who *don't* try to elevate their social status by acquiring the trappings of gentlemanly wealth are accorded more respect by their social superiors than those who *do*. At the same time, those below them can only dream of marrying the sons and daughters of such upwardly mobile farmers. When the working-class weaver Samuel Bamford tries to marry the girl of his dreams, a farmer's daughter, he is told in no uncertain terms by her mother that her daughter is not going to marry any man who cannot take her away on his own horse. For some the benchmark is a parlour, for others it's a horse – but there is always a benchmark of some sort.

THE WORKING CLASSES

There are more than eight million working-class people in Great Britain in 1812 – just over 70 per cent of the population.[41] That includes at least a million men working as general labourers and craftsmen and a further 742,000 employed as agricultural labourers or miners. Some of these craftsmen are highly skilled: stonemasons, cabinet-makers, harness-makers, blacksmiths and wheelwrights. Most women in this class are workers too. They and their children are employed in factories, mills and mines, spinning cotton or weaving cloth; scrubbing doorsteps and saucepans as domestic servants; or hawking goods and trinkets through marketplaces and from door to door.

How much do they earn? At the highest end, a manservant in a wealthy household might receive £20 or more per year. The footmen in the duke of Devonshire's employment are paid £35 per year, the head coachman £60 and the butler £80. However, such jobs are few and far between. A clergyman is unlikely to pay his manservant more than £10 per year, and a boy might earn as little as two guineas.[42] In 1790 a factory worker might earn 7s–8s per week with a good employer like Josiah Wedgwood, and a few experienced, skilled workers in his company can hope for 12s or more. But that's still only between £18 and £30 per year – barely enough to raise a family. Very few working-class jobs pay more than this. Coal miners receive between 10s and 15s per week. Skilled workers in the London building trades occasionally see 20s or more in their weekly pay packet in the 1820s but that is unusual. An agricultural labourer in the 1790s is lucky to earn 7s per week. Even in 1830, he will only receive 10s in summer and 9s in winter.

As a result, women and children are often forced to work in the same dangerous and unhealthy occupations as their husbands and fathers. In 1813 the author Richard Ayton descends a coal mine near

Whitehaven in Cumbria. After being winched down 630 feet in complete darkness in a coal bucket, he traces his way through the dark passages until a light appears in the distance. It is fixed to a horse drawing a long line of wagons 'driven by a young girl, covered with filth'. After that, he recounts:

> We were frequently interrupted in our march by the horses proceeding in this manner with their cargoes to the shaft, and always driven by girls, all of the same description, ragged and beastly in their appearance, and with a shameless indecency in their behaviour, which awestruck as one was by the gloom and the loneliness around one, had something quite frightful in it, and gave the place the character of a hell. All the people whom we met with were distinguished by an extraordinary wretchedness; immoderate labour and a noxious atmosphere had marked their countenances with the signs of disease and decay; they were mostly half-naked, blackened all over with dirt, and altogether so miserably disfigured and abused that they looked like a race fallen from the common rank of men and doomed, as in a kind of purgatory, to wear away their lives in these dismal shades.[43]

For youngsters growing up in such an environment, questions about status and wealth seem irrelevant and absurd. These people have neither. A boy or girl employed in a mine will normally be paid just 1s a week. Children as young as three or four are sometimes 'down pit', if only to fight the rats off their parents' packed lunches.[44]

Daily life is a real struggle for many working-class families. In 1795 the Revd David Davies publishes *The Case of Labourers in Husbandry Stated and Considered*, which examines the incomes and outgoings of the rural working class in great detail. From his own parish of Barkham in Berkshire he gives the example of an agricultural labourer and his wife who earn 8s and 6d per week respectively, amounting to an annual household income of £22 2s. With this they have to feed not only themselves but five children under the age of eight. Most of their money goes on bread; their total food bill comes to £23 4s 9d. In addition, they have to pay for rent, fuel and clothes, and cover the costs of illnesses and the mother's lying-in. According to Davies's calculations, every year their income falls short of their necessary expenses by £7 2s 9d. Or, to put it another way, they only earn 75 per cent of what they need.[45] All across the country you'll find people in a similar situation. And it's getting worse. About one in five families in Great Britain does not have enough to feed, house and clothe themselves, and keep themselves warm.[46]

THE DESTITUTE

If those in employment are often only paid a pittance, many working-class men and women are unable to find any work at all. Others lose their jobs when they fall ill or after experiencing a personal tragedy. The story of George Purnell illustrates how easily it can happen. He was once a gentleman's servant but, at the age of sixty-six, he lost his wife and his job. He had no pension and his only income was 2s per week from part-time gardening. With so little money, he could not maintain his cottage, which eventually collapsed. He was turned away from the parish workhouse on account of his filthy condition and forced to live in the rickety hayloft of an inn. He stayed there for several months until some drunken colliers and their boys found him and threw stones at him for a laugh, injuring his leg. After that he sleeps rough. He is found dead on a roadside in November 1812, at the age of seventy-one.[47]

You will still find people who believe that the poor have only themselves to blame for their condition, on account of their not working hard enough, but it is becoming more and more apparent that there are real problems facing society. As the population grows, the working classes inevitably increase at the fastest rate. But employment opportunities do not keep pace. In 1812 there are more than 308,000 vagrants and 387,000 paupers in the British Isles; in 1829 there are more than 30,000 beggars in London alone.[48] But what can people do? Vagrants are arrested and escorted back to the parish of their birth, where they can seek 'outdoor relief' from the Overseer of the Poor. This is a small weekly sum that allows an individual or a family to remain in their own home and do some work, thereby lessening the burden on the community. The Revd David Davies gives the example of a woman who, having been abandoned by her husband and left with six children, only earns 1s a week. Her two eldest children earn a further 3s. The Overseer of the Poor pays her an extra 5s per week, thus bringing the household income to £23 8s per year.[49] This still does not cover all the family's basic needs, which amount to £28 15s, but at least it means they don't starve. In this respect the system works. The only problem is that there are so many people in need of support that poor relief is becoming more and more of a financial burden on the rest of society. By 1800 over a quarter of the population is dependent on parish relief. Whereas the bill nationally amounted to £2 million in 1784, in 1818 it reaches £7.8 million.[50] When the harvest is poor and wheat prices go up, the fixed sums handed out to destitute families are not enough. Men then have no option but to risk the mantraps and gamekeepers' guns in order to feed their families.

Outdoor relief is only for the able-bodied. The old and infirm and orphan children are forced to resort to 'indoor relief' – otherwise known as the workhouse. Workhouses have proliferated over the last hundred years and are now to be found in every large town and many rural areas. The Bristol workhouse, for example, accommodates 61 men, 190 women and 36 children in 1797. Most of the adults are lame, mentally ill, old or blind. Their sole occupation is picking oakum for ships' caulking. They sleep in dormitories of twelve to fifteen beds and have to put up with swarms of lice and other vermin.[51] Unsurprisingly, there is a real stigma to entering the workhouse, and people do all they can to avoid it. But on the positive side, they are sheltered, fed and clothed, and given medicine when sick. If they die, they will be buried by an Anglican minister. That last point is not a trivial matter. The philanthropist Jonas Hanway estimates that an infant under the age of four has a life expectancy of just one month after entering a London workhouse. As he puts it, 'parish officers never intend that parish infants should live'. The simple reason is that, if they survive, they will be a burden on the community ever after. In some workhouses the officers are distressingly successful, with infant mortality rates of 100 per cent.[52]

This brings us to a crucial point about poverty: it falls hardest on the very young. Obviously a child who is not fed enough will not grow properly. But that is not all. Sometimes a desperate couple will resort to selling their children to a chimney sweep, professional beggar or brothel-keeper to be a slave in all but name. As you can imagine, the very fact that there is a market for children means they are vulnerable to being stolen – and you'll be surprised to hear that stealing a child is not against the law until 1814.[53] Even harsher fates await some unfortunate youngsters. Parents can insure their offspring with a burial club by paying a small amount each year. If an insured child falls ill when the family experiences hard times, the parents may not send for a physician, whom they cannot afford, but rather let nature take its course, so they can claim on the insurance. On one occasion, a wealthy Lancashire gentlewoman hears that her wet nurse's child is ill; she kindly offers to send her own physician to help but the mother replies, 'Oh, never mind, Ma'am, it's in two burial clubs.'[54] In some extreme cases, infants are starved or smothered, to net the parents up to £20 in cash. Rent collectors report that they are sometimes asked to wait until an insured child has died. The children of the destitute in Regency Britain are not only without status; they are sometimes denied the right to life.

Women

Generally speaking, a woman's status depends on her father when she is unmarried, on her husband while he is alive, and on her income when she is a widow. As a result, although women suffer a welter of legal disqualifications and prejudices against their sex, they still have higher status than men of a lower social standing. For example, if a countess and a gentleman were to arrive at an inn at the same time, the countess would get the best suite, even if the gentleman be a baronet. As a countess, she outranks him in the official order of precedence. Similarly, even though the landed gentry in Yorkshire think Anne Lister is a very strange lady – defiantly single, somewhat arrogant and sexually attracted to other women – they all pay her a great deal of respect as she is a gentlewoman in her own right, worth about £1,500 a year.[55] Society might bar women from all sorts of activities but it upholds their status without prejudice.

What discrimination will you face as a woman in Regency Britain? You cannot go to university or practise a profession requiring formal qualifications. Noblewomen cannot enter the House of Lords. You cannot stand for election as an MP. Tradition dictates that women do not vote. However, the principal constraints on your freedom will not be these legal prejudices but the laws relating to marriage. According to the eighteenth-century jurist Sir William Blackstone, husband and wife are a single entity represented in law solely by the man. That carries with it some advantages for women: it means that a husband is legally responsible for his wife's debts; that she can expect her husband to support her; and that he has to accept any child of hers as his own offspring, even if he believes she has been seeing another man. But it also carries many limitations. A wife must obey her husband in all respects. All her property is legally his, including any money she makes by her own labour. She has no rights over their children if they live apart. She may not make a will without her husband's consent. She cannot allow anyone into her house without her husband's permission. And because she cannot legally accuse him of anything or give evidence against him in court, her husband has the right to force himself on her sexually and to beat her, even to the point of maiming her.

Women are at a disadvantage in the workplace too. Even when they do the same job as men, they are generally paid between half and two-thirds as much as their male colleagues. In Mr Wedgwood's factory, the men who gild the porcelain are paid £31 4s per year but the women only £19 10s for doing the same job.[56] In a wealthy household in Bristol, a female cook receives £15 per year for her culinary skills but this is overshadowed by the fact that the man-servant in the same house is paid £35.[57] Normally wages for women in domestic service are much lower than this: £3 per year for a maidservant is not unusual and five guineas is good.[58] Nor is low pay the only indignity that working women have to suffer. In Scotland, female domestic servants are expected to work barefoot.[59] In many large houses in England, all the below-stairs females are called 'Betty' or a similar name, thus being denied their identity.[60] And then there is the matter of sex. All employers expect women and girls to be chaste – unless, of course, they seduce them them-selves. The Revd James Woodforde sacks his pregnant servants even when their boyfriends promise to marry them, on each occasion giving them twenty-four hours to leave the house.[61] Young women are thus left with nothing but their babies to feed and their reputa-tions in tatters. No one wants to employ an unmarried, demon-strably unchaste female.

Women in Regency Britain are thus constantly required to make compromises. Wealthy, independent women have to make the fewest; poor girls have to make the most. At the age of seventeen, William Jackson is caught heading up the back stairs to rape his mother's maidservant in her bedroom. When confronted by his angry father, the young man doesn't deny what he is planning to do but defends himself on the grounds that 'she is no thing of beauty'.[62] Lord Byron writes to Sir Walter Scott in 1822 of 'the tremulous anxiety with which one sometimes makes love to a beautiful woman of our own degree with whom one is enamoured in good earnest – whereas we attack a fresh-coloured housemaid without ... any sentimental remorse'.[63] These men should feel ashamed of themselves: lives are ruined in this way. But the very fact that 'gentlemen' can have such attitudes shows you why many women are happy to sacrifice their freedom for the security, support and affection of marriage. The key thing is to find a husband who is able and willing to provide that support and affection. Divorce is almost impossible: it requires a private Act of Parliament, which you can only afford if you are exceedingly rich. For most young women, the choice of husband is thus the most important one of their lives.

Many parents, knowing how significant the decision is, take it upon themselves to arrange their daughter's marriage, and understandably they sometimes place a little too much emphasis on the bridegroom's status and not enough on the support and affection he might be able to give their daughter. But what should you do if want to marry the man of your dreams rather than the crooked-nosed old duffer whom your father has lined up for you? If you are over twenty-one years of age, you can marry whom you like. However, if you are under twenty-one, in England and Wales, you need your father's permission. Your trump card in such circumstances is a Scottish marriage. North of the border you can be married without parental consent as long as you are over the age of twelve and your bridegroom is over fourteen. This is why so many young ladies and gentlemen elope to Gretna Green. Sarah Anne Child, the only daughter and heiress of Robert Child, the owner of Child's Bank, runs away at the age of seventeen to marry the dashing John Fane, tenth earl of Westmorland. Henrietta, the underage illegitimate daughter of the marquess of Cholmondley, does the same when she falls in love with John Lambton. Even Lord Eldon has a Gretna Green marriage when he is nineteen. Considering what an arch-conservative he later becomes, it is quite amusing to think of him waiting on his horse as his sixteen-year-old sweetheart climbs out of an upstairs window and down a ladder into his arms.

For some women, marriage to a rich man is the best way to elevate themselves socially. For others, though, *not* marrying is an even better way – flaunting their sexual desirability and promiscuousness, thereby trading respectability for notoriety and riches. The prime example is Kitty Fisher, the greatest sex symbol of the eighteenth century. Although she dies long before the Regency period begins, in 1767, her story sets a pattern for later women to follow. Seduced by a rich and handsome officer at a young age, by seventeen she is the talk of London on account of her vivacity, beauty and charm. Thereafter she shares her favours with many of the great and the good – and the not-so-good, the devilish and the downright bad. The list of her lovers contains the names of so many eminent men that you cannot help but think that they were *her* conquests, not she theirs. Men feel compelled to try to add their names to her *curriculum amorum*, but you need a title, great wealth or some other mark of high distinction to be invited to join her elite club. One day in St James's Park she falls from a horse and exposes herself: a print of the event soon appears, with her legs shown all the way up to the tops of her stockings. Becoming a pin-up only adds to her fame. Sir Joshua Reynolds paints her portrait not once but four times – which itself gives rise to rumours. It is said that she once ate a £100 note on a slice of buttered bread; and that she banned Prince Edward from her house after he only paid her fifty guineas for the night. Tragically, she does not grow old but dies aged just twenty-six, thereby becoming a legend.[64]

Most of the Regency women who follow in Kitty Fisher's footsteps are actresses who catch the eye of a wealthy man at the theatre. Mary Robinson's appearance as Perdita, for example, not only secures the affections of the young Prince George but opens the door to her taking a progression of rich and famous lovers. This in turn enables her to publish poetry, novels, essays and plays and to become fashionable, famous and independent.[65] However, the best known of all the courtesans of the Regency, Harriette Wilson, bypasses the stage altogether. She sets off for Brighton at the age of fifteen to find herself a rich lover. She succeeds in attracting the attention of Lord Craven, the Hon. Frederick Lamb (the son of Viscount Melbourne), Lord Frederick Cavendish-Bentinck (the son of the duke of Portland, the prime minister), Lord Lorne (the son of the duke of Argyll), Lord Ponsonby, Lord Hertford, Lord Brougham, Lord Worcester (the son of the duke of Beaufort), Lord Deerhurst, the duke of Devonshire, the duke of Leinster and even the duke of Wellington. In her late thirties Harriette retires from horizontal social climbing and embarks on writing her memoirs, publicly announcing that any gentleman willing to pay £200 would not be named therein. This allegedly elicits the duke of Wellington's famous response: 'Publish and be damned!' The work appears in four volumes in 1825 and causes quite a stir: it is reprinted thirty times in its first year, making her and her publishers a further £10,000.[66] Obviously not every poor woman can make a fortune in this way – or would want to – but those who do so demonstrate that a sexist society can be turned to their advantage. Indeed, those who make it often find that the greatest social obstacles they face later in life are put up by other women – who never let them forget exactly how they made their money.

We can't end this chapter without mentioning the greatest rags-to-riches story of the age. The woman at the heart of it is not a courtesan but her rise in status is so extraordinary that she attracts just as many waspish insinuations, envious remarks and snobbish insults. Her name is Harriot Mellon and her origins are about as lowly as you can possibly imagine. She is the illegitimate daughter of a peasant woman from County Cork, Ireland, who makes a living by looking after the clothes of a group of travelling actors in the north of England. Having grown up among such people, it is only natural that Harriot also wants to be onstage. She gives her debut in a barn at the age of ten and strikes some people as having star potential, which eventually brings her to the attention of Richard Brinsley Sheridan. He casts her in his play *The Rivals* in 1795. Although not a natural leading lady, her beauty, intelligence, vivacity and rustic humility make her so popular that twenty years later she is earning £600 a year from her stage appearances. This, however, is her pocket money. By this time she has acquired an elderly admirer in Thomas Coutts, who just happens to be the principal partner in Coutts Bank. His wife suffers from dementia; when she dies in 1815, the seventy-nine-year-old Thomas asks thirty-seven-year-old Harriot to marry him. She says yes, and for the remaining seven years of his life they are very happy together. Mr Coutt's three daughters are not so pleased, however, as they fear their father will disinherit them. They are decidedly unfriendly to the new Mrs Coutts. Mr Coutts, disappointed that they should treat his new wife so meanly, bequeaths his entire estate to Harriot, including his 50 per cent partnership in the bank. She lives up to his confidence in her by running the business very efficiently. She remains generous to his daughters too, giving them each an annual allowance of £10,000.

Despite this, she is ridiculed in the press and criticised in society. The *haut ton* see her as an upstart intruder trying to enter the fashionable world. Then, in 1827, she marries the young duke of St Albans, who is twenty-three years her junior. This is too much for the ladies who guard the gleaming gates of British aristocratic society and who now shun Harriot for rising above her station. Yet her second marriage is also a happy one. Thus the illegitimate daughter of a penniless Irish peasant woman becomes a duchess and one of the richest people in the kingdom, with a personal fortune of about £2 million. This she controls herself through her partnership in the bank, not having to yield to her husband, even though he is a duke.[67] It may well be a man's world but Harriot Mellon manages to overcome poverty, sexual prejudice and all the degrees of class snobbery to lift herself above it – and never has to trade respectability for respect along the way.

4

Character

An old, mad, blind, despised, and dying king;
Princes, the dregs of their dull race, who flow
Through public scorn – mud from a muddy spring;
Rulers who neither see nor feel nor know,
But leechlike to their fainting country cling
Till they drop, blind in blood, without a blow.
A people starved and stabbed in th'untilled field;
An army, whom liberticide and prey
Makes as a two-edged sword to all who wield;
Golden and sanguine laws which tempt and slay;
Religion Christless, Godless – a book sealed;
A senate, Time's worst statute, unrepealed –
Are graves from which a glorious Phantom may
Burst, to illumine our tempestuous day.

Percy Bysshe Shelley, 'England in 1819'[1]

All societies contain a mass of conflicting traditions, beliefs and aspirations but Regency Britain is particularly full of contradictions. The American ambassador, Richard Rush, openly expresses his dismay at a country with so many apparent anomalies: how can anyone, let alone a foreigner, possibly hope to understand a nation with so much wealth and so much poverty; so much meanness yet so much charity? One moment you encounter 'ignorance and crime so widely diffused as to appal' he writes, and the next, you meet with 'genius, learning and virtue'.[2] The answer, as Robert Southey explains, lies in not trying to reconcile these extremes but in understanding that the people of Regency Britain are themselves contradictory. As he puts it:

This spirit of contradiction is the character of the nation. They love to be at war, but do not love to pay for their amusement; and now that they are at peace, they begin to complain that the newspapers are not worth reading, and rail at the French as if they really wished to begin again. There is not a people upon the Earth who have a truer love for their Royal Family than the English, yet they caricature them in the most open and insolent manner. They boast of the freedom of the press, yet as surely and systematically punish the author who publishes anything obnoxious, and the bookseller who sells it ... They cry out against intolerance and burn down the houses of those whom they regard as heretics. They love liberty [yet] go to war with their neighbours because they chose to become republicans, and insist upon the right of enslaving the negroes. They hate the French and ape all their fashions, ridicule their neologisms and then naturalize them, laugh at their inventions and then adopt them, cry out against their political measures and then imitate them ... And the common people, not to be behind-hand with their betters in absurdity, boast as heartily of the roast beef of Old England, as if they were not obliged to be content themselves with bread and potatoes.[3]

Southey is undoubtedly right. The English are a self-contradictory lot – and so, it might be added, are their neighbours in Wales and Scotland. It all makes Regency Britain a very complicated place. And trying to understand it is not so much a walk in a park as a jungle exploration.

The Spirit of the Age

If you ask a Regency person to sum up the spirit of the age, he or she will probably use the word 'evil'. This is not necessarily because of any of those things that we would condemn as 'evil' – sexism, racism, childhood mortality, ignorance and violence. All these things can be justified in the Regency mind as natural and sent by God. For many, the real evil is change or, as some people call it with horror, 'innovation'. The introduction of machinery to take men's jobs is an evil. Chimneys belching smoke are another evil. The possibility of a French-style revolution is an even greater evil. Threats to the status of the old landowning class are, again, an evil. In short, people fear the future. As Mary Shelley puts it in *Frankenstein*, 'nothing is so painful to the human mind as a great and sudden change'.

Although Jane Austen's books have come to be seen as epitomising the Regency period, *Frankenstein* is the novel that best sums up the spirit of the age – its magnificence and terror, its power and pity. When the book is published in 1819, it asks some unsettling questions. If Dr Frankenstein can create life, does he not become like God? And does he not also become responsible for the moral welfare of his creation? When Dr Frankenstein sets about making a mate for his monster, he fears that the female may be just as destructive as the male, and if they have children, they will breed and destroy humanity. But what right does he have to bring a creature to life and then deny him a means to find happiness? The scientist thus has grave responsibilities. And so does everyone who wants to change society. Mary Shelley's husband may well write of 'a glorious Phantom' bursting forth to bring light to England in 1819 but she herself paints a far more distressing picture – and anticipates a far more disturbing future for humankind. For the first time in history, we are becoming the architects of our own fate.

At the same time, there are those who welcome innovation as a 'new dawn'. For them, the real evils are the terrible working conditions in factories and mines, the immoral behaviour of the rich and the exploitation of the poor. As Shelley's poem suggests, ordinary people can now dream of the day when their hard labours, indignities and suffering are diminished or even extinguished. They can hope that, in the wake of the French Revolution, the days of the ruling classes are numbered. As they see it, the common interests of the British people are advancing steadily against the bastions of privilege and, little by little, the old world is giving way.

Many of the intellectuals in this latter camp take their lead from a book by the marquis de Condorcet, *Outlines of an Historical View of the Progress of the Human Mind*, published in French in 1795 and in English later the same year. Condorcet divides human history into ten epochs, each of which constitutes a stage in the progress of humanity. For example, the third epoch sees our 'progress' from the age of farming to the invention of writing. However, it is Condorcet's discussion of the last epoch that has the greatest impact on contemporaries. He argues that, on the basis of seeing how people behaved in the past, we can establish the laws of human nature as fully as we can the laws of physics, and thus predict the future 'almost with certainty'.[4] This is an extraordinary statement in the 1790s. People simply don't expect the future to be markedly different from the present or the past. They certainly can't imagine predicting the differences. But most surprising of all is the sort of future that Condorcet predicts. It includes three things in particular: 'the destruction of inequality between different nations; the progress of equality in one and the same nation; and lastly, the real improvement of man'.[5] And by 'man' he also means women. In his words, 'among those causes ... that are of most importance to the general welfare must be included the total annihilation of the prejudices which have established between the sexes an inequality of rights'.[6] This is truly radical. So too is his prediction of the inevitability of the abolition of slavery. And the development of a national insurance system to pay old-age pensions. As he sees it, the fact that such policies will ultimately benefit the whole of society means that it is only a matter of time before they are generally adopted.

Condorcet's argument that change is *inevitable* is alluring to some and terrifying to others. Those who want women to have equal rights with men read Condorcet and learn that it *will* happen. Radical politicians like Thomas Hardy, the founder of the London Corresponding Society, are inspired by the idea that one day all men will be able to vote. Intellectuals like Mary Wollstonecraft welcome the inevitability of all men and women being equal. Anti-slavery campaigners like William Wilberforce find encouragement in Condorcet's work. But some people look at these predictions and shudder. If you are a plantation owner, the idea that the end of slavery is inevitable is a dire warning. If you are one of the few people in your parish who has the vote, you may be aghast at the idea of all your socially inferior tenants also having a say in choosing your MP. Some men don't want their wives to have equal rights. For such people, Condorcet and every innovation he represents is another 'evil'.

Religiosity and Evangelism

Religion still permeates almost every aspect of life. In marked contrast to the twenty-first century, in which your spiritual outlook is largely a personal matter and secularism the social norm, the opposite is the case in Regency Britain: a common religious understanding is the social norm, and any non-religious thoughts are generally kept private. Most people in 1789 still believe that the Earth was created on the afternoon of 23 October 4004 BC, according to the biblical calculations of Archbishop Ussher in the seventeenth century. Although one free-thinking antiquary, John Frere, suggests in 1790 that some flint axes excavated at Hoxne in Suffolk indicate humanity is much older than the Bible suggests, the implications of his letter on the subject to the Society of Antiquaries are ignored. The dominant Creationist framework lasts well into the nineteenth century and goes a long way to explain the widespread acceptance of social disparities such as gender inequality and differences in wealth. As the eighteenth-century English poet Alexander Pope expresses it in his attempt to vindicate God's plan for the world: 'whatever is, is right'.[7] People believe that it is God's will that there are rich and poor, weak and strong, male and female – and they do not presume that they have the right to question the divine order of things.

Not everyone sees religion in the same way, of course. There are many different interpretations of God's will within the Church of England, as well as among communities of Jews, Roman Catholics and nonconformist Protestant congregations. Nevertheless, despite their differences, they all believe in God's presence in the world. That is also true for the majority of non-religious people; their reluctance to attend church is mainly due to their idleness or distrust of authority, not an expression of disbelief. There are virtually no atheists. The first atheistic tract in the English language is a two-page pamphlet, *The Necessity of Atheism*, published by the nineteen-year-old poet Percy Bysshe Shelley in 1811. This leads to him being sent down from the University of Oxford in disgrace. No one else openly advocates atheism in England until after the end of the Regency period.

In addition to this deep-seated religiosity, the dominant churches – the Anglican Church in England, and the Kirk, or Church of Scotland, north of the border – are still responsible for much of the day-to-day running of the country. Many public services are administered within the framework of the established Church, including the probate of wills, the burial of the dead and education. In order to become a judge, a magistrate, a university lecturer or an MP, you need to swear a Protestant oath. Thus these positions are closed to nonconformists, Jews and Roman Catholics (although the restrictions on nonconform-ists are lifted in 1828 and on Roman Catholics in 1829). It is still frowned upon if you don't go to church, especially in rural parishes: the official penalty is 1s for every Sunday you are absent but you can also be fined £20 per month on top of this.[8] Mr Skinner, rector of

Camerton in Somerset, regularly admonishes the local colliers and labourers if they don't turn up on Sunday. They tell him they do not have smart enough clothes or that they now go to a Methodist chapel, but more often than not, their real reason is a dislike of the ties between ecclesiastical authority and the establishment.

Morality is still fundamentally a religious matter, and it continues to be shaped by Britain's puritanical past. 'Sunday at Bath is like Sunday everywhere else in England,' writes Christian Goede: 'no music, no dancing, no cards are suffered; and the assembly rooms open merely for promenade and conversation.'[9] Scotland is even more religious. Visiting Glasgow in 1814, the Swiss industrialist Hans Caspar Escher notes that 'even the coffee we drank after dinner in another room was preceded by grace and was followed by a grace. I reckon that we have been to divine service for four hours today and that we have listened to grace eight times.'[10] At the same time, the evangelical movement of the eighteenth century is having an impact on many people's perceptions of morality and the social good that religion can do. John Wesley's emphasis on reading the Bible and living a moral life – in marked contrast to the debauchery, pride and corruption of the rich – attracts hundreds of thousands of ordinary people. His preaching inspires them to take up their own moral crusades. If you want to hear his last sermon, you can in October 1790, when he speaks beneath the boughs of an ash tree in Winchelsea, Sussex, at the age of eighty-seven.

The fervour of evangelism is not just restricted to nonconformists; it also emerges in the mainstream churches. When the Revd Dr Thomas Chalmers moves from rural Fife to central Glasgow in 1815, he is appalled to find that his new parish consists of a huge slum of 11,000 souls. He can't possibly visit every house to tend to his flock. So the good doctor does what he does best: he preaches. And in so doing he seeks to teach people that the Christian faith is the religion of the poor – 'she can light up the hope of immortality in their humble habitations,' as he puts it. Thus, 'a man in rags may become rich in faith'.[11] It works. People who have little financial wealth find they derive deep satisfaction from counting their Heavenly blessings. Dr Chalmers builds schools and urges people to become missionaries. He also speaks of the virtues of scientific discovery and technological development and, in this way, combines the trusted language of religion with the social benefits to be gained from 'innovation'. Before long, he becomes a celebrity in his own right, with hundreds of people attending his sermons.

In England, many pious middle-class people share the idea that Christianity, morality and social improvement all go hand in hand. Some of them form the Clapham Sect: a group of wealthy and well-connected men and women who collaborate on supporting such causes as penal reform and the abolition of slavery. Others are the editors and writers of the many new religious journals, which help to carry the message of spiritual salvation to the urban masses. Still others are the founders of new institutions with moral or religious purposes at home and overseas, such as the Society for the Suppression of Vice, and the Missionary Society for Propagating the Gospel in Heathen and Unenlightened Countries. As you can see, while half of the Regency elite are 'mad, bad and dangerous to know', it seems the other half are doing their best to be sane, good and angelic.

Radicalism and Repression

As a time traveller, you would be well advised to avoid politics. After all, none of the political fights is yours. However, you will not be able to ignore certain issues, particularly the repeal of the Corn Laws and the reform of the House of Commons. Thus I suggest you make note of the reasons why people become so agitated and what the consequences are of getting caught up in the unrest.

We need to begin by returning to the problem of people having enough to eat. As William Cobbett so eloquently puts it in his *Weekly Political Register*, 'I defy you to agitate any fellow with a full stomach.' It is the shortage of food during the war with France that makes the London mob attack the royal carriage and smash its windows as the king is driven to the House of Lords in 1795. Similarly, it is the fear of long-term unemployment that triggers the Luddite riots in Yorkshire in 1811. Hundreds of skilled weavers and textile workers professing to follow 'Ned Ludd' – a mythical, Robin Hood-like figure – break into factories and smash the power-driven looms and torch the buildings. They see their jobs being taken and their wages undercut by an unskilled workforce operating the new machinery. The government responds by making machine-breaking punishable by death, which

does nothing to alleviate their fears. In April 1812, the situation esca-
lates into a crisis when William Horsfall, a public advocate of
machinery in Huddersfield, is attacked and murdered. Local magistrates authorise the use of force, and mill owners hand out firearms
to their trusted foremen to defend their property.

Although the Luddite riots die down the following year, the end
of the war with France in 1815 sees huge numbers of ex-soldiers and
sailors left without employment. Their availability for work makes
things tougher for the hard-pressed artisans and labourers who have
already seen their wages cut. To make things even worse, the government passes an Act for Regulating the Importation of Corn – a tariff
on imported grain when the price is below a certain level – to prohibit
merchants buying it cheaply overseas. Although the idea is to preserve
agricultural jobs, the effect of the legislation is to increase the price
of bread for urban workers. Riots break out in London, where citizens
attack the homes of politicians who are thought to be in support of
the policy. When the harvest fails in 1816, corn prices escalate even
further. Meat prices follow suit. Food riots break out from Norfolk
to Devon. In Suffolk, 1,500 farm workers break threshing machines
and burn barns and hayricks, yelling 'bread or blood' as they ransack
bakeries and butchers' shops. Early the next year, a crowd pressing
in around the Prince Regent's coach in the Mall turns violent and
someone throws a stone, smashing one of the windows. Coming
after the assassination of the British prime minister, Spencer Perceval,
in 1812, people fear a revolution. As the upper-class Welsh army
officer Rees Gronow later remarks in his memoirs, 'in the riots and
meetings of those troublesome times the mob really meant mischief,
and had they been accustomed to the use of arms and well drilled,
they might have committed as great excesses as the ruffians of 1793
in France'.[12]

Despite the burning hayricks and smashed looms, no one listens
to the protesters. Thus in 1817 a crowd of textile workers decide to
march from Manchester to London to present a petition to the Prince
Regent. It becomes known as the March of the Blanketeers, as each
worker carries a blanket not only to keep warm but to show his trade.
The march is ruthlessly broken up by the King's Dragoon Guards and
many of the demonstrators are arrested or forced to flee. Three
months later, an unemployed textile worker called Jeremiah Brandreth
plots the overthrow of the government from Derbyshire. The Pentrich

Rising, as the plot becomes known, is foiled but serves to remind people that a French-style revolution could easily break out in Britain. Brandreth and two of his co-conspirators are beheaded but such draconian punishment does nothing to calm the febrile atmosphere. It grows over the next two years and reaches its climax on 16 August 1819 when more than 60,000 people gather in St Peter's Fields, Manchester, to hear Henry Hunt speak on the subject of parliamentary reform and the recent Importation of Corn Act. Seeing the huge crowd and the banners of 'No Corn Bill' and 'Equal Representation or Death', the magistrates order the cavalry to help arrest the ring-leaders. Ten minutes later the ground is strewn with the bodies of dead and injured men, women and children. Eleven are killed at the scene and 600 are injured, several of whom die shortly afterwards. One of those fatally injured, John Lees, is a veteran of the Battle of Waterloo. The juxtaposition of military courage in the defence of the realm four years earlier and military cowardice now in killing unarmed protesters is shocking. The atrocity soon becomes known as the Peterloo Massacre.

While the hard-pressed workers and unemployed weavers try to make the government listen to their pleas about unemployment and the price of bread, others are looking to change the political system. How can it possibly be right that the upper classes completely dominate both Houses of Parliament? They don't just sit in the House of Lords: more than 500 seats in the House of Commons are controlled by members of the nobility and landed gentry, to which they appoint their family and friends. In addition, certain groups such as Roman Catholics and Jews are specifically barred from voting in elections or standing as candidates. It is hardly surprising that so many people want to see Parliament reformed. Some are militant, calling for all men to have the vote. Others demand specific changes, such as the abolition of anti-Catholic or anti-Jewish legislation. The most radical thinkers call for a bloody revolution, because they believe that only a total shake-up of society will bring some fairness for working people.

On top of the disenfranchised, the persecuted and the unemployed, you have the dreamers. People are fired up with the possibility of a better society, drawing from such works as Thomas Paine's *Rights of Man*, published in two parts in 1791 and 1792, and William Godwin's *Enquiry Concerning Political Justice*, which appears in 1793. Paine calls for a written constitution, the abolition of the aristocracy, the setting up of a republic in place of the monarchy, a graduated income tax, the education of the poor and the introduction of old-age pensions. Godwin pioneers the anarchist argument that the only justification for government is to provide security against injustice, violence and corruption, so if the government itself promotes all these things, it is part of the problem, not the solution. Followers of Jeremy Bentham's concept of Utilitarianism – the view that the morally correct course of action is that which will result in the greatest happiness for the greatest number – also want parliamentary reform. Another campaigner, Major John Cartwright, establishes Hampden Clubs up and down the country to unite middle-class liberals and working-class revolutionaries in the pursuit of a new constitution. In 1820, a 'provisional government' in Scotland issues a proclamation calling for a radical war and mass strike action to achieve equal rights. William Cobbett promotes reform through his *Weekly Political Register*, and Henry Hunt continues to shout for it at demonstrations, demanding universal male suffrage, annual parliaments and voting by secret ballot.

With so many people calling for political change, why is there no revolution? One reason is that the reformers are so divided they have no hope of agreeing on a single agenda. Francis Place calls Henry Hunt 'an ignorant, turbulent, mischief-making fellow'. Jeremy Bentham describes William Cobbett as 'a microbe struggling with a swarm of his elemental kind in a drop of water'.[13] Britain's geography is also a factor. The industrial areas of the Midlands and the North are a long way from Westminster, and reformers cannot easily march on the capital in large numbers, as the fate of the Blanketeers demonstrates. But the principal force holding back the revolutionary tide is the widespread 'dread of innovation'. As the French Revolution turns into the Terror, and people see the smiling lips that once promised equality draw back to reveal teeth in the form of guillotine-blades, many lose their faith in political change. For them, Napoleon's coronation as emperor in 1804 is the last straw. What is the point of a revolution if it only hands power to another autocrat? As for the propertied classes, they are prepared to back almost any level of repression to reduce the threat of revolution. The British government is thus able to deal firmly with radicalism, employing spies wherever it can and meeting the upturned palms of the hungry workers with a firmly clenched fist.

Cruelty and Compassion

People have always done cruel things, and you don't need me to tell you that they still do. But that does not mean that society is inherently cruel. Plenty of horrific acts arouse widespread condemnation in Regency Britain, just as they would today or, indeed, in any age. It is rather those acts of harshness that do *not* arouse their horror that mark the period out as a crueller place than modern Britain.

Consider slavery, for example. Most Regency people have no knowledge of the terrible conditions experienced by enslaved people in the West Indies. However, everyone understands what it means for individuals to lose their freedom. Despite this, the transatlantic slave trade continues until 1807, and even after the buying and selling of humans is prohibited, the status of slavery overseas is officially upheld. The reason is that slaves are seen primarily as assets and only secondarily as human beings; and most people agree that safeguarding wealth is more important than upholding the rights of low-status individuals. Who is going to recompense the plantation owners if their workforce is emancipated? And who is going to do the necessary hard labour? In 1823 there is a large-scale slave revolt in British-ruled Demerara. Hundreds of enslaved people are killed in a protest about their appalling living conditions. Dozens more are hanged on the orders of the British governor. Yet public sympathy in Britain lies initially with the slave owners, not with those who are suffering.

Another area of life in which you will come across habitual cruelty is the punishment of felons. Although the abhorrent practice of burning women at the stake for petty treason is abolished in June 1790 – after the burning of Catherine Murphy the previous year for making false coins – men and women are still regularly hanged. The mass of eighteenth-century legislation that makes more than 200 offences punishable by death, known as the Bloody Code, prevails throughout most of our period. You can be executed for arson, murder, rape, rioting, robbery and theft. No surprises there, you might say. But you can also be hanged for being out at night with a blacked-up face, sheep-stealing, damaging a fishpond, taking rabbits from a warren, pickpocketing, forgery, cutting down trees, consorting with Gypsies, damaging a road and concealing a stillborn child (if you are an unmarried mother). Even teenagers are executed. John Old and

Patrick Murphy, both aged seventeen, are hanged for burglary in 1803. Eighteen-year-old Sarah Shenston is hanged in 1792 for killing her illegitimate baby. Elizabeth Marsh is hanged in 1794 at the age of fifteen for killing her grandfather.[14] Moreover, almost everyone condemned to death is executed in public. This does not just add to their personal humiliation and the distress of their families: it brutalises those who witness these punishments. Thousands of people attend public hangings. Parents take their children to watch. Shop girls and apprentice boys take the day off especially. The bustle and excitement as the crowd waits for the killing is like a carnival. Someone's agonising death is public entertainment.

Having said all these things, society is gradually becoming more humane. Certain punishments, such as the pillory and the whipping of women, are curtailed in this period. Mantraps are outlawed in 1826 and, although reintroduced in 1830, they have to be licensed thereafter. However, the clearest indications that society is becoming less cruel are to be seen in three important humanitarian movements: namely, prison reform, the restriction of the death penalty and the abolition of slavery.

With regard to prison reform, we need to go back to the 1770s to get the full picture. In 1773, John Howard, high sheriff of Bedfordshire, is astonished to discover that some people are kept in prison after they have been found Not Guilty. The reason is that they cannot pay the gaolers' fees they incurred while awaiting trial. He succeeds in changing the law, so that innocent people are not detained any longer than necessary. But in the course of his investigations, he realises that conditions in British prisons are appalling. Not only are the buildings themselves filthy, damp and unventilated but also the systems in place are unnecessarily harsh. Prisoners are made to bear heavy chains all the time. When Howard visits, few gaolers dare accompany him into the cells, so great is their fear of infection. On leaving, his clothes stink too much for him to travel in a coach.[15] Nevertheless, he inspects 230 institutions and publishes the results in 1777 as *The State of the Prisons in England and Wales*. It shocks everyone who reads it. Sir Samuel Romilly, MP, a lawyer and legal reformer, describes it as 'one of those works which have been rare in all the ages of the world – being written with a view only to the good of mankind'.[16] From that moment on, people begin to press for an improvement in the state of the prisons.

The other name associated with prison reform at this time is even more famous. Elizabeth Fry is a Quaker who is appalled by the state of Newgate Prison, where hundreds of women are locked up with their young children in squalid and overcrowded conditions. In 1816 she sets up a small school there and introduces a set of rules and activities for the children and their mothers, ranging from prison dress and supervision to education, Bible-reading and moral codes. She is remarkably successful in rehabilitating some of the hardest women in the prison. The following year she establishes an association to help reform the conditions in Newgate, which in 1821 becomes the British Ladies' Society for Promoting the Reformation of Female Prisoners. Like Howard, she visits prisons up and down the country, suggesting ways of improving conditions and publishing a handbook to encourage other prison reformers in 1827.

'When one creature is murdered, another is immediately deprived of life in a slow torturing manner; then the executioners, their hands yet reeking with the blood of innocence, believe that they have done a great deed.' So writes Mary Shelley in *Frankenstein*, summing up the attitude of the more liberal-minded to the hanging of criminals. Opposition to the death penalty has been growing for decades, and in our period the momentum is with the reformers. Juries now frequently find someone Not Guilty if they believe a Guilty verdict will result in a death sentence. Judges similarly employ transportation to Australia as an alternative to hanging. But the reformers still have a mountain to climb. The landowners who control Parliament are keen to preserve their right to shoot thieves or to see them hanged. The campaign against the death penalty is led by Sir Samuel Romilly. In 1808 he manages to persuade Parliament to repeal the Act that makes pickpocketing a hanging offence. Two years later, he denounces the Bloody Code in the Commons, declaring that 'there is no country on the face of the Earth in which there have been so many different offences according to law to be punished with death as in England'.[17] Over and over again he introduces Bills to have capital offences removed from the statute books. Five times between 1810 and 1818 he tries to abolish the death penalty for shoplifting, every time without success; but his persistence raises awareness and even the most intransigent landowners realise that they are winning battles but losing the war. Romilly dies in 1818 but his legacy is profound: in 1823 an Act is passed that removes the sentence of death from more than fifty crimes. Even more importantly, every judge who finds a felon guilty from then on has the legal power to pass a lesser sentence. The death penalty only remains compulsory for treason and murder.

When it comes to the abolition of slavery, one name still rings out above all others: that of William Wilberforce, MP. On 12 May 1787, under an old oak tree in Kent, he has a conversation with William Pitt in which he tells the prime minister that he is going to propose a Bill to abolish the slave trade. Pitt encourages him, thereby setting him on his life's mission. Wilberforce is assisted by many others, most notably Granville Sharp and Thomas Clarkson, who are both founding members of the Society for Effecting the Abolition of the Slave Trade, and Hannah More and her friends in the Clapham Sect. They lobby politicians and peers, write books and give lectures to promote the cause. But ultimately the success of the campaign owes most to Wilberforce's leadership, charm, deep Christian faith, gregariousness, eloquence and single-minded determination. After the abolition of the trade in slaves in 1807, Wilberforce turns his attention to the total eradication of slavery. Gradually, he turns opinion round. As he lies dying in his London house in July 1833, the Bill for the Abolition of Slavery is being debated in the House of Commons. It is passed on the evening of the 25th. Wilberforce is told the following morning. He dies three days later, his life's work complete.

Cruelty and Kindness to Animals

Given that people can be so vicious to one another, it is hardly surprising that they are especially brutal to animals. Again, the principle of property applies, so that the animal's welfare is less important than its value. That is why you'll find donkeys and horses kept down in mines in darkness, never brought up above ground but forced to pull wagons of ore or coal until they die. Similarly, work horses are whipped almost to death – indeed, foreigners frequently note that England is a 'hell for horses'. Anne Lister is annoyed with her old mare Diamond when she embarks on a journey just before Christmas 1821. The poor animal is still recovering from hauling her gig 32 miles across the hills the previous day but Anne declares that she 'never saw an animal so idle and sluggish' and therefore gives the poor beast 'more whipping even than yesterday'.[18] A month later Anne has

Diamond put down – by having her stabbed through the heart. It takes five minutes for the poor creature to die.

You will, of course, come across people who are not cruel to animals. 'I was taught by my mother from my earliest infancy to be tenderly kind towards the meanest living thing,' writes the poet Samuel Rogers, 'and, however people may laugh, I sometimes very carefully put a stray gnat or wasp out at the window.'[19] A few horses are extraordinarily prized and pampered: the duke of Wellington's favourite mount, Copenhagen, which he rides at the Battle of Waterloo, is a good example. Some dogs are much loved. The twenty-year-old Lord Byron erects a splendid monument over the grave of his 'firmest friend', Boatswain, a Newfoundland, at Newstead Abbey in 1808, declaring in the epitaph that the animal 'possessed beauty without vanity, strength without insolence, courage without ferocity, and all the virtues of Man without his vices'. The practice of keeping exotic pets becomes ever more popular. Many families will proudly show you their parrot or songbird in its cage. One traveller in East Devon in 1805 strikes up a conversation with a boy carrying a wooden box: he is the proud possessor of a guinea pig and three Angora rabbits.[20]

The real test, however, is not how people treat their precious pets but what consideration they show for livestock. Herein, again, you will find that Britain is a nation of extremes. 'Cattle are slaughtered with the clumsiest barbarity,' writes Robert Southey, 'the butcher hammers away at the forehead of the beast; blow after blow raises a swelling which renders the following blows ineffectual, and the butchery is completed by cutting the throat'.[21] The American clergyman Nathaniel Wheaton visits Smithfield Market in June 1824 and reports on the manner in which animals are driven there. He is particularly distressed by the transportation of calves:

> Their legs are all brought together and bound so tightly with cords as to stop the circulation. In this state, they are piled into a cart, like a load of butchered hogs, and transported twenty or thirty miles, their heads being suffered to hang out of the cart at each end, and to beat against the frame at every jolt of the vehicle. In this state of torture, I have often met them on the road, with their eyes rolled up in the agonies of death. Many actually expire on the way and may be seen strewed about the pavement of Smithfield on market days, where they

are sold to the manufacturers of veal pies and sausages. Let a person whose nerves are strong enough to endure the sight of brute misery in all its varieties and degrees give a few days' attendance at the markets for livestock and he will look upon the whole tribe of butchers, drivers, carriers &c as no better than a hardened, relentless, unfeeling race of fiends, in human shape. I am convinced that the lowest classes of the English are either by nature or custom, cruel.[22]

The other side to this story is far more heartening. The English are leading the way in promoting the better treatment of animals. The spark is the evangelical idea that, because God loves all Creation, it is the duty of every Christian to respect and care for living things, and that to cause them suffering is a sin. This moral message receives support from the secular philosopher Jeremy Bentham, in his *Introduction to the Principles of Morals and Legislation*, published in 1789:

There is very good reason why we should be allowed to eat such non-human animals as we like to eat: we are the better for it ... There is also very good reason why we should be allowed to kill ones that attack us: we would be the worse for their living ... But is there any reason why we should be allowed to torment them? None that I can see. Are there any reasons why we should *not* be allowed to torment them? Yes, several ... The day may come when the non-human part of the animal creation will acquire the rights that never could have been withheld from them except by the hand of tyranny ... A full-grown horse or dog is incomparably more rational and conversable than an infant of a day or a week, or even a month old. Even if that were not so, what difference would that make? The question is not *Can they reason?* Or *Can they talk?* But *Can they suffer?*[23]

Over the next two decades several Bills to outlaw bull-fighting, cock-fighting and other forms of cruelty to animals are presented to Parliament. They are all unsuccessful until, in 1822, the Cruel Treatment of Cattle Act is passed. The tide has at last turned. In June 1824, the Society for the Prevention of Cruelty to Animals (later the RSPCA) is established. In its first six months it undertakes sixty-three prosecutions. Ironically, the coffee house where the society is founded is called Old Slaughter's.

The changes in attitudes to animals are vividly exemplified by Chunee, an elephant in Pidcock's Royal Menagerie in the Strand. He is kept upstairs in a cage for fourteen years, never seeing another elephant, never being allowed out. By 1826 he has had enough. When he tries to break through his bars, his terrified owner, Edward Cross, decides to kill him. First, he attempts to poison the animal, which has no effect; then he tries to have him shot. He summons military help but 152 bullets fail to kill Chunee. In the end, Mr Cross savagely hacks through the poor beast's neck with a soldier's sabre.[24] Some people conclude that enough is enough. Very shortly afterwards, *The Times* publishes the following letter:

> To place an elephant or any beast without a mate in a box bearing no greater proportion to his bulk than a coffin does to a corpse, is inhuman; and there can be no doubt that confinement and the want of a mate caused the frenzy which rendered it necessary to destroy the late stupendous and interesting animal in Exeter 'Change.
>
> In France ... the Jardin des Plantes contains a menagerie at once humane, safe and a national ornament. A pair of elephants are to be seen there, walking about in a field, provided with a pond (through which they frequently promenade), sheds, etcetera, and enjoy themselves with but little restraint, without disgusting the spectator with offensive scents, and the cruel spectacle of an animal cooped up in a den little larger than his own body.[25]

The menagerie never recovers its popularity. Mr Cross closes it in 1828 and transfers the remaining animals to his new Surrey Zoological Gardens in south London, where they roam in the open air.

Duelling

Is Regency Britain a violent place? Yes, there is an awful lot of fighting, thrashing and beating – but it does not often result in people killing each other. The annual homicide rate is only two people per 100,000.[26] This is roughly twice what it is in Britain today but only one-third of what it is in the twenty-first-century United States. So you should be safe. However, there is one particular risk that you need to bear in mind when visiting, for it may well claim your life.

Duelling is a matter of upper-class male honour. No gentleman would deign to fight someone from the middle or working classes: it would be beneath him. Besides, the lower classes have less dangerous ways of sorting out their differences: the middle classes take their opponents to court; the working classes simply punch each other. As for women, there is no expectation that two ladies should resort to violence; there is rather an expectation that they should not. The only notable duel between women in this period, the so-called Petticoat Duel of 1792, is a somewhat contrived affair, following Lady Almeria Braddock's inaccurate estimate of the age of her friend, Mrs Elphinstone. They meet in Hyde Park and shoot at each other, but without injury. Then they fight with swords, until one of the ladies is nicked in the arm – after which they make up and become friends again.

What is the etiquette if you are challenged to a duel? First, before your adversary issues a challenge, he should ask you for a written apology. Obviously there are some insults that cannot be remedied in this way: if he has just caught you in bed with his wife, a note saying 'sorry' is unlikely to make amends. However, he should take every step necessary to minimise the need to fight. This is not only because you might kill him but also because, if he kills you, he might be tried for manslaughter or murder. Duelling is against the law and sometimes the man who delivers the fatal blow is hanged as a result.[27]

Supposing that you refuse to apologise for casting doubt upon your adversary's honour, he should then send you a letter giving details of the challenge, which will be delivered by his 'second' or personal assistant. The time set for the meeting will normally be very early, about 5 a.m., to avoid detection. If you refuse to attend, people may well think you a coward for not being prepared to defend *your* honour. If you accept the challenge, you will need to appoint your own second. He will be equally culpable if you kill your challenger, so you will only choose a very close friend for whom you'd be prepared to do the same favour. You may safely presume that you will fight with pistols. Normally you'll be expected to bring a pair of them, so that you can fire twice without having to reload. It is rare after 1780 for men to fight with swords; only those who are hell-bent on killing each other resort to blades – and then only after they have shot at each other twice and failed to obtain satisfaction.

On the designated morning you will face your opponent and listen to the seconds' formal request to settle the disagreement in a peaceful manner. If you refuse, you and your opponent will face each other at a distance agreed by the seconds, usually between eight and twenty paces. Note that this is not a Wild West gunfight – you do not normally draw and shoot at the same time, although the seconds might agree to this. The challenger usually fires first. When being shot at, you would be wise to stand sideways, looking at your adversary over your shoulder and presenting him with as small a target as possible. If you survive the first shot, you may then take a shot at him. Do not steady your pistol on your arm or spend too much time taking aim: you must simply raise your gun, aim and shoot. According to James Gilchrist, writing in 1821, out of 172 duels fought over the previous sixty years, three have resulted in both men being killed, sixty-six have seen one man expire, and ninety-six combatants have been seriously injured.[28] Although this is undoubtedly an underestimate of the total number of duels fought, the proportions of fatalities may be taken as representative. Thus, if you fight a duel, you have a 21 per cent chance of dying and a 28 per cent chance of being wounded. Rarely has anything been so formal and yet so visceral, so controlled and yet so furious, so honourable and yet so ludicrous, all the same time.[29]

What induces gentlemen to risk life and limb in this way? Frequently it is a woman's virtue. When a naval lieutenant challenges an army captain in March 1803 on account of the dishonour the latter has done to his sister, the animosity each man feels towards the other is so great that they tell their seconds there is no point in attempting to mediate. Duels like this are the most dangerous sort: fought over the honour of a third party, on whose behalf one of the duellists is determined to kill the other. In this case the two men shoot at each other simultaneously, twice. The first time, the lieutenant has the pistol blown out of his right hand, losing two of his fingers. Taking out a handkerchief and binding it around the bleeding stubs, he assures his second that God gave him another hand for good reason. Holding the second pistol in his left hand, he waits for the signal. When he hears 'Gentlemen, are you ready? Fire!' he hits the captain in the head but at the same time receives a bullet to his chest. As he lies dying, he is informed that he has killed his sister's seducer. He begs his second to take the ring from his finger and deliver it to his sister 'that she might be assured this was the happiest moment that he ever knew'.[30]

Duels are often fought over far more trivial matters, especially by military men who cannot accept even the slightest questioning of their honour. In June 1788 Captain Tonge challenges Captain Paterson to a duel after the latter repeatedly steps on his heel in the Strand; it ends with Captain Tonge being shot in the thigh.[31] In March 1794 Captain Parkhurst and Lieutenant Kelly fight a duel over their seats at the opera house; they are both injured in the ensuing exchange of fire.[32] In April 1803 Captain James Macnamara of the Royal Navy is out walking his Newfoundland dog in Hyde Park when the animal scuffles with another Newfoundland belonging to Colonel Robert Montgomery. Montgomery angrily demands to know whose dog it is and threatens to 'knock down' any animal that attacks his own. Macnamara accuses him of arrogance, Montgomery levels the same accusation at Macnamara, and the two officers agree to fight a duel at Chalk Farm. They shoot and injure each other; Montgomery dies of his wound.

I am sure you would agree with me that there are better ways of settling an argument with someone than by allowing him to point a loaded gun at you and pull the trigger. However, there is much more going on here than meets the eye. The real reasons for fighting the above-mentioned duels are not because someone trod on someone else's heel, or one dog attacked another, but because gentlemen with public reputations cannot afford to have them called into question. When the duke of Buckingham fights a duel with the duke of Bedford in 1822, he tells his opponent: 'My Lord Duke, you are the last man I wish to quarrel with, but you must be aware that a public man's life is not worth preserving unless with honour.'[33] You cannot be a public figure in Regency society if you don't stand up for what you believe in – even in the face of death. It follows that the greater your reputation, the more important it is that you do everything you can to defend it. Even a prince might fight a duel. In 1789 Colonel Lennox, heir to the dukedom of Richmond, challenges Prince Frederick, duke of York, the king's second son, and the prince accepts. The two meet on Wimbledon Common and Colonel Lennox fires first. The bullet 'grazes his curl' but does not draw blood. His Royal Highness then refuses to return fire, thereby winning much praise – both for putting his honour ahead of his royal privilege and for not trying to exact revenge.

Even more revealing of the importance of honour in the mindset of the Regency elite is the fact that not one but *two* serving prime ministers and two prominent Cabinet ministers fight duels – the latter with each other. In 1798 the prime minister, William Pitt, accepts the challenge of George Tierney, MP, to resolve a dispute about the defence of the realm. Both men fire and miss. Nevertheless, the significant issue is that the prime minister's honour is so important to him that he is prepared to risk his life defending it. Personally, I find that quite admirable. After all, how many modern-day politicians have such integrity that they would willingly face a man with a loaded gun in defence of their policies? And Pitt is not the only prime minister to think this way. In 1829 his successor, the duke of Wellington, follows his example – even though he is nearly sixty and famously detests heroic causes. The duke takes issue with some snide remarks that the earl of Winchilsea has made about his proposed reforms to the anti-Catholic legislation. As the challenger, the duke fires first and misses; the earl then deliberately shoots wide.[34] But the most extraordinary political duel of all takes place in 1809 between the then Secretary for War, Lord Castlereagh, and the Foreign Secretary and future prime minister, George Canning. These two ministers are from the same political party and are serving in the same Cabinet. When Castlereagh learns that Canning is plotting to have him removed from office, it's pistols at dawn. Moreover, the two ministers have no intention of shooting wide: they agree to fire at each other simultaneously. On the first round, both men miss. On the second, the War Secretary hits the Foreign Secretary in the thigh, forcing him to return home to seek medical attention.

Sensitivity

All this talk of honour and staring down the barrel of a pistol might give you the impression that Regency gentlemen have nerves of steel. Some do. But the modern trope of the 'strong, silent type' is almost nowhere to be found in this period; the duke of Wellington is one of the very few. Men are much more emotional than you might expect. Of course, there's no surprise that the prince of Wales sheds tears when his beloved mistress, Mrs Fitzherbert, threatens to abandon him. But you would not expect the same prince to burst into tears in public when his friend Beau Brummell criticises the cut of his new coat. Nor would you expect a man like Richard Brinsley Sheridan to weep over the fact that his government sinecure – worth £800 a year – will not be inherited by his son. Judges sometimes cry in court when delivering their verdicts. When Samuel Whitbread, MP, kills himself in 1815, many members in the House of Commons who rise to pay him compliments cannot control their tears. It is the original instance of there being 'not a dry eye in the House'.[35] When George Tierney gets to his feet to speak he is sobbing so much that he is unable to say a word – which is perhaps surprising, considering that he has a reputation as a duellist.

This contrast between the resolute man of honour and the weeping politician seems to be yet another contradiction in the Regency character. However, I suspect these two things are both examples of a rawness or thin-skinned vulnerability that many men share. The sensitive man who is easily made to cry is also likely to be moved to passion by an insult. This is, after all, the Romantic age, when extremes of feeling are considered normal, even desirable. In the words of Lord Byron:

> The great object of life is sensation – to feel that we exist, even though in pain. It is this 'craving void' which drives us to gaming – to battle – to travel – to intemperate but keenly felt pursuits of every description, whose principal attraction is the agitation inseparable from their accomplishment.[36]

Sometimes, when we consider the hard lives of our forefathers, we imagine them to be emotionally as well as physically tougher than us. But whereas the sheer physicality of their lives can hardly be doubted, when you examine their feelings, they are just as vulnerable as us, if not more so. It is striking how many gentlemen in this period commit suicide in the most dramatic fashion, with a razor through the throat. Samuel Whitbread, Sir Samuel Romilly and Lord Castlereagh all choose this method. The female equivalent is to drown yourself, like Jane Toulmin, mentioned at the start of this book, and Shelley's first wife, Harriet Westbrook, who writes sad farewell letters to her family and husband and is found dead shortly afterwards in the

Serpentine, aged twenty-one. Such extremes of passion will leave you deeply saddened – and aware that the true intensity of being alive can hardly be contained in the pages of a history book or a novel.

Glorious Uncertainty

Regency people love to gamble. It fits into their daily lives as naturally as watching TV fits into ours. And, generally speaking, the people born to the greatest privileges are the biggest risk-takers of all. Many fortunes that took generations to build are lost in one night at a London club. People love the thrill, as Lord Byron explains:

> I have a notion that gamblers are as happy as most people – being always *excited*. Women – wine – fame – the table – even ambition – sate now & then, but every turn of the card & cast of the dice keeps the gambler alive ... [I love] the glorious uncertainty not only of good or bad luck – but of any luck at all.[37]

Up and down the country, in London clubs, provincial assembly rooms and the houses of the rich and fashionable, men place bets as solemnly as they take communion in church. Silence reigns, with just the murmur of spectators' hushed voices around the table. The players sit with their coats turned inside out for luck and wear high-crowned hats with broad rims to conceal their emotions.[38] Women too gamble for high stakes; they arrange salons in their houses at which both men and women can play together. This brings additional thrills. When you catch the eye of a member of the opposite sex, with both of you feeling the tingling excitement of a large bet, the risk itself takes on a seductive character.

The most common forms of gambling are dice and card games but bets are placed on anything – from parliamentary decisions to when a public figure might die. Lord Malden bets 1,000 guineas that none of his friends can seduce his mistress, the actress Mary Robinson. What a foolish bet! He stands to lose both the girl and the money – especially when she finds out that he is taking her constancy for granted. Sure enough, Colonel Tarleton soon reaps both rewards. If you look in the betting book at Brooks's, a gentle-man's club in St James's, London, even more bizarre wagers are recorded. Gentlemen bet which one of two fellow members will get gout first; whether Mr Sheridan will be married before a certain date; and whether Mr Beckford will ever be made a peer.[39] Once the new pastime of ballooning arrives, club members have a fresh subject for their speculations. Mr Webster bets Lord Derby 100 guineas that he will not rise 100 yards above the ground in a balloon. Lord Cholmondley goes one better and places a bet of 500 guineas, payable – in the words of the betting book – 'whenever [Lord Derby] fucks a woman in a balloon a thousand yards from the Earth'.[40]

While the dice and card tables see the heaviest betting, men will light-heartedly gamble on almost anything. Eating feats are particularly popular. When in 1812 two gentlemen meet a coal carrier on Ratcliffe Highway in east London, they bet £5 with each other that the man cannot consume 9lbs of roasted bullock's heart, 3lbs of potatoes, a 1¾lb loaf of bread and a pot of porter within three-quarters of an hour. The coal carrier accepts the challenge and rolls up at the Queen's Head to demonstrate his capacity, with spectators paying 6d a head to place bets of their own. The contestant finishes well within the allotted time and calls for rum, downing four glasses of that as well.[41] Other wagers are not so appetising. The Revd James Woodforde is told of two men eating a leg of beef, bone and all, for a bet, and another drinking a half-pint glass of beer and then eating the glass too.[42] On 26 May 1811 the *Morning Chronicle* records that a blacksmith at Stroud 'ate on Tuesday for a trifling wager a pint of periwinkles with the shells in the space of ten minutes. Being desired to repeat this disgusting feat he readily did it but he is now so dangerously ill that he is not expected to recover.'[43] *The Sporting Magazine* carries a report of a man eating a live cat for a bet in Windsor in January 1790. The exponent incurs much bloodying of his head as the poor animal puts up a spirited defence but eventually all that is left are its bones.[44]

Sexual Immorality

Morality and immorality in the Regency period are not like two separate countries with a border between them, so that people are either inhabitants of one or the other. The courtesan Harriette Wilson is hardly a bastion of morality, yet the public delights in reading her memoirs when they are published. They are impressed by her 'virtue' of never taking more than one lover at any one time (although her lovers do sometimes overlap, even to the point of two dukes meeting on her doorstep). One of her bedfellows, the duke of Wellington, is a much more respectable public figure, yet *his* reputation is tarnished by his womanising: people expect a strong, upstanding commander like him to be more restrained in his sexual appetites. Another military hero, Lord Nelson, evades criticism for publicly conducting an affair with Emma, the wife of Sir William Hamilton. Instead it is his wife, Lady Nelson, who is criticised for not tolerating her husband's *ménage à trois*. It seems that attempting to draw a line between morality and immorality is like trying to draw the shape of the wind. Princess Lieven, the wife of the Russian ambassador, complains about the behaviour she witnesses at an English ball, noting that 'so many couples wandered off into the bushes that by the end of the dance almost the only people left in the ballroom were debutantes, chaperones, and the host'. Yet she herself has an affair with Prince Metternich, the Austrian diplomat.[45] Virtue and sin, which in previous centuries were seen as absolutes, now lie – like beauty – in the eye of the beholder.

The royal family has a lot to answer for in this respect. You've already heard about the prince of Wales and his many mistresses. His brother, Prince Frederick, also keeps a mistress, Mary Anne Clarke, who causes a scandal in 1809 when she admits selling army commissions on his behalf. The king's third son, Prince William, duke of Clarence (the future William IV), sets up house with a famous actress, Dorothy Bland, better known as 'Mrs Jordan'; they have ten children in the twenty years they are together. But in 1811 William abandons her because he is heavily in debt and needs to marry a wealthy heiress. Here it is not the 'living in sin' that is morally shocking but his cruelty and despicable cynicism. A similar story may be told of the king's fourth son, Prince Edward, duke of Kent. He lives with the married Madame de Saint-Laurent for twenty-eight years before he leaves her to marry a younger woman, in order to try to produce an heir to the throne. The less said about George III's fifth son, Prince Ernest, duke of Cumberland, the better. He does not conduct his affairs openly, like his brothers, but in secret, which many people think is even worse – especially after his valet, Joseph Sellis, apparently slashes his own throat in the duke's apartment. People suspect Cumberland of having seduced Mrs Sellis, thereby bringing about the tragedy. The king's sixth son, Prince Augustus, duke of Sussex, marries Lady Augusta Murray in contravention of the Royal Marriages Act and has two children by her. He then leaves her, paying her off with an allowance of £4,000 per year. The only prince to stay clear of accusations of sexual impropriety is the king's seventh son, Prince Adolphus, duke of Cambridge. As for the princesses, they are closeted within the court and unable to meet any suitable men. Perhaps unsurprisingly, they fall in love with unsuitable ones. At the age of twenty-two, Princess Sophia becomes infatuated with a retired general thirty-three years her senior. It is even said that she gives birth to his illegitimate child.

With the royal family setting such an example, you can just imagine how the upper classes behave. If lords wish to maintain mistresses, they do. Where they wish to have a string of occasional lovers, again there is nothing to stop them except their crossed-armed, foot-tapping wives. And if those wives themselves choose to swing naked from the chandeliers, then both parties are at liberty to dance freely through society, trailing the ribbons of free love. Lady Harley, countess of Oxford and Mortimer, has so many affairs that her children are collectively described as the 'Harleian Miscellany' as no one is quite sure who their fathers are. The daughters of Earl Spencer – Lady Georgiana and Lady Harriet – both marry well and bear children by their aristocratic husbands but then proceed to seduce their way through the rest of society. Harriet has an affair with Richard Brinsley Sheridan, among others, and gives birth to two children by Earl Granville. Georgiana – a heavy-drinking, hard-gambling fashion icon of immense popularity – has an affair with Charles James Fox, the leader of the opposition, and a daughter by Charles Grey, the future prime minister, before joining her husband in a long-term *ménage à trois* with Lady Elizabeth Foster, who also has affairs with the duke of Dorset, the duke of Richmond and the earl of Dunraven. Frankly, it is difficult to keep up with who is sleeping with whom among the well-to-do.

Ask Harriet or Georgiana whether it is right for married women to behave like their men in taking lovers and you will receive an unequivocal 'yes'. Other people are not so certain. A conversation in James Boswell's *Life of Dr Johnson*, published in 1791, expresses what is probably the majority view, which is that infidelity is not such a sin for husbands as it is for their wives. As Dr Johnson puts it, 'the man imposes no bastards upon his wife'.[46] This difference between male and female infidelity is acknowledged by many women too, even by some of the most free-thinking. A female friend of Boswell's says to him, 'I do not see why I should not indulge myself in gallantries with equal freedom as my husband does, provided I take care not to introduce a spurious issue into his family.'[47] Most high-status women plan accordingly to provide 'an heir and a spare'. Despite this, it is not unknown for a grand title and a vast estate to be inherited by a love child, as in the case of William Lamb, the second Lord Melbourne. His mother provides the first Lord Melbourne with an heir but no 'spare', so when the heir tragically dies, it is her son by the earl of Egremont who inherits her husband's fortune and title – and goes on to become prime minister.

How do people justify this in such a religious society? One answer is provided by the Scottish philosopher David Hume, who argues that it is unnatural to suppress any appetite, including lust. Another is provided by Boswell's lady friend, quoted above, who sees it as a matter of 'equality' with her husband that she should be as free as him to indulge herself in 'gallantries'. Boswell's own mistress, Jean Home, provides a third answer to the question, when her husband divorces her for adultery (with another lover, not Boswell): 'I hope that God will not punish me for the only crime I can charge myself with, which is the gratification of those passions which He Himself implanted in my nature.'[48]

The divinity of human passion may help you to understand one of the more unusual sides of sexual immorality: gentlemen's sex clubs. These are not so much established for the purpose of arranging sexual encounters – that is easily done with a prostitute – but for celebrating sex. You will arrive too late to join Sir Francis Dashwood's 'Monks of Medmenham', who until 1778 worship naked nymphs, fornicate in cells, drink to excess and do all sorts of libidinous, sacrilegious and at times satanic things by night in the ruins of Medmenham Abbey. However, you can still view their Temple of Venus, built in the shape of a giant vagina.[49] And you can still read the immortal words of John Wilkes, MP, whose *Essay on Woman* was composed for the club:

> Let us (since life can little more supply
> Than just a few good fucks and then we die)
> Expatiate free o'er that lov'd scene of Man;
> A mighty Maze! For mighty pricks to scan.[50]

The luxurious side of the Regency: Brighton seafront in 1825, showing the long line of fashionable houses facing the sea, and the Royal Chain Pier, with a steamship about to depart for Dieppe. Proportionally, Brighton is the fastest growing large town in the whole of Regency Britain.

The working side of the Regency: New Lanark Mills, Scotland, in about 1815. The emphasis on the welfare, health and education of the workforce leads to commercial success and is widely seen as the epitome of responsible entrepreneurship.

The cotton factory in Union Street, Manchester, in 1829. Thousands of people daily spend 14-hour shifts in such buildings, dealing with the stifling heat, dust, constant noise of the steam engines and rattling of the cotton-spinning machinery.

Until 1750, Old London Bridge (on the left) was the only permanent river crossing. By the time it is replaced with New London Bridge, in 1830, there are six more. Collectively these permit the city to expand south of the river. This engraving by E. W. Cooke shows how fine mass-produced illustrations are by the end of our period.

Looking down Regent Street in 1828. The building on the left is the Argyll Rooms, a concert venue where the Philharmonic Society of London holds the British premiere of Beethoven's Ninth Symphony on 21 March 1825.

St James's Park, London, in the early nineteenth century. Note that the lake is still a canal, half a mile long, stretching from in front of Buckingham House (later Buckingham Palace) to the Parade Ground at Whitehall.

Thomas Telford is one of the great engineers of the age. Brought up in poverty, he builds roads extending for thousands of miles across Wales, England and Scotland, as well as harbours, canals and bridges. This is his 579ft-long suspension bridge over the Menai Straits, completed in 1826.

The Point of Honor decided, or the Leaden argument of a Love affair.

Duelling in Hyde Park in 1825. Although it might seem ridiculous in modern eyes, the duel is a deeply serious demonstration of dignity. Two serving prime ministers fight duels in this period. You have to respect politicians who are willing to put their lives on the line to defend their policies and principles.

The ancient market at Smithfield remains the major London venue for the wholesale trade of cattle and sheep. However, observers are increasingly appalled at the conditions in which the animals are kept, eventually giving rise to the Royal Society for the Prevention of Cruelty to Animals.

Just as Smithfield represents the old ways of selling food, so the Fish Market in Newcastle, built in 1823–6, illustrates the new. Increasingly marketplaces are covered over, to give well-heeled customers a more comfortable shopping experience.

This Manchester calico factory in 1834 shows why working conditions are so dangerous. Imagine these machines thundering away in dim light, surrounded by dust and heat – you can see it is all too easy for a sleeve or skirt to get caught up in the cogs, and for workers to lose their fingers or limbs.

A London greengrocer's shop or 'fruit seller' in 1819. Increasingly such shops are becoming the usual place for obtaining fresh food – rather than in the traditional old marketplaces. Almost half of the old markets in London close over the period.

James Lackington's 'Temple of the Muses', on Finsbury Square, London, is the largest bookshop in Britain, reputed to have 500,000 volumes.

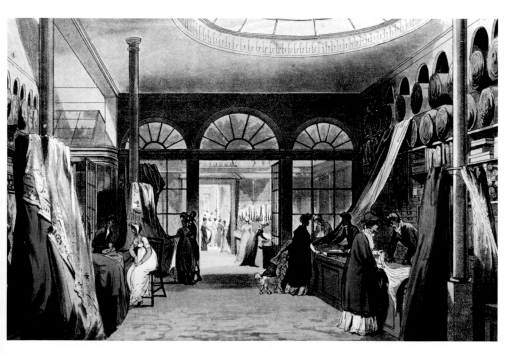

Messrs Harding, Howell & Co., on Pall Mall, London, is one of the earliest department stores, with glazed partitions separating the five departments.

Prince Hermann Pückler-Muskau comes to England in 1826 in search of a wealthy wife to rebuild his fortune – with the acquiescence of Lucie, his much-loved existing wife, who divorces him to assist in the project. His voluminous letters to her are hugely revealing of upper-class life in England.

Lord Byron, at the age of 25. Few portraits of the poet and maverick peer are as revealing of his character as this one, by Richard Westall. With unrestrained honesty, he shows us the best and the worst of the Regency gentleman.

Anne Lister. Famous in the modern world as the first lesbian to describe her love life at great length, her diaries are just as interesting for their mass of detail about gentry life in the Regency period.

The Chevalier d'Eon. He is required to wear women's clothes by the king of France in order to continue receiving his pension in exile in London. He may frequently be seen giving demonstrations of his fencing skills – always in a dress, of course.

Furthermore, there is at least one sex-worshipping society that you can still join (if you are so inclined). This is the Most Ancient and Puissant Order of the Beggar's Benison and Merryland, founded at Anstruther in Scotland in 1732. Gentlemen members drink together from phallus-shaped wine glasses and engraved punch bowls. They read out pornographic poems and stories to each other, recount their recent sexual exploits and watch young women undressing and performing naked. They normally end their evening's frivolity by collectively masturbating and ejaculating onto a pewter 'test platter' engraved with the words 'the way of a man with a maid'.[51]

Not everyone approves of all this libidinous activity, as you may well imagine. This is especially the case as you look further down the social hierarchy. Middle-class men might visit prostitutes, read pornographic novels and buy erotic prints, but very few keep a mistress. The general opinion is that a prostitute is no danger to a marriage but a mistress undermines the husband's marital devotion and reduces the wife to subservient misery. A middle-class woman who fancies taking a lover similarly threatens to make her husband a cuckold, destroying the social respectability of her family. Jean Home tells Boswell that 'I love my husband as a husband and you as a lover, each in his own sphere. I perform for him all the duties of a good wife. With you I give myself up to delicious pleasures.'[52] That might be acceptable for the upper classes, whose social standing and wealth are unassailable; but it is too great a risk for those trying to make their way upwards in society. The combination of 'the duties of a good wife' and 'delicious pleasures' is not something middle-class women can afford.

Further down the social hierarchy, there are still other concerns. Among the poor, the question of respectability matters less than daily survival. Unmarried women may lower their moral standards in order to attract men whom they hope will be willing to look after them and their children. Inspectors visiting the slums in Liverpool, Manchester, Ashton-under-Lyne and Preston comment on the sleeping arrangements of the poor in these densely populated places, where four or more people might sleep in one bed – fathers and daughters, brothers and sisters, male and female lodgers, and women with their married sisters and their husbands. Thus there is little that can be done to stop the general promiscuity. In Hull, one inspector asks a prostitute how she fell into her way of life. She tells him:

> She had lodged with a married sister and slept in the same bed as her and her husband; that hence improper intercourse took place and from that she gradually became more and more depraved; and at length was thrown upon the town because, having lost her character, the town was her only resource.[53]

By 1800 one in twelve children is illegitimate.[54] The highest rates are, unsurprisingly, in those areas that suffer the greatest levels of deprivation. In Ashton-under-Lyne, for instance, the parish register notes that one in eight children is born out of wedlock.[55] And on top of these day-to-day sexual transgressions, people will stoop to horrifyingly low levels of immorality. One man in a London prison sells his sixteen-year-old daughter's virginity to a fellow prisoner – payment to be taken on their release.[56] Of course there are many more horror stories along these lines. Overall, you can depict the extent of sexual immorality in society in the shape of an hourglass: ample to overflowing at the top, narrowing around the middle, and burgeoning again among the lower classes, for whom it is just another aspect of daily life.

Education

In 1808 the Irish writer Richard Edgeworth observes that 'obstinacy of ignorance and imaginary self-importance used to be one of the common ludicrous characteristics of our English squires but ... the ignorant, hunting, drunken, obstinate, jovial, freedom-loving tyrant is no more to be seen, except in old novels and plays'.[57] He is right: gentlemen are far more ashamed to be ignorant now than they used to be. In fact, people of all classes feel they should be as well educated as their peers. As a result, over the period from 1754 to 1840, the literacy rate in England rises from 60 to 67 per cent for men and from 40 to 50 per cent for women. It is even higher north of the border: almost all Scottish men can read and write by 1800, due to the excellent provision of parish schools there, although female literacy is much lower.[58] As for adult education, across the whole of Britain, educational facilities are established on an unprecedented scale: most towns now boast a literary society, several circulating libraries, Bible-reading classes, a scientific institution and a debating club.

All that sounds very positive but, as usual, there is a contrary view that cannot be ignored. Many people do not go to school. In some places the educational horizons of unskilled workers are shrinking; their skills diminishing as they only operate one machine, day in, day out. In Ashton-under-Lyne in the 1830s, only 12 per cent of bride-grooms can sign their name in the marriage register – a drop of 70 per cent since the 1760s.[59] Women's literacy has halved over the same period, down to 8 per cent. The fact that life expectancy here has dropped to just eighteen goes a long way to explaining why: people simply have other priorities. Among those at the very bottom, there are horrifying levels of ignorance. An investigation into the gaol in Preston shortly after the end of our period reveals that 40 per cent of the inmates can't name the king or recite the Lord's Prayer; 50 per cent can't name all twelve months of the year; and 20 per cent can't count up to a hundred.[60]

One of the more encouraging developments of the drive for better education is the focus on teaching those who have some physical disability. In 1764, Thomas Braidwood opens the kingdom's first school for the deaf in Edinburgh, where he teaches sign language as well as reading and writing. In 1783, the school moves to Hackney, near London. In 1792, it is joined by the London Asylum for the Deaf and Dumb. As for the visually impaired, the Liverpool School for the Indigent Blind opens in 1791. Here the emphasis is on teaching the pupils specific skills, such as manufacturing curtain lines, baskets and slippers, playing music and tuning instruments. Given the large number of people who go blind because of smallpox, such an institution marks a great step forward.[61]

BOYS' EDUCATION

With such massive disparity in knowledge between rich and poor, it is perhaps not surprising that education is seen as an indicator of status. Wealthy parents start their sons off at the age of six or seven with a private tutor or a few years at a preparatory school. Neither of those options is cheap. A private day school is likely to cost £20 a year, sometimes twice as much, and a tutor may charge a lot more. Boarding can double these costs. When the Revd John Skinner looks at his three children's school bills one day in March 1823, he is shocked to realise that they add up to £304 for the year.[62] Most expensive of all are the old public schools or 'foundation schools', as they are known: a year at Winchester College might cost more than £200.[63] What will your son get in return? Poor-quality food, spartan lodgings, bells waking him up at 5.30 a.m., fagging (having to act as an unpaid servant to a senior boy) and the prospect of being beaten up regularly by the sons of some of the greatest landowners in England. And a first-rate education in classical literature.

You might be surprised at how much emphasis schools place on studying Ancient Greek and Latin texts. Even after the arrival of the great reforming headmasters – Dr Samuel Butler at Shrewsbury in 1798 and Thomas Arnold at Rugby in 1828 – most lessons are still ordered around classical literature in the original languages. The main reason is that the classics include the philosophical, moral and strategic writings of some of the greatest orators, thinkers and leaders who have ever lived. Schoolmasters are keen to impress on their pupils that they are the heirs of Cicero, Plato and Caesar, and they use the ancient texts to impart lessons in diplomacy, responsibility and judgement. Another reason is that Latin and Greek are taught in a highly systematic way, so that through studying them, boys learn the basic rules of grammar as well as how to organise information. A third reason is that the classics are a time-honoured and worthy alternative to the Bible. Teaching Cicero in Latin and Homer in Ancient Greek might not seem to us the most appropriate forms of education for the future leaders of the most advanced industrialised nation in the world but these texts offer secular views of society to balance the more introspective influence of divinity.

For the next tier in wealth, the best option is a grammar school. Most of these establishments also place great weight on studying the classics and the Bible. Your son will start off by learning to read texts in English before advancing first to Latin and then to Greek, which prepares him for matriculation to university. If you want him to have a more modern education, in which he is taught geography, history, modern languages and the sciences, you will need to send him to one of the private academies run by nonconformist ministers.

An alternative would be a private commercial school, of which you will find many in urban areas, normally run by a single master whose wife will be the matron. These charge fees of £30–50 per year for board and education. Some of them are of a very dubious quality, however. When the merchant's son John Bowring is sent to a small school in Devon, he finds he is one of eight mischievous boys who run rings around their one and only teacher. They cut up his cane into small lengths and put it back together carefully on his desk, waiting for him to attempt to beat one of them. They put gunpowder into his candle snuffers, and saw the bottom two stairs off the staircase leading into his cellar, which they fill with water.[64] In this way they make up somewhat for the lack of organised sports from which they might have benefited at a larger school. Whether this is the sort of education you want for your son, however, I will leave you to decide.

If you have very little money for education, do not despair. One option is to send your son to one of the many Bluecoat charity schools established around the country. Another is to send him to a free school that follows the system established by Joseph Lancaster in 1798, in which the older boys teach the younger ones how to read and write and do arithmetic. In 1811 the National Society for Promoting the Education of the Poor in the Principles of the Established Church in England and Wales is founded, which promotes 'National Schools' in all the major towns. By the 1830s, there are fifty-seven charity establishments in Liverpool alone, catering to the needs of 25,000 young people.[65] In towns where there are no charity schools, you will be able to find day schools charging as little as 2d per week.[66] Some places give you the option of buying modules of learning: 1s 6d for three months of being taught to read and write (not including pens, penknives, ink and paper), and 2s 6d for Latin lessons.

The other form of education available is an apprenticeship. There are two forms: private and public. Private apprenticeship is used to teach a specific trade, normally after a boy has attended school and learnt the basics of reading, writing and arithmetic. At the age of about fourteen he will sign an apprenticeship indenture, a legal document by which he is bound to serve a master for seven years or until the age of twenty-one, learning in that time how to practise the trade in question, with the master feeding him and generally being in charge of his well-being. Fees normally consist of a one-off payment. It will set you back £10 to send your son to be an apprentice miller in South Petherton (Somerset), and £50 to teach him to be a cabinet-maker in Chertsey (Surrey), but you'll have to fork out £210 if you want him to be a lawyer in Usk (South Wales).[67]

Public apprenticeship is a form of social relief. From about the age of seven, disadvantaged and orphaned children are sent by their parish overseers to the households of prosperous local people, who take them in as servants and educate them in husbandry or some other trade from which they will one day be able to earn money. If the master happens to be a cotton-mill owner, then the boys may well end up sleeping, eating and working in his mill. It's completely unpaid labour, which hardly counts as education. Not until the Factory Act of 1802 comes into force are mill owners required to teach their apprentices to read and write and do arithmetic. Nor can the apprentices leave until they reach the age of twenty-one. As you can see, prior to this, public apprenticeship is not so much a form of education as a sentence of hard labour.

BOYS' HIGHER EDUCATION

If you are very wealthy, you might consider heading off on a Grand Tour after you finish school. This is an extended journey, normally in the company of a friend and a tutor, to see the parts of Europe that are essential to understanding its customs, culture and history. It can last between one and four years. Ideally you would head to Italy through France, but the revolution and the wars that follow make France a problematic destination for young aristocratic Englishmen, so most go through Germany down to Italy. Alternatively, if you prefer to stay at home, you might complete your education at one of the Inns of Court in London, where you can qualify as a lawyer. Or, if your chosen career is in the armed forces, you might opt to study artillery at the Military Academy at Woolwich, or to train as a professional army officer at the Royal Military College, which from 1812 is located at Sandhurst. If, however, you are not keen on either judging or killing people, and can't afford to spend a couple of years travelling around Europe, then perhaps you should consider reading for a university degree.

There are six universities in Great Britain at the start of our period: the venerable institutions of Oxford and Cambridge, and the smaller and only slightly less venerable Scottish ones of St Andrew's, Glasgow, Aberdeen and Edinburgh. But how well they will prepare you for life is a matter for debate. If you run your eye down the staff list at Oxford, you will quickly see that the university is just as traditional as the public schools. It appoints professors in divinity, Hebrew, Greek, Arabic, civil law, common law, medicine, clinical medicine, ancient history, modern history, botany, astronomy, geometry, natural philosophy, experimental philosophy, music and poetry. That list sounds quite impressive but note the lack of mathematics and economics – or anything to do with mechanics or industry. The problem lies in the fact that Oxford is heavily dominated by clergymen and they see themselves as primarily being responsible for teaching the next generation of the nation's clergy. And the university, being very old and set in its ways, is slow to adapt. Between 1795 and 1830 professorships are established at Oxford in Anglo-Saxon, anatomy, chemistry, mineralogy, geology, political economy, moral philosophy and Sanskrit but, overall, the university's approach to the changing times is best illustrated by its reaction to the steam engine. In 1828 the vice-chancellor has a model locomotive displayed at the university – not so that the students can investigate its mechanical workings but so it can be the subject of that year's prize for the best poem in Latin.[68]

As a result of this intransigence, the impetus for educational reform shifts away from the old universities and focuses on the establishment of new ones. The changes begin in Scotland, with the foundation of the Andersonian Institute in Glasgow in 1796 and the Edinburgh School of Arts in 1821, both of which provide lectures on technical and scientific themes. In 1826 Jeremy Bentham and his friends set up London University. Here the range of subjects is broad and modern, with professors lecturing in French, Italian, German, Chinese language, Chinese literature and other Oriental languages, as well as the classics. You can also read history, political economy, geography, mathematics, logic, natural philosophy, astronomy, chemistry, botany and zoology. The new university particularly prides itself on its medical education, employing professors in anatomy, physiology, surgery, clinical surgery, 'morbid anatomy', midwifery, pharmacy, medical jurisprudence, and the principles and practices of medicine.[69] Most significantly, students don't need to be members of the Church of England. Alarmed by this secularist march on the brightest young men in the capital, Church leaders respond by setting up an Anglican alternative, King's College, in 1829.

For some wealthy young men, it doesn't matter what the university teaches. Their prime reason for attending is social, not educational. Lord Byron's career at Cambridge is a classic example. He goes up to Trinity College in 1805 and immediately starts living the high life. He does buy books and pays a tuition fee but you are unlikely to see him in any lecture hall. As a nobleman, he is not required to sit exams. He describes his life at Cambridge as 'a villainous chaos of dice and drunkenness, nothing but hazard and burgundy, hunting, mathematics, and Newmarket, riot and racing'.[70] He buys a carriage and keeps a team of horses. Most memorably, he marks his objection to the university's rule that he may not keep a dog in college by bringing a bear, called Bruin; he then further mocks the university by announcing that Bruin is going to sit for a Fellowship. But his time at Cambridge is not wasted – quite the opposite. He makes many good friends, including some who will be his companions for the rest of his life. He perfects the art of appearing in public and holding a conversation. He writes poetry and publishes his first book, *Hours of Idleness*. He arrives as an overweight boy of seventeen and leaves as a graceful, lean, urbane, dashing, romantic poet of twenty – sufficiently confident to launch himself into London society and then head off on a Grand Tour. In other words, Cambridge teaches Lord Byron how to be Lord Byron. And you can't really argue that he could have had a more appropriate education than that.

GIRLS' EDUCATION

You'd have thought that William Holland, the vicar of Over Stowey in Somerset, would be a great believer in female education – especially as he is a tutor to a girl prodigy and has a daughter of his own – but he declares, 'I should not like any woman the better for understanding Latin and Greek. All pedantic learning of this kind makes them conceited.'[71] His prejudice is commonly shared. Most men and women believe that girls require nothing more than instruction in religious duty, morality and those accomplishments befitting their future station in life. For the rich, this includes sewing samplers; playing the piano, flute and harp; dancing; speaking French and Italian; and practising penmanship. For the poor, suitable accomplishments do not extend beyond housewifery and cookery, darning socks and sewing clothes and helping on the farm. Even bright middle-class girls might find their education ignored. Mary Wollstonecraft is barely taught to read and write while her older brother, Ned, is prepared for a career in the law. This makes her very unhappy. 'Such indeed is the force of prejudice that what was called spirit and wit in him, was cruelly repressed as forwardness in me,' she later recalls.[72]

How should you set about obtaining an education for your daughter? If you are wealthy, you will normally employ a full-time governess, as well as a part-time French teacher, and music, drawing and dancing masters, to teach her all the skills you wish her to acquire. If you lack that sort of money, many of the new charity schools also have classes for girls. In addition, private and public apprenticeships are available. Thus a grocer's daughter might learn to read and write at a charity school and then, at the age of eleven or twelve, sign up to learn the skills of a seamstress or dressmaker. Poor girls might go straight into the public apprenticeship system at the age of six or seven. This is nearly always to learn housewifery, and needless to say, it does not involve learning to read and write but simply being the unpaid skivvy around the house, working for nothing but bread and board through her childhood, until she finds a position as a domestic servant or marries.

If you have higher hopes for your daughter but cannot afford a governess, you will have to send her to a private, fee-paying school. In Brighton in 1815 there are nine 'academies for young ladies' (compared to seven for young gentlemen) and a 'female Sunday school'.[73] Fees are cheaper than at a boys' school because they employ female teachers, whose salaries are a mere fraction of those paid to their classically trained male counterparts. As to what your daughter will actually learn, most schools do not teach anything more intellectually challenging than those 'accomplishments' listed above. As Elizabeth Ham recalls, of her time at a private girls' boarding school in Tiverton:

> Our studies were not very extensive, nor very edifying. We learnt by rote either from the dictionary, the grammar or geography. Wrote no exercises, nor were we asked any questions about our lessons. We read

from the Bible in the morning, and the history of England or Rome in the afternoon. A master came to teach us writing and cyphering from eleven to twelve, and a dancing master twice a week.[74]

When it comes to living conditions, such places are just as harsh as boys' schools. The girls are made to share beds and are not given anything like enough food. The women in charge of a 'dame school' relish wielding the rod quite as much as the masters at a boys' school. Anne Lister is even *whipped* at her school in Ripon.[75]

Girls' schools do not teach Latin or Greek – and it goes without saying that no higher education is available for girls. If you want your daughter to have a classical education comparable with a boys' one, you should teach her yourself. That is what the Revd George Austen, rector of Dean and Steventon, decides to do with his daughters. One of them, Jane, spends less than twenty months at boarding school before leaving at the age of eleven, after which she is educated by her father. She learns to read French fluently and acquires a working knowledge of Italian, and studies British history in some depth.[76] It is quite adequate, as it turns out. In fact, thirty years later Miss Austen's *Pride and Prejudice* is the prince of Wales's bedtime reading.

SELF-EDUCATION

Perhaps the most impressive educational advances in this period are not down to any particular masters of schools but to the growth in self-education. Thousands of people yearn for what we often take for granted today, and cherish every fragment of learning they acquire. Some of them turn out to be among the greatest minds of the age. Engineers like Thomas Telford and Richard Trevithick are largely self-taught; George Stephenson receives his first education in a coal mine. But perhaps most remarkable of all is the child prodigy George Parker Bidder, 'the calculating boy' from Moretonhampstead in Devon. From about the age of seven he teaches himself to do enormously complicated sums very quickly in his head. Realising the boy's genius, his father shows him off at country fairs, where ladies and gentlemen pay to ask him the hardest questions they can imagine. 'If a coach-wheel is 5 feet 10 inches in circumference; how many times would it revolve in running 800 million miles?' George takes fifty seconds to come up with the answer: '724,114,285,704 times, with 20 inches remaining'. 'What is the square root of 119,550,669,121?' This takes George thirty seconds: '345,761'. This is incredible, considering he cannot even read and write. In 1815, at the age of nine, he is presented to the queen, who asks him this question: 'From the Land's End, Cornwall, to Farret's Head, in Scotland, is found by measurement to be 838 miles; how long would a snail be creeping that distance, at the rate of 8 feet per day?' '553,080 days,' he replies after just twenty-eight seconds.[77]

Master Bidder is not simply a mathematical fairground attraction. He goes on to work with George and Robert Stephenson in laying out many of the great railways, becomes a co-founder of the world's first electric telegraph company, oversees the building of a large section of the London Docks and eventually becomes president of the Institution of Civil Engineers. As you can see, self-education can take you a long way in nineteenth-century Britain.

Attitudes to Foreigners

What do the English think of their Continental cousins? One set of answers is given in a book on English manners, published in 1816. 'We do not scruple to regard Frenchmen, in a mass, as volatile, loquacious and impertinent; Germans as blunt and phlegmatic; and Spaniards as pompous, haughty and indolent.'[78] And what do they think of Americans? Sydney Smith speaks for many when he declares:

> They are but a recent offset indeed from England; and should make it their chief boast, for many generations to come, that they are sprung from the same race with Bacon and Shakespeare and Newton ... In the four quarters of the globe, who reads an American book? Or goes to an American play? Or looks at an American picture or statue? What does the world yet owe to American physicians or surgeons? What new substances have their chemists discovered? ... Who drinks out of American glasses? Or eats from American plates? Or wears American coats or gowns? Or sleeps in American blankets? Finally, under which of the old tyrannical governments of Europe is every sixth man a slave, whom his fellow creatures may buy and sell and torture?[79]

From all this you might gather that the English regard foreigners in one of two ways: if they are from the New World, then they are inferior to the English; and if they are from Europe, the English are superior to them.

Having said this, the ways in which individuals treat foreigners depends on their own status, education and familiarity with other cultures. While the lower classes have always been suspicious of strangers – and are particularly hostile to the French – the upper and middle classes have generally welcomed high-status travellers with open arms. So too have those who benefit financially from them, such as innkeepers and ferrymen. Londoners too are normally welcoming to foreigners – not surprisingly, as one in fifty citizens was born overseas.[80] In the 1790s there are fifty-four French Protestant churches in the city, plus eight German ones, and six Dutch, three Swedish, four Swiss, four Danish, eight Roman Catholic and four Greek Orthodox places of worship. Consequently, you will come across a wide range of attitudes. In some quarters, hatred of foreigners goes with singing 'God save the King', eating roast beef and drinking warm beer. Among Londoners and the well educated, being generous to overseas visitors is part of a different patriotism that holds up the United Kingdom as a great world power and celebrates its ruling class as sophisticated men and women whose taste and refinement should be the envy of every civilised nation.

Anglo-French relationships remain volatile. This is perhaps unsurprising as, by 1793, the English and French have been at war with each other for almost 200 of the last 600 years. After that, they fight almost constantly for twenty-one years. The Aliens Act is passed in 1793, controlling the immigration of people from all nations but particularly the French, 4,000 of whom have recently arrived in England, fleeing from the revolution. Most of these new arrivals are high-born yet devoid of income, so in a Brighton restaurant you may have a French nobleman waiting on you at table, or you might find a *chevalier* cleaning your windows. Of course the large influx of Frenchmen does not endear them to the common folk. Louis Simond can but sigh when he is victimised yet again for 'the sin of being born in France', as he puts it. The ongoing war also leads to a genuine fear of invasion. Parson Woodforde records in his diary for April 1798 how all men between the ages of fifteen and sixty-three are being put on a reserve list because French troops are expected to land any day.[81] This fear is, of course, heightened by the fact that, during the Terror, French revolutionaries massacre their own people – the peasantry of the Vendée and aristocrats and middle-class professionals all over the country. Robert Jenkinson, the future prime minister (as Lord Liverpool), witnesses the revolution at first hand and is convinced the French people are simply 'robbers and assassins ... murderers and regicides, whose hands are still reeking with the blood of a slaughtered monarch'.[82]

The French, however, remain a great inspiration to the British. French fashions are greatly admired; French furniture is much sought after – as are French paintings – and French cooking delights people who seek culinary pleasure beyond simple roasting, baking and boiling. And let's not forget the unsurpassed excellence of French wine. When in each other's company, many aristocratic people speak French in preference to English – partly to show that they can, and partly so the servants don't understand what they are saying. If they could, they would travel to France too. In 1802, the Peace of Amiens briefly allows them to rush across the Channel and see the famous places and buy French clothes and paintings. But that respite is all too brief: the war recommences the following year. Then the English have to wait until June 1815. After Napoleon's defeat, the British upper and middle classes treat France as a sort of promised land. Whole families excitedly cross the Channel to see the sights of Paris, or go to Belgium to visit Waterloo, where they can buy a souvenir jawbone or a piece of tattered uniform from the many guides to the battlefield.

Opinions of the Irish do not follow the same path, especially not in England. In the Irish Rebellion of 1798 the Society of United Irishmen attempts to provoke an American-style War of Independence from Great Britain. It fails, with the loss of tens of thousands of lives. In addition, the extraordinary population growth in Ireland in recent decades does not make the Irish popular in Britain. Thousands of working-class Irishmen sail to Liverpool and settle in the city's slums. They are said to be 'so notoriously dirty in their habits that ... English workmen will not reside in the same courts'.[83] In London, where the Irish form 9 per cent of the population, their labourers offer to work for half the wages paid to the English. This leads to disturbances, with English workers shouting, 'Down with the Irish' and smashing the windows of Irishmen's houses.[84]

The three nations within Great Britain are more relaxed in each other's company. London is particularly open to the Scots: they account for 7 per cent of its residents in the 1790s.[85] Although relatively few English people make the reciprocal trip north of the border, and those who do tend to be offended by the poor living conditions they encounter, the Scots themselves are equally welcoming. By the 1820s, many lairds are following English ways and even living in England. Conversely, Sir Walter Scott's hugely popular novels open English eyes to the romance of old Gaelic culture. Thus you will occasionally come across a Scottish clan chief at a society gathering in London or Brighton, clad in his traditional plaid and holding forth upon the Highland way of life – and perhaps on how much contempt he and his countrymen still have for the English.[86]

Homosexuality and Lesbianism

You might have thought that a society in which gentlemen can indulge in mutual masturbation sessions might be one that is relatively tolerant of homosexuality. If so, think again. Attitudes against male–male sexual acts are appallingly harsh: *nothing* is more likely to make you the object of widespread detestation. A guilty verdict on a charge of sodomy usually results in the death penalty: at least forty-five men are hanged for this offence between 1805 and 1830.[87] It does not matter how old you are or how privileged. Thomas White is just sixteen when he is accused of having sex with the forty-two-year-old John Hepburn in 1810. Both the boy and the man are hanged.[88] The following year the Honourable William Courtenay – the future earl of Devon – is forced to flee the country to avoid prosecution for being sodomised twenty-five years earlier, as a sixteen-year-old boy, by William Beckford. In 1823 the duke of Newcastle accidentally opens a letter from a young man, Henry Hackett, addressed to 'My beloved Benjamin ... ' The duke quickly discovers that the intended recipient is his own valet, Benjamin Chandler, who turns out to be a member of a homosexual ring centred on nineteen-year-old Hackett. The duke immediately reports the case to the magistrates, and Chandler and his homosexual friends are arrested. They are all hanged on Hackett's evidence.[89]

There aren't many areas in life where women have it much easier than men but same-sex love is one of them. People simply don't talk about lesbianism. The nearest they come to publicly admitting its existence is to acknowledge that the Ancient Greek poetess, Sappho, may have composed erotic poetry about women. Famously, the two 'ladies of Llangollen', Lady Eleanor Butler and Sarah Ponsonby, maintain a very discreet 'romantic friendship' for many years at their retreat in North Wales. Having both run away from their oppressive families in their youth, they live together, sleep together, dress in men's clothing and refer to each other as 'My Beloved' and 'My Better Half'. Yet no one thinks they might be lesbians or 'sapphists', to use the contemporary term. It's the same case for the poetess Anna Seward and her romantic friend, Honora Edgeworth, and for the sculptress Anne Damer and her lover, Elizabeth Farren. It is not against the law, and two women spending time together is utterly harmless in the eyes of the public.

The independent gentlewoman Anne Lister records much of her romantic and sexual life in her diaries. As these reveal, she has affairs with a number of women near her home, Shibden Hall in Yorkshire. Indeed, you might be surprised to find out through her writings how many Regency women can be persuaded to try sapphic love for themselves. It would be untrue to say she entirely avoids negative attention: groups of working-class men occasionally insult her with questions like 'Does your cock stand?' as she passes them, and women also sometimes assail her with an elbow-knock to the breast.[90] But no one seriously threatens her respectability. When one of her lovers asks whether what they are doing is sinful, Anne tells her that sapphism is not forbidden in the Bible, as male homosexuality is.[91] There are times when she has to be cautious – finding bedrooms with lockable doors or making sure that she and her girlfriends are very quick in their embraces – but her only significant fear is making too fast an advance on a woman who might be shocked. However, Anne is lucky. And she obviously has a way with women. At the age of twenty-five, she notes, she has 'never been refused by anyone'.[92]

Transvestitism

Transvestitism is not a problem for women. Men, however, can be ruined by it. It is not so much the wearing of women's clothes itself that is the issue as the reasons why. If it is done to encourage the sexual attentions of other men, it is tantamount to importuning a member of the same sex, and thus punishable as a misdemeanour. In 1792 a transvestite club is raided at the Bunch of Grapes in St Clement's Lane, London, after an anonymous letter is received by the magistrates. The report states that:

> The officers, upon rushing into a room up-stairs, discovered two wretches dressed in women's apparel, and painted in the face, walking a minuet. Sixteen other wretches were at this time sitting round the room on the benches, laughing spectators of the degradation of man, and in indecent familiarities with each other; they were all immediately secured, and conveyed to the watch-house; and yesterday morning they were taken, amidst the general execration of an immense mob, to Bow Street.

At the subsequent trial, the accused admit that, in their club, they all go by female names, such as Lady Golding, Countess Papillion, Miss Conveniency, Blood-Bold Nan, Miss Frisky, Betsy Dash, Moorfields Moll, Miss Fancy and Little Cockatoo. In reality, they are shoemakers, tailors, servants and other ordinary working men. But such is the opprobrium in which they are held that no one speaks up for them. No one sees their dressing up as a bit of innocent fun. 'Execration' is indeed the right word.[93]

In marked contrast, one male transvestite in London manages to wear a dress openly every day. This is the émigré French gentleman Charles d'Éon de Beaumont – known as the Chevalier d'Éon. Formerly a French diplomat and a spy, with a brilliant military career, he poses as a woman to enter the circle of Empress Elizabeth of Russia. He also seduces Madame de Pompadour while dressed as a woman at a ball at Versailles Palace. He has in his keeping letters that incriminate Louis XV in some secret business. After that king's death, his son Louis XVI pays the chevalier a royal pension in order to buy his discretion but bizarrely insists that he should wear female attire for the rest of his life. Charles accepts – but only on the condition that he can continue to wear his military medals. Thus he dresses as a woman every day for the next three decades, most of which are spent in London demonstrating his fencing skills. He is feted by society and genuinely mourned when he dies in 1810.

There are a few men who simply want to live as women do, quietly and without fuss. If you consider the disadvantages faced by women

– the sexual prejudices, the lack of power over their own property and the limited opportunities – you have to admit that they have not chosen the easy option. Spare a thought for those men who really do identify as female in this period and who, until the day they die, live in fear of discovery. In Colchester, a housemaid lives and works in the same household for thirty years until her death in 1811, when she is discovered to have been a man.[94] In Yorkshire, in 1820, a cook and housekeeper called Mrs Ruspin falls in love with another housemaid, who leaves the house in distress after an argument. Mrs Ruspin goes after her – and takes her to London, where she reveals herself not to be a woman at all. Shortly afterwards they get married. They set up a cookshop together and, we may hope, live happily ever after.[95]

Women who dress up as men tend to do so for a particular purpose. When the playwright Lady Wallace wants to observe proceedings in the House of Commons, she puts on male attire to enter the public gallery, as women are forbidden from entering the House. Many actresses wear male clothes onstage: audiences love them for it. However, the most common reason for women to dress as men is to go to sea or take part in an army expedition. You've already heard about Phoebe Hessel fighting alongside her lover at the Battle of Fontenoy; she serves in the army for seven years, dressed as a man. Hannah Snell serves as a soldier for twenty-one years, losing part of her finger in battle.[96] In *The Female Shipwright* (1773), Mary Lacy writes about her time in the navy, first as a servant on board a warship and later as a 'male' shipwright at Portsmouth. Then there is Mary Anne Talbot, who dresses up as a common sailor to go to sea with her lover. She ends up fighting at the Battle of Camperdown in 1797, when her knee is shattered by a bullet, putting an end to her military career. Nevertheless, *The Life and Surprising Adventures of Mary Anne Talbot* hits the bookstands in 1809.

Of all the female cross-dressers of the Regency period, James Barry deserves a special mention. From the age of ten she dresses and acts like a boy, which allows her to receive a classical education and later read medicine at the University of Edinburgh – something she could not have done as a woman. After being awarded her degree, she joins the army as a doctor. Over the course of her career she pioneers new nursing methods and introduces strict levels of cleanliness into military nursing. But her big day comes on 25 July 1826, in South Africa. Normally a Caesarean section is an attempt to save the life of the infant when a mother is dying in childbirth. Only once has it ever been achieved without resulting in the death of the mother, in Zurich in 1818; James Barry's own tutor at Edinburgh has twice tried the operation and failed. But that day Dr Barry saves both the child and the mother. As for her being a woman: she keeps that a secret until the day she dies. But you might find it sad nonetheless that someone has to flout conventions to such an extent in order to fulfil her calling to save lives.[97]

Racism and Anti-Semitism

If you happen to be one of the approximately 15,000 black people in Britain at the end of the eighteenth century, you will experience discrimination on every conceivable level.[98] The basic assumption is that you have until recently been an enslaved person, or that you are a sailor who has abandoned his ship. You can be verbally assaulted and physically abused – and no one in authority will particularly care. People might casually describe you as a 'Nigger' or a 'Negro' and call you 'Blackey' or 'Mungo' to your face. You will also have difficulty finding work. At the colliery in Camerton, the bailiff openly declares he is 'happy to employ anyone except a black'.[99] You won't find life much easier if you're of mixed-race parentage, as people will presume that you are the illegitimate progeny of black slaves by their white owners and thus doubly tainted – once with your ethnic impurity and a second time with your supposed illegitimacy.

One woman who has it particularly hard comes from the Khoisan people, otherwise known as the Hottentots. Like many Khoisan women, she suffers from steatopygia, which makes her buttocks protrude extraordinarily and gives her thighs an exaggerated roundedness. Having been named Saartjie Baartman by a Dutch farmer, she comes to England in 1810, where she is known as Sara 'the Hottentot Venus'. She is exhibited naked at public exhibitions so that people can view her enormous behind and inspect her hugely enlarged labia, which many believe to be a separate organ unique to the Hottentots. Cartoons satirise her features and express the strong feelings of lust or disgust she inspires in viewers. When she dies in 1816 after years of misery, she is subjected to a post-mortem humiliation worse than that reserved for murderers. A plaster cast is made of her body, and wax models of her genitals. Then she is dissected and her skeleton put on permanent display.

Despite such pitiable individual cases, the position of black people in Regency Britain is much better than it was in the past. The question of whether an enslaved person who has been brought to Britain is legally still a slave has been emphatically answered by the Lord Chief Justice, Lord Mansfield. In 1772 he rules that the state of slavery does not exist in English common law, nor has it subsequently been created by a royal decree or Act of Parliament. Thus a slave owner has no power to compel an enslaved person in his service to board a ship to return to the West Indies. Horrified slave owners immediately petition Parliament to pass an Act recognising slavery. Parliament refuses. In 1778 a Scottish judge makes a similar ruling with regard to Scottish law, declaring that the laws supporting slavery in the West Indies do not apply in Scotland any more than the laws of Virginia do in England. Therefore, if you are a slave and you set foot in Regency Britain, to all intents and purposes you become free. For this reason several talented black writers and artists come to Britain, where they hope to be able to earn an independent living without the stigma they receive in other countries. In 1789 the ex-slave and mariner Olaudah Equiano, who has settled in London, publishes his autobiography, which becomes a bestseller; when he dies in 1797, he is able to leave an estate worth about £1,000 to his daughter. In 1825 the great African-American actor Ira Aldridge makes his debut on the London stage, beginning a long career that sees him cast in almost every role open to a person of colour. The Afro-European violinist George Bridgetower – for whom Beethoven composes one of his best-known sonatas – also comes here to perform in the 1820s.[100]

It has to be said that most black artists and showmen still depend on the support and protection of a wealthy white patron. Julius Soubise is a charismatic ex-slave who excels at riding, fencing, singing and playing music, and dresses in the latest fashions: he comes to prominence through the patronage of the duchess of Queensberry. Dido Belle, the illegitimate daughter of Sir John Lindsay and a black woman, grows up in the household of her great-uncle, who is none other than Lord Mansfield, the Lord Chief Justice: you may be familiar with her famous portrait. Even the renowned black boxers of the day owe something to the patronage of enlightened aristocrats. Bill Richmond is born into slavery in New York and brought to England by Hugh Percy, heir to the duchy of Northumberland, who gives him an education and has him apprenticed to a cabinet-maker in York. But Bill ends up getting into fights on account of the insults he receives for his colour. One day a brothel-keeper sees him with a white woman on his arm and calls him a 'black devil'. Bill challenges the man and very soon the brothel-keeper is on the ground, regretting his comment. Gradually Bill's fame spreads and he comes to London to fight professionally. He becomes famous, winning bouts that sometimes go on for more than an hour, and ends up teaching the rudiments of his art to gentlemen of fashion, including William Hazlitt and Lord Byron.

Looking around the larger towns you will realise just how many non-white groups there are living in Britain. Near the docks in London there is a community of lascars – Indian sailors, who stay here between voyages for weeks or months at a time. There are also small numbers of Chinese sailors in Liverpool and London. A few of them reside here permanently.[101] William Macao is a Chinese man who makes his home in Edinburgh and works for the Board of Excise for more than forty years.[102] Gypsies are another minority, although they never settle in a town. They roam the country, living outdoors all year round. They are particularly prone to racial abuse. In August 1797 *The Times* reports that thirty Gypsy men, women and children are uncovered when their tents are struck down while they are sleeping on Norwood Common. All are arrested as vagrants. People don't like their lack of religion, their different language (Romani) and the fact that they do not attend church, even to marry. Many look down on them for their illiteracy. Others don't trust them for having no fixed abode. A settled job is out of the question for them. So too is paying taxes or contributing to the parish rates.

Jews represent the largest minority group living in Britain, with between 15,000 and 20,000 in London by 1800 and another 5,000–6,000 scattered in towns around the country. About a quarter of them are Sephardic Jews, who have been here for the last 140 years, after they were expelled from Spain and Portugal. The remaining three-quarters are Ashkenazi from Eastern Europe, Germany and Turkey, whose predecessors arrived in Britain after 1700. All are victims of prejudice in one form or another. Jews cannot vote in elections or stand for any public office or a post in a university or Anglican school. Nor can they be licensed medical practitioners. They are denied poor relief and are not allowed in a Christian hospital. But these are just the official lines of discrimination; more hurtful are the personal attacks. Francis Place records that he has seen many Jews 'hooted, hunted, cuffed, pulled by the beard, spat upon and so barbarously assaulted in the streets, without any protection from the passers-by or the police ... dogs could not be used in the same manner'.[103] Karl Moritz reports that, one day, when the crowded stagecoach he is on stops in Kensington:

A Jew wanted to join us but there was no room inside and he didn't want to ride on the outside. This caused my travelling companions to demur. They couldn't understand why a Jew should be ashamed of travelling on the outside; anyway, as they said, he was nothing but a Jew! I have noticed that here in England this antisemitic prejudice is far stronger than it is among us Germans.[104]

It's not all bad news for Jews, though. For a start, some Jewish businessmen, like Benjamin and Abraham Goldsmid, Levi Barent-Cohen and Moses Montefiore, start to break down the walls of anti-Semitism in the city of London. Nathan Mayer de Rothschild proves exceptionally successful. After setting up a textile business in Manchester in 1799, he moves to London to invest in gold bullion and becomes one of the first great international merchant bankers, working in collaboration with his German relatives. The family's rise is astonishing. In 1815 the Rothschilds are worth £136,000, of which Nathan's share is £90,000. But just three years later they are sitting on a fortune of £1.17 million and Nathan's share has grown to about £500,000. When he dies in 1836, he is worth more than a million.[105] That brings a significant benefit to the status of British Jews. It is difficult for middle-class people to regard someone as 'nothing but a Jew' when a Jew can be richer than a duke.

Working-class Jews gain their own hero in Daniel Mendoza. Emerging as a prize fighter in 1787, he wins several high-profile fights in and around London and then opens his own school for teaching the art of self-defence. Francis Place notes that, as a result of his success, people start to be more cautious about insulting Jewish men, who are taking up the art of pugilism.[106] Jewish writers too emerge, including Isaac Disraeli, father of the future prime minister, Benjamin Disraeli. His *Curiosities of Literature* and his historical works are popular with readers as well as scholars: he is awarded an honorary doctorate by the University of Oxford. But perhaps most striking of all, non-Jewish writers start to portray Jews in a positive light, thereby reflecting new standards of respect and consideration. In Sir Walter Scott's *Ivanhoe*, published in 1819, the Jewess Rebecca is the romantic heroine – and far braver and more interesting than the hero's socially acceptable Saxon love interest. Lord Byron composes a suite of beautiful poems for his *Selection of Hebrew Melodies, Ancient and Modern* (1815); these are written and published in response to an advertisement published by a Jewish composer, Isaac Nathan, and are sung by the leading tenor, John Braham, who also is Jewish. Byron even includes in his *Hebrew Melodies* a poem that quickly becomes a favourite with his many readers: 'She walks in beauty, like the night / of cloudless climes and starry skies ... ' With Byron's poetry and Scott's romantic figure of Rebecca, there are clear signs that respect for Jews is improving, despite the restrictions and prejudices they continue to suffer.

Wife Sales

You will recall from the last chapter how working-class women are penalised in several legal and social respects. Unfortunately, the indignities they suffer do not end there. They can still be forced to undergo the ritual humiliation of the ducking stool (described in chapter 11). Another custom to put women in their place is the smock wedding. This is based on the belief that, if a man marries a woman in a state of nakedness – that is, in the state in which she came into the world – he does not have to take responsibility for her debts. Like ducking stools, smock weddings are on the decline and probably die out in this period, but they do still take place. In 1797 a Birmingham bride arrives at church in a large cloak, in which she waits until the wedding ceremony is about to begin. At that point she throws off the garment and stands before the altar 'in the exact state of Eve in Paradise', as the *Derby Mercury* puts it. She clearly is very determined to wipe out her debts, as churches tend to be cold at the best of times – and it is December.[107]

Possibly the most extreme examples of the ritual humiliation of women are the hundreds of wife sales that take place around the country. The rules vary from region to region but generally they conform to the following pattern. First, there should be some prior announcement of the impending sale, either by means of a town crier or a printed poster. The wife must be sold openly – in a marketplace or public house – so that the public can witness the proceedings. She must be led to the place of sale with a rope halter around her neck or, in some places, around her waist. Sometimes the rope is tied up to some railings or a post. She must be sold to the highest bidder, and there can be no reserve. Only unmarried men are allowed to bid, because the winner will take the woman home as his common-law wife. Prices vary from a few farthings to £100 for an attractive young woman. In some cases, the husband throws in their children too. It is hard to say what's worse: if he does sell the children with their mother or holds on to them himself.

The most surprising thing about this custom is that – unlike other forms of ritual humiliation – it is *not* in decline. In fact it is increasingly being seen as a form of liberation for women. How come, you may ask? A clear example is presented in *The Times* for 15 January 1827. A Plymouth innkeeper, having found his wife in bed with a certain Mr Boots on several occasions, and having forgiven her repeatedly, one day finds her departed from their home with their children. He learns she has gone to the next town; he pursues her there – only to find her in the arms of the said Mr Boots. What can he do? He *could* drag her home again – he has that right – but clearly neither of them will be happy. They cannot get divorced, as that requires an Act of Parliament. So he agrees to sell her and their two children by auction as the means of resolving the matter, with Mr Boots present at the auction. The key to the whole business is that a wife has to give her consent. It isn't legal according to the law of marriage but it is a neat way for a woman simultaneously to escape an unhappy relationship and find someone else to take responsibility for her and her children. It is therefore not surprising that wife sales are on the rise.[108]

Women's Rights

As you will recall, women are denied an education that would allow them to be the intellectual equals of men. They are not taught the classics as it is assumed they will never be the leading orators, thinkers and statesmen in society. The advice normally dished out to society ladies who do manage to acquire a deep knowledge of literature is to 'conceal all your learning'. As Jane Austen puts it in *Northanger Abbey* (admittedly with her tongue somewhat in her cheek), 'a woman especially, if she have the misfortune of knowing anything, should conceal it as well she can'. And that is exactly what a lot of bright women do. They play the piano or the harp not just to entertain people but so they can demonstrate that they are intelligent and full of understanding without threatening other people with too much knowledge and reasoning.

Some women don't accept this state of affairs. Catharine Macaulay, for one, is determined to become a serious historian. But the mere idea that a woman can demonstrate the necessary intellectual rigour, wisdom and judgement to contribute significantly to human knowledge is risible in most Regency salons. When the first volume of her eight-volume *History of England* appears, the *Monthly Review* expresses the wish that 'the same degree of genius and application had been exerted *in more suitable pursuits*', for writing history is not an appropriate occupation for 'our lovely countrywomen'.[109] Over and over again her work is diminished by being described as that of 'the *fair* Macaulay' or 'our *fair* historian'. How patronising! And that after dedicating her life to examining the rise of the concept of liberty! Macaulay believes that it all comes down to the poor education that women receive. As she puts it, it is 'absurd ... that the education of females should be of an opposite kind to that of males'.[110]

That view is shared by all the surviving members of the informal 'Blue Stocking Society', established by Elizabeth Montagu in the 1750s. They are unashamedly intellectual upper-class women who are fervent in their desire to broaden their intellectual horizons and debate with men on an equal level. But they are constantly frustrated in their ambitions. Indeed, the very phrase 'bluestocking' quickly becomes a term of abuse and remains so throughout our period.[111] The only area of intellectual excellence open to women without fear of scorn is that of writing novels and poetry aimed at other women. It is therefore hardly surprising that women develop intellectual inferiority complexes in which they put each other down and tell their daughters to conceal their learning and opinions. And that is just among the well-to-do. Lower down the social spectrum, women are intellectually ground down to the level of functionaries. You cannot help but feel sorry for Elizabeth Ham when she writes in her memoir that 'I know I have had a most oppressive feeling of my own inferiority to everyone about me, and this feeling, I am convinced, has influenced the whole of my life.'[112]

Clearly there is dry tinder here waiting for a spark to set it alight – and the French Revolution provides several such sparks. One is the marquis de Condorcet's treatise *On the Admission of Women to the Rights of Citizenship*, published in 1790, in which he declares that 'either no individual of the human species has any true rights, or all have the same; and he or she who votes against the rights of another, whatever may be his or her religion, colour, or sex, has by that fact abjured his own'. Another is a book by Olympe de Gouges, *A Declaration of the Rights of Women and the Female Citizen*, which emphatically declares in its first line that 'woman is born free and remains equal to man in rights. Social distinctions may be founded only on the common good.' These have no effect on the French constitution but their ideas and boldness set some minds blazing in England.

One woman who takes a keen interest in women's citizenship is Mary Wollstonecraft, the future wife of the radical writer William Godwin and the mother of Mary Shelley. In 1792 she publishes *A Vindication of the Rights of Women* to provide a vision of how the revolution could result in greater happiness for the whole human race. For her, women are held back and made to look stupid by being denied a decent education. Thus they are forced to define their virtues in terms of greater sensitivity and sensibility but, she argues, to claim that women are more emotional is to imply they are weaker than men. This further undermines their position. To remedy this, Wollstonecraft insists that 'there must be more equality established in society, or morality will never gain ground'. She finds supporters in women like Frances Wright, who denounces organised religion and all forms of inequality, and promotes free education and the sexual liberation of women. Some men eagerly support her cause, especially on account of her espousal of free love. Richard Carlile, the editor of *The Radical*, regards love-making as 'the very source of human happiness' and declares that 'a true moralist sees no crime in what is natural and will never denounce an intercourse between the sexes where no violence nor any kind of injury is inflicted'.[113] But such messages of support do not go down well with other reform-minded men and women, let alone the general populace. Hannah More's reaction to *A Vindication of the Rights of Women* is typical of the middle classes.

'There is something fantastic and absurd in the very title,' she declares; and later she writes, 'let us take comfort [that] these atrocious principles are not yet adopted into common practice'.[114] Thus the fire of women's liberation does not flare up all of a sudden but remains small, and intense, until later in the nineteenth century.

Superstition

Of all the contradictions you will come across in Regency society, none seems more extreme than the coexistence of superstitious beliefs and scientific knowledge. In order to avert bad luck, people still avoid crossing each other on staircases, walking under ladders, killing money spiders, chopping down holly trees and putting any book on top of a Bible. Advertisements appear with increasing regularity in the newspapers offering advice on 'planetary influence as it relates to ... marriages, legacies, possession of wealth, attainment of any particular desire [or] the state of an absent friend by sea or land ... '[115] People still cling to their favourite portents too. The Revd James Woodforde writes down all his dreams, believing them to be indicators of the future. At dinner he may suddenly inform you that the weather will change, his certainty being based on the fact that he noticed his cat wash herself behind *both* ears after breakfast.[116]

Although the Witchcraft Acts were repealed back in 1736, people still hang up 'witch balls' in their houses. These are spherical mirrors that force any witches in the room to confront their reflection, which they cannot bear. In Suffolk in 1795 you can even witness one of the last instances of a mob subjecting a suspected witch to the ordeal by water. This is when the poor woman has a rope tied around her waist and is flung into a watercourse: if she floats, she is considered to be guilty, for the water of baptism is rejecting her. If she sinks, she is innocent and should be hauled out. Needless to say, if the crowd have taken the step of immersing her, they have already deemed her guilty.[117] You will find many such superstitions unshakably rooted in people's minds. The reason why they gradually diminish is not because science changes the way they think but rather because the old guardians of such knowledge gradually die off, leaving the differently educated next generation with their more scientifically calibrated understanding of how the world works.

Science

For those with scientific interests, this is one of the most exciting times to be alive. As Mary Shelley puts it, 'none but those who have experienced them can conceive of the enticements of science. In other studies you go as far as others have gone before you, but in a scientific pursuit there is continual food for discovery and wonder.' Few people understand the term 'chemistry' in 1789. That year, however, sees the publication of Antoine Lavoisier's *Elements of Chemistry*, which appears in English the following year. Here, presented for the first time, is the modern theory that all matter is made up of compounds of elements. After Lavoisier's career is tragically cut short by the guillotine, other scientists continue his work. Among them is the British chemist John Dalton, who in 1803 develops a theory of atomic weights. In the first volume of his *New System of Chemical Philosophy*, published five years later, Dalton postulates that all matter is composed of a limited number of elements; that atoms can neither be created nor destroyed; and that all atoms of an element are identical. European scientists also contribute to the rapid advance of chemistry, including Amedeo Avogadro, the Italian who coins the term 'molecule'; the Swede Jacob Berzelius, who discovers the elements cerium and thorium and establishes chemical notation based on the first letter of the element's name; Johan Arfwedson, another Swede, who discovers lithium; and the Danish polymath Hans Christian Ørsted, who first isolates aluminium. All these discoveries do not remain locked up in their respective nations but feed into a collective whirlpool of scientific knowledge circulating throughout Europe and America. In Britain, John Dalton is merely the foremost of a group of chemists who between them discover palladium, rhodium, osmium, iridium, potassium, sodium and calcium.

A similar story can be told about many other branches of science. Astronomy is hugely advanced by William Herschel and his family from their house in Bath; William discovers the first new planet since antiquity, Uranus, and with his sister builds ever larger and better telescopes for seeing further into space, recording more and more moons, constellations and galaxies. Although zoology and botany have been studied for many years, it is only in 1800 that the term 'biology' acquires its modern scientific sense. By then, the physician Erasmus Darwin has already published *Zoonomia, Or the Laws of Organic Life,* in which he suggests a basic theory of evolution, including a degree of natural selection and a series of primeval urges that are common to all animals – lust, hunger and security – thus foreshadowing not only the work of his grandson Charles Darwin but also that of Sigmund Freud. If Erasmus Darwin's work on evolution raises some serious questions about the Creation story, so too does the work of two Scotsmen, who transform our understanding of the Earth's geology. In 1795 James Hutton puts forward the theory that our planet was not simply created but evolved through natural processes, such as erosion and sedimentation, over the course of thousands of years. Right at the end of our period, in 1830, Charles Lyell takes up the theme and develops it further in his seminal work, *The Principles of Geology*. Again, a scientific discipline that barely existed in 1789 has come to wide public attention.

'Electricity is the plaything of the English. Anyone who can air views about it is sure to make a stir,' writes Karl Moritz as he travels around England in 1782.[118] He is right – and his words remain true for the nineteenth century too. Electricity amazes people: it is mysterious and fantastical. Imagine you found a new way to move objects without touching them, or make things light up without applying a match. Just a list of the names of those working in this field will show you its importance. You have probably heard of Luigi Galvani, who in 1791 conducts the famous experiment in which he stimulates the legs of dead frogs with electricity to make them jerk, thus suggesting to people that electricity can bring things to life. You have almost certainly heard of the galvanometer, named after Galvani by André-Marie Ampère, another scientist researching the properties of electromagnetism. His name in turn will make you think of amperes or amps, units of electric current, which are named after him. Then you have Alessandro Volta, the Italian physicist who creates the voltaic cell, and who lends his name to volts and voltage. As for the unit of electrical resistance, the ohm, you have to thank the German physicist Georg Ohm. He is responsible for Ohm's law, which stipulates that 'voltage (in volts) equals current (in amps) multiplied by resistance (in ohms)'. All these men, working across Europe in these years, share their knowledge with British scientists and open up new possibilities for scientific discovery.

If you were going to choose a time and a place in which to be an inventor, Regency Britain would have to be a contender for the ideal one. The arc lamp – the first practical electrical light – is invented by Humphry Davy in 1807. Michael Faraday sets about summing up the discoveries in the field of electromagnetism and in so doing discovers the principles of the electric motor in 1821. And who could not be impressed by Francis Ronalds's work? His name might not be famous in the modern world but in 1815 he builds the world's first electric clock. The following year he rigs up eight miles of wiring in his garden in Hammersmith and sends the world's first electric telegraph message. If you're wondering why he is not more famous, the answer lies in the reaction of the Admiralty when he offers them the technology. Sir John Barrow replies on behalf of the government that such an invention is 'wholly unnecessary'. The armed forces do not need an *electric* means of instant long-distance communication when they have flags and semaphore signals.

If any single invention represents the technological brilliance of the age, it is the steam locomotive. Long before it is a reality, people can see that it represents the transport of the future. Erasmus Darwin writes in his poem *The Botanic Garden*, published in 1791:

> Soon shall thy arm, unconquered steam, afar
> Drag the slow barge, or drive the rapid car;
> Or on wide-waving wings expanded bear
> The flying chariot through the fields of air.

The challenge is how to make a steam engine efficient enough for it to drive its own weight as well as whatever else it has to pull. But Mr Darwin does not have to wait long to see his prediction come true. In 1801 Richard Trevithick cracks the problem and builds the world's first steam locomotive, *Puffing Devil*, in Cornwall. Four years later, one of his engines hauls 10 tons of iron and a number of men for 10 miles at Penydarren in South Wales. Its successor, called *Catch-me-who-can*, is stoked up for a series of demonstration rides on a circular track just to the north of London in 1808: rides cost 1s a head. Within six years, steam trains are employed at four or five collieries in the Newcastle area, and by the end of our period they are drawing passengers too. Suddenly, everything seems possible. People can fly in balloons, use electromagnetism to make things move, and draw enormous weights along rails at great speed. In 1824 Lord Byron reflects on how much scientific understanding has progressed since Isaac Newton's time and suggests that 'ever since, immortal man hath glow'd / With all kinds of mechanics, and full soon / Steam-engines will conduct him to the moon'.[119] And although the 'moon' bit is somewhat tongue-in-cheek, it illustrates how closely imagination and technology are intertwined. Basically, if you can imagine it, one day it will probably happen. In the fields there are threshing machines where you once saw only flails. Henry Maudslay's screw-cutting lathe, developed in 1800, makes it possible to cut a standard screw thread in a nut and bolt, allowing the use of interchangeable parts. Paper is increasingly made by machines in long rolls, after the Fourdrinier brothers set up the first modern paper mill at Frogmore in Hertfordshire in 1803. One of the most startling glimpses of the future is revealed in 1827, when the Frenchman Joseph Nicéphore Niépce comes to show half a dozen of his 'heliographs' – photographs – to the Royal Society. Exhibitions are held to showcase the technology that will transform people's lives. In July 1828 Prince Hermann Pückler-Muskau visits one in London and sees:

> a machine which draws of itself all the objects visible within its horizon, in perspective; a pianoforte that plays ... a hundred pieces by itself, which you may accompany with extemporary 'fantasie' on the keys; a very compendious domestic telegraph, which spares the servants half their labour ... [and] a washing machine, which only requires one woman to wash a great quantity of linen.[120]

From now on, technology and changes in daily life will increasingly go hand in hand. By 1830, people across the country realise that, whatever they think of 'innovation', there is no turning back.

Romanticism and History

Some people are not so happy with the old ways of life disappearing so quickly. While mechanisation, industrialisation and standardisation mean profit for some, they ring the death knell for the old craftsmen who create unique things in their individual ways. At the same time, families who have been masters of their lands for generations now feel under threat from urban radicals who demand the vote for everyone. Just as Mr Puddicombe is stopped from writing his chronicle-like burial register and obliged to fill out a printed form instead, so people's lives are becoming standardised. Many of them instinctively insist upon their individuality. The resultant vision combines personal liberty and political freedom, looking back as well as forward for inspiration, finding it in the glories of the natural world and the passion of romantic love. Above all else, they long to escape the humdrum of everyday life and to pursue self-defining noble causes.

This, you might say, is a coupling of the last moments of the decadent old world and the dreams of the new dawn, instilled by the French Revolution. The two merge powerfully in calls for political reform, as we have seen in Shelley's sonnet 'England in 1819' at the start of this chapter. The dream that all countries might one day be free from foreign rulers attracts many would-be revolutionaries. The Irish rebels in 1798 share the dream that Ireland will one day be independent and united. Similar aspirations take Lord Byron to Greece, to help the people of that country in their quest for independence from the Ottoman Empire. Fittingly he dies there in 1824, ensuring his lasting fame as a hero of the Romantic movement, sacrificing his life in the name of liberty. It is the pinnacle of political romanticism – a matter of dying for one's ideals, as serious as a duel but imbued with the modern virtues of liberty, equality and fraternity.

The man who lives in a dashingly independent way, regardless of the rules, laws and expectations of society, thus becomes a romantic hero. Highwaymen are dangerous thieves if you happen to meet one on a dark road but some now see them in a positive light, simply for living outside the law. The stories of eighteenth-century pirates are also told with far greater admiration than when murderous thieves actually sailed around the Caribbean. People hail the wild Scottish laird because he will take no orders but lives as free as an eagle on his untamed moors. Most significantly, you have the romantic lover. In Ancient Greek mythology, every night Leander swam across the Dardanelles to be with his sweetheart. People believe that in their own time the passionate hero is similarly driven to go that bit further than ordinary, less-inspired people. Thus Byron swims across the Dardanelles in 1810, in emulation of Leander. Romantic love makes the lover greater than any mere mortal, and he becomes truly heroic through acting upon his emotions.

Romanticism has another side, which stresses the beauty of nature. This is the age in which artists reach for the sublime, especially in the natural world. This might be a perfect sunset or a mountain view; or a terrifying storm at sea – any situation that will move you emotionally. Painters are also obsessed by the picturesque, especially the wild beauty of the Highlands, a Welsh valley, a ruined abbey by moonlight, a dark forest or a clifftop castle. In their portraits, men and women of fashion regularly have themselves depicted walking in a wild rural scene, thereby demonstrating their appreciation of the perfection of the trees, mountains and lakes in the background.

All this desire for freedom has an unexpected consequence in that people start to become more interested in history, especially pre-Roman and medieval history. They become fascinated by the archae-ology of ancient sites and burial mounds. Soon scholars are producing editions of early poetry and chronicles in order to satisfy public curi-osity in the medieval period. For many, its bloodshed, superstition, fear and valour resonate with their own romantic ideals. They start visiting ruined abbeys and castles to marvel at the passage of time. A hundred years ago, people would have looked at a crumbling medieval ruin and seen it as nothing more than a spoil heap of cheap rubble; now they contemplate its overgrown splendour and find it difficult to imagine anything more picturesque.[121]

Sense of Humour

In this chapter we have looked deep into the Regency soul and glimpsed many dark corners. We have seen cruelty, sexism, immorality, ignor-ance, racism and many more aspects of misery. How can people put up with such things, you might ask? The obvious answer is that they have no choice. But having a sense of humour no doubt helps. Laughter is one of humanity's greatest blessings. Sometimes it's all we've got.

Lord Alvanley takes great offence at being called 'a bloated buffoon' by Daniel O'Connell, the Irish Catholic politician, and challenges him to a duel. Mr O'Connell refuses to fight – he has already killed one man in a duel, to his enormous regret, and has vowed never to fight another. But his son, Morgan, is of a different disposition. After Lord Alvanley attempts to have Mr O'Connell senior ejected from Brooks's Club for the insult, Mr O'Connell junior takes offence at the slight to his father and *he* challenges Alvanley to a duel. That evening Lord Alvanley solemnly makes his way to the appointed place, just a short distance out of town, in a hackney cab. He tells the driver to wait. The seconds press the men to settle peacefully. They cannot. Having resolved to shoot each other, the order of process is announced by Alvanley's second: at just twelve paces apart, the two men will fire simultaneously. Young O'Connell does not wait and fires immediately but the bullet goes wide. The seconds agree that the shot was accidental and that he should be allowed to reload. When they both fire, neither man is hurt. They shoot once more, and again no blood is spilt. At that point they agree that honour has been maintained and decide to withdraw. Lord Alvanley gets back into his hackney cab and asks to be driven home. When he arrives at his front door, he reaches into his pocket and hands the driver a gold guinea. The man is astonished at the generosity and protests that he did not take him very far. Lord Alvanley replies, 'My friend, the guinea is not for taking me out but for bringing me back.'[122]

Regency life tumbles with jokes, japes and jocularisms. This is the great age of the political cartoonists, James Gillray, Thomas Rowlandson and George Cruikshank, whose unfettered satirical wit delights the nation and humiliates the rich, the famous and the fashionable. Everything is up for mockery; nothing is sacred. Witticisms abound – from the facetious and the macabre to the elegantly astute. When the politician John Wilkes asks a friend if he will vote for him in a forthcoming election and receives the reply, 'I would rather vote for the devil', Wilkes responds: 'Naturally. And if your friend decides against standing, can I count on your vote?' Another time Wilkes provokes the earl of Sandwich to exclaim, 'Sir, I do not know whether you will die on the gallows or of the pox!' To which Wilkes calmly replies, 'That depends, my lord, on whether I embrace your principles or your mistress.' Jane Austen's understatements are particularly enjoyable. You may be familiar with her verdict on historical writing in *Northanger Abbey*: 'I often think it odd that it should be so dull, for a great deal of it must be invention.' Sometimes it is those private quips, never meant for the public ear, which make you laugh. 'Miss Fenton is about forty,' Anne Lister writes in her diary. 'Large and fat and ready to marry almost anyone. She is fruit that would fall without shaking.' Robert Southey makes a joke about a man who has taken out no fewer than seventy patents for pointless inventions: the most useful of them, he declares, is 'the hunting-razor, with which one may shave oneself while riding full gallop'.[123] And who can fail to be amused by

Daniel O'Connell's description of Sir Robert Peel: 'His smile was like the silver plate on a coffin.'

The lines that will probably stay with you the longest, however, are those coined by the most famous wits of the day. Therefore I will conclude this chapter with a few quips by two men who undoubtedly make Regency Britain a happier place.

The Revd Sydney Smith is something of a Dr Johnson of hyperbole. His speciality is to take an ordinary subject and extemporise on it to ridiculous extremes. Excessively fond of his food, and somewhat corpulent, he is put on a strict vegetarian diet by his doctor. One day a visitor overhears him moan, 'Oh, I wish I were allowed even the wing of a roasted butterfly.' When told firmly that, if he wishes to lose weight, he must take walks on an empty stomach, he shoots back: 'Whose?' He always manages to find a perfectly graceful way of putting someone down. His verdict on the historian Thomas Babington Macaulay is both charming and utterly damning at the same time: 'He has occasional flashes of silence that make his conversation perfectly delightful.' And one day he says to a friend: 'I am just going to pray for you at St Paul's – but with no very lively hope of success.'

The man who has the best claim to the title of 'wit of the age' is Richard Brinsley Sheridan. Plays on words and aphorisms pour from his pen. 'A bumper of good liquor will end a contest quicker than justice, judge or vicar.' 'Wit loses its point when dipped in malice.' 'Pity those whom nature abuses, never those who abuse nature.' Sheridan is the man who, when hearing that the duke of York has retreated before the French advance, rises and proposes a toast: 'To the duke of York and his brave followers'. One day he is found by a constable lying inebriated in the street. The man roughly shakes him and demands to know who he is. 'A Member of Parliament,' replies Sheridan. The constable is not impressed and demands to know his name. Sheridan says he will only tell him on condition of the utmost secrecy. When the constable agrees, Sheridan whispers the name in his ear: 'William Wilberforce'.

Ah, Sheridan … or Sherry, as he is known to his friends. He is in many ways the epitome of the Regency gentleman, throwing himself with passion into everything he does. Everything in excess! He successfully fights a duel over the girl he wants to marry – only to have to challenge the same man again when the cad lies about the outcome of the first duel. Unfortunately, second time around, Sheridan comes off worst. But what a romantic! 'Won't you come into the garden? I would like my roses to see you,' he famously says to a young lady. The author of several successful plays, he borrows heavily to buy an interest in the Drury Lane Theatre. He is invited to all the great aristocratic houses and drinks in all the clubs in London, impressing everyone from Lord Byron to the prince of Wales. When he enters the House of Commons, Sheridan almost single-handedly raises the standard of political rhetoric. One day he responds to a speech by Henry Dundas with the immortal words, 'The right honourable gentleman is indebted to his memory for his jests and his imagination for his facts.' Refreshingly, he rises above the crass sexism of his day, showing more respect for women in his humour than perhaps any of his male contemporaries. As he puts it in his play *The Rivals*, 'Through all the drama – whether damned or not – love gilds the scene, and women guide the plot.' One of his favourite causes is the education of women. This gives rise to the wonderful line: 'It is by woman that nature writes on the heart of man.'

Even when facing a personal disaster or financial ruin, Sheridan can produce a line that effortlessly delights the listener. He delivers what is perhaps his finest quip when the Drury Lane Theatre burns down on the evening of 24 February 1809. Fortunately, no performance is in progress at the time. Sheridan is still debating the war in Spain in the House of Commons when the news arrives. He takes his leave and heads straight for Covent Garden. Surveying the inferno, he retreats across the street to the Piazza Coffee House where he calls for a drink. There he sits, thoughtfully watching the blaze. A friend interrupts the contemplation of his financial ruin, asking how he could possibly sit there so calmly? Sheridan looks at him and replies: 'A man may surely be allowed to take a glass of wine by his own fireside.'[124]

5

Practicalities

You like the details of daily life and have often told me that you feel
the want of them in most travel books, and that nothing gives you a
more lively conception of a foreign country. You must therefore forgive
me if I go into trifles.

Prince Hermann Pückler-Muskau (1826)[1]

When we survey periods of history it is very easy to be overwhelmed
by the big picture and to miss the little details. If you look closely,
however, you'll find that simple everyday tasks that you wouldn't have
thought could be done any differently can be performed in all sorts
of ways. Where should you go to buy a pint of milk? Do you always
use coins to pay for things? What should you do if a fire breaks out
in your home? These details might seem insignificant when we think
about the great sweep of history but they are quite important if you
are there at the time. What's more, it is often through asking the
most straightforward questions that you discover how little you know
about the past. Suppose you need to send a letter to your mother in
Scotland: how much will it cost to post it? Are there any post boxes?
It is from such 'trifles' as these that our knowledge is tested and some
of the most interesting aspects of life revealed.

The Weather

In the vast majority of paintings from the period the sky is clear and
the sun is shining. But don't be fooled: it rains more in Regency Britain
than it does in modern times. Manchester, for example, sees an average
annual rainfall of 36 inches, compared to just under 32 inches today.[2]
In some years, the weather is atrocious. The summer of 1816 stands

out as particularly bad. After one of the biggest volcanic eruptions in
history – that of Mount Tambora in Indonesia – weather patterns
around the world are thrown into disarray. In Britain there are frosts
and floods in June; snow falls in London in August.[3] People thus refer
to 1816 as the 'year without a summer'. It's not particularly cold – the
average temperature in June, July and August is only three degrees
below the modern equivalent – but it rains incessantly. Food shortages
and high prices inevitably follow. Depression gives way to despair. As
winter sets in and overnight temperatures drop to minus 20 degrees
Centigrade, the poor are more desperate than ever.[4]

Regency people talk about the weather just as much as we do in
the modern world.[5] It unites people like nothing else: the rain pours
just as heavily on the parklands of the gentry as it does on the vegetable
patches of the poor. Hence quite a few gentlemen make a special
study of it. They buy a barometer and a thermometer and record
their readings for posterity. As a result, we know that the central-
England temperature in this period averages between 8 and 10 degrees
Centigrade but three years drop below this range (1799, 1814 and
1816) and three rise above it (1822, 1826 and 1828). If you want to
know how those figures compare with modern times, twenty-one of
the last thirty years (1989–2018) have averaged in excess of 10 degrees,
and none has fallen as low as 8.[6]

Regency winters are harsh, particularly at the start of our period.
The year 1789 opens with a great frost that lasts from 24 November
1788 to 13 January 1789. That is when the Thames freezes and a frost
fair is held on the river, complete with puppet shows, roundabouts,
booths, ice skating and bear-baiting. Even an ox is roasted on the ice.[7]
Five years later, in January 1794, the Revd James Woodforde watches
the mercury level dip lower than he has ever seen it before. It snows
heavily and the wind is so strong that it blows the thatch from his
barn and the tiles from the roof of his house. Two local women freeze
to death on their way home from market.[8] In 1795, the surgeon-
apothecary Matthew Flinders notes in his diary that the winter is
'uncommon severe' because it snows incessantly for three months.[9]
The average temperature that January is minus 3.1 degrees Centigrade
– the coldest monthly average *ever* recorded in England. In rural
Norfolk, James Woodforde finds that the milk pans in his dairy are
frozen solid and the apples in his barn covered with a thick carpet of
frost. Crows and rooks queue up at his kitchen door to be fed

alongside the chickens. Most disconcertingly, when he wakes in the morning after using his chamber pot in the night, he sees that his urine has frozen solid.[10]

What about the warm days? It's perhaps not surprising that people tend to write little about the sunshine: they just venture outside and enjoy themselves when the sun's out. I can particularly recommend spending the summers of 1798, 1808, 1818 and 1826 in England. But I have to add that those four years are the only ones in our period in which average temperatures in June, July and August rise above 16 degrees Centigrade. There are very few days like 7 July 1794, when Mr Woodforde's thermometer reads 102 degrees Fahrenheit (38.9 degrees Centigrade).[11]

Hours of the Day

If in the modern world you agree with a friend that you will call at ten o'clock, he or she will expect you to turn up on time (or thereabouts). Things are a little more complicated in Regency Britain: you and your friend both know that your clocks may tell different times. The problem is not one of accuracy – people have had reliable pendulum clocks for well over a hundred years – but the lack of a standard. Anne Lister notes that her friend arrives 'at 5 p.m. by the kitchen clock, ¾ past 4 by the Halifax, & ¼ past 4 by [the] Leeds & York', referring to the clocks of various stagecoach companies in the vicinity.[12] Time might be universal but its reckoning is highly localised. If you carry a pocket watch with you when you travel, one of the first things you will do on arrival in a new town is adjust it to the time of the most ostentatious public clock.

With this caveat about time-keeping in mind, when should you get up? Agricultural workers will normally rise before dawn, to make the most of the daylight. Farmers selling livestock will be making their way to market even earlier. Traders at Newgate Market in London start doing wholesale business at 2 a.m. even though the official opening for retail sales is 6 a.m. At Smithfield, livestock is sold from midnight.[13] Household servants also rise before dawn, long before their masters and mistresses. Builders tend to work from 6 a.m. to 6 p.m., the hours being sounded by the bell of the parish church. A typical urban labourer rises around 5 a.m., works from

6 to 8 a.m., stops for a short breakfast, then works until noon or 1 p.m., when he'll take an hour for dinner (the main meal of the day). After that he'll work through to tea at about 5 p.m. Shop workers carry on to 8 p.m. or 9 p.m. As an apprentice bookseller, James Lackington has to work from 6 a.m. until 10 p.m. every day, even in winter.[14] Although London shops are usually open from 7 a.m. to 8 p.m., some grocers and haberdashers don't bring down their shutters until 10 or 10.30 p.m. If a great deal of tidying up is needed on the premises, staff may have to stay there until past midnight.[15] Most working people are in bed by this time.

The wealthy don't get up so early. Members of the gentry often sleep until 7 or 8 a.m., and then rise to dress. They will take a leisurely breakfast at 10 or 11 a.m., after which the 'morning' properly begins. The time of dinner depends on how posh you are: 4 or 5 p.m. is not unusual, or even later if you're very grand.[16] Afterwards the fashionable world comes to life. For the wealthy, social engagements can go on very late. If you're going to a ball I'd suggest having dinner beforehand, about six o'clock. Expect to drink and dance until about midnight, then you'll have supper, which will be followed by songs and other entertainments. Often the dancing will start again and continue until carriages arrive between 3 and 5 a.m.[17]

Christmas

There are no such things as Bank Holidays in Regency Britain – they're a Victorian invention. Christmas is widely celebrated, however, although not quite as you know it. Christmas cards won't be invented until 1843. There is no commercial run-up to Christmas Day as in modern times; indeed, many people work on the day itself. Nor are you likely to see a Christmas tree. Although Queen Charlotte has set them up in the past, the custom won't catch on until the royal family resurrects it in the 1840s.[18] However, mince pies, roast chestnuts and plum puddings are ubiquitous, and people are keen to restore the old tradition of decorating their houses with evergreens, such as mistletoe, holly and ivy. They now hark back to the days of Merry England, when the lord of the manor flung open the door of his hall to his tenants and offered them a handsome feast. Thus Regency people might invite friends to join them and their family at Christmas in eating a joint of roast beef, a turkey or a goose, and perhaps brawn, sausages and oysters, as well as apples, oranges and pears. Twelfth Night sees the baking of twelfth-cakes, made of flour, honey, ginger and pepper. Employers also give their workers presents or money in small boxes on Boxing Day, and some people give similar boxes to the poor. And that is probably the most firmly established thing about Christmas: its spirit of generosity. The ways in which people express their goodwill might alter down the ages but that general mood remains the same. As a result, you are more likely to feel at home in Regency Britain on 25 December than perhaps on any other day in the year.

Indoor Lighting

Although towns start illuminating their streets with gas in this period, the same is not true for private houses, which continue to use candles and oil lamps. In the houses of the rich, elaborate candlesticks and multi-armed candelabra of solid silver are often the prize pieces decorating the dinner table. In their drawing rooms and dining rooms, chandeliers of cut glass holding a dozen or more candles are lowered each evening to be lit by the servants, then raised again so the golden light might brighten the room. In a fine house the candles will be made of beeswax; in the homes of the less well off, they are produced from tallow (beef, bacon or mutton fat). Beeswax candles burn with a bright flame and are odourless, while tallow candles are smelly and burn with a dirty flame. They also start guttering if you don't regularly trim the wick. Beeswax is taxed as a luxury item, which makes it even more costly. Expect to pay 3s 3d per lb for the finest wax candles, compared to about 6d per lb for tallow ones. Given that an ordinary family gets through about 2½lbs of candles per week, you might want to use your wax candles sparingly.

The most common alternative is an oil lamp, which burns a wick in a bath of vegetable or whale oil. This frequently takes the form of a metal dish on short legs with a 'spout' to support the wick. You will also find elaborate metal-and-glass varieties, especially the new Argand lamps, invented in the 1780s, which are popular among the urban middle classes. In an Argand lamp, a mesh of cotton is curled around a small metal tube in the centre to form a cylindrical wick and, through having a glass funnel above it, air is drawn up from beneath so that it burns with a much brighter light than one or two candles. The downside is that it can burn through a pint of oil in twelve hours. In his London home the architect John Soane uses whale oil, which he buys at 7s 6d the gallon; including replacement wicks, it costs him roughly twice as much per hour as it does to burn a beeswax candle – but the price is worth paying for the extra brightness.

The poor, by comparison, spend their evenings in comparative darkness. In fact, the very poor tend to avoid using artificial light altogether in the summer months. In winter they use rushlights rather than candles. These are long rushes that have had most of the bark stripped off, leaving a narrow part to hold the dried pith intact. This is then soaked in tallow and fastened to a metal rushlight holder. The light is only a modest flame but it is cheap. Each rush burns for roughly three-quarters of an hour, so a poor family can have 1,200 hours of light for just 3s, or thirty hours for less than a penny.[19] John Soane's oil lamps cost thirty times as much.

What about matches? At the start of our period, people habitually use tinderboxes – striking a metal scraper against a flint to get a spark in the time-honoured fashion. But in 1788, one G. Watts tells readers of the *Morning Post* that he has invented:

A large variety of machines of a portable and durable kind, with Promethean fire, paper and match enclosed, most admirably calculated to prevent those disagreeable sensations, which frequently arise in the dreary hour of midnight, from the sudden alarm of thieves, fire or sickness, as, by procuring an instantaneous light, the worst calamities and depredations might often be prevented.[20]

Mr Watts's 'Promethean fire' does not quite, er, set the world ablaze. It isn't even wholly original – the idea for sulphur-headed matches comes from medieval China – but he is still in business forty years later. That is when the London chemist Samuel Jones starts selling similar matches from his shop in the Strand. These he also calls 'Prometheans', directly stealing Mr Watts's idea. Mr Jones even takes a patent out on his Prometheans, claiming to be the inventor himself. When John Walker of Stockton-on-Tees invents 'friction lights' in 1826, which he calls 'Lucifers', Mr Jones starts manufacturing that type of match too, also borrowing that brand name. Mr Watts then starts selling 'Lucifers' as well. So, if you want an easy way of striking a light in 1830, you have a choice of Prometheans or Lucifers. Expect to pay 1s for a box of fifty matches of either variety.

Now for the safety warning: Regency matches are dangerous. For a start, a box of Lucifers exposed to direct sunlight can explode. In addition, the chemicals are potentially lethal. The head of a Promethean is a small glass bulb containing sulphuric acid, which has an igniting agent such as phosphorus on the outside. The idea is for you to break the bulb with a pair of pliers and allow the two chemicals to ignite. However, some people break the bulbs with their teeth when they can't find a pair of pliers in the dark. If they don't burn themselves with the flame, they are likely to do so with the acid or the phosphorus. As for Lucifers, even the unscrupulous Samuel Jones has a health warning printed on the packets: 'Persons whose lungs are delicate should by no means use the Lucifers.' All in all, you might just want to keep that old tinderbox to hand.[21]

Fire and Fire Insurance

The risk of fire is enormous. One night, James Lackington props a candle against a pewter flagon and nods off. He wakes to find the heat has melted the handle off the flagon so that the candle has fallen on to a chair, which it has then burnt almost entirely.[22] Even carrying a light to your bedroom is risky. If the flame brushes against a curtain or the drapes of a bedstead, the whole neighbourhood might go up in smoke. Ladies' clothing is very vulnerable, especially a muslin dress. Seventeen-year-old Lady Isabella Courtenay is standing before the fire in her father's house in Grosvenor Square when a spark sets her skirt alight. She panics and runs through the house – and her clothes turn into a coat of flame. She dies of her burns eight hours later, 'in the greatest of agonies'.[23]

Every year there are hundreds of house fires in London and a thousand chimney fires.[24] The city's industries add to the danger. In July 1794, a barge carrying saltpetre catches alight at Ratcliffe. The raging fire that ensues destroys 400 homes and twenty warehouses on the docks. But perhaps the most dangerous places in terms of fire are the theatres. From the late 1810s, the trend is for eerie colour effects onstage to support and enhance the gothic themes then in

PRACTICALITIES   157

fashion. Impresarios who buy a copy of Claude-Fortuné Ruggieri's
Principles of Pyrotechnics, published in French in 1801 and in English
in 1825, gain access to a whole catalogue of sensational ways in which
to burn down their theatres. 'Red fire' – filling the whole stage with
a red glow – is created by burning a mixture of strontium nitrate,
potassium chlorate and antimony trisulphide. Replace the strontium
nitrate with copper nitrate and you get 'blue fire' – ideal for re-creating
an underworld scene. Lycopodium powder thrown into a flame creates
a bright flash and, for sound effects, stage managers employ small
amounts of gunpowder.[25] However, throwing explosive matter around
in the dark, night after night, is a recipe for disaster. Covent Garden
Theatre burns down in 1808, Drury Lane in 1809 and the Lyceum in
1830. Nor are provincial venues any safer: Exeter's Bedford Circus
Theatre goes up in smoke in 1820, when a gas-lit chandelier sets light
to the rafters. And the Theatre Royal in Glasgow – said to be the
largest and most impressive venue outside London – is consumed after
a rehearsal in 1829.

Insurance is part of the solution. Ever since the Great Fire of
London in 1666, property owners have chosen to pay a premium of
between 2s 6d and 5s per £100 of goods or buildings.[26] You will be
amazed to see how many fire-insurance offices there are by 1830.
Honiton, a small town of 3,200 people in Devon, has sixteen fire-
insurance agencies on its High Street that year (compared to one bank,
six butchers and six schools).[27] That is admittedly exceptional but most
places of that size will have three or four offices, often agencies for
one of the big London companies, such as the Alliance, the Hand in
Hand, the Phoenix, the Provident and the Sun. In 1788, £135 million
worth of property in England is insured; by 1830, that has increased
to £482 million. Scotland sees an even bigger proportional increase,
from £1.9 million to £34 million.[28]

The prospect of having to pay out large sums on a regular basis
makes insurance companies set up their own fire-fighting services in
large towns. Many villages also acquire fire engines of their own. Thus
by 1800 relatively few settlements don't have access to a fire service.
However, these remain highly inefficient. First, when you discover a
fire, you must send a message to the master of the nearest fire engine.
Then, after the volunteers have been summoned and gathered, and
the horses made ready, they have to drag the heavy wooden engine
and leather hoses to the danger. Once they are there, finding sufficient

water is frequently a major problem, especially in towns. Built-up areas often don't have a river or pond nearby, so the firefighters need to open the fireplugs in the pipes supplying the local houses. But private water companies do not consider fighting fires one of their responsibilities, so it is rare that they include fireplugs in their pipes. Even when they do, the water supply might be intermittent and it can take up to twenty minutes for sufficient pressure to build to operate a hose.[29] In rural areas it can take *hours* for the fire engine to respond. When Belvoir Castle catches alight on the night of 26 October 1816, the nearest fire engines are stationed at Grantham and Melton, both eight miles away; it takes the firemen over nine hours to arrive.[30] For this reason, many owners of country houses acquire fire engines of their own, which they generally keep near their stables in case of disaster.

Cometh the hour, cometh the man. In this case the hour is about 10 p.m. on 15 November 1824. The place is an engraving workshop on the second floor of an alley near the High Street in Edinburgh, and the man is twenty-four-year-old James Braidwood, the newly appointed chief of the city's fire engines. His men are undertrained and ill-equipped to deal with the inferno that confronts them that night. Many of Edinburgh's houses are more than ten storeys high, situated in lanes far too narrow to be reached by fire engines. As a result, the fire spreads from the workshop and rages for five days. But Braidwood, being young and keenly responsible, learns a great deal from the Great Fire of Edinburgh. Over the next six years he devises new training methods, designs new fire engines, develops more efficient hoses, and pioneers the use of breathing equipment for those entering smoke-filled buildings. He carries out fire-prevention surveys and examines the causes of fires in order to guard against their repetition. In 1830 he publishes the first manual on firefighting, entitled *On the Construction of Fire Engines and Apparatus, the Training of Firemen and the Method of Proceeding in Cases of Fire*. Some of the principles he advocates will still be quoted 200 years later, saving many thousands of lives. Of course, if you're visiting Regency Britain, this will come a little too late for you. But if you wish to shake hands with all the Regency people who make the world a better place, remember that you need to shake James Braidwood's hand just as vigorously as you do those of the great social reformers and engineers.

Newspapers

Daily newspapers have grown considerably in number and circulation over recent years. In London in 1790, you can choose between fourteen morning papers, including such influential titles as *The Morning Herald*, *The Morning Advertiser*, *The Morning Chronicle* and *The Times*, each with a circulation of 2,000–3,000 copies.[31] In addition there are evening papers, such as *The London Evening Post* and *The St James's Chronicle*. There are even – God forbid! – Sunday papers. Yes, despite the religious frowns, the first Sunday paper, the *British Gazette and Sunday Monitor*, appears in 1779 and is still going strong at the turn of the century, inspiring a number of other Sabbath-breaking publications, including *The Observer*, which first sees the light of day in 1791, and *The Sunday Times*, first printed under that title in 1822.[32] Gradually *The Times* pulls ahead of its rivals, achieving a circulation of 5,000 by November 1814, when it switches over to steam-powered presses. In 1821 it is selling 7,000 copies a day while its nearest competitor, *The Morning Chronicle*, is managing just 3,100.[33]

Most of these papers are broadsheets consisting of only four pages – a large single sheet, folded once. A single copy will cost 3d or 4d until 1797, when there is a substantial increase in stamp duty, raising the price of most of them to 7d or more. A large proportion of readers are subscribers, who pay a premium for the paper to be delivered to their door. Expect a subscription to cost you about £4 8s per year in the 1790s and about £10 in the 1820s. Many London papers are hired out – even though this is against the law, as it deprives the government of stamp duty. Some are sold on to provincial newsmen. Thus the London papers reach many more people than their circulation figures suggest. Robert Southey calculates that, if each copy of every newspaper sold is read by five people, at least 250,000 people in England read a London newspaper every day.[34]

In addition to the London press, at least one weekly title (if not a daily paper) is published in almost every major town – more than a hundred titles in all by 1810. Among the many you will recognise are *The Salisbury Journal*, *The Yorkshire Post*, *The Glasgow Herald*, *The Scotsman*, *The Westmorland Gazette* and *The Manchester Guardian* (subsequently renamed *The Guardian*). Like the London papers, most charge 3d per issue for four pages until 1797, when they are hit by the increased stamp duty; thereafter their price doubles to 6d or more. The effect on their circulation is dramatic: *The Leeds Mercury*, for example, sees its weekly sales fall from around 3,000 copies in 1794 to about 800 in 1801. Nevertheless, the industry keeps growing. By 1830 there are more than 150 provincial papers on sale.[35]

Regency newspapers take some getting used to. The small print is difficult to read; the language will strike you as being rather formal; and there are no headlines as such. Nor are there any pictures, except for the odd image advertising a stagecoach company or insurance firm. If you pick up *The Times* for Saturday 15 February 1823, you'll see that the whole of the front page and almost two-thirds of the back page are covered in small ads. These offer everything from places on board vessels sailing to the Cape of Good Hope to the contract for 'maintaining the poor at Greenwich'; from music lessons on the harp to situations vacant and valuable freehold estates for sale. *The Morning Post* is unusual in that its front page actually carries some news. Court cases are given a lot of attention, especially those that have an exciting story attached to them, such as a well-planned murder or the antics of smugglers and highwaymen. Most London papers are keen to report the elopements of girls from wealthy families with unsuitable men, especially if they are currently being pursued to Scotland by the girls' irate fathers.

Speed of Communications

It goes without saying that the speed of producing the news depends largely on how quickly it can be obtained – which at this time is only as fast as someone can travel. Nevertheless, information can move at impressive speeds. In London one summer's evening, Nathaniel Wheaton reports that:

> a hawker is now under my window bawling 'A true account of the fight between Spring and Langan for £500.' This took place this after-noon at 3 o'clock, and sixty miles from London. It is now ten in the evening. In the space of seven hours, then, the battle has been fought – the intelligence has been transmitted sixty miles – thousands of handbills have been struck off and are now selling in all the quarters of the town.[36]

This is indeed prompt publishing, considering that even the best long-distance riders, with two changes of horses, will struggle to cover 60 miles in less than five hours – leaving less than two hours after the end of the fight for it to be written up, typeset, printed and distributed. Nevertheless, it is not uncommon for events taking place more than 100 miles from London to be reported in the newspapers the next day. News of Princess Charlotte's death at Claremont House, Esher, which occurs in the early hours of 6 November 1817, is received 200 miles away, at Northgate, Halifax, on the morning of the 8th.[37]

European news travels at similar speeds. Lord Byron's death at Missolonghi in Greece on 19 April 1824 appears in *The Times* on 15 May, having arrived the previous morning after a journey of almost 2,000 miles – a speed of nearly 80 miles a day. Usually the French newspapers published in Paris on, say, a Wednesday, will travel the 234 miles to London in two days, arriving on the Friday; their news is then reported in *The Times* on the Saturday. Personal communications take a comparable amount of time. In 1818, Anne Lister receives a letter from Brussels at her home in Yorkshire (a distance of about 670 miles) six days after it was written.[38] The duke of Wellington sends his famous despatch about the victory at Waterloo to Lord Bathurst on the evening of 19 June 1815, the day after the battle. It arrives in London – 227 miles and a sea crossing away – a little before midnight on the 21st. Unfortunately, the messenger does not know where Lord Bathurst is. He asks the first gentleman he meets – the artist Benjamin Haydon – who, in his excitement, directs him to the wrong house, where there is a late-night party going on. It is more by luck than good judgement that the news makes the pages of the *London Gazette* the following morning.[39]

While intercontinental news can sometimes travel surprisingly quickly, it is normally frustratingly slow. New York's daily newspapers go on sale in London three weeks after their publication.[40] News from Latin America takes even longer to arrive. A riot in Mexico on 10 December 1826 is reported in a Philadelphia newspaper on 10 February 1827 and announced in a London paper, *The Courier*, on 10 March. In other words, the story takes two months to travel 2,500 miles across America and then one month to cross the 3,500 miles by sea to London. Personal communication can take even longer. A letter sent from Rio de Janeiro on 7 May takes four months to reach Donington in Lincolnshire, where Matthew Flinders receives it on 11 September

1795. It takes ten months for two letters to reach him from Port Jackson, Australia, in 1797.[41] This is unusually slow. Nevertheless, if you write to a friend in the Antipodes, you'll be lucky to receive a reply within twelve months.

The Postal System

The Regency postal system is one of the most complex things ever invented. To start with, there are actually two systems in operation: the Royal Mail, administered by the General Post Office for the whole of Great Britain; and the Penny Post, arranged on a local basis. And that is just the beginning of the complications. As you will see, the fact that there are neither public post boxes nor postage stamps is the very least of the problems facing a letter writer. I apologise for the complexity of what follows but anything simple on this subject would be misleading.

Let us suppose you are in London. Despatches leave the General Post Office in Lombard Street at 8 p.m. but the gates are shut at 6 p.m. for sorting, so you need to deliver your letter by that time if you wish it to go out that evening. If you can't get to the General Post Office, you can post your letter instead at one of the 400 post offices around the city, as long as you take it there by 5 p.m. for it to be transferred, or by 6 p.m. if you are prepared to pay an extra penny. If you're really desperate, you can ask the man on the gate at the GPO to take in a letter as late as 7 p.m. on payment of an extra 6d. Note that there is no collection or distribution on a Sunday.[42]

So far, so good. Calculating how much postage you need to pay on top of these collection fees is where it gets difficult. The task is not made any easier by the fact that every relevant Act passed by Parliament alters the rules as well as the rates, with major changes taking place in 1794, 1797, 1801, 1805 and 1812. One important point to bear in mind is that a two-sheet letter costs twice as much to send as a single-sheet one, and three sheets costs three times as much. From four sheets up, you are charged by weight: each extra quarter-ounce requiring the same payment as a single sheet. Thus to send one sheet a short distance from London in 1790 costs 2d, to send two sheets costs 4d, and five sheets (weighing 1¼oz) costs 10d. However, if your letter is addressed to a place more than one stage from London – a stage being the inn where the postboy or mail coach will change horses – then you need to pay more. In 1790, up to two stages costs 3d per page, and more than two stages but less than 80 miles, 4d per page. To send it up to 150 miles costs 5d per page; and more than 150 miles, 6d. Thank goodness, in 1797 distances are standardised, so you no longer have to guess how many stages your letter is travelling. From then on, to send a letter up to 15 miles is 3d per sheet; up to 30 miles is 4d; and so on, with every sheet sent more than 150 miles within England costing 8d, plus an extra 1d for passage into Scotland. In 1801, most of the prices are changed again, with greater amounts set for long distances and the abolition of the extra penny for Scotland. They're changed again in 1805 and 1812. To send a two-page letter 150 miles after 12 March 1805 will cost 1s 6d; and to send a three-page letter that distance after 9 July 1812 will cost 2s 6d.

The basic idea behind the Penny Post is simple: letters collected from about 570 receiving offices in London, Westminster and the borough of Southwark are delivered at a cost of 1d to any address in the same districts or up to 10 miles from the city, with an additional cost of 1d if the destination is in that 10-mile hinterland. The extra 1d is paid by the receiver. This is a cheap and efficient system. Letters sent within the bounds of the city are collected four times a day (at 7 a.m., 11 a.m., 3 p.m. and 7 p.m.) and delivered the same day. Letters to the suburbs are collected in most offices twice a day. At first the system operates only in London but from 1793 Birmingham, Bristol, Manchester and Edinburgh also have their own Penny Posts, with Glasgow following in 1800, Liverpool in 1801 and many other towns from 1808. But this is where postal rates start to get *really* complicated, because these local rates are combined with the national ones to produce an overall postage cost, on top of the fees for delivery. And to add to the confusion, in 1801 the rate for the Penny Post is raised to 2d. Some people call it the 'two-penny post' as a result – which is not helpful when posting to the hinterland now costs 3d.

So far we have only discussed sending a letter from London. You won't be surprised to hear that it gets even more complicated when sending between provincial towns. If you have to send a letter via London, say, from Southampton to Norwich, you will pay postage twice – once for the journey to London and then again for the journey to its final destination. Send a letter from Southampton to Aberdeen and you will pay postage three times – for the journey to London, the journey to Edinburgh, and finally the journey to Aberdeen, with each extra sheet increasing the amount of postage. Also, you need to remember that if you want your letter to go via London, you have to measure the mileage via that city and not by the direct route. Then you've got to factor in the cost of the actual delivery in a provincial area. So, to send a two-page letter from Morpeth to Torquay in 1811 costs 2s 2d for its transit from Morpeth to London and from London to Torquay via Newton Abbot – that's a total of 462 miles, not the 392-mile direct route. And then you need to add an extra 1d for local delivery, the last part being paid by the recipient.[43]

As you can see, the postal system is an absolute nightmare. And with so many highwaymen on the road, there is no guarantee that your letter or parcel will even arrive at its destination. Your precious letter will also be subject to the dangers inherent in mail coaches, which thunder along the highways at night and risk careering off into a ditch or breaking an axle on a rock or a pothole. Yet in some ways the Royal Mail is remarkably accommodating. Anne Lister remarks on live hedgehogs being sent by the mail in 1821.[44] I can't advise you on the postage rates for hedgehogs but I can guarantee that the calculations will be fiendishly complicated.

Language and Politeness

In previous ages, you'd have found a visit to Britain problematic on account of the different languages spoken. You'll be pleased to hear that's no longer an issue. With the exceptions of some Gaelic-speaking Highlanders and Welsh speakers, most Regency people will understand your English, and vice versa. Yes, you will find some dialects a little tricky – no one is going to pretend that Scots and the Devonshire dialect are easy – but even before the start of our period, Dr Johnson notes that in Scotland 'the great, the learned, the ambitious and the vain all cultivate the English phrase, and the English pronunciation, and in splendid companies Scotch is not much heard, except now and then from an old lady'.[45]

There are, however, a few complications – not the least of which is the slang. This isn't only used by the lower classes: the well-to-do have their own abbreviations and linguistic peculiarities. For example, the term 'crim. con.' stands for 'criminal conversation', meaning the evidence of an adulterous affair. You will hear the upper classes refer to the '*haut ton*' (the fashionable set), 'chaney' (china) and 'Corinthians' (fashionable men about town). Ordinary Londoners have slang words for everything, particularly women of easy virtue. 'Lady-birds', 'wantons', 'trollops', 'bachelor-fare', 'light-skirts', 'barques of frailty', 'Paphians', 'Cythereans' and 'demimondes' are just a few. In addition, in male conversation, 'straw-chippers' are ordinary females; a 'bit of muslin' is a more attractive woman; a 'fair Cyprian' is a rather special young lady; and a 'prime article' is a born-again Kitty Fisher. If you hear the phrases 'blue ruin', 'strip-me-naked' or 'flashes of lightning', the speaker is talking about gin. A 'flash house' is a pub used by criminals. 'Free-traders' are smugglers. 'Gingerbread', 'blunt', 'dibs' and 'rhino' are all words for money. A 'windsucker' is a bore. A 'snyder' is a tailor who happily allows you to put your new clothes on credit but then charges an extortionate rate of interest. A 'gullgroper' is a money lender. 'Punting on River Tick' means to be in debt. 'Tap-hackled' and 'bosky' both mean drunk. My own favourites of all the slang phrases of the period are 'to lush some slop', which means 'to drink tea'; and 'Slubberdegullion', which, according to Captain Grose's *Dictionary of the Vulgar Tongue*, published in 1811, means 'a dirty nasty fellow'.

But I'm getting ahead of myself. Here we are, discussing bad language, and I haven't yet told you how to introduce yourself. My apologies.

In a society as hierarchical as this one, there is plenty of scope for making mistakes. If you're overfamiliar with someone of higher status than you, you will have great difficulty recovering from a negative first impression. Similarly, to be too welcoming to someone of significantly lower status will probably create bad feeling with members of your own class. Anne Lister is shocked to see her father, a landed gentleman, shake hands with a mere publican.[46] The best course of action is to play it safe. With people of very high status, just remove your hat and bow or curtsy, and don't turn your back on them. Likewise, when leaving the presence of a member of the royal family or a duke or bishop, you should bow or curtsy. If you see someone in the street whom you know, you don't need to take off your hat as people do on the Continent; it is sufficient merely to make the mark of a bow, with a nod of the head or a motion of your hand to the brim of your hat.[47] If you meet someone indoors with whom you are already acquainted, presuming he or she is from the same class as you, you will shake hands on both greeting and departing. Note that women do this as well as men, although not quite as vigorously. Gentlemen will often say hello to friends by offering them a pinch of snuff. Slapping someone on the back is a form of salutation only employed by very close male friends. Likewise, kissing someone on the hand (a formal mark of greeting or parting) is only done between family members and close friends. Don't kiss someone's hand unless you know them very well. You certainly should not try to kiss them on the cheek.

What if you are not yet acquainted? It is said that if one English gentleman sees another drowning, he won't rescue him if they have not been properly introduced.[48] The American Nathaniel Wheaton notes the 'coldness and reserve' with which English gentlemen make an acquaintanceship:

> It is seldom that an Englishman extends his hand to a stranger who is presented to him. He bows slightly and formally, and with a grave composure of his features, which produces a rather repulsive effect until you recollect that such is the manner of the English and that it does not necessarily infer unkindness. It is not until after two or three interviews and you have been admitted to the hospitality of his fireside that you give him credit for all the warmth of feeling which he really possesses.[49]

Of course, even after you advance from handshaking terms to offering your snuffbox, you will still only refer to each other by surname. Years will go by – in some cases, *decades* – before a gentleman will even think of using another gentleman's first name. As for ladies, introductions are frequently arranged by letter in advance, entailing a whole dance of excessive politeness in ensuring that the lady to be called upon is not inconvenienced in any way. Like the men, the use of first names is a stage of intimacy that few friendships reach. Most members of a lady's acquaintance outside her own family will never be called anything other than 'Lady ——' 'Miss ——' or 'Mrs ——'.

Among ordinary folk, less importance is placed upon formalities. Men and women address each other by their first names on first meeting because they don't have an alternative; they cannot use

'Mr ——' or 'Mrs ——' because that would denote too high a status. They will shake hands without a second thought on first meeting too. Similarly, you will shake hands on doing business with people, such as the landlord of a pub, an auctioneer or a trader in the market. Lower-status individuals are neither stifled by refinement nor hypocritically polite. You might find their informality something of a relief.

Money

As you are no doubt aware, money is reckoned in terms of pounds, shillings, pence and farthings: four farthings make a penny, twelve pence make a shilling, and twenty shillings one pound. The wealthy also reckon in guineas – £1 1s – as gold coins are multiples of this denomination. That's the easy bit. The problem is that not all these coins are available. This is partly due to the low output of the Royal Mint in George III's reign: just £1,800-worth of silver coins are produced between 1788 and 1815. The minting of gold coins ceases altogether in 1797, when the price of gold rises to the point where the metal in a guinea is worth more than the face value of the coin. As for copper, the introduction of steam power in 1797 results in massive new 'cartwheel' copper pennies and two-penny pieces being minted; these are very handsome but people don't like carrying them because they are so heavy.[50] It is only in 1816, after the war is over, that the government starts to address the problem.

What do people do in the meantime? They manage with whatever coins they can find. This includes using silver dollars and half-dollars, which are large silver Spanish 8-reales coins countermarked with the head of George III and circulated with a value of 4s 9d. The Royal Mint starts issuing 'bank tokens' for 3s and 1s 6d as an interim measure. Traders start issuing their own copper tokens: pennies, halfpennies and farthings. Astonishingly, at the height of its prosperity, Britain cannot mint enough basic coins to meet its everyday needs.

In the face of this cash shortage, the wealthy start to rely on banknotes. In 1789, the Bank of England issues notes in multiples of £10 up to £100 – so you might well come across a £90 note – as well as larger amounts, up to £1,000. In Scotland, both the Bank of Scotland and the Royal Bank of Scotland issue notes as low in value as £1 and as high as £100. It is the low-value notes that are the most useful. Provincial English banks realise this and start producing their own promissory notes in small denominations – normally £1, 1 guinea or 5 guineas. In 1793 the Bank of England follows their example and starts issuing £5 notes, and in 1797 £1 and £2 notes. Inevitably, forgers do their best to 'help': between 1801 and 1811, the value of fake notes identified by the Bank of England exceeds £100,000.[51] This complicates matters for shoppers, as traders will sometimes charge you a premium for paying with paper money. Also, using a fake banknote, even unwittingly, is tantamount to passing it off – which is punishable by death or, in special cases, transportation. Just having a fake £1 note in your possession can be enough to warrant a one-way ticket to Australia.[52] If you're worried about this, and you're wealthy enough to have a bank account, you can always write a cheque instead. By 1800 these carry an intricate swirling design on the left-hand side to make the forger's life as difficult as possible. They are also numbered, in case you need to stop a payment.

The other solution to the lack of currency is credit. You can easily see why it is popular with all classes: even a £1 note is going to be a cumbersome way of paying for a pint of milk costing 1d – and the dairyman selling it to you won't thank you for asking him for 19s 11d of change. Thus most customers don't normally hand over coins to their regular supplier of food, drink or coal. Tradesmen provide credit, recording each transaction in their 'shop book'. Your account should be settled regularly – either quarterly or annually, at Christmas.

For larger amounts of credit you'll need a bank. In 1784 there are about a hundred outside London; by 1810, the total has mushroomed to 721. They all face a problem, however, in that they are limited by law to a maximum of six partners and there is no limitation on their liability. Therefore many of the smaller institutions fail when things get tough. In 1825 there is a stock-market crash. In the ensuing run on the banks, six London partnerships and hundreds of provincial ones go bust, taking with them all their clients' money. When the dust settles, only about 500 are still in business. So, although cheques and banknotes go some way to solving the nation's currency problems, don't give up on gold and silver coins just yet.

Shopping

Shopping is a cultural barometer. When we only buy essentials we are in a very different situation from when we browse for novelties and luxuries that might improve the quality of our lives. In this respect, the nineteenth century is a golden age – in terms of choice, range, luxury, opulent shops and service. At the top end of the market, as Louis Simond puts it, 'you are caressed for your money'.[53]

In London, the old street markets are closing at the rate of one every two years: by 1830, fifteen of the thirty-four will have disappeared. People are choosing to visit shops rather than outdoor market stalls. They are increasingly prepared to pay for convenience – even though it can be expensive. For example, a mackerel from a fishmonger located near a fashionable square will cost you twice as much as in a retail market.[54] The well-off are also beginning to enjoy window shopping, which is now possible on account of glass manufacturers' ability to make larger panes. Shops have awnings that can be pulled down to protect you during bad weather. Seeing these changes afoot, market-place proprietors try to rival the high-street shopping experience by building covered spaces for their stalls. The rather splendid St John's Market in Liverpool is fully enclosed by 1822 under a roof supported by 23ft-high cast-iron columns, with glass panels in part of the roof and gas lights illuminating the rest of the space.[55] This is the future of market selling and it is no surprise that many other marketplaces are rebuilt on similar lines.

Many of the best shopping experiences in London are to be gained in the specialist retail outlets in the West End. Perhaps you have already visited some of them. Berry Brothers, suppliers of wine to George III, has been at 3 St James's Street since 1698; Lock & Co. has been selling hats from 6 St James's Street since 1765; and Fortnum & Mason has been piling up the groceries at its Piccadilly store since 1707. You'll know the London auction houses too: Christie's and Sotheby's are already several decades old by the start of our period; they are joined by Bonhams in 1793 and Phillips in 1796. But there are many more emporia that you will not know. Gunter's Tea Shop in Berkeley Square is a must – if only so that you can try the fresh Italian ice creams and frozen mousses. Wedgwood's magnificent showrooms on York Street are a shopping marvel. Huge, high-ceilinged salons with massive windows hold glass-fronted wooden display cabinets stuffed with the finest dinner services, bowls, urns, dishes, lamps – you name it. Another fine emporium is James Lackington's bookshop, otherwise known as 'The Temple of the Muses', whose large arched windows face on to Finsbury Square. Enter and you will find yourself in a hall with book-shelves on the far wall that reach from the floor to the ceiling. In the middle is a substantial round desk where assistants take your money and package your books for you. Note that Lackington does not offer credit. The only way he can justify his cheap prices is by insisting on cash.[56]

Luxurious though these shops are, probably the most popular estab-lishments for the well-to-do are the arcades, 'bazaars' and 'magazines'. The idea comes from the old Royal Exchange in the City: a building full of small units where pretty shop girls tempt customers with the highest-quality merchandise. Further Exchanges are built, including Exeter Exchange on the Strand. Here an indoor pavement passes between glass-fronted shops at the front and then down a central aisle flanked by glass-topped display cases, where expensive trinkets are on sale. By 1807 the 'Change, as it is affectionately known, is being advertised as a 'bazaar' – the Oriental term being used to imply a covered market but with an exotic twist. In 1816, John Trotter opens a rival, the Soho Bazaar, in a disused warehouse in Soho Square. Here he creates a large selling space hung with red cloth interspersed with tall mirrors and surrounded by mahogany counters selling milli-nery, gloves, lace, jewellery and flowers. At the rear there is a grotto decorated with climbing plants and a kitchen to provide sustenance for the well-heeled customers. There's even a ladies' dressing room. At the same time, the model of the single-arcade shopping mall – adapted from the 'Change – is copied in other upmarket establish-ments, such as the Royal Opera Arcade and Burlington Arcade off Piccadilly. You'll find them outside London too – at the Lower Arcade in Bristol and the Pelham Arcade in Hastings. All these bazaars and arcades point the way to the department store of the future. The very earliest such examples are already doing business: Hanningtons in Brighton, whose departments in 1808 include linen drapery, mercery, haberdashery and hosiery; and Harding, Howel & Co.'s Grand Fashionable Magazine in Pall Mall, established in 1796, where glazed partitions separate the five departments: furs and fans; haber-dashery; jewellery, ornaments and clocks; perfumery; and millinery and dresses.

Taxes

Every so often you read an article in a modern newspaper or magazine suggesting that some of the taxes in the Regency period are the
'most ridiculous', 'stupid' or 'strangest' that the government has *ever*
inflicted on the people of Great Britain. These invariably include such
things as window tax, wallpaper tax, clock tax, watch tax, hat tax,
salt tax, hair-powder tax, candle tax, soap tax, playing-card tax and
brick tax. Yes, it's true that all these things are taxed at some point.
But the modern journalist never seems to notice that they are all
taxed in our own day too, through the VAT system. Indeed, if you
were to tell a group of Regency people that, one day, we'd tax *everything* except a handful of necessities, they'd no doubt shake their
heads in disbelief. As far as they are concerned, it makes sense to tax
wallpaper when only wealthy middle- and upper-class households can
afford it. You can say the same thing for the manservant tax and the
tax on coats of arms. If you keep a liveried servant in uniform, such
as a footman on the back of your carriage, you'll be taxed a guinea
or more. As for heraldry, from 1798 painting your armorial bearings
on your carriage requires a certificate costing two guineas. It's quite
sensible really: a taxation system that does not harm the poor.

Taxation is an important subject in this period. The reason is that
Britain fights expensive wars. Even before the beginning of the conflict
with France, £9 million is required annually to pay the interest on the
national debt, as the government still owes more than £230 million
for the American War of Independence. This is a real headache for
ministers, as the four main forms of state revenue – customs, excise,
stamp duty and taxation – collectively only bring in about £13 million
in 1784. Unfortunately, there seem to be few opportunities for
squeezing more money out of the economy. The customs system is
already frightfully efficient – as anyone who has seen their luggage
ransacked by customs officers can testify. Nor can the government
raise excise duties much further, for fear that it will lead to an increase
in smuggling. That doesn't leave many other options. The country
may be growing richer by the year but the government is practically
bankrupt.

The man who steps up to the mark is the prime minister, William
Pitt. He decides to raise more money, partly through loans and partly
through stamp duty and taxation, with a heavy emphasis on charging

the rich for their luxuries. In the 1780s he increases many existing taxes and introduces new ones on bricks, tiles, saddle horses, coach horses and racing horses. He also imposes a stamp duty on licences to kill game, pawnbrokers' licences, the sale of men's hats, gloves, mittens, hair powder, perfume and cosmetics. He reduces the duty on tea – because smuggling tea is almost as common as drinking it – and instead raises the window tax. With regard to the tax on manservants, he increases it and establishes the principle that those who employ more than two servants should pay incrementally more, with the rate rising to £3 per manservant if eleven or more are employed. It works. By the 1790s the government is running a budget surplus. But then, in 1793, war breaks out with France.

Pitt's determination to defeat the French economically as well as militarily forces him to become more and more inventive with his taxes. He places a premium on non-working dogs. He tries taxing clocks and watches but that proves damaging to the trade, so he replaces that tax with the stamp duty on coats of arms. He increases existing taxes with each succeeding budget. Then, in 1797, he announces that he will increase *all* assessed taxes. Massively. If you pay less than £25 on your manservants, carriages and horses, then your tax liability will simply treble; if you pay more than that, it will quadruple; and if you pay more than £50 in assessed taxes, it will increase five times. At the same time he introduces income tax, on a sliding scale. An incremental amount – starting at 1/120th – is due on incomes of £60 or more, rising to 10 per cent on incomes over £200. This is the first levying of income tax in British history. Pitt's mistake is to trust people to make their own tax assessments – and an extraordinary number decide they earn *just* under £60. The following year, he appoints independent commissioners properly to assess the amounts due. At the same time a scheme for voluntary donations is established, so people can pay more tax, if they wish. Surprisingly, this nets the Treasury an extra £2.8 million. Thus in 1798 you have the extraordinary situation of people complaining about tax collectors knocking on their door to ask how much money they earn, and counting their horses and windows; and, at the same time, patriotic peers writing cheques for £3,000 or more as voluntary contributions to the war effort.[57] Pitt somehow manages to keep it all together. So too do his successors, and they do so without ruining the country. As the economist David Ricardo remarks after the end of the war, 'the annual

revenue of the people, even after the payment of their taxes, is probably greater at the present time than at any former period of our
history'.[58]

It has to be said that the new taxes are not popular. Income tax in
particular is 'universally disliked', according to James Woodforde.[59] It
is briefly suspended during the short peace of 1802 but reintroduced
on the resumption of hostilities in 1803 (at 5 per cent on incomes
over £150). It is increased further in 1805, by which time it is bringing
in more than £5 million per year. It remains in place until the end of
the war and is dropped in 1816. The tax on manservants is hardly any
more popular. The sum payable goes up and up until, in 1812, a family
with eleven or more manservants will pay a tax of £7 13s for each
one. Combined with the carriage tax, horse tax, land tax, income tax
and window tax, it causes many middle-class people to reduce the
number of male servants they employ, thereby increasing the total of
men without work. They also cut down on how many horses they
maintain, and thus the grooms and stable boys in their service. They
start to block up their windows too. 'This tax now being very high,
we have stopped up the spare garret window, which will be a saving
of 12s per annum,' writes Matthew Flinders in 1800. The following
year he replaces four small windows with two large ones, 'costing £20
but saving 22s annually'.[60]

Perhaps the only taxes that are not 'universally disliked' are the
lotteries operated by the government: the state-run National Lottery,
for instance, has a prize of £20,000 and runs from 1784 to 1824. Good
luck. Otherwise, you will probably agree with Sydney Smith when he
publishes his great fulmination against taxes in 1820:

The schoolboy whips his taxed top, the beardless youth manages his
taxed horse, with a taxed bridle on a taxed road; and the dying
Englishman, pouring his medicine, [on] which he has paid 7 per cent.,
into a spoon [on which] he has paid 15 per cent., flings himself upon
his chintz bed, [on] which he has paid 22 per cent, and expires in the
arms of an apothecary who has paid ... a hundred pounds for [a licence
for] the privilege of putting him to death. His whole property is then
immediately taxed from 2 to 10 per cent. Besides the probate, large
fees are demanded for burying him in the chancel; his virtues are
handed down to posterity on taxed marble; and he is then gathered to
his fathers – to be taxed no more.[61]

6

What to Wear

Dress is at all times a frivolous distinction, and excessive solicitude
about it often destroys its own aim ... It would be mortifying to the
feelings of many ladies, could they be made to understand how little
the heart of man is affected by what is costly or new in their attire ...

Jane Austen, *Northanger Abbey* (1818)

Does it matter what you wear? Jane Austen doesn't seem to think so.
No matter how much a girl frets over the cut of her muslin gown,
the man she most wants to impress will probably pay little attention
to it. Impressing the other sex, however, is not the only criterion by
which this question should be judged. Dress says a great deal about
your class, and that *certainly* matters. It affects your ability to get credit
in a shop, rent a house and gain entry to a ball. If you are a young
woman, fine clothes will act as a caution to any gentleman who might
think of taking advantage of you; makeshift clothes, on the other
hand, will send the signal that you have no powerful connections.
Then there is the matter of political outlook. Flamboyant or foppish
fashions are likely to enrage those who sympathise with egalitarian
values. In the wake of the French Revolution, when hard-pressed and
starving Londoners are bold enough to attack the royal coach, it can
be nothing short of dangerous to walk down Piccadilly in a waistcoat
embroidered with gold thread. In addition, fashion is an international
concern and Paris continues to set the trends that Britain, the rest of
Europe and North America follow. Therefore the French Revolution
gives rise to a new sartorial philosophy throughout the Western World.
It sees high-status men give up dressing in colourful and exotic clothes,
instead adopting a style of understated elegance.

Fashion constantly changes, of course. With only five natural fibres
to choose from – silk, wool, linen, hemp and cotton – and a limited

range of buckles, furs and feathers with which to embellish them, it is essential that the cut and colour of your clothes remain up-to-date. At the start of every month *The Times* publishes a report on London female fashion, giving details of the latest style in 'full dresses', 'walking dress', 'travelling dress' and headdresses, as well as providing observations about which colours are in vogue. Also at this time, patterns for making your own dresses are becoming available. Fashion magazines are published from the 1790s, among them *The Lady's Magazine, The Gallery of Fashion* and *The Lady's Monthly Museum*. Some of these even carry hand-coloured, engraved illustrations. Of course there is no substitute for visiting London or Brighton to see for yourself what the well-to-do are wearing and exactly how the newest styles should be worn. Many people in the South-east do exactly that.

Gentlemen's Clothing

The prince of Wales's wardrobe illustrates the extremes to which fashionable gentlemen go to make an impression. On the occasion of his mother's birthday in 1790, he wears a brown velvet coat and breeches of the same cloth with small blue spots, richly embroidered with gold and silver; and his waistcoat and coat cuffs are covered with gold tissue. Later that evening he changes into 'a brown and pink-spotted velvet coat and breeches [with a] silver tissue waistcoat embroidered with a very rich appliqué of silver stones and coloured foils'.[1] When he takes his seat in the House of Lords he wears a pink-and-gold-embroidered black velvet coat and pink high-heeled shoes. All this costs a fortune. Some of his coats cost as much as £300 – and he orders more than a hundred suits to be made for him, even before he becomes regent in 1811. Throw in an average of fifty new shirts per year, handkerchiefs that cost more than £12 each, and no fewer than 300 whips, epaulettes made of *solid* gold and feathers that cost 16 guineas *each* – and you can see why the prince's attire excites attention throughout his life.[2]

People tend to emulate their social superiors but, even if you are very wealthy, you would be wise to take your lead from other gentlemen and not try to copy the prince. If you go to the House of Commons in the early 1790s, for example, you'll see that almost everyone there is wearing flat-heeled, black-leather shoes with silver buckles; white stockings; breeches that end just below the knee; a short waistcoat beneath a thigh-length cutaway coat with a high collar; a white cravat; and hair combed back and powdered silver-grey or concealed beneath a curled silver-grey wig. As for hats, you might see a few early versions of the top hat with wide brims. Otherwise the most common are 'cocked hats' – with the brim either folded up on three sides to form a 'continental' (later called a 'tricorne') or folded up on two sides to make a 'navy' (later, a 'bicorne'). This form of clothing – the breeches, stockings, waistcoat and coat – is employed in every dimension of a gentleman's life.

Evening wear differs from day wear in 1790 by virtue of the fabric and embellishment of the garments. Your dress shirt, for example, will have full flouncy cuffs and lace trimmings down the front. Likewise, the waistcoat you wear to a grand event will be embroidered whereas the one you wear every day will be plain. Everyone of rank dresses for dinner, even when travelling alone and staying at an inn; the appropriate clothing might be a velvet waistcoat or a smarter, cutaway coat. As for hunting in the country, you need a fuller riding coat with a turned-down collar and small cuffs (called a frock coat) and looser-cut breeches of a hard-wearing wool. Don't forget to pack your hard-heeled boots; the soft, flat leather pumps you wear in town won't do in the country.

Into this world strides George Bryan Brummell – better known to us as Beau Brummell. Born in 1778 and educated at Eton College and briefly at Oxford (where he studies the art of ostentatiously ignoring his inferior contemporaries), he comes to the attention of the Prince Regent, who appoints him an officer in his own regiment, the 10th Hussars, in 1794. Over the next four years the teenage Brummell becomes a close friend of the prince and gains a reputation for style, wit and sheer effrontery. On turning twenty-one, he inherits £30,000 from his late father and sets up house in Mayfair, becoming a full-time dandy. He and his friends sit in the bow window of White's Club judging everyone who dares walk or ride down St James's. Unsurprisingly, they make enemies. Captain Gronow thinks of the group as 'unspeakably odious' because 'they hate everybody and abuse everybody ... swear a good deal, never laugh and have their own particular slang'.[3] You could add that they never work or contribute in any way to the well-being of others. However, Brummell's astounding preference for style over rank permits him to put down the most pompous men for their sartorial errors. 'Bedford, do you call this thing a coat?' he exclaims loudly one day – to the duke of Bedford.

So what is Brummell's contribution to fashion? What is the legacy that will last two hundred years?

For centuries, men have demonstrated their power, wealth and prestige through extravagant clothing. And since the late Middle Ages they have deliberately dressed in impractical ways to demonstrate how little physical work they need to do. Brummell sees how French fashion in the wake of the revolution has turned against all that. He realises that, from now on, men who wish to show they are in command must dress in practical clothing, like men of action. Furthermore, he sees that this new French style has much in common with traditional English values, especially the love of self-control and almost-puritanical dislike of showiness. He thus forges a composite of French post-revolutionary fashion and typical English restraint, banishing vulgar ostentation from men's day wear. Clothes, he insists, should be admired for their perfection of cut and how well they fit the wearer. In this respect, he is helped by the development of the tape measure. Previously, tailors used strips of parchment or paper to trace their clients' dimensions.[4] But now they can quickly and easily measure them precisely, and cut clothes to fit perfectly. And, according to Brummell, nothing less than perfection will do.

Following Brummell's lead, a gentleman should be fastidiously clean, slim and elegant. His day clothes should be made up of subtle, muted shades: a pair of buff pantaloons or trousers, a plain-coloured waistcoat, a black- or dark-coloured coat, and natural, unpowdered hair. If you want bright buttons, they should be brass, not gold or silver. Breeches and stockings are right out, unless you are attending a formal event, in which case old-style dress is still *de rigueur*. If wearing pantaloons, they should come down to the calf and be made of buckskin and tight-fitting. They are to be worn with either low-heeled, black-leather Hessian boots, which have rising fronts and tassels just before the knee, or 'top boots': black-leather riding boots with flat tops turned down to reveal the lighter tan leather at the crest of each boot. Shirt collars should be clean, crisp and high, and the cravat should sit right up under the chin. Dark overcoats or greatcoats can be worn to provide a contrast to fawn- or buff-coloured trousers, thus creating a dramatic effect. Alternatively you may wear a short practical overcoat with virtually no tails, called a 'Spencer' after the Earl Spencer, who invented it after his tailcoat was singed when he fell asleep in front of the fire. But whatever you choose, it is understatement, not vulgar ostentation, that matters. Gentlemen should *wear* their clothes – and demonstrate their virtue and merits through their actions, manners and words – and not simply drape themselves in symbols of wealth and power.

The new style has great resonance with social reformers and active young gentlemen. However, it does not immediately catch on with everyone. The Prince Regent has become used to being described in *The Times* as the best-dressed man at every event he attends – largely due to the amount he spends – so he is reluctant to give up his jewelled waistcoats. But as more and more gentlemen start to follow Brummell's understated style, even the prince is forced to pay attention. And he realises that Brummell's standards are not ones he can meet: they require considerable self-restraint, especially with regard to keeping a slim figure. In the end, the two men grow to hate each other. Of course it is Brummell who makes the break – and he does it with characteristic style. One day in 1811 he is walking along St James's with Lord Moira when the Prince Regent approaches. The prince greets Lord Moira but cuts Brummell by ostentatiously ignoring him. Brummell delivers his famous response with all the finality of a guillotine blade slicing through a royal neck. He turns to Lord Moira and says in a loud voice, 'Pray, who is your fat friend?'

The prince is by no means the only gentleman who is reluctant to embrace the new style. Fellows of university colleges continue with clerical dress or academic gowns. Schools still expect their pupils to don black breeches, white cotton stockings, a blue waistcoat and a white neckcloth. The very fact that breeches and white stockings are old-fashioned makes them seem formal, and thus professional men wear them to appear more dignified. Older men naturally refuse to adopt the style of the young bucks. As a result, if you visit Britain in the years around 1810 you will have to decide what to wear according to how old you are and where you want to go. If you wander into the Royal Academy, all the young men there will be dressed in 'demo-cratic' coat and trousers and none will have powdered hair. In the Board Room at the Admiralty, however, all the military gentlemen will not only be wearing breeches and white stockings but powdered wigs too. Walk into any upmarket shop and it is more likely that the customers are wearing trousers and the staff old-style breeches and stockings.

Jump forward to the 1820s and things have changed. In the streets and shops, in the offices of government, in the libraries and board-rooms, almost all the men are wearing trousers. Although Beau Brummell has left England for Calais by this time, his style lives on. But fashion has not stood still since his departure. Nowadays, the dashing young man about town is wearing a coat with padded shoulders and an even narrower waistline than Brummell himself sported. Many gentlemen have corsets or stays made for them, aiming for an idealised athletic, triangular shape to the upper torso. Their trousers may swell out slightly below the narrow waist, to be wider at the hip, and long and tapered.[5] Single-breasted, knee-length frock coats are popular: these are gathered at the waist and not cut away like a tailcoat but conceal the thighs entirely; the lapels are often trimmed with fur. Those who wear them frequently also sport a top hat and cane. Shirts are always white, made of linen and fastened at the cuffs with gold buttons or cufflinks. Cravats, which, according to Brummell, should always be of the purest white linen, now are sometimes coloured and even made of silk. They can be tied in different ways too: in 1828 Monsieur le Blanc publishes *The Art of Tying the Cravat*, detailing thirty-two varieties of knot around your neck. Top boots remain popular for riding but now you might choose instead to wear Wellington boots. These, made famous by the duke, are knee-high at the front but cut lower at the back for ease of movement, and (unlike modern-day wellingtons) they are made of leather.

What is all this going to cost, you might wonder? In the 1790s a suit of a high-quality cloth – consisting of a coat, waistcoat and breeches – is available from a London tailor for 4 guineas. If you are happy to accept a lower-quality cloth, you can bring the price down to £3 10s. Shirts are of white cotton or linen and are very often made at home, lovingly stitched together by wives, sisters and daughters. If you want to obtain one from a fashionable London shirt-maker, you can expect to pay £1 10s or more. Cravats are normally in the range of 3s–7s. Socks are made of cotton or wool; an everyday pair might set you back 4s–5s. Stockings can be expensive, especially if made of silk: 8s–10s will get you a good pair; 4s should be your minimum. Finally, you might consider wearing drawers. These come in two forms: long and short. The long ones are like modern long johns, worn beneath pantaloons and trousers. The short variety are for wearing under breeches. Expect to pay in the region of 3s–5s, depending on length. Not everyone wears them, though: many men just make do with folding their shirt tails underneath their backsides.

In 1790, you will still find most men of high status wearing a wig or powdering their own natural hair with hair powder. For the latter you first need to cover your hair in pomatum (made from beef or mutton lard, beeswax and scent), which will help the powder stick. Then you need to get your manservant to apply a pair of bellows to blow the powder into the hair. The powder itself is made from starch and coloured according to the desired end result, silver-grey being the most popular. Obviously there is a great deal of wastage. Despite this, in the 1780s almost every gentleman in the country is observing this expensive ritual. The introduction of a hair-powder tax by Pitt in 1786 goes some way to reduce its use. From 1795 you also need a licence to powder your hair, costing a guinea: the penalty for not obtaining one is £20. By the end of the century, more and more gentlemen are sporting a short hairstyle known as the Bedford crop and forgoing powder altogether. Brummell's notions of democratic dress do the rest of the damage. By 1812, only old gentlemen and their servants powder their hair. At the same time, the half-beard known as 'mutton chops' becomes fashionable. On that point, most gentlemen shave themselves at home but, should you wish to go to a barber, it will cost you a shilling to emerge with a smooth chin.[6]

Eyewear

Before 1727 spectacles consisted only of a pair of round lenses in a frame that sat on the bridge of the nose but in that year the London manufacturer Edward Scarlett begins making them with metal arms or 'sides'.[7] It's a minor change but an important one: if you wear spectacles all the time they become an item of your dress whereas if you only put them on when needed, they remain utilitarian tools, which anyone might use. As a result, the design starts to matter that much more. Those who want to wear spectacles regularly choose examples with frames of silver or polished steel. As they tend to be worn by older people and the more bookish sort, so they increasingly become associated with wisdom. Hence eyewear becomes popular with the dandies, who like to carry lorgnettes (spectacles held up to the eyes with a handle) or a quizzing glass on a ribbon, for scrutinising things. Such articles serve as a metaphor for their view of themselves as meticulous critics of the world. You can't help but feel, though, that when a dandy holds up a quizzing glass to view a picture or a young lady's face, he is not concerned with what he is seeing so much as with being seen.[8]

Ordinary Men's Clothes

Much of what needs to be said about the clothes of ordinary men has already been said – because people tend to ape their social superiors. Most self-respecting working men wear coat, stockings and breeches until the early nineteenth century because that is what the upper and middle classes wear. However, there is a considerable difference between the cut and cloth of a suit costing 4 guineas and the equivalent garments worn by a shopkeeper in a provincial town. If you rifle through the wardrobe of the Plymouth dyer William Mortimer in 1823 you'll find that his four coats all have a second-hand value of between 3s and 6s. Similarly, his best cotton shirts are worth only 1s 6d each and his trousers all 5s or less. Three of his flannel shirts, four pairs of woollen stockings and his one and only pair of drawers are valued together at 9s. I assume that William Mortimer is not a man who believes in wearing drawers every day. At least, I hope not.[9]

Perhaps the most significant exception to the above generalisation – that working men ape their social superiors – is that, in the country, they continue wearing breeches for many years after the upper and middle classes have switched to trousers. In addition, they often have to wear protective clothing. Richard Rush notes in 1818 that 'the few peasants whom we saw were fully and warmly clad. They wore breeches, a heavy shoe, which lacing over the ankle made the foot look clumsy; a linen frock over the coat, and stout leather gloves, which they kept on while working.'[10] Nathaniel Wheaton similarly observes five years later that:

breeches are universally worn by the labouring classes. These are commonly of a coarse corduroy, the legs being embraced by sheepskin gaiters reaching from the heels to the ham, and sometimes above the knee. Shoes of the most formidable size and weight, stuck full of hobnails, complete the lower part of the labourer's attire. Over his coat he commonly wears a frock of brown linen, gathered at the breast into a vast number of fine plaits – the use of which it is difficult to conjecture.[11]

This 'frock' is also known as a smock-frock. Made of coarse linen, it goes over the head and covers the whole body, reaching down to the knee, or even lower. The plaits allow it to expand over very bulky clothes, for its prime purpose is to provide protection for those who are out in all weathers – shepherds, cowhands, carters and suchlike. Shorter versions and smocks without arms are made for men engaged in more active work. Most men in the country complete the ensemble with a bully-cock hat.

The smock-frock, breeches, sheepskin gaiters and hob-nailed boots might be the most common labourers' dress to be found in Britain but there are many others besides. Just as recognisable are the sailor's loose striped trousers, short blue jacket, shirt and waistcoat – often worn without socks or shoes. You will probably be familiar with the butcher's apron but expect to see keepers of public houses also wearing aprons, as well as weavers, barbers, carpenters, bricklayers, masons and road builders. More distinctive occupational clothes include such items as the carpenter's paper hat and the coal heaver's fan-tailed hat, which covers the back of his neck. Many workers in the coal trades wear white clothing. Colliers wear white suits. Coal whippers, who unload the coal from ships in baskets, wear white shirts with a blue stripe along with their fan-tail hats.

Another key difference between the clothing worn by the upper and middle classes and labouring men lies in the use of neck decoration. Barbers, butchers and shopkeepers sometimes sport a cravat in order to appear respectable to their patrons, but the large majority of ordinary working folk do not normally wear anything around their necks. If they have any neckwear at all, it will be a handkerchief loosely tied below their chin, like sailors do. The weaver Samuel Bamford describes setting off with his uncle in the first decade of the nineteenth century, his uncle wearing 'a green woollen apron twisted around his waist; his clean shirt showing at the open breast of his waistcoat; his brown silk handkerchief wrapped around his neck; a quid of tobacco in his mouth and a broad and rather slouched hat on his head'. Meanwhile young Samuel himself is following along in a 'rough jacket, knee-breeches, strong stockings and shoes [and an] open-collared shirt ... '[12] Like most workers who do not have to face the public, Samuel can dispense with neckwear and other unnecessary items.

Ladies' Clothing

Are the signals that British women send out in their dress – or state of undress – part of a universal language or special to their own time? You might think that, if a woman wears a low-cut top in the Regency, she is trying to draw attention to herself. But just because this is a modern interpretation does not necessarily mean it is the correct Regency one. Dress signals vary. In some periods in the Western World, it is taboo to reveal the naked arms, shoulders and legs. On other continents, near-nudity is an everyday form of attire. Furthermore, the subtleties of dress signals go way beyond sexual attraction. As we have seen with male clothing, there are messages about status and political outlook in the wearing of certain garments that have signifi- cance for contemporaries but which are not immediately obvious to visitors.

Ladies are expected to dress appropriately at all times of the day. This means wearing morning dress or 'undress' in the morning – until dinner time – and 'full dress' or evening dress for a formal dinner or going out to a ball. These expectations imply a series of restrictions. Morning dress is only worn when the lady is at home; it must completely cover her arms and wrists, and also her neck. Hence morning clothes are high-necked and long-sleeved, and might be topped with an informal hat or cap. However, if you leave the house, you will be wearing 'half dress', which is more formal, more showy and more revealing. 'Full dress' permits the lady to reveal more still – to be quite risqué, in fact – by exposing her arms above the elbow and as much cleavage as she dares to show. Low-cut dresses are titillating but not taboo. The irony is not lost on contemporaries that a woman in 'full dress' is showing much more flesh than when she is in 'undress', when all you can see of her skin are her fingers and her face.

In 1789, women don't normally wear drawers and ladies *certainly* do not wear them. This is because they are associated with prostitutes who tempt men by displaying (but not wholly revealing) their wares. Instead, the closest garments to a woman's body are her stockings and her chemise or shift. Stockings are self-explanatory, held in place above the knee by silk garters, which are sometimes embroidered with a motto (for young men to find out). The chemise generally reaches down to the thigh; it is cut low over the breast and has loose sleeves that are drawn in around the arm just above the elbow.

Next, if it is one of the cooler months, your maid will help you with your underskirt, which is normally plain and tubular but can occasionally be quilted for warmth. Your petticoat goes over this. If you're wearing full dress, your petticoat will be reinforced with a series of hoops, increasing in circumference from the waist down, to create a wide skirt around you – the hoops being made of wire or bamboo. These can be very wide indeed, although perhaps not quite as wide as earlier in the eighteenth century, when some women could not pass through a doorway without having to tilt their skirts up. An alternative to the hooped petticoat (but now on the way out) is a pair of paniers – large extensions to the hips to extend the skirt sideways. If you intend simply to be wearing half dress, you can dispense with the hoops and paniers and wear a bustle: a tube normally stuffed with cork that goes around the back of the waist, to extend your skirts. Over your chemise or, rather, around your torso, your maid will then wrap your stays and lace them up tightly at the back, pulling hard on the whalebone-reinforced garment to produce the narrow-waisted conical shape so favoured by ladies of fashion. I'd like to be able to tell you that it doesn't hurt – but that would be a lie. Elizabeth Ham recalls that her first pair of stays 'was nearly purgatory, and I question whether I was sufficiently aware of the advantage of a fine shape to reconcile me to the punishment'.[13] It is not surprising that under their morning dress, many ladies prefer to have their stays only loosely tightened or to leave them off altogether, so they can move more freely.

Now for the dress that goes over the top. This might be a front-opening gown, a frock that fastens at the back, a 'redingote' or riding coat for outdoors wear, or a 'sack' – which is not as frumpy as it sounds but an elegant dress with pleats at the back. Some older ladies might still prefer to wear a mantua, a loose gown with a bodice attached to an overskirt with a train. All of these dresses might be made of satin, wool, muslin or silk and embroidered or otherwise decorated with sophisticated gatherings and pleats, creating a stunning effect. The very finest examples are exceptionally expensive: it is possible to spend as much as 100 guineas on an evening dress, should you wish to do so. However, most ladies will be quite satisfied with something that costs between £2 and £5. In another irony of women's dress, the ones that cost the most are those low-cut, revealing numbers that cover you the least.

The dress does not complete the appearance of the lady of fashion. Necklaces and earrings are as regularly worn with evening dress as now. Your shoes will hardly be seen under the voluminous skirts that cover a hooped petticoat and brush the ground, so their appearance is less important. Consequently, most women wear comfortable low-heeled or flat footwear, composed either wholly of leather or of leather soles with cloth uppers. Gloves are, of course, *de rigueur*, even if you only carry them. If formally dressed, you will wear long fine silk ones over your bare arms, leaving a small expanse of skin visible at the top. Pockets are separate from your dress – like linen bags that hang from your waist – but they are invisible beneath the folds of your skirt and are reached through slits in the cloth.

Undoubtedly the most striking element of your dress, apart from your gown, will be your hairstyle and headdress. Ladies as well as gentlemen still wear pomatum and powder in their hair until the early 1790s, with the most prized colour being grey. Sometimes, for a special occasion, the hair is built up into a great edifice of curls and tresses, using cushions concealed inside the hairstyle, so that it is very high indeed. On top of this, you will wear a tall feather or two. Even if you are not dressing your hair up in a great tower, and are simply wearing a large wide-brimmed hat or a fashionable turban, you will decorate it with a high-standing feather. The most sought-after examples are from egrets, ostriches, birds of paradise and peacocks. Of course competitive ladies start increasing the height of their feathers and headdresses so that, within a few years, dressing rooms have to be provided at assembly halls where ladies can put on their feathers after arriving, as no coach can accommodate a 3ft- or 4ft-high feather-topped mound of hair and the lady herself beneath it.

So there you are, resplendent in your flounces, fluffs and feathers, when along comes the French Revolution. As with male dress, there is a sudden and drastic rethinking of what is appropriate. Those arbiters of Parisian fashion realise they must be seen to eschew everything that is showy and ostentatiously aristocratic. But how do you demonstrate elegance and refinement without appearing in awe of aristocratic values? What role does taste play when society is brutally killing its arbiters in the bloodiest way imaginable?

The Parisians find the answer in reaching back to Ancient Greece, the cradle of democracy. Classical sculptures of female figures show a beauty that does not rely on hooped petticoats and feathers but on the natural female shape, made more modest and yet at the same time more alluring by draping it in thin material. This aesthetic is now adopted both for morning dress and half dress and very quickly it makes its way across the Channel to London. From the early 1790s, ladies' daytime clothing turns decidedly neoclassical, with very fine muslin 'chemise dresses' becoming all the rage, especially among younger women. The style is even adopted for evening wear. Dresses are cut to be free-flowing, with a very high waist just beneath the breasts, which allows the girdle to push up the bosom for greater effect. The neckline is cut low and held gathered on a drawstring, which has the effect of making the front of the dress look pleated. Muslin being so fine, it clings to the body and moves with it, giving the impression of nudity beneath its flimsiness. Coral beads are the ideal accompaniment: their timeless pinks and reds contrast beautifully with pale skin and the white of the muslin dress.

Unsurprisingly, the new style is hugely popular with men. Never before have women appeared in public covered in so little! But most women are just as keen on it, for it allows them to move freely without being hampered by heavy petticoats. If you are naturally slim, you don't even need to be laced into your stays. Oh, the freedom! The beauty of the folds of muslin cascading over the limbs means there is no need for elaborate and costly embroidery, yet pleats and gatherings can still be used to enhance the sophistication of the dress. Many women make their own muslin gowns, as they are so much simpler than the mantuas, sacks and frocks of the 1780s. For twenty years this Grecian style becomes the basis of fashionable day wear in Britain.

The new style allows ladies greater latitude with their hair too. You may have it cut to reflect the Ancient Roman style, wearing it short and ruffled *à la Titus* or *à la Brutus* – marking the first occasion since classical times when it has been acceptable for high-status women to have short hair. If you prefer to keep your hair long, you can draw it up into a bun on the back of the head, as certain ladies did in Ancient Rome. Another popular style is to hold your hair above your forehead with a comb and allow the tresses to fall down each side of the face, in imitation of a Greek sculpture – or 'the coiffure of nature' as one fashion writer describes it.[14] Powdering such hairstyles would be ridiculous, of course, so the practice quickly falls out of favour among fashionable gentlewomen. This love of the classical styles means that, for the first time in centuries, it becomes fashionable for women to leave the house without a hat, cap or bonnet of any kind – not even a 4ft feather.

The changes in fashion following the French Revolution also affect how much skin women can reveal. *The Times* reports on 18 June 1798 that Parisian women 'are every day divesting themselves of some of the customary articles of dress, and the rage for *nudity* is so great that it is apprehended, even by the Parisian journalists, they will shortly have the effrontery to present themselves to the public eye in a state of pure nature'. And what is good for Paris is good for London: muslin dresses are sometimes so thin that you can see the lady's garters beneath. Those who are not inclined to such exhibitionism turn their thoughts to what to wear under a muslin dress, mindful of the fact that anything substantial will negate the effect of the flowing cloth. Fine petticoats are thus developed to maintain modesty. Nor can pockets be concealed in their skirts. 'Those heavy appendages are no more worn at present than keys at girdles,' declares *The Times*, adding:

> Every fashionable fair carries her purse in her workbag. Her handkerchiefs, her toothpick case, her watch and her keys, if she has any, are the constant concomitants of her visits; and while no part of the symmetry of her shape is altered or concealed by the old-fashioned paniers, she has the pleasure of laying everything that belongs to her upon the table wherever she goes.

The usual word for what the journalist calls a 'workbag' – and we would call a handbag – is a 'reticule', which is inevitably mocked as a 'ridicule' by opponents of the new fashion.

Another consequence of the greater freedom of female dress is that respectable women start wearing drawers. At a ball in 1796, a fashionable lady appears in 'flesh-coloured pantaloons, over which [is] a gauze petticoat, tucked up at each side in drapery, so that both thighs [can] be seen'.[15] The style catches on, with the word 'pantaloons' quickly being feminised to 'pantalettes'. A pair of pantalettes differs from drawers in that they extend to below the calf and are intended as an item of flirtation – to be seen, with lace frills around the bottom. In contrast, drawers are loosely cut, made of linen and knee-length in this period, and are not meant to be seen. By 1815 even respectable married ladies like Mrs Eliza Soane, wife of the architect John Soane, are wearing 'long cotton drawers' beneath their chemises. It still takes a certain boldness to wear them, however, given their erotic connotations. One lady writes a letter in 1817 to say that she is 'insulted' by another obviously wearing pantalettes at a function. Unsurprisingly, Anne Lister is not put off: she not only wears them herself but receives them as gifts and lends them to female friends to copy.[16]

You can't help but feel that one of the reasons why long drawers become popular with women is the warmth they offer. Wearing a thin muslin dress is something you don't really want to be doing in the cold. Thus the Grecian style is accompanied by a wave of Indian shawls and fur and feather boas, as well as fur muffs from a wide range of animals. Women wear the short 'Spencer' coat like men, and adapt the full-length redingote to be worn as an overcoat over a thin chemise dress. Pelisses too are developed for warmth in the 1790s: they are high-waisted coats made of wool or velvet that go over the dress but follow its lines. Walking around your own home in private, you might wear nothing but a pelisse over your underwear. Anne Lister only has to take off her pelisse and drawers to make love in a snatched seven minutes alone with her girlfriend in 1817.[17]

As the nineteenth century enters its second decade, the fascination with the dress of the ancient world extends to British history too. The 'democratic' urge weakens and women start to emulate Mary, queen of Scots, and Elizabeth I in their costume, even to the extent of adding mock-Tudor ruffs to their ensembles. Muslin dresses with a high waistline continue to be fashionable but the sleeves, which are generally short, are puffed out in 1820. A diaphanous petticoat beneath the muslin now gives a shimmering effect beneath the skirt, which is complemented by sequins and costly jewellery. Strings of corals remain in vogue. The hair is still normally parted in the centre and curled, so that clusters of ringlets fall on each side of the face.

From 1821, the waistline of the dress starts to descend and continues to do so year by year until in 1825 it is about two inches above its natural position. If you really want to cut a dash as you walk down Bond Street or St James's in the 1820s, you will be wearing a narrow-waisted, brightly coloured, full-skirted silk dress in a strong colour like scarlet, black or gold, which is cut very low to reveal your chemise just covering your breasts. That should be accompanied by flat-heeled shoes and long silk gloves, a long scarf or a boa of a contrasting colour draped over your shoulders, together with a large wide-brimmed hat of the same colour as your dress, tilted to one side and topped with three or four tastefully placed feathers of exotic birds. You could say that we have returned to the ostentation of the 1780s. But in fact the style expresses the exuberance of the Romantic movement and the freedom of the individual, quite unlike the formal drapery of the earlier age.

Cosmetics

At the start of our period, the prime purpose of cosmetics is to cover up the blemishes and signs of ageing that afflict a woman's face and limbs. Its application is not therefore to enhance nature but to conceal it. The philosophy may be summarised as 'paint and powder' – in which the paint is a mixture of white lead and vinegar, and the powder is made from rice flour or talcum powder. The cheeks are rouged with another white lead-based compound; the eyebrows are blackened with burnt cork or fine soot; and the lips reddened with a coloured lip salve. Many of these are available over the counter in an apothecary's shop. Unfortunately, white lead is highly toxic, so many women ruin their looks by too frequently painting their faces.[18] In some cases it proves fatal. Other means of concealing ageing or unfortunate facial features include shaving off the eyebrows and replacing them with false ones made from the hides of mice; applying lipstick made from coloured plaster of Paris; daubing on rouge composed of rock alum and Brazilwood shavings; and rubbing lotions such as Gowland's

Lotion into the face to remove pimples and freckles. Obviously, if you want to fit in with the society ladies in 1789, you will follow suit. But I cannot recommend any of these things. Not only do you not want to poison yourself with white lead, but Gowland's Lotion has mercury in it, so it will not only remove your freckles but also some of the skin on your face.

The desire to present a more natural appearance to the world following the French Revolution alters women's approach towards make-up. People start to believe that cosmetics should enhance natural beauty, not cover it up. Books such as *The Mirror of Graces* (1811) and *The Art of Beauty* (1825) outline the more sophisticated modern approach. Only natural ingredients should be used in pastes, washes, salves, balms and lotions to keep the hands soft, remove freckles and suntan, remedy cracked lips and tighten the skin. For a red lip salve, for instance, the author of *The Mirror of Graces* recommends that you take:

> A quarter pound of hard marrow from the marrow-bone. Melt it over a slow fire; as it dissolves gradually, pour the liquid marrow into an earthen pipkin; then add to it an ounce of spermaceti, twenty raisins of the sun, stoned, and a small portion of [alkanet] root, sufficient to colour it a bright vermillion. Simmer these ingredients over a slow fire for ten minutes, then strain the whole through muslin and, while hot, stir into it one teaspoon of the balsam of Peru. Pour it into the boxes in which it will remain; it will there stiffen and become fit for use.[19]

Similarly, a recipe for a natural face-wash 'for the removal of tan' includes half a pint of milk, the juice of a lemon and a spoonful of brandy all boiled together, skimmed and allowed to cool. As you can see, the look now sought after is one of pale-skinned, rosy-cheeked youth. 'Natural' beauty in Regency Britain is nothing like the suntanned look that many women aspire to in the modern world.

Ordinary Women's Clothes

While the principle that the lower social classes emulate their superiors is as true for women as it is for men, there are limitations. A working-class housewife cannot afford separate day and evening wear, or to trim her best gown with lace and bedeck her head with feathers costing £10 a piece. Nor is it necessary; she is unlikely ever to be invited to an event at which full dress is required. While many women are highly skilled seamstresses, they wouldn't dream of making for themselves clothes as elaborate as those they make for the wealthy. All they need is something attractive, hard-wearing and easy to clean.

The garments a working townswoman will put on in the morning at the start of our period include a plain linen shift, a linen or woollen petticoat (unsupported by hoops or paniers), a pair of pockets, stays, stockings, a dress (usually called a gown), low-heeled or flat shoes, a bonnet or linen cap and a shawl or cloak. The cost of such an ensemble is likely to be significant – the shift will cost 6d, the petticoat 1s–2s and the gown 3s–5s – so one set of clothes can easily cost between 16s and £1. For this reason, you will probably buy some of your clothes second-hand or make them at home from fabric bought in the market. Most towns have second-hand clothes dealers. It is always a little unnerving to find yourself looking at what other people have worn – especially if you happen to witness the pitiful sight of someone trying to sell their clothes in order to get food – but by doing so, you might be able to halve or even quarter the cost of acquiring your basic day wear. Even so, many working-class families aren't able to spend 3s or 4s on a dress. An agricultural labourer with a wife and five children under the age of eight whose annual income amounts to £22 2s cannot afford to spend more than 13s each year on cloth and thread.[20] That's less than 2s per head. Thrift is extremely important when clothes cost so much.

The general outfit worn by ordinary women does not alter a great deal over the period. Many women working in service receive cast-offs from their employers – after the lace and trimmings have been removed – and are able to rework them into something they can wear with pride. If you were to compare a maid doing the cleaning in a gentleman's town house about 1800 with her daughter doing the same job twenty-five years later, you'd see that although the types of garments have remained consistent, the fashion has changed. The older woman wears a long undecorated woollen gown with a fash-ionably high waist, a straight skirt over an unsupported petticoat, and short sleeves ending above the elbow. On her head she wears a plain linen mob-cap, into which she has tucked up her hair; suspended from her high waist is the inevitable white apron. In wet weather or when mopping the floor, she might wear 2-inch-high iron pattens to keep her shoes dry: Southey notices in 1802 how these make women 'clatter along the street like horses'.[21] Her daughter's generation may well still be wearing a mob-cap and iron pattens indoors but the cap is likely to be decorated in some way, and the improved state of the streets means she probably won't need the pattens outside. The hem of her dress is likely to be pinned up by about a foot to make it shorter when she is working, and the skirt puffed out with the support of a fuller petticoat or a bustle. Her apron will probably be red-checked cotton. She may well be wearing drawers, and her arms will probably be bare from the fashionably puffed short sleeves that don't come much further down than the shoulder. Indeed, as there is no uniform for ordinary servants, and many women are highly skilled with needle and thread, the styles of their clothing are often almost as up-to-date as those of their employers. The London fashions are quickly emulated on the streets of country towns by the wealthy, and their keen-eyed servants and the local seamstresses quickly grasp a way to copy the latest style. If the fabric has been handed down, the servant may well pass for one of the family. Many a gentleman has visited a new acquaintance at home and mistaken the parlour maid for his host's sister or daughter.

Regional Dress

The Highlander's traditional attire – the tartan plaid, long socks, buckled shoes, belt, sporran and sword – is sometimes to be seen on the streets of Lowland towns in Scotland as well as in the Highlands and islands. Some Scottish gentlemen will even wear it at society events in England, although a Scotsman in tartan is quite an unusual sight on the streets of London.[22] By the 1820s, it is most likely that a Scottish gentleman in England will be wearing a kilt rather than the full plaid of ancient times. In case you are unaware of the difference, the kilt is a pleated tartan skirt, whereas the plaid is a very long piece of cloth wrapped around the body, covering not only the torso and thighs but also the upper body and shoulder. In the Highlands, both are still worn by men of all classes. When George IV ventures north of the border in 1822 at the invitation of Sir Walter Scott, he has a traditional tartan kilt and coat made for him, to show off his

Scottish ancestry. He poses in them proudly for a portrait by the Scottish artist Sir David Wilkie, with a brace of pistols, dagger, sporran and sword, and with a green sash across his breast. Apart from those Highlanders who wear tartan trews (trousers) or tartan breeches when riding, the key feature of the dress is the display of bare legs and knees, which you simply don't see in men of distinction anywhere else in Britain.

A bare leg is also the most striking aspect of female dress in Scotland, although this is to be noted only among the working class. When Louis Simond crosses the border he describes the women he meets as going 'barefooted and bareheaded ... We see them at the fords of their little brooks, exhibiting very innocently, I believe, higher than the knee'.[23] Likewise, when Hans Caspar Escher is entertained in an industrialist's house in Glasgow in 1814, he remarks that 'all working-class women and children always go about barefoot'.[24] Otherwise the basic garments – chemise, petticoat, skirt and bodice or gown – are broadly the same as those worn in England. Towards the end of our period, shawls are becoming popular, being used coquettishly as well as for warmth. You may also see working women wearing the arisaid, the female equivalent of the long plaid, although it is not as popular as the male version. As for hats, ordinary women rarely wear them, although you will see plenty of women wearing a mutch or linen cap, rather like a mob-cap. If you travel into the Highlands, you might find a lady wearing a tartan gown, or wrapping a small silk tartan cloth around her head when attending church. Otherwise the fashionable styles seen in the assembly rooms and salons of London will govern those seen north of the border.

Women's dress in Wales is very different from that worn in England or Scotland. You will not be able to miss the black hat, sometimes tapered but more often straight, looking like a top hat. Another distinctive item is the large cap worn under it, which hangs down to the chin and frames the face. The petticoat or skirt is worn beneath a bedgown: a short-sleeved garment that comprises a bodice with tails, like a gentleman's tailcoat but which is normally made of striped flannel. Over the front of the petticoat goes an apron, which is very often checked. Around the shoulders, women wear a whittle or large square shawl. Most married women and those of marriageable age wear woollen stockings and shoes but younger women and girls may go barefooted and bareheaded.[25] Given that temperatures are colder than in modern times, you won't envy Welsh girls and Scottish women stepping across cold flagstones and pavements in bare feet.

Laundry

As we have seen, clothes are expensive. You therefore need to look after them – and this begins with keeping them clean. If you live in a large town, you might consider sending your linen out to a professional washerwoman. Even before the railways revolutionise the industry, some women have already set up services whereby they receive dirty clothes, towels and bed linen from near and far on a regular basis, launder it and return it.

Before you rush to package up all your dirty things, give some thought to the risk you are taking by sending out all your valuable clothes. In 1822, the London wine merchant James Cowie has his servant pack up all his family's dirty laundry to be sent to a washerwoman. The contents are worth in excess of £30, and include a fine dress belonging to his wife worth £6. At half past three, the carrier's boy comes by with the clean linen from the previous week and tells Mr Cowie that he will collect the new dirty load in about half an hour. At four, another person calls and collects the box of dirty laundry. It is only when the first carrier's boy comes by again at six for the laundry that the fraud is discovered. Fortunately, Mr Cowie and his wife have all their clothes and sheets embroidered with their initials, so they are able to identify them at a pawnshop, and thereby discover who took them.[26]

Most households up and down the country still do their own laundry. In Scotland, the traditional washing method among the poor is for women to lift up their skirts and simply stamp out the dirt from the clothes in a tub of hot water. In some parts of the country, stale urine is kept for the purpose of cleaning clothes, because it contains ammonia. In Lancashire the collected urine is called 'lant', while southerners refer to it euphemistically as 'chamber lye'. You won't be washing your dirty laundry in your own urine, though: neighbours tend to empty their chamber pots into a common vat, which is then used by the whole street. The stench is nauseating, so it is essential to rinse the clothes very thoroughly after their immersion and beating in the lant. In other parts of the country, people still wash with lye or wash balls, which are small lumps of potash made from burnt ferns. These clean your linen effectively, but because they are acidic they are unfortunately very tough on the skin. Thus the best way to wash your clothes is by using soap. Having said that, many women complain about the smell. In fact, they complain about the smell of soap more than they do about the stench of urine.[27]

How often you do your laundry depends on your status. If you are wealthy and have enough linen to see your household through a whole month, then you might only do the laundry every four weeks. In James Woodforde's parsonage, it is done every five weeks, when two washerwomen come by on a Monday and Tuesday to help his maids clean all the linen and clothing. The parson feeds them at mealtimes and pays them 1s each on their departure.[28] In poorer houses, the washing is normally done once a week. Women start very early in the morning to make sure it is all done in a day. Most large houses have a 'copper' – a large vat sunk into a brickwork hearth – which is used to heat the water. This is then baled into the washtub with soap and the items to be cleaned, which are beaten with a dolly (a stick with between three and six short legs at one end). Some very dirty garments have to be scrubbed on a scrubbing board prior to everything being rinsed clean and put out to dry either on a washing line or a hedge.

When it comes to smoothing the clean clothes, you might use a mangle. In all probability, this won't be the iron-framed pair of rollers with which you might be familiar: those don't start to become common until after 1830. Instead the washerwoman will use a 7ft-long chest containing several hundredweight of stones that is rolled across the wet cloth, forcing out the water and flattening the garment at the same time. Such 'box mangles' are so efficient that, for sheets and towels, you won't need to do any further smoothing or ironing. They are expensive and take up a lot of space, however, so you will only find them in large houses and professional washerwomen's premises. If you can't afford one, your next best option is to wait for the clothes to dry and then use smoothing irons. These cool quickly, so you'll want to heat up two or three near the fire before you start, so you can exchange each iron for a hotter one after it begins to cool. Alternatively, if you have no ironing equipment, you could do what some Scottish women do: they take their washing to the local grave-yard and beat it flat on a tombstone.[29]

Finally, I should point out that cleaning is considered exclusively women's work, as it has been for centuries. This won't change until men start to involve themselves in laundry as a large-scale commercial enterprise, after the advent of the railways. If a Regency man has to do any cleaning – for example, if he is a widower and too poor to send out to a washerwoman – then he usually does it furtively, late at night, to avoid the shame of being seen.

7

Travelling

Nobody is provincial in this country. You meet nowhere with those persons who never were out of their native place, and whose habits are wholly local – nobody above poverty who has not visited London once in his life; and most of those who can, visit it once a year. To go up to town from 100 or 200 miles distance is a thing done on a sudden, and without any previous deliberation. In France the people of the provinces used to make their will before they undertook such an expedition.

Louis Simond (1810)[1]

Regency roads are different from ours. Indeed, considering how consistent roads have been in their function over the last 2,000 years or so, they have altered tremendously in their form. In a fashionable city like London or Bath, you'll see wide avenues covered with flag-stones. Other towns have paved or gravel-covered streets and squares. Many have alleys cobbled with large stones. In the countryside you will come across highways and lanes that are frequently flooded and mud-clogged. Anne Lister, travelling from Chester to Manchester in 1822, declares the road 'shockingly bad for two or three miles, full of great holes and pools of water' – and that is in *July*. In December it can take her almost two hours to travel just 7½ miles.[2]

Generally speaking, the further you are from a major city, the worse the condition of the roads. Visitors to Devon and Cornwall encounter ruts cut into the mud that are more than a foot deep. Even more annoying is the fact that the old lanes are so narrow that two vehicles cannot pass each other. When you remember that carriages and wagons have no reverse gear, you can see the problem. If two meet, one of the drivers will have to get down and either back up the horses or unharness them and use them to draw his carriage backwards into a passing place. Thus travelling in the wilder parts of the country in the 1790s is a slow process. Do not expect to travel at more than 5mph in Devon and Cornwall, Scotland or North Wales, even if you have an excellent coach, an experienced driver and a fresh team of good horses.[3]

The roads are improving rapidly, however, even in these remote areas. Over the last century or so, many hundreds of Turnpike Acts have been passed by Parliament. These allow local people to set up a trust charging travellers for using a public highway, so tolls can be levied to raise money for repairs. By 1809 almost 23,000 miles of road are maintained in this manner, covering about one-fifth of the entire road system of Great Britain. As a result, travelling by coach is becoming far more efficient and pleasant. In towns like Bristol, the wheels used to judder and shake the occupants when they passed over street paviours, whereas they now tend to revolve smoothly on a gravelled road.[4] But be warned: these new, improved roads are not cheap. It might cost you just 9d to drive a coach and four along a stretch of road but this will only get you as far as the next turnpike: you will have to pay a similar sum on every section of improved road. If you are travelling a long distance, you may well spend 2d or 3d per mile on tolls. In 1795, James Woodforde pays 6d, 3s 6d and 5s 6d at various toll houses when travelling in a hired carriage from Cole in Somerset to Bath via Shepton Mallet; this amounts to almost 4d per mile.[5] While on this subject, you'll notice that many tolls are in multiples of 6d. This is because turnpike men are not obliged to give you any change, so if you only have a shilling for a 6d toll, you'll end up paying the full shilling.[6] You would therefore be well advised to carry a number of sixpences with you on your journey.

It is one thing to recognise the need for road improvement and quite another to bring it about. Fortunately, the Regency is an age of great innovators, and many of them are also road builders. One of the earliest is John Metcalf, a blind working-class lad from Knaresborough. In his long career he works as a professional musician, jockey, horse dealer, gambler, transporter of fresh fish, coach-hire merchant, smuggler of tea and rum – and expert road builder. Using only his staff as his guide, he surveys and lays out highways in his native Yorkshire as well as the surrounding counties. By the time he dies in

1810, at the grand old age of ninety-two, he has built more than 120 miles of roads.[7] And to what does he attribute his success? To his blindness, he says, because it makes him concentrate hard on every little detail of the project in hand.

Notwithstanding Metcalf's achievements, the greatest road builders of the age are Thomas Telford and John Loudon McAdam. Telford has already been mentioned as the builder of some of the most important docks, canals, aqueducts, tunnels and bridges in the country. But it is not from any of these that he gets his nickname. The poet Robert Southey calls him 'the Colossus of Roads' because, in just eighteen years, he oversees the construction of more than 1,200 miles of new roads in the Scottish Highlands. Telford is also responsible for the long-distance highways from London to Holyhead and from Bangor to Chester. He lays deep stone foundations beneath a regular smooth surface, which is carefully engineered to make sure it remains well drained. His work is excellent but expensive: some of his roads cost more than £1,000 per mile.[8] His fellow Scot, McAdam, takes the opposite approach and tries to balance engineering and cost. His method is carefully to prepare the subsoil, levelling it but incorporating a drop of one inch in the yard towards the edges for drainage, and then laying a bed of small stones 10 inches deep. This creates a surface that should only get better as more and more vehicles travel along it, compressing the stones further. By the 1820s, roads built in this way are referred to as 'macadamised'. McAdams's engineering might not be as robust as Telford's but his roads are just as satisfactory as far as most travellers are concerned.[9] The only problem is how much dust they create in dry weather – hence the water poured on them in residential parts of London in summer.

Various other improvements are made as the number of road users increases. For example, it is not yet compulsory to drive on the left – it won't be until the Highway Act of 1835 – but it is increasingly becoming normal practice.[10] Another improvement is the building of better bridges. The pleasure of travelling along a newly macadamised highway – at considerable expense in tolls – is somewhat lessened if your journey comes to a halt at a rickety old wooden bridge or a muddy ford. Thomas Telford's 1,200 miles of roads in the Highlands require no fewer than 1,100 new river crossings. In England, although many fine bridges still stand from the medieval and Tudor periods, new ones are now built wherever the existing one is inadequate, often making use of new technologies. The first iron bridge, at Coalbrookdale in Shropshire, is already open, having been completed in 1780. A second is built at Wearmouth in 1796, designed by Thomas Paine (better known as the radical writer Tom Paine, author of *Rights of Man*). A third, at Buildwas in Herefordshire, is also completed in 1796, designed by Thomas Telford. Many more follow.[11] As you would expect, these are all supported by tolls. If you wish to cross Tom Paine's bridge in a gig with one horse, expect to pay 2s 6d. Crossing in a coach and four will cost you a whopping 7s. Even pedestrians have to pay 3d on a weekday or 6d on a Sunday.[12]

The earliest suspension bridges in this country are pedestrian-only. After 1800 the Americans construct several large enough to carry carriages but the technology is taken to a new level by Commander Samuel Brown of the Royal Navy, a specialist in producing heavyweight chains. In 1813 he builds a 105ft-long model of a suspension bridge, which receives the approval of the engineers Thomas Telford and John Rennie.[13] Together with Rennie, Brown constructs the Union Suspension Bridge over the Tweed, between Horncliffe in England and Fishwick in Scotland. When it opens in 1820, it is the longest single-span bridge in the world, at 449 feet. From then on suspension bridges are all the rage. Three particularly noteworthy examples are Thomas Telford's magnificent 579ft-long bridge over the Menai Straits, which is finished in 1826; William Clark's crossing over the Thames at Hammersmith, completed in 1827; and the Stockton Railway Bridge, the world's first train-carrying suspension bridge, designed by Samuel Brown and built in 1830. Aesthetically as well as practically, these constitute some of the most impressive engineering achievements of the age.

Walking

You don't need to spend much time in Regency Britain before you notice that people are far more accustomed to walking long distances than we are. Travelling by coach is expensive, and even maintaining a riding horse is more than most people can afford. Thus the working class see 'Shanks's pony' – their own legs – as their only means of getting about. When James Woodforde sends his servant boy to do some shopping in Norwich, 10 miles away, the lad walks into the city and back in a day.[14] But that's just a short walk by Regency standards. The Lancashire weaver Samuel Bamford thinks nothing of walking the 260 miles from Middleton to London. Sometimes walking can be faster than travelling by coach. John Metcalf meets an old friend, Captain Liddell, in London and is offered a lift home in the captain's carriage to Harrogate. John declines on account of the fact that, even though he is blind, he can walk the distance faster than Captain Liddell can drive it. The captain bets him he can't. John covers the 210 miles on foot in five and a half days – and wins the bet.[15]

It isn't only men who walk long distances. Groups of young women and girls appear on the highways in summer, walking from Wales or Shropshire to London to work in the seasonal fruit and vegetable sales. Once they arrive in the South-east they transport loads of up to 50lbs on their heads between the market gardens west of the city and the central markets, doing the 11-mile trip from Isleworth to Covent Garden twice a day. Often they catch a lift back on a cart to the market garden but, even so, they regularly walk more than 130 miles a week, mostly with a load. And at the end of the season they walk the 160 miles or more back home.[16]

If you choose to see Regency Britain on foot, you'll be grateful for the many milestones and fingerposts that have been put up over the last 150 years showing the direction to nearby towns, together with their distances. You can also buy maps of the country, easily folded for the pocket, which show all the major roads and towns.[17] Despite this, very few people of quality walk any great way. If you arrive somewhere on foot, it will be presumed that you cannot afford any other form of transportation. 'A pedestrian seems in this country to be a sort of beast of passage – stared at, pitied, suspected and shunned by everybody who meets him,' writes Karl Moritz during his walking tour of the country. Entering an inn at Eton, he recalls:

> I could see at once from the expression of the waiter that I was unwelcome. They served me like a beggar, with muttering and neglect, but charged me like a gentleman. I honestly believe the fellow thought it not proper for him to wait on a miserable mortal who went afoot.[18]

Riding

Riding is not only good exercise, it is also one of the fastest forms of transport. Walking 30 miles takes a whole day but most reasonably fit people can ride that distance in less than five hours.[19] To go any faster than that – or to go much further at the same speed – requires at least one change of horses and increasing levels of endurance on the part of the rider. The record is set by the sportsman George Osbaldeston, who rides 200 miles using a team of twenty-eight horses at Newmarket racecourse, just after the end of our period, in 1831. His finishing time of 8 hours 42 minutes equates to an average speed of 23mph. This is exceptional, more than twice as fast as most mail coaches and far quicker than Lieutenant Lapenotière's epic journey in bringing the news of the Battle of Trafalgar from Falmouth to the Admiralty in London in 1805. That 267-mile dash takes him thirty-seven hours, an average speed of 7.2mph.[20] Frankly, if you want to travel faster than George Osbaldeston, you'll need to catch a train.

The drawback to riding is the expense. First there is the cost of buying a suitable mount, which can set you back anything from £8 for a barely adequate old beast to ten times that for a young, well-trained horse suitable for a cavalry officer. Anne Lister buys a colt for £25 in 1822, hearing on good authority that in two years' time he could be worth 100 guineas. She calls him Hotspur. After just one year, a veterinary surgeon assures her that Hotspur is already worth 50 guineas and in another year or so, if he stays healthy, 'a dealer would match him and sell the pair for 400 guineas'.[21] That would be an exceptional price but if you want a matching pair for a smart carriage you will have to pay at least £70, with highly prized pairs normally in the range of £200 and upwards.[22]

The expenses of riding mount up further when you factor in maintenance. If you have your own stable and are in the London area, expect to fork out about £120 every year for one horse, including the services of a groom and occasionally a farrier.[23] If you live in a city, a livery stable is likely to cost you just over £60 per year.[24] Perhaps you should consider whether you really need your own horse: you might be better off hiring one from a reputable establishment. Expect to pay 6d per mile, plus a deposit for the animal and its harness. At 15s for a 30-mile journey, you can see why riding is such a mark of social distinction – and why innkeepers are far keener to welcome clients on horseback than those arriving on foot.

Private Carriages

The author of *The Traveller's Oracle* reports in 1827 that 'the art of coach-making within these last thirty years has been improved greatly in beauty, strength and convenience, and a carriage is now considered as a distinguishing mark of the taste of its proprietor'.[25] Two important innovations are crucial to this development. One is the invention of elliptical springs, which give carriages proper suspension. The other, even more significant, is the iron-hooped tire. A Regency wheel is put together by fitting the wooden spokes into the central hub and hammering on the felloes (which form the rim of the wheel), and then heating up the iron tire, so that it expands and can be placed around the outside of the felloes. When the tire cools, it contracts onto the assembly, fastening the whole wheel together much more firmly and providing one long uninterrupted running surface all the way round the wheel. This is an enormous improvement on earlier tires, which used to be nailed on as separate pieces. These did not hold the component parts together as a unit, so the wheel lacked strength and could easily break if it struck a rock. Also, the separate pieces of iron made for a bumpy ride. Thus travelling in a carriage in the 1790s is a much more comfortable experience than it was a couple of decades earlier.

Generally speaking, you can divide vehicles into two categories: those that you drive yourself and those in which you are driven. Among the former there are four-wheeled, lightweight carriages, like the phaeton, pulled by two horses. There are also several types of fast two-seater, two-wheeled vehicles for going around town or making short journeys in the country. The most common of these is the gig, which is drawn by one horse. If you enter the showroom of a coach-works you'll see many variants on this, including the Tilbury, designed by the Hon. Henry Fitzroy Stanhope in about 1812; the Stanhope, designed by the same gentleman in about 1815; and the Dennet. The different types relate to their suspension, the size of wheels, location of luggage space and whether they have splashboards (to protect the driver from being soaked by puddles) and canopies. Alternatively, the carriage salesman might offer you a curricle, drawn by two horses; or a cabriolet, with a covered double seat, pulled by a single horse. If you want a fast single-seater, you have the option of a whisky, which has two high wheels and is just the thing for driving around your estate, or, if you are very daring, a skeleton gig, which has a single seat on a central shaft and no other surrounding bodywork. These are for racing – and are fast to the point of being dangerous.

A coach is the catch-all term for a large, enclosed carriage with four wheels, normally drawn by four horses, harnessed in pairs. It generally has four or six seats inside, windows in the doors on each side, and exterior seats at the front. The coachman sits on one of the exterior front seats. Often there is standing room at the rear for footmen, or a trunk for luggage. A larger, slower form of a coach is a diligence, which is much longer and more like a bus. The wealthy do not travel in such vehicles. They do, however, use the post-chaise, which is an enclosed, four-wheeled carriage, with two or three front-facing seats. The cab is much smaller than that of a coach, with windows to the front as well as the sides. Rather than being driven by a coachman, the two horses are guided by a postilion, riding the left-hand horse. Sometimes there is also a dickey seat above the rear luggage chest for exterior passengers. Or children who can be trusted to hang on.

For those who can afford it, travelling in style around town on a summer's day calls for a barouche or a landau. Both these types of luxurious convertible carriage have two pairs of seats facing each other: in the barouche the collapsible canopy (called a calash) only covers the rear pair of seats; in a landau there is a separate canopy covering the front ones too. Both are driven by a coachman, of course, who sits on a raised seat at the front. Another type of upper-class vehicle that you might come across is a travelling chariot: a lightweight four-wheeled carriage, with only a pair of back seats within the closed body and a separate raised seat up front for the coachman.

What will you have to pay for one of these carriages? At the bottom end of the market, you can buy a new gig for around £40 or a second-hand one for half that sum. At the top end, you can spend more than £1,000 on a grand coach to be drawn by six horses. In 1821 Anne Lister visits a coachbuilder in York and is offered a Dennet for £44, with £2 extra for lamps; a Tilbury for £52 10s; and a Stanhope for £47,

including the harness. Or, the salesman tells her, she can buy a travelling chariot for £180.[26] These prices are not exorbitant. The travelling
chariot made for the Lenthall family of Abingdon in 1817 – complete
with gun compartment, in case of highwaymen – costs £344.[27] At that
price, you might opt instead to hire a carriage and let someone else
take care of the maintenance and the harness. An ordinary post-chaise
will cost a standard 1s per mile, and a coach and four 2s 6d per mile.
Don't forget to allow for food and drink for your coachman at every
inn where you stop, and for tips too – normally at the rate of 1s for
every 20 miles.

How fast will you be able to travel in a private carriage? Most people
drive at 5–7mph. James Woodforde usually does the 10 miles from
Norwich to his rectory in Weston in two hours. Louis Simond similarly
travels at a steady 5mph in Devon, and at 6mph or more in Somerset.
Anne Lister personally drives her new gig eight miles in ninety minutes
in North Wales.[28] These speeds reflect the normal rate at which people
go about their business.[29] But if you want to go somewhere fast, you
will probably opt to use public transport. As you will see, coachmen
who work for transport companies don't care how hard they have to
whip their horses, whereas those who use their own animals usually
do.[30]

Public Transport

There are about a thousand hackney cabs in London. You can recognise them from their yellow-painted coachwork and black roofs, as
well as the licence number on a tin plate fixed to the bodywork. Unless
the driver has already been working for twelve hours, he is compelled
under the terms of his licence to take you to any place you want to
go within 10 miles of the city. Even after dark he is obliged to carry
you up to 2½ miles from London if the highways are illuminated
with street lights. The fares are a standard 1s for a journey of up to
1¼ miles and 2s for up to 2½ miles, with an additional 6d being
charged for each additional half-mile. Note that after dark you'll have
to pay an extra 6d per half-mile on top of these sums. You'll also have
to pay if you keep your driver waiting (when you go shopping, for
instance): 1s for up to 45 minutes, 1s 6d for an hour, and then 6d for
every twenty minutes beyond that.[31]

In well-to-do cities like London and Bath you have the option of using one of the hundreds of sedan chairs available. These are already a little old-fashioned but they are convenient in wet weather, or where your journey takes you along a narrow passageway or up a flight of steps, or where the pavement is simply too filthy. They are, however, an expensive way to travel. In Bath, where all the chairmen wear a distinctive dark-blue livery, the set fees are 6d for a journey of less than 500 yards, 1s for a journey up to two-thirds of a mile, and 6d for every third of a mile beyond that. And they are slow. The chair and poles are quite heavy, and even if you're not particularly over-weight, two men won't be able to carry you very far without regular rests. And if you're a bit chubby – well, the carriers will hope for a tip in proportion to your size.

If you need to travel further afield, you have a choice. One option is to take a ride in a carrier's wagon. These are long and wide, and covered with an arched canvas awning bearing the name of the propri-etor and the inns where they start and end their journey. The carrier himself walks beside his animals with a long whip over his shoulder.[32] The problem is that such vehicles are designed to transport bundles, crates, trunks and boxes, not people. With an average speed of just 3mph, you could walk faster. They are only useful for personal trans-port if you are poor and unable to walk, and then only for local trips. It takes a carrier a full five days to travel from Bath to London. The expense of being on the road that long, and having to stay four nights at inns, defeats the purpose of opting for cheap travel. Thus your real choice of public transport between towns comes down to taking either a stagecoach or a mail coach.

STAGECOACHES

The type of stagecoach known as a diligence has a long body with three windows on each side, with steps up to the single door at the rear. Inside, there are two benches facing each other, each one having space for between eight and twelve people.[33] Passengers always seem to take the extreme seats first – at the far end or by the door, so latecomers will need to sit in the middle. These coaches are not built for speed: those with sixteen seats might do 4½mph when drawn by four horses.[34] But they serve their purpose in conveying many people faster than they can walk, at low cost. In July 1829 one such vehicle appears on the Marylebone Road, with yellow-painted wheels and a decorated blue superstructure. Drawn by three horses abreast, this is the world's first 'omnibus', designed and operated by George Shillibeer: it does the journey between Paddington and central London four times a day. But while long coaches are fine for short urban journeys, especially when it is raining, you don't want to spend too much time in them. Robert Southey illustrates why in his description of a trip in a sixteen-seater from Bristol to Birmingham in 1807:

> The atmosphere ... was neither fresher nor more fragrant than that of a prison ... I never before passed five hours travelling so unpleasantly. To see anything was impossible; the little windows behind us were on a level with our heads, the coachman's seat obstructed the one in front, and that in the doorway was of use only to those who sat by it. Any attempt which we made at conversation by way of question was answered with forbidding brevity; the company was too numerous to be communicative. Half of them went to sleep and I endeavoured to follow their example.[35]

The faster types of stagecoach differ principally according to their size and the luxuriousness of their fittings. The best have leather upholstery and opening-and-closing glass windows to protect you from the elements and the dust of the street. You might have a lamp above your head and even a hot-water bottle for your feet. You can quite comfortably read a book in such a vehicle, even at night. Prince Hermann Pückler-Muskau writes to his wife that 'I lit the lamp in the carriage and read Lady Morgan's latest novel with great pleasure while we rolled swiftly over the level road.'[36]

Such journeys are expensive, of course. Thus many people opt instead to travel as outside passengers. Most stagecoaches can only accommodate six people within the cabin, but by elongating the section at the rear where luggage is stowed (the 'trunk'), and by lengthening the space at the front between the coachman's bench and the cabin, you can create more space for seating and standing. Passengers can also sit on the roof. As Karl Moritz informs us:

> Poor people who cannot afford to pay much ride in this way – on the top of the coach without any seat or handhold being provided. They

sit there anyhow they can, with their legs dangling over the side. This is called 'riding on the outside', for which they are only charged half as much ... We had another six passengers over our heads in this way and they made a terrific clatter with their frequent mounting and dismounting ... If you can keep a level balance on top of a coach you can sit there well enough, and in some ways you should be better off than those riding on the inside, especially on a hot day, and the view of the surrounding scenery is better, but the companionship is a trifle plebeian and the dust a nuisance. Those riding on the inside can at least shut the windows.[37]

But then Herr Moritz tries riding on top for himself and reports that:

When I got on top I made straight for a corner where I could sit and take hold of a little handle on the side of the coach. I sat over the wheel and imagined I saw certain death before my eyes as soon as we set off. All I could do was to take a firmer grip of the handle and keep my balance. The coach rolled along the stony street at great speed and every now and then we were tossed into the air; it was a near wonder that I always landed back on the coach.[38]

Fear won't be your only problem if you choose to travel on top. Those at the back can't see where they're going, which makes many of them feel sick.[39] Those travelling at the front get the weather full in their faces. For this reason many people carry an umbrella with them. Then there is the modesty problem: women and girls can hardly climb up on to a roof without showing their legs.[40] It is especially risky on the way down, when skirts and petticoats can easily get snagged on a hook or door handle. The cold can be bitter, especially in winter, with the added wind chill of the carriage's speed. Occasionally passengers get frostbite or even die of exposure on the roof, as happens to two people in March 1812, travelling between Bath and Chippenham.[41] Many coaches don't depart from an inn until after midnight, so if you're travelling as an outside passenger in winter, you had better wrap up warm.

How much will a stagecoach cost you, and how fast will you go? The answers to these questions differ from year to year and from route to route. Take the London to Brighton road, for example. In

1789 only a handful of daily coaches do this 54-mile journey. Leaving London at 5 a.m., you should arrive before 7 p.m., making it a fourteen-hour journey. It will cost you about 23s, or 13s if you travel on the outside (not including tips). However, the following year a partnership starts up with the aim of providing a flying coach that does the journey in just eight hours. Very soon more companies enter the market. Prices fall, speeds increase and the number of vehicles on the roads mushrooms. By 1811, twenty-eight coaches are doing the journey every day; the fastest time is now six hours and prices have plummeted to 10s for an inside seat and 5s for an outside one. Two years later, you can catch a stagecoach from London that will take you to Brighton *and back* in a single day. In 1815, fifty-two coaches are on the route, their competitive coachmen all lashing their horses mercilessly; fifteen horses die in just one week the following year. Thereafter there is a period of consolidation. By 1822, the journey time has dropped to four hours, an average speed of more than 13mph.[42]

Similar changes can be seen on other routes. In 1700 you could spend ten days travelling the 378 miles from London to Edinburgh; by 1830 this has come down to forty-six hours. Whereas there used to be only one coach plying the trade between Manchester and London in 1700, by the end of our period there are more than thirty, and the time taken to do the journey has fallen from ninety hours to eighteen – an average speed of 10mph.[43] On the whole, you can assume a stagecoach will transport you at an average 5–7mph in the 1790s and 7–10mph in the 1820s. Perhaps the fastest performance on record for our period is set on May Day 1830, when the coach known as 'The Independent Tally Ho' travels the 109 miles from London to Birmingham in 7 hours and 39 minutes – an average speed of 14.25mph.[44] By this time, the entire coaching business has acquired a much greater sense of urgency. Now, servants bring refreshments out from an inn to serve you as you wait in your carriage while the horses are changed. The changes themselves are much faster, as timetables force stable boys to have the replacements ready and waiting. Inns on coaching routes have become twenty-four-hour establishments as travellers prepare to leave in the early hours. Lights in the yards burn all night as grooms ready themselves for the sound of urgent hooves clattering over the cobbles in the dark.

MAIL COACHES

Mail coaches are not stagecoaches as such but a transport system designed to move packages as quickly and as efficiently as possible. The vehicles selected for the task are post-chaises – the same four-wheeled closed carriages that you might hire for private use – and their teams of four horses are changed every 10 miles, with stops sometimes taking as little as a minute. They also carry fare-paying passengers: three inside the coach and two on top, at most. You can take nothing bulkier than hand luggage with you. You aren't allowed more than twenty minutes for meals, and the post boy, who rides postilion, will make sure you stick to these times. Whereas stage-coaches are often delayed by their passengers and innkeepers en route, the mail coaches are governed by a strict timetable. Indeed, they have to travel even if there are no passengers, whereas stagecoach drivers often delay departure until all the seats are full. Dependability and speed are thus their main selling points. Mail coaches also have greater security in that they are protected by an armed guard, who rides with the mail sacks at the back. And they are exempt from having to pay tolls. Considering you'll be forking out 1s per mile, and 1s to the post boy as a tip every 10 miles or so, that last point is worth bearing in mind.

SAFETY

The presence of armed guards will remind you that travelling between towns carries the risk of being accosted by highwaymen. But although there are numerous attacks up and down the country, the truth is that you are more likely to be injured in a traffic accident. Therefore you might like to bear in mind the following health-and-safety issues when considering a coach journey.

First, if you have a large number of people sitting on top of an 8ft-high carriage, plus two dozen suitcases and travelling bags stacked up behind them, the centre of gravity is significantly raised, making the coach top-heavy. This is especially the case in summer, when more people want to save money and travel in the open air. Stagecoach drivers can be prosecuted for allowing more than six on the roof: fines of 40s per person are introduced in 1795. Despite this, you often see twelve or fourteen passengers on the top of a long coach. Louis Simond once counts seventeen.[45] As he himself remarks, this increases the likelihood that it will overturn on a bend, especially if it is going at speed.

Second, coachmen increasingly drive as fast as they possibly can. In so doing they are not only supported by their employers, who want to claim that they run the fastest coaches on a particular route, but also by the passengers, who want to reach their destinations as quickly as possible. However, this means the vehicles are often driven in a reckless manner – at great danger to pedestrians and even greater peril to the occupants. As a result, accidents are common, and they happen to every class of traveller. In 1806, the princess of Wales has an accident when she urges her coachman to drive faster and he does so, overturning on a corner and leaving one of the princess's companions fatally injured. James Wyatt, the prince of Wales's architect, is killed in a coach accident in September 1813. The landscape gardener, Humphry Repton, spends the rest of his life in a wheelchair after an accident on the way home from a ball in 1811. You may think that coaches are quaint and slow-moving but the truth is they are anything but. In the circumstances, it is not entirely surprising that one company on the London to Brighton route puts on a service that is deliberately slow. The proprietor targets his advertising at old ladies and people of a nervous disposition, calling his coach 'The Life Preserver'.[46]

New Forms of Road Transport

In such an age of invention, it is hardly surprising that people put some thought into other potentially lucrative forms of transport. On the streets of the capital you cannot miss the velocipedes that suddenly appear in 1818, after their invention in Germany the previous year. Also known as 'dandy-horses' or 'hobby-horses', these wood-and-metal contraptions are effectively bicycles without pedals. You use your feet to push yourself along. Denis Johnson, a coachbuilder in London, realises their potential and improves the design, patenting his 'pedestrian curricle' in December 1818. More than 300 are manufactured the following year, each priced at £8, with four being ordered by the Prince Regent to be sent to Brighton.[47] Although the craze is only temporary, it fuels a wider interest in alternative modes of transport. In February 1820, Anne Lister pays a visit to the Museum Room in Albion Street, Leeds, to see 'the newly invented carriage propelled by the feet of the person going in it'. She describes it as a 'very simple mechanism, like a small gig on three wheels', noting that the price of this model is £35 and that of a larger example able to carry two people is £45.[48] A few years later Prince Hermann Pückler-Muskau inspects a kite-drawn vehicle invented by a schoolmaster that is reputedly capable of attaining a speed of 45mph.[49] The drawbacks of such a contraption are obvious but, nevertheless, people have clearly begun to think of ways of travelling that were previously unimaginable.

The widespread interest in improving transport is evident when you look at the dozens of relevant patents granted in these years. Patent number 1,767, taken out in July 1790, is for an extendable carriage with six wheels and three sets of springs that overcomes the problems of potholes and may be extended to have up to forty-eight seats. Patent number 2,431, granted in 1800, is for 'driving carriages of all kinds, without the use of horses, by means of an improved Aeolian engine, driven by compressed air'. However, the real game-changer comes in 1802, when Richard Trevithick and his cousin Andrew Vivian are granted patent number 2,599 for 'a carriage for common road purposes to be propelled by steam'. This relates to Trevithick's experimental steam engine, *Puffing Devil*, which the two men have demonstrated is able to travel at 9mph in Camborne. Driven on by public enthusiasm, Trevithick and other engineers push ahead with the development of steam locomotives. The success of Matthew Murray's *Salamanca* at the Middleton colliery near Leeds in 1812 inspires a flurry of others: William Hedley designs *Puffing Billy* and *Wylam Dilly* for Wylam colliery in 1813; William Chapman and William Brunton build experimental steam engines for collieries in 1813 and 1814 respectively; and George Stephenson produces his first locomotive, *Blücher*, in 1814. Stephenson then goes on to build at least a dozen more locomotives and to establish the basic principles that underpin the railways of the future.

For the purposes of passenger transport, the key date you'll want to put in your diary is 27 September 1825 – the opening of the Stockton and Darlington Railway, engineered by George Stephenson to connect all the collieries of south-west Durham. That day, a train of passengers and goods wagons is hauled along at speeds of up to 16mph. Most people have never travelled so fast. The Canterbury and Whitstable Railway starts carrying both passengers and goods in May 1830, using a steam engine, *Invicta*, built by Stephenson's company. At the same time, Stephenson is overseeing the construction of the Liverpool and Manchester Railway. In September 1830 his famous *Rocket* enters service, pulling the first scheduled passenger train on the line between Liverpool and Manchester at speeds of up to 30mph. Soon 30,000 people are travelling on the line every month. At the end of the year there are about 100 miles of track in use in England. The Railway Age has truly begun.

Water Transport

The advantages of living on an island often go unappreciated. People tend to stress the defensive aspects of being surrounded by a large body of water, thinking of it as a barrier, whereas the sea is really a superhighway. If you want to transport large quantities of coal or iron ore from one place to another, it will take you a very long time if you use wagons that can only carry a ton. Much greater loads can be transported by ship. Moreover, as Great Britain has so many estuaries, all you need to do to maximise the value of your cargo is to convey it to a navigable river. Thus the rivers and the sea are as much an asset to Great Britain's economic development as its burgeoning workforce and mineral resources.

Landowners and entrepreneurs have been aware of this fact for many years. Since the mid-seventeenth century they have been improving waterways by dredging rivers, removing boulders, straightening tight bends and widening narrows. In addition, they have been building canals between major rivers. These not only enable raw materials to be shipped to the industrial towns but also provide routes for finished goods to reach wholesalers and retailers. The engineer James Brindley is the first to see the commercial advantages of joining up the four most important rivers in England – the Trent, the Mersey, the Severn and the Thames – in a 'grand cross' of waterways, thereby linking the four great trading ports of Hull, Liverpool, Bristol and London. His vision is finally completed in 1790 when the Midlands waterways are connected to the River

Thames by means of the Coventry Canal and the Oxford Canal. Now cargoes can be transported between the Irish Sea and the North Sea without having to go around Land's End or John O'Groats. That same year, a 35-mile canal linking the Forth and the Clyde opens, allowing vessels to travel across the middle of Scotland.[50] Such is the enthusiasm for canals that more than fifty are given the go-ahead by Parliament between 1790 and 1794. Even after 1800, dozens are constructed, some of them incorporating remarkable engineering feats, such as tunnels more than three miles long and inclined planes, which lift boats from one level of a canal to another. By 1830, the canal system amounts to some 4,100 miles, approximately three times its extent in 1760.[51]

SEAFARING

Shipping sees a similar level of investment as canals and stagecoach routes. In 1788, there are 12,464 registered vessels in the United Kingdom; thirty years later, the number has grown to more than 22,000.[52] The country requires more merchant ships and a more substantial navy to respond to the needs of a burgeoning population, increased trade and a growing empire. In addition, there are thousands of small, unregistered boats dotted in and around the coast: from the estuarine fishing smacks and oystermen to the ketches, hoys and sloops you'll see tied up in every harbour. It is only when you watch all the comings and goings along an estuary that you fully realise how much the British depend on the sea.

With regard to your own journey plans, you'll need to think about how much a passage to your destination will cost you, where you need to sail from and what sort of conditions you can expect on board. Let's suppose you are looking at a voyage aboard a packet boat. This is normally a medium-sized, two- or three-masted vessel of about 200 tons burden, sailing out of one of the packet stations maintained by the Post Office until 1823, and after that by the Admiralty. Their prime purpose is to take parcels and letters to British colonies and overseas embassies. Thus each of these stations facilitates access to specific sea lanes. Milford Haven and Holyhead serve the south and the north of Ireland respectively; Dover sends ships to France; boats from Harwich and Great Yarmouth head across the North Sea; and Falmouth has

the important role of despatching vessels for North and South America,
the Mediterranean and the Far East.

Turning up at a packet station and entering the office, you might
well see a printed list of prices on the wall. In Falmouth, for example,
you can buy tickets to New York, Nova Scotia, Rio de Janeiro, Buenos
Aires, Madeira, Lisbon, Cadiz, Gibraltar, Jamaica, the Leeward Isles
and Surinam. Note that the prices for outward-bound and return
voyages can differ considerably. In 1811, a cabin to Rio de Janeiro will
cost you £86 but the return voyage will set you back £107. The main
reason is that the outward trip normally takes only thirty-five days
whereas the return is usually fifty-two. With Jamaica, the reverse is
true: getting there takes fifty-two days and costs £60 but returning
normally takes forty-five days and will set you back just £54.[53]

As you can see, cabins are not cheap. And these prices aren't all-
inclusive either: you will have to provide your own furniture, candles,
candlesticks and bedding, as well as any utensils you might need on
the voyage. If you want any food above the most basic rations, you'll
need to take it yourself. I recommend packing your own sugar, jam,
eggs, biscuits, cheese and ham and perhaps pickles and potted meat,
as well as anything else you fancy that can be kept at room temperature for up to eight weeks at sea. But the difficult question is whether
you should save money by travelling steerage? This will cost you a
mere £46 to Rio and only £56 on the return journey – saving almost
half the price of a cabin. But a cabin is considerably more comfortable. It will normally be a panelled room at the stern of the lower
deck, extending to half the width of the boat, with angled windows
at the rear, overlooking the rudder. It might even have space for a
sofa or a table and chair, as well as a bed. Steerage berths, on the
other hand, are kennel-like bunks built into the cargo areas of a large
ship or, on a packet boat, around the middle and forward section of
the lower deck. They are arranged in tiers of three, each one being
1½ feet wide, with barely 2 feet of headroom. They open directly
on to the central area of the lower deck, where there is a long
communal dining table, and offer no privacy except when you lie in
your bunk, with the curtain drawn across. Washing has to be done
in public – or, rather, *male* passengers have to wash in public. Women
are not permitted to disrobe publicly, so they cannot normally wash
at all, if they are travelling steerage, for the entire duration of the
voyage.[54]

Whether you are travelling cabin-class or steerage, a sea voyage is generally not a pleasant experience. The days are governed by a routine that is grimly monotonous. You will rise by seven o'clock. There is a time set for meals and for prayers, and a time for cleaning the berths and the cabins. Afternoons are generally given over to conversation, journal-writing and card playing (but no gambling). Alternatively, you might opt to do a little exercise on deck, if the weather is good enough, although passengers are forbidden from climbing the rigging. When darkness falls, candles are lit – but in communal areas they have to be extinguished by 9 p.m. and in cabins by 10 p.m., due to the danger of fire. This means you'll probably lie awake in your berth in darkness, listening to the constant creaking of the ship's timbers and the whistling of the wind in the rigging. You may hear some of your fellow passengers vomiting into buckets with the pitching and rolling of the ship. When the weather takes a turn for the worse, you will feel anything but comfortable. Huge waves hit the ship with a massive dull thud. You might hear glass tinkling in your cabin as a large wave crashes into the stern. The water running across the floor in the darkness will no doubt cause you to pray, even if you are not religious. You'll clutch your blanket in your bunk and thank God that you're not up on deck, having to haul in a sail or make the equipment safe.

The one form of sea voyage you want to avoid above all others is an involuntary one – being pressganged for the navy. As the war with France creates a desperate need for naval manpower, pressgangs kidnap working men when they are out drinking with their friends in a port late at night. Sometimes the pressgang will ransack every public house they come to and take away all able-bodied men within. *The Times* regularly reports 'hot presses' in which 500 or 600 men are taken in London in a single night and forced on to rowing boats and galleys, which take them straight out to sea. If people are held in prisons, prior to being taken on board, they will go to almost any lengths to avoid being pressed into the navy. When Samuel Caradise is held in Kendal Prison, waiting to be transferred to a ship, he sends for his wife. What happens on the evening before his intended departure is described in *The Times* for 3 November 1795: 'He was in a cell and she spoke to him through the iron door. After which, he put his hand underneath and she, with a mallet and chisel, concealed for the purpose, struck off a finger and thumb, to render him unfit for his majesty's service.'[55]

STEAMSHIPS

In 1800, a steamship is still an object of curiosity for most members of the public. But that year Lord Dundas, the governor of the Forth and Clyde Canal Company, commissions William Symington to build the *Charlotte Dundas*, a 56ft-long steamboat driven by a single rear-mounted paddle. It is launched in January 1803. Nine years later, the first regular steam passenger service opens on the Clyde. When Hans Caspar Escher looks out over the river in August 1814, he can see six steamers at once. A year later, there are thirteen on the same stretch of water and, by the end of our period, seventy-one. Across the whole kingdom, 300 steamships are plying the rivers, canals, estuaries and the high seas by 1830.[56]

The year 1815 is when most people in Britain become aware of the potential of steamboats. First, one leaves the Clyde and docks in Liverpool. Soon afterwards another, the *Marjory*, puffs eastwards along the Forth and Clyde Canal, enters the North Sea and steams all the way down the east coast to London. Then the *Duke of Argyle* does a similar journey from Glasgow down the west coast and around Land's End to London. Advertisements appear for new steamboat services in the capital. The *Marjory* goes up and down the old ferry route on the Thames between London and Gravesend; the *Duke of Argyle* is renamed the *Thames* and put on the London to Margate route. Steamboats start running the sea lanes between Greenock and Belfast in 1818 and between Glasgow, Liverpool and the Isle of Man in 1819. In 1821 Anne Lister takes a steam packet called the *Favourite* from Selby in Yorkshire to London. She embarks at 9.25 one morning, docks in Hull that evening, stays at an inn, re-embarks the following morning and arrives in London at 6 p.m. A few days later she takes a stagecoach to Dover, stays there overnight and boards another steam packet, which takes less than three hours to convey her in rough seas to Calais.[57] Apart from being sick eight times during the Channel crossing, her whole journey is untroubled and unhurried – yet it would have been a furious dash to cover the distance of almost 300 miles by stagecoach and sailing boat in as little time.

Early steamships are wooden and mostly between 80 and 100 feet in length. The majority have two paddle wheels between 9 and 12 feet in diameter, one on each side, but some are powered by a single wheel at the rear. Many have additional masts and sails, in case of problems with the engine or poor-quality coal. Inside, the main cabin is normally an open-plan, carpeted area occupying the full width of the ship, with a series of windows above the deck on both sides. Benches run the length of the interior, beneath the windows, with tables arranged around the cabin for playing chess, draughts, backgammon or cards, to eat cake and drink tea, and read books from the ship's library.[58] As long as you stay inside, steamships are clean; but if you go out on deck you will be covered in smoke. Overall, they give a sense of style, modernity and luxury, and high prices are charged accordingly. A ticket on the London to Margate service, for example, costs between 7s and 15s, with children going half price.

Despite the cost, steamships grow popular as a form of travel. In 1822, more than 27,000 passengers travel on them between London and Margate; three years later, more than 50,000 do so.[59] By then they have crossed the Atlantic and even reached India. Their great advantage is that they can be operated even if the wind is blowing in the wrong direction. No more will you arrive at a port to find your ship has already left on account of the wind having been on the turn a few hours earlier.[60] Both operators and customers can be much more confident of sailing times.

SAFETY AT SEA

Hundreds of vessels of all sorts go down around the shores of Great Britain every year, sometimes with the most appalling loss of life. In 1789, the *Adventure* sinks off Tynemouth Haven, in front of many onlookers, who cannot help but watch in horror as the crew drown before their eyes. Another case of lives being lost very close to land occurs in 1800, when HMS *Brazen* hits the rocks near Newhaven. She is less than half a mile from shore, yet only one member of her 105-strong crew survives. And so on. If you go to sea, there will inevitably come the day when you spot the sad, blackened hulk of something that was once part of a ship drifting by – and you will realise that the same thing could easily happen to your vessel.

The good news is that in 1789 there are already more than two dozen lighthouses around the shores of Great Britain – from the Lizard in Cornwall to Kinnaird Head in Aberdeenshire. Soon dozens more are being built or rebuilt. By 1830 another twenty-five lighthouses have been constructed around the coast of Scotland under the direction of Thomas Smith and his stepson, Robert Stevenson, working for the Commissioners of Northern Light Houses. As many again are constructed in those years around the coasts of England and Wales, under the guidance of Trinity House. Moreover, these new lights are much brighter than their predecessors, using Argand-style lamps rather than tallow candles or coal fires. In addition, they come to incorporate clockwork-driven revolving frames, so the lights seem to blink a signature – two flashes of white light and one of red per minute, for example – allowing mariners to know exactly which light they are looking at in the darkness.

Accidents still happen, however, as Henry Greathead knows only too well. He is a boat builder from South Shields and one of the men who watches the *Adventure* sink off Tynemouth Haven in 1789. He is appalled at his own helplessness and resolves to build a lifeboat for use in such circumstances. The same thought occurs to others, among them Lionel Lukin, a London coach builder, and William Woodhave, the parish clerk of South Shields. After a competition to design a lifeboat, these men's ideas all come together in a single design, which Greathead builds in 1796. It is 28½ feet long, 9½ feet wide and can carry ten passengers in addition to its crew of ten oarsmen, who are equipped with cork life jackets. Greathead calls it the *Original* and it serves as the prototype for another thirty-one lifeboats. As a result, sailing within sight of land is far safer after 1800 than in 1789.

Lifeboats by themselves do not save lives, of course: the volunteers who man them do. With this in mind, Sir William Hillary, a gentleman from the Isle of Man, publishes a thin volume in 1823 entitled *An appeal to the British nation on the humanity and policy of forming a national institution for the preservation of lives and property from shipwreck*. He enlists the help of two influential MPs and a meeting is accordingly held in the City of London Tavern, in Bishopsgate, on 4 March 1824. There it is agreed to establish the Royal National Institution for the Preservation of Life from Shipwreck. It seeks to obtain lifeboats and train men for their use. Most impressively, Sir William does not consider his work finished with this foundation; he undertakes to save lives himself. Back on the Isle of Man, he buys lifeboats for all four of the chief harbours and takes an active role in leading rescue missions. In December 1827, at the age of fifty-seven, he and his crew save seventeen Swedish sailors from going down with their ship. That same year Hillary suffers six fractured ribs when rescuing the crew of the *St George*. Three years later, he forms part of a crew of fourteen men who save sixty-two lives from another shipwreck. In the course of the storm he is swept overboard but, just when you think it would be a terribly sad end for the founder of the organisation that will one day become the RNLI, he manages to clamber back on to the lifeboat. He is simply indefatigable and an inspiration to all who know him. Obviously I would not want you to go down on a sinking ship, but if you did, I hope it might be near the Isle of Man, somewhere within reach of Sir William Hillary.

8

Where to Stay

It is generally acknowledged by all travellers in England that they have been most agreeably surprised with the elegance of inns throughout the kingdom. The sleeping beds and rooms are uncommonly neat: it is true, beds are that sort of luxury among the English which are always carefully attended to.

Christian Goede (1807)[1]

Where are you going to spend the night? The obvious answer is an inn. These are quite numerous: you will see them throughout the country, and they are widely praised by travellers, especially in England. But they are not your only option. Increasingly you will find hotels catering to the wealthy. Private houses and furnished rooms are available for rent in all the principal tourist attractions, such as the seaside resorts, cathedral cities and picturesque places in the Lake District. What's more, you are bound to make friends on your visit, perhaps with the owners of country houses and even aristocrats. Maybe you will join them for a shooting party or a ball. Or perhaps you will find yourself in an industrial town going home with someone from a very different walk of life – perhaps after a few too many beers in the pub. And what if you find yourself with no money, looking for a cheap boarding house in somewhere like London or Liverpool? This chapter will give you a glimpse of the vast range of places you might stay in Regency Britain, whether you are destined to sleep in squalor or slumber in splendour.

Inns

Generally speaking, inns fall into two sorts: those large town-centre establishments, often built around a central courtyard, from which stagecoaches depart on their rapid journeys around the country; and quieter country hostelries, which are independent of the stagecoach trade and might be as modest as a couple of letting rooms above a public house. It is far more likely that you will find yourself staying at one of the former. Stagecoach companies often have arrangements with landlords that they will only take their passengers to a certain inn for food or accommodation. Also, if you arrive in the country via a major port, such as Liverpool, as soon as you step off your ship you'll be surrounded by a small crowd of boys waving cards printed with advertisements for inns, all offering to carry your luggage for you to their recommended establishment.[2] You may well feel that you have no choice but to select one of them.

There are advantages and disadvantages to staying at a coaching inn. On the downside, they are nearly always noisy. Robert Southey illustrates how annoying this can be when he stays at an inn in Falmouth:

> Doors opening and shutting, bells ringing, voices calling to the waiter from every quarter, while he cries 'Coming' to one room, and hurries away to another. Everybody is in a hurry here; either they are going off in the packets, and are hastening their preparations to embark, or they have just arrived and are impatient to be on the road homeward. Every now and then a carriage rattles up to the door with a rapidity which makes the very house shake. The man who cleans the boots is running in one direction, the barber with his powder-bag in another; here goes the barber's boy with his hot water and razors; there comes the clean linen from the washer woman; and the hall is full of porters and sailors bringing in luggage, or bearing it away. Now you hear a horn blow because the post is coming in, and in the middle of the night you are awakened by another because it is going out.[3]

On top of the noise, you might be bothered by the indiscriminate mix of the clientele – the carriers in their smocks drinking a quart of ale while they wait to depart, and crowds of irritated travellers clambering off a long coach and harrying the waiters and chambermaids or ringing the bell for attention. Also, the rapid turnaround of guests means that some things are not attended to properly. Some hard-pressed chambermaids don't change the sheets if they've only been used once; either that or they just dampen them and dry them hurriedly before reusing them.[4] This gives rise to infections and irritants. You might be plagued by bedbugs even at a major London inn, like the Bell Savage – to the extent that you will be forced to sleep in a chair.[5]

On the upside, however, staff at coaching inns don't worry about people coming and going through the night, as stagecoaches arrive and depart on a twenty-four-hour basis. You can even order a meal after midnight in some establishments.[6] They have many rooms, and so are unlikely to turn you away. Even if they're full, they will often find you a place in a nearby lodging house.[7] There will be locks on the doors of the bedchambers, and the beds will not be damp from having been unused and unheated for several days, as in some quiet village inns. Most of all they are welcoming. This, for example, is how you might be greeted at a leading hostelry in Bath. As your coach or post-chaise comes to a standstill before the main door, one or both of the two footmen waiting there will open your carriage and arrange the fold-down metal step, and take your arm if he perceives any danger of you falling. While his colleague deals with your luggage, he will take a note of your name and escort you inside to an elegantly furnished parlour or sitting room, warmed by a blazing fire and decorated with gilt-framed paintings. There will be a table with all the latest newspapers laid out. You will be invited to sit on one of the chairs or sofas and your footman will summon a boy to help you remove your boots (which will be taken away for polishing) and give you a pair of slippers. A waiter will offer to bring you a drink. A chambermaid will next appear, with a white apron, who will show you to your bedroom. On entering, she will light the lamp, draw the curtains and point out the washing table and facilities, such as the bell rope to call for attention and the chamber pot or close stool (a seat enclosing a chamber pot beneath). If the fire is not already burning in the grate, she will light that too. The room will often be decorated with framed prints – sometimes of famous actresses and actors, or hunting scenes – and covered in wallpaper. The bed with its four mahogany posts and curtains will dominate the room, its thick feather mattress covered with sheets and blankets. There will also be a mirror, a towel and a jug and basin for washing yourself. Some of the best inns have sofas and tables in their larger chambers, as well as a sideboard with crockery. There will also be a desk for you to write letters.[8]

What will it cost you to stay at an inn? In the 1790s, a bed in London should be between 1s and 18d.[9] James Woodforde stays at the best coaching inns and usually pays around 9s per night for himself and two companions, including dinner.[10] Rural inns are rarely more than 1s per night – although they will often charge more for stabling your horse than they do for accommodating you. By the 1820s, however, you can treble these sums. Sir Walter Scott notes that servants' travelling expenses in the 1820s amount to 4s 6d a day – four times what they had been in his youth.[11] Of course you can spend much more than this at the best inns in the most fashionable towns. When Louis Simond and two guests spend a night in Bath at an inn like the one described above, in 1810, the bill for all three of them, including tea, dinner and breakfast, comes to £2 11s – that's 17s each.[12]

On top of the bill, you have to allow for tips. Waiters and chambermaids are often unpaid – they generally receive only board and lodging – so tipping is very important. Generally, you can expect to hand over an extra 10–20 per cent of the bill. Note, however, that you don't pay a tip with the bill but rather pass a sixpence or shilling to each individual member of staff who serves you. If you are not careful, this can end up costing you much more than 20 per cent, as a letter writer to *The Times* in 1795 complains, following a night at Ingatestone:

> The innkeeper's bill was as follows: supper, 1s; beer, 3d; bed, 1s; horse and [oats] 1s 7d – together 3s 10d. I gave away as follows: waiter, 1s; chambermaid, 6d; jack-boot, 6d; ostler the change out of 2s I paid him for the horse, being 5d ... Yet the ostler was so abusive because I did not give him more than the odd 5d change that he actually threatened me that he would mark me if I came there again.[13]

Hotels

Hotels, like inns, provide bedchambers, sitting rooms and dining rooms but they differ in that they cater exclusively for guests travelling by stagecoach who have no need of stables and no desire to

encounter the sort of riff-raff you meet at a traditional inn.[14] The
first such enterprise was the German Hotel in Suffolk Street, London,
which opened its doors 'to all foreign nobility' shortly before 1710.[15]
The second was 'The Hotel' in the centre of Exeter, established in
1769. These two hotels inspire about a dozen more in London by
1789. You might stay at the English Hotel in Leman Street; Wood's
Hotel on Covent Garden Piazza; or the Adelphi Hotel on the Strand.
If you are French, you'll probably head to La Sablonières in Leicester
Square; if you are German, you might stay at the German Hotel
mentioned above; and if you are Italian, you won't have long to wait
before John Baptiste Pagliano opens the Italian Hotel in St Martin's
Street.[16]

Over the next two decades the leading London hotels establish
themselves as suitable places for the grandest foreign visitors. In 1814,
Louis XVIII of France stays at Grillon's Hotel in Albemarle Street.[17]
That same year Tsar Alexander I stays at the Pulteney Hotel on
Piccadilly, whose excellent reputation makes him turn down the Prince
Regent's offer of accommodation at St James's Palace.[18] Equally
renowned are Mivart's Hotel in Brook Street (on the site of what is
now Claridge's); Thomas's Hotel in Berkeley Square; Stevens's Hotel
in New Bond Street; and the most splendid of them all, the Clarendon
Hotel, also in New Bond Street. In 1826 Prince Hermann Pückler-
Muskau describes his room at the Clarendon:

> Everything is far better and more abundant than on the Continent.
> The bed, for instance, which consists of several mattresses laid one
> upon another, is large enough to contain two or three persons ... On
> your washing table you find not one miserable water bottle with a
> single earthenware or silver jug and basin, and a long strip of a towel,
> such as are given you in all the hotels and many private houses in
> France and Germany, but positive tubs of handsome porcelain in which
> you may plunge half your body; taps which instantly supply you with
> streams of water at pleasure; half a dozen wide towels; a multitude
> of fine glass bottles and glasses, great and small; a large standing
> looking-glass; footbaths, etcetera ... As soon as you are awake you are
> allured by all the charms of the bath ... Good carpets cover the floors
> of all the chambers, and in the brightly polished steel grate burns a
> cheerful fire, instead of the dirty logs or the smoky and ill-smelling
> stoves to be found in so many of our inns.[19]

Such luxury is not cheap. *The London Adviser and Guide* for 1790 notes that hotels charge around 5s per night for a bedchamber, 5s for the use of a parlour, 2s for a fire and 1s per head for breakfast, plus extras – such as 1s for the hairdresser.[20] By the 1820s, top hotels are charging much more: a guinea per night to sleep and another guinea per head for dinner, not including wine. If you have family or staff with you, the cost can mount up significantly. Tsar Alexander I's bill at the Pulteney amounts to 210 guineas for a week. But if you enjoy being served dishes cooked by Parisian chefs in a restaurant lit by crystal chandeliers, before listening to a string quartet in an opulent sitting room – not forgetting the plentiful provision of flushing loos – you can easily see why West End hotels quickly take over from inns as the best places to stay in London. By 1830 you'll find establishments calling themselves hotels all over the country.

Town Houses

As you will no doubt remember from chapter 1, there is a massive difference in quality between the mansions of the upper classes and the living quarters of the urban poor. It is thus impossible to generalise about what it's like to stay in a town house, whether as a friend of the family, a paying guest or a tenant for the season. Will your bedroom be decorated with Chinese wallpaper and have a view of a well-paved square? Or will it be a corner of a damp cellar and shared with a large family? Clearly, you need to see what it's like to stay in a range of places. Aside from your own comfort, you can hardly begin to understand the people until you see what life is like for them at home.

TRADESMEN

William Mortimer, the dyer and scourer of cloth mentioned in chapter 6, lives in Drake Street, Plymouth, next door to his shop and dyehouse.[21] At the time of his death in 1823, he is a widower with two children, aged twelve and ten. His home is a typical middle-class dwelling: three-storeys, 18 feet wide, constructed of brick, and with two sash windows on each of the upper floors and one at ground level, to the side of the door. It is now about ten years old, having been built when the old town gate was demolished and this area developed to accommodate the new marketplace, which is next door but one to his house. If you were to rent it unfurnished, it would cost you in the region of 20 guineas per year, or furnished, one guinea per week.

Inside the front door, you find yourself in a stone-floored passage covered by a woven rush mat. Open the white-painted door to your right and you will enter the parlour. The first thing you'll notice will probably be the light coming through the south-facing window and the patterned wallpaper all around the room. But you will no doubt also observe how much dark wood there is. There is mahogany everywhere in a Regency house. A mahogany dining table stands in the centre of the room with eight chairs around it, all of them stained black to look like ebony, with cane seats. Beyond, on one side of the fireplace, there is a mahogany sofa; on the other side is a glass-fronted bookcase – again, made of mahogany. Nearby there is a mahogany Pembroke table with brass castors, and on top of it, a mahogany tea caddy. In front of the fireplace there is a copper coal scuttle and what we would call a companion set: tongs, brush, shovel and poker. A brass fender shields the room from tumbling hot coals, and an old hearth rug lies in front of that, protecting the Kidderminster carpet that covers the floor. This is the only room in the house which is 'close carpeted' – that is, carpeted from wall to wall. Above the painted wooden mantelpiece is a gilt-framed mirror reflecting the rest of the room. There are patterned cotton curtains to cover the windows and a linen roller blind to pull down, to prevent passers-by from peeping in. Against one wall there is a bell-pull to summon a servant. It all looks satisfyingly solid and reassuring. But notice that there are no paintings or prints on the walls. There are no musical instruments. If it strikes you as a serious space, well, it *is*. In a house like this, the front parlour is often a showpiece: unused except for when visitors come to dinner, and by the family on Sundays. The real buzz of life goes on elsewhere.

Before leaving the parlour, take a closer look at that fireplace: it represents a small revolution in living standards. It is cast-iron, decorated with neoclassical motifs and set within a 3ft-wide hearth. However, the semicircular fire basket in the centre is small – barely 15 inches across. It might seem like an inefficient use of space. So much metal, such a big hearth and yet so little fire. But the chimney above is relatively narrow – not only to increase the draw and take up more smoke but also to prevent the heat from escaping. Instead, the warmth is conducted into the cast-iron flanks of the fireplace, from where it radiates out into the room. The space below the fire basket allows ashes to fall down on to a tray, where they can easily be cleared up. Far from being inefficient, this fireplace gives out much more heat for a limited amount of coal than anything available before our period.

Back in the hall, you'll pass a grandfather clock in a mahogany case as you make your way to the stairs. Its slow, loud tick accompanies you as you climb. Above the parlour is the main bedroom, where you'll find William's bed: a mahogany four-poster. The bed itself has chintz curtains, a mattress stuffed with feathers, and a pair of bolsters; it is made up with linen sheets, woollen blankets and topped with a heavy quilt and cotton counterpane. On the far side of the room is a chest of drawers, and beside that a chair and a full-length mirror on a stand-alone frame. Of course, they are all made of mahogany: even the hearth brush has a mahogany handle. What else is there to see in here besides the dark wood? The carpets, in the form of three matching runners that surround the bed; the blue-and-white china washbasin and matching jug on the mahogany washstand; a white linen 'rolling blind' over the window; and the curtains. It is all very elegant and tasteful and, dare I say it, a trifle puritan. Again, there are no prints on the walls, no paintings, just a patterned wallpaper. This is a room in which to sleep, to wash, to dress and undress, and to say prayers at night. There is nothing here that has even a whiff of self-indulgence about it. Unless, that is, you consider the appreciation of quality an indulgence. That bed, and everything on it, is worth a total of £15.

There are two other bedrooms on this floor, both furnished much like William's own, although one has a 'tent bed' rather than a four-poster. Both rooms otherwise have similar pieces of mahogany furniture, as does the servants' room on the second floor. Washing in each place is facilitated by a china jug and basin of cold water. There is no separate bathroom. Nor is there a water closet. If you need the toilet, you have a choice between going downstairs and out to the privy in the yard or using a chamber pot, which you will have to take out into the yard later.

Downstairs there are two kitchens, front and back. Normally a back kitchen is where all the wet and dirty work is done and the front kitchen is where the cooking takes place. In this house, though, the front kitchen is used as an informal dining room, or breakfast room. Six Yealmpton chairs stand around a single-pillar breakfast table. The only other items of furniture are a table with drawers, a nursing chair and a glass-fronted corner buffet. Some work does get done in here: the ironing, for instance – hence the set of box irons (in which you put hot coals to heat them up). Here too the tea is made. There are a couple of kettles ready to put on the fire, and on a nearby shelf there are two tea caddies and a couple of blue-and-white china teapots. To one side there are mugs, cups and saucers, and two black-lacquered tea trays. Open the drawers of the table and you'll find the cutlery: a dozen table knives and forks, eight dessert spoons and forks, six skewers and a carving knife.

The back kitchen is where William's housekeeper and maidservant do all the washing and cooking. The wide fireplace holds a bar grate: a series of horizontal iron bars fixed into the hearth walls, which enable a large coal fire to burn at a convenient height. To one side of the fireplace is the 'copper': a bricked-in cauldron beneath which a small fire is lit to heat large quantities of water with the minimum of heat loss. On the other side is an oven with an iron door, heated in a similar fashion. Food is stored in baskets and cooking utensils, including earthenware dishes, tin baking pans, iron saucepans, a steamer, flour dredge and a fish kettle, are stacked on the lower shelves of a built-in dresser.

This kitchen might be very different from yours, with your cooker and electric appliances. It is even more markedly different after dark, when you have to work in it by candlelight; but the sight of many of these objects will make you feel at home. Here is William's knife box, with a selection of good knives, a sharpening steel and a rolling pin. His white-china dinner service is arranged on the upper shelves of the built-in dresser, each piece facing outwards. And look at his wine glasses – here is a man after my own heart! No fewer than *five* decanters, seven wine glasses and fifteen rummers (wine glasses with short stems and wide bases, so you don't knock them over). William might have few objects of curiosity in his house but I can see myself sitting down with him and sharing a bottle of wine or two by candlelight – and putting the Regency world to rights.

THE WEALTHY

The typical gentleman's town house is a three- or four-storey terraced building, with three rooms on each floor, plus a basement and an attic. The large rectangular windows are all composed of a number of smaller panes of glass: the wealthier the owner, the larger the panes. Architectural decoration otherwise is kept to a minimum, being nothing more than a few recesses or arches in the masonry and pillars on either side of the front door. Occasionally you see elements of fashionable decor, such as classical pediments, Grecian urns and Egyptian sphinxes, but these are low-key and restrained. There will often be railings in front of the house and a light-well to illuminate the basement, sometimes with a staircase leading down to a trades-men's entrance and the coal hole.

Entering from the street, you'll find yourself in a wide passageway with a hat stand and hooks for umbrellas. Beyond is the main hall, fitted with a rich carpet, and a wide stone staircase. Another carpet rises up the middle of the stairs, held in place by brass rods. Stand at the bottom of the stairs and look up: the banisters and mahogany handrail turn in ovals between all the floors of the house. As you can see, a gentleman's town house is built around its staircase. Each floor has its purpose: the basement is for the service areas; the ground and first floor for social functions; the second and third floors for bedrooms; and the attic for the servants' sleeping quarters and storage. As a result, people are always nipping up and down the stairs – the gentle-man's family on the main staircase, the servants on the back stairs. As Louis Simond playfully remarks, 'the quickness with which the individuals of the family run up and down and perch on the different storeys, gives the idea of a cage with its sticks and birds'.[22]

The ground floor is sometimes called 'the parlour floor'. If you turn up at no. 1, The Royal Crescent, Bath, in the early 1790s – the house of the retired Irish MP, Henry Sandford – you'll find that his parlour is a large close-carpeted room, simply and tastefully decorated with a modest plaster frieze just below the ceiling. The polished dark-mahogany furniture includes a glass-fronted bureau-bookcase, a side table, a breakfast table and a set of dining chairs. The fireplace – a polished steel basket with a serpentine front – sits in a recessed chimney and is surrounded by the most beautiful carved marble surround, as architecturally refined as the building itself. The windows have white-painted wooden internal shutters which, when open, reflect light into the room. The whole space is much larger and brighter than a tradesman's house. It also has many extra refinements: there are gilt-framed paintings on the walls; the furniture is of a superior design with better fittings, the candlesticks are gilt, and the table-top clock discreetly tells the time in a way that does not wake the whole house with the clanging chimes of doom.

The dining room in Mr Sandford's house is a handsome space with a high ceiling, cream-coloured panelling and a polished steel fireplace. In the middle is a large Oriental rug. On this stands the dining table – mahogany, of course – which can be made longer by drawing out the end sections and inserting extra leaves in the middle, enabling up to twenty people to dine together. The additional chairs required for such an occasion stand around the room like sentries, with their backs against the wall. There is a sideboard with drawers, in which the best cutlery and linen are kept. Notice too the fine porcelain and solid-silver candlesticks on show. Blue-and-white china and other *objets d'art* enhance the subtle impression that there is more to this room than its simple function. Dinner in here is not just a meal. It is an event.

Informal meals tend to be served in the breakfast room. This is normally a south-facing room on the ground floor, with a round pedestal breakfast table of mahogany or rosewood in the centre. Robert Southey remarks in 1802 that 'our breakfast table is oval, large enough for eight or nine persons, yet supported upon one claw in the centre. This is the newest fashion, and [as] fashions change so often in these things ... it is easy to know how long it is since a house has been fitted up, by the shape of the furniture.'[23] The main differences between the breakfast room and the dining room, besides the shape of the table, lie in the quality of the furniture and fittings. The better sort of everything – chandeliers, paintings, sideboards, clocks and porcelain – is to be found in the dining room. Thus the breakfast room is where a gentleman sits with his morning coffee and reads the paper, paying no particular attention to those around him; and the dining room is where he entertains his guests – and would never dream of ignoring anyone.

The drawing room – or 'withdrawing room' to use the old-fashioned word still favoured by elderly gentlemen and ladies – is normally located on the first floor. Its primary function is entertainment and so it is decorated to match or even outdo the dining room. Walls are covered with gold silk damask; the largest gilt-framed paintings are on display; and chandeliers provide plenty of light. Here you may also find a piano or a harpsichord, and a satinwood table for card games. This is where a gentleman keeps his best tea urn and his finest teacups or tea dishes (teacups have handles; old-fashioned tea dishes don't). But most of all, it is where he and his guests sit in comfort. Thus you may also find upholstered mahogany sofas in here, as well as several armchairs and that newfangled item of furniture, the chaise longue, which appears around the year 1800.

Bedrooms are furnished with fine rugs and carpets, metal fireplaces, chests of drawers and free-standing mirrors. Framed prints or paintings decorate the walls. In the best bedrooms, the four-poster beds have silk damask hangings; printed cotton or linen is used in the less-showy ones. Sheets are of holland (fine linen). Every bedroom has a washstand with a china basin and ewer. The best bedrooms also have a dressing room, joined by an interconnecting door. This will be furnished with a full-length mirror, chest of drawers, dressing table, clothes horse, shaving table, shaving mirror, laundry baskets, wig stands, hat boxes and a tall wardrobe for fine dresses and coats, as well as all the brushes, razors, towels, cosmetics and perfumes that are personal to every occupant. Occasionally you'll find a washbasin with running water situated in here and, in a *very* few cases, a bath. John Soane's house has a separate 'bathing room' (as he calls it) near his dressing room. It is close-carpeted and has a plumbed-in cast-iron bath beside the window, a thermometer and all the luxuries you could wish for: a large fireplace, a longcase clock, oil paintings, two mahogany sofas, porcelain on the mantelpiece and a large mirror above the fire.[24]

The basement is where you will find the front and back kitchens and the pantry, scullery, larder, wine cellar and housekeeper's room. If there is a central heating system, it will be located here. This normally takes the form of a coal furnace from which hot air rises to vents in the ground floor of the house. John Soane has hot air piped to his museum, offices and dressing room through brass grilles – although it only takes the chill off, leaving the house in winter at a none-too-cosy 11–13 degrees Centigrade.[25] As for the kitchens, these are much larger than in a tradesman's home. The front one is lined with shelves holding dozens of copper saucepans and frying pans as well as utensils – jelly moulds, sieves and ice-cream-making machines.

Kitchens that have recently been upgraded will probably be fitted with a large cast-iron range. Coomb's Patent Kitchen Range, for example, is designed 'to roast, boil, bake, stew and fry at the same time' using only one fire; it also incorporates a copper to give hot water on demand.[26] Mr Soane's front and back kitchens, which he renovates in 1812, both have huge ranges in their wide fireplaces. The one in the back kitchen – a magnificent example made by Thomas Deakin – has a bar grate in the centre, a baking oven to the left, a boiler to the right, and hot plates on top of both the oven and the boiler. It is such a dramatic piece of equipment, so fiercely blackened and bold, that it lurks in the massive fireplace like a shining black dragon.

The last room that counts as an essential requirement in a gentleman's residence is the smallest one. The term 'water closet' has been in regular use since the early eighteenth century but, up to now, very few town houses have been equipped with them. In 1775 the Scottish watch-maker Alexander Cummings does humanity a great favour when he invents the S-bend (which we call the U-bend) by which water can create an airlock to trap the smells of everything that has been flushed away. Three years later, Joseph Bramah obtains control of the patent and starts manufacturing his famous water closets; over the next twenty years he produces more than 6,000 of them.[27] Of course gentlemen are quick to embrace the fashion, installing them in closets where previously they had a close stool. John Soane puts in three flushing loos in his house: one adjacent to his dressing room, another next to his wife's morning room, and a third in his servants' quarters. Notwithstanding this improvement, ladies and gentlemen do not immediately give up on the alternatives. Chamber pots are tucked away in suitable cupboards. Likewise, china bourdaloues are hidden around a drawing room or parlour for ladies to use. Toilet paper is available, although not yet manufactured in commercial quantities. Soft, absorbent paper is a preserve of the rich; those who cannot afford it make do with old rags, old newspaper, brown paper or whatever else comes to hand.[28]

How much will it cost to rent a gentleman's town house? That depends on where it is and when exactly you are visiting. A good property in a fashionable part of London will be between 100 and 150 guineas per year in 1790 and three or four times as much in the 1820s. The most expensive houses in the best London squares can fetch up to 1,000 guineas per year by the end of our period. Note that these prices are for unfurnished properties and therefore, if you fail to pay the rent, your landlord has the right to seize your furniture. You will also be liable for all the taxes. Renting a furnished building avoids these problems but is considerably more expensive. A house costing about 100 guineas unfurnished in 1790 will be 4–8 guineas per week furnished, depending on the season. If you rent a single floor as lodgings, the first floor is generally valued at half the rent of the whole house; the parlour floor and the second floor are each a quarter. A prime house that is 1,000 guineas per year unfurnished will go for as much 60 or even 80 guineas per week, if furnished. These, however, are never let out as lodgings.[29]

If you want to see how the truly grand live when in town, you will have to explore their London palaces. What do these have that the above-mentioned gentlemen's houses do not? Space, in a word – with reception rooms in which thirty or forty people can sit down to dinner at once. They also have grandeur. Imagine marble pillars on either side of every doorway and a gold-leaf-decorated plaster frieze around the top of each reception room. There's more light – both natural and artificial – more gold and silver, more design, more woven carpet, more artwork, more crystal glass and more *objets d'art* than you'd ever see in an ordinary gentleman's town house. The exceedingly wealthy live in a world of red, blue, gold and glass – rich red carpets and silk damask wall hangings; gold everywhere you can possibly put it; and multi-tiered crystal chandeliers hanging from the ceiling in every room. And if you ever step foot inside Carlton House, you will never forget it. Heavens above – the gold. The gold! Gold-leaf-covered columns and cornices, gilt furniture, gold clocks, gold sculptures, gilt frames around paintings, gold candlesticks, gilt bookcases and so on. The Prince Regent is surrounded by gold as ordinary gentlemen are surrounded by mahogany. Every item of furniture in every reception room – from the chairs and pier tables to the sofas and sculpture pedestals – is covered in gold leaf. The porcelain is mounted on gold. The mouldings of the wall panels are covered with gold, the plaster-work on the ceiling has so much gold decoration it is difficult to take it all in, and the immense chandeliers are also bedecked with gold. How does one describe this as a town house? It isn't one. Even calling it a palace doesn't do it justice. The only phrase that seems appropriate is that which the poet Samuel Taylor Coleridge uses to describe Kubla Khan's residence: it is 'a stately pleasure dome'.

THE URBAN POOR

In the poorer parts of London, 60 per cent of working-class families have only one rented room in which to eat, sleep, cook, wash and often work – sometimes with a large number of children. Much the same can be said for Liverpool and Manchester.[30] Rents are not cheap: between 2s and 5s per week for a room in London and about 2s 3d in the industrial towns.[31] You might come across cheaper rooms in the London slums – for as little as 1s a week – but these, measuring barely 10ft x 8ft, are very small for a couple, let alone a family.[32]

Let us suppose you are renting a furnished room in London costing you 2s 6d a week in the 1790s: what can you expect to find? A bed, a mattress, a bolster and blankets; a small table; a couple of old chairs and perhaps a bench; a small looking-glass (normally fixed to the wall), a window curtain; an iron stove in the fireplace with a poker, shovel and tongs; an iron candlestick and tin candle-snuffer; a quart bottle for water; a tin pint pot; a glass vial for vinegar and a stoneware cup for salt.[33] You will have to provide sheets yourself. If the house was once occupied by a tradesman's family, there may be the remnants of their wallpaper; otherwise the plastered walls will simply be white-washed. Do not expect the window to open, as the sashes have usually broken. Wood, rags or paper take the place of any broken panes of glass.[34] The furniture will be old and made of oak or elm. As for plumbing, there is none. Most landlords believe that, if they were to provide a water supply, the lead pipes 'would be there in the evening and gone in the morning'.[35]

'It will scarcely appear credible,' writes one physician at the end of the eighteenth century, 'that persons of the lowest class do not put clean sheets on their beds three times a year'. He adds that curtains are never washed at all and that 'from three to eight individuals of different ages often sleep in the same bed, there being in general one room and one bed for each family'.[36] Sharing beds is indeed very common – so much so that it is considered normal. In Preston, out of 852 beds in one poor district, almost all are shared – 129 of them by four or more people.[37] You can imagine the results. Or, rather, you can't. People suffer in all sorts of ways. A London doctor visiting an old Irish woman with a broken rib discovers that she rents one corner of a first-floor room. Her landlady occupies the bed in the middle of the room, in front of the fire; the beds in the other corners are rented out to three other families, one of which comprises a widow and her three children. The old Irish woman is in so much pain she cannot go out to work, selling vegetables. So her landlady suggests she sublets half her bed. This she does but the woman who comes in is much larger than the old Irish woman, and presses against her broken rib in the night, making her pain worse.[38]

As we saw at the opening of this book, the lack of drainage has a huge impact on the living conditions of the urban poor. When you consider that in some places there are more than 200 people using each latrine, overflowing cesspits present a real problem.[39] But the worse the problem gets, the more expensive the solution. So no one does anything about it. Is it any wonder that people are not too bothered about washing their sheets? Or themselves? As for the water supply, water companies do not serve the houses of the poor. In most areas the inhabitants have to rely on water carriers who deliver a few gallons for a penny, but the purchasers rarely know where that water has come from. When you look at it closely in a glass, you can see larvae and other animalcules wriggling in it.[40] People are generally not so foolish as to drink such noisome stuff, but they use it to rinse their hands, faces, saucepans and dishes, so diseases quickly spread.

If you can't afford to rent a corner of a room, you might apply for a place in the parish workhouse. These range from small establishments catering for thirty people to large ones housing several hundred. The sexes are segregated in separate dormitories or wards. Medical help is available for those who are sick. The sheets are cleaned in the laundry and your clothes might be washed there too. Young children are allowed to accompany their mothers and some institutions even provide a rudimentary school. But the food is sparse and the beds, blankets and other comforts few and far between. And, as the name suggests, you have to work for your keep. Strict discipline is imposed. People enter a workhouse only when necessity forces them to do so. In the late eighteenth century, forty-five London workhouses are home to more than 10,000 inmates, coming and going as their individual states of desperation wax and wane.

Some people will not be accepted by the workhouse authorities. If they reject you, then you might be forced to take a place in one of the sheds around the larger towns. These are old barns and disused stables where straw mattresses are rented out for 2d per night or, if you take one on a weekly basis, between 6d and 9d. There are no facilities – no latrines, no water, no heating and no cooking apparatus – and you will share your accommodation with criminals and alcoholics. But they are better places to stay than the cellars. These are unspeakably grim. Don't imagine any furniture or refinements. The floor and walls are likely to be soaked. In Clitheroe there is 'a range of cellars ... occupied as lodging-houses, in which the beds are raised on bricks, to keep them out of contact with the water, which, during periods of much rain, rises above a foot in depth'.[41] As for the underground lodging houses in Liverpool, one inspector writes:

> At night the floor of these cellars, often the bare earth, is covered with straw, and there the lodgers, all who can afford to pay a penny for the accommodation, arrange themselves, as best they may, until scarcely a single available inch of space is left unoccupied; and in this way as many as thirty human beings or more are sometimes packed together, each inhaling the poison which his neighbour generates, and presenting in miniature a picture of the Black Hole of Calcutta.[42]

Rural Houses

Whereas all the rooms in a town house are stacked on top of one another, in the country they are arranged on just two or three floors. The servants still sleep in the attic but there's no need for the kitchens and service rooms to be in the basement; they can be on the ground floor. The whole architectural approach is much more easy-going. The building spreads across its plot and those who live in it similarly spread out and relax.

THE MIDDLE CLASS

Twenty years before the start of our period you would walk into a yeoman's farmhouse and see a hall with a flagstone floor and a log fire blazing away in a 7ft-wide fireplace. The middle of the room would be dominated by an oak table, with an oak or elm chair at either end for the yeoman and his wife, and benches along the sides for the children and helpers on the farm. The chambers above would be furnished with beds and chests, as you would expect, but the bedsteads would be made of oak, and sacks of corn might be stacked in the chests, where they could be preserved from the rats and the damp. Now these signs of old-style, solid prosperity have mostly disappeared, especially from England. The middle classes live with greater elegance. Their houses might well date from the sixteenth century but the hall is now close-carpeted and called a dining room. The table is mahogany, and the benches have been replaced by mahogany chairs. China has replaced pewter. Knives, forks, spoons and glasses are laid around the table at mealtimes, and the farm helpers eat elsewhere. In some farmhouses, the only wide hearth you'll find will be in the kitchen: the one in the hall has been mostly filled in and a smaller, cast-iron fireplace installed instead, which burns less wood. In the evenings, the yeoman withdraws to his parlour and sits in a comfortable chair, reading a newspaper or magazine by the light of a lamp. Upstairs you will find four-poster beds, carpets, chests of drawers and swing mirrors. The rural middle classes are adopting all the refinements introduced by their siblings and cousins in their town houses.

Not all middle-class rural residences are farmhouses. Many are rectories and vicarages, or the houses of professional men, such as physicians and surgeons, or gentlewomen. Chawton Cottage in Hampshire is where Jane Austen lives from 1809, together with her sister, Cassandra, their mother and a friend, Martha Lloyd. If you look at the house from the street you'll see a red-brick frontage with five sash windows on the first floor and, on the ground floor, a central front door with one large window on either side. Entering, you'll find yourself in a hallway, which, if you turn to your left, will take you through to a parlour decorated with a yellow patterned wallpaper. On the walls you'll see pictures of family members. There's a piano, which Jane likes to play before breakfast, and a card table, for games in the evenings. Otherwise it is very similar to the Plymouth tradesman's parlour, with a mahogany bureau-bookcase, mahogany Pembroke table, comfortable sofa, elegant chairs and a bar grate in the fireplace.

If you step the other way from the hall and open the creaking door, you'll enter a dining room decorated with a patterned green wallpaper and furnished with a mahogany dining table and chairs. There is also a small walnut-topped pedestal table on which Jane writes when she has time. Again, many things in here will remind you of William

Mortimer's house in Plymouth, from the longcase clock and the tea-making facilities to the cast-iron fireplace and the carpet. However, individual touches, such as the high-quality plaster surround of the fireplace and the Wedgwood dinner service, will remind you that this house is owned by a gentleman – Jane's brother – and lived in by his relatives. Whereas there are only three downstairs rooms in the trades-man's house, here there are five, not including those in the outbuild-ings. Next to the dining room you'll find a front kitchen or breakfast parlour. At the rear of the property is a back kitchen, equipped with a bar grate and oven. Next to that is a scullery. Across the other side of the yard there is a bakehouse for making bread and doing the laundry. The Austens have much more space for both work and relax-ation. And whereas a middle-class town dweller has no room for a stable or a coach house, the Austens have both – although they actu-ally ride around the parish in a donkey carriage.

Moving upstairs, the bedroom that Jane and her sister share is at the back of the building. Their mother occupies a large room at the front. Also at the front is a guest room with an adjoining dressing room. There is another small bedroom on the other side of the corridor and two rooms in the rear wing, above the back kitchen and scullery, one of which is used by Martha Lloyd. A second flight of stairs leads up to the attic, which is lit by two dormer windows facing the street. All of the first-floor bedrooms are heated by fireplaces. They are furnished like those in Mortimer's house in Plymouth: mahogany four-posters and tent beds; ewers and basins on mahogany washstands; looking glasses, and so forth. Chamber pots are concealed under beds or in cupboards. There is no bathroom. As Jane's nephew will remember when reminiscing about this house in future years, it contains relatively few *objects*. As far as the middle classes go, con-sumerism is still a thing of the future.[43]

The real joy of a house in the country is the amount of external space. Whereas town houses hardly ever have more than a small yard or flower garden, middle-class rural houses may have several acres. Each one has its own well and can gather rainwater from the roof in a cistern, so there is no need for the servants to queue up at a communal pump. There is no difficulty in disposing of effluent or kitchen waste as you can simply dig a hole somewhere away from the house. And there is space for such luxuries as a vegetable garden, a lawn and a 'wilderness' – a place of natural beauty where you can wander undisturbed. In the case of Chawton Cottage, although the house faces the road, a high wooden fence and a hornbeam hedge shield the garden, so there is a pleasant area for the ladies to exercise without being seen or disturbed.[44] In this way, a rural family can live in greater comfort than an urban one with an equivalent income. Indeed, due to the extra space, their style of living has more in common with that of a gentleman than a tradesman. And if your family is as large and supportive as the Austens, who could ask for more?

THE WORKING CLASS

Rural labourers and their families enjoy a far higher standard of living than their urban kinsfolk. Not only are their working conditions much better, there is more space to accommodate them. The difference is demonstrated by the comparative life expectancy. Whereas the average age of burial in an industrial town is nineteen, in rural counties like Wiltshire and Rutland it is thirty-six.[45]

Not that agricultural labourers' cottages are palaces, mind you. Enter some of them and for a moment you might feel you are back in the Middle Ages. A few are indeed medieval hall houses that have yet to be converted to two-storey living. In these places you'll look up to see the underside of a thatched roof: all the eating, drinking and sleeping here takes place in the same barn-like space. However, most hall houses that are inhabited by working-class families have been divided up into two or three cottages. If you are invited to stay at one of these, you'll walk into a wide, low-ceilinged room about 15 feet square with roughly plastered walls and a large fireplace. The floor is packed earth except for the area near the hearth, which is laid with flagstones. The fireplace itself is still a wide area for cooking and brewing: few cottages have yet taken advantage of Count Rumford's cottage stoves, which increase efficiency and reduce the consumption of firewood.[46] On one side of the fireplace is an old, curved wooden settle, where a grandparent sits during the day and the rest of the family gather of an evening. Nearby there is a washtub and cauldron, as well as a pile of logs for the fire; a pair of bellows stands at the ready. Inside the fireplace a pot-hanger waits for a kettle or the cauldron to be hooked up to boil. Prized possessions such as brass candlesticks, a copper kettle or an old Delftware serving plate are displayed on the mantelpiece. The window is wide and glazed, throwing light on the grain of the oak table, which is a cast-off from a local yeoman's house. Similarly, some of the oak chairs and benches that were in the yeoman's house twenty years ago are now here, demoted to being sat on by the labourer rather than his master. Earthenware and stoneware jugs and bowls are stacked on the shelves. Strings of onions and a flitch of bacon hang nearby. In one corner is the spinning wheel on which the housewife makes a few extra pennies.

To go to bed in such a cottage you'll need to climb up the ladder in the corner, carrying your rushlight with you. As you go up, the flame illuminates the room, which is open to the rafters – you can see the beams and underside of the thatch, replete with cobwebs.[47] The beds are plain oak bedsteads and the mattresses are filled with straw. There are also old chests for clothes. The floorboards are bare. There is no fireplace. Sometimes there is no window either, but where there is, it is normally at the level of the floor, as this space has been created out of the upper part of the old hall. With neighbours so close – on the other side of a partition wall – you might conclude that this is little better than the houses in town. But here your host's family have two large rooms to themselves, and easy access to a water supply from the well in the yard. And fresh air, a vegetable garden and a pigsty not far from the back door. And all the community capital of a village. If they need firewood, fallen branches may be obtainable locally in the woods. Blackberries and damsons may be taken from the hedgerows, apples and pears scrumped from orchards and, in many cases, a cow or ewe pastured on the common. People even cultivate roses around their front doors – something they definitely can't do in an urban slum.

· In Scotland, the houses of the rural poor generally take the form of single-storey stone structures about 30 feet long by 16 feet in breadth with clay floors and turf roofs, a central front door and two front windows. In the past they were heated by a peat fire that burnt in the middle of the room, with the smoke escaping through an opening in the roof. Now, however, the majority of Lowland houses have a coal fire in a hearth set against the gable-end wall, beneath a chimney. Often two families share a house, one living at either end, the head-boards of the beds serving to partition the interior into 'rooms'. Don't be surprised to find potatoes stored under the beds: it is only practical when people are cooking, eating and sleeping in the same space. You will also find houses divided between a stable at one end and a home at the other. The smell inside is powerful, especially as the windows do not open and the door offers the only ventilation. When you see the dark liquid or 'runnings' seeping out of the piles of dung and peat outside the front door and trickling across the road, it might put you off knocking on the door.[48]

In the Highlands you will still come across crofts without fire-places or chimneys. Nathaniel Wheaton visits one in 1824 and records that:

> It was built partly of stones and partly of logs, the crevices being filled with clay and moss. It contained but a single apartment and was without floor or chimney, a hole being left in the roof for the smoke to escape. As this was in no haste to make its exit and glass windows being unknown in this region, the room was so dark that we could not at first discern the inmates, consisting of a Highlander lazily stretched out on a bench; his blear-eyed wife; two or three half-naked children and as many pigs – all dirty beyond description. The earthen floor was strewed with the refuse of fish and the smells that saluted our nostrils from this receptacle of filth were far from being savoury.[49]

Such a description might challenge your idea of what a Regency dwelling should look like. But Wheaton's account is supported by other travellers. Louis Simond describes the interior of a similar home in 1810:

> The only door is common to men and beasts and, of course, very dirty. You see as you come in, on one side, a small stable ... The other side is separated by a rough partition: this is the dwelling place of the family. You find in it not a chimney but a fireplace on the ground with a few stones round it immediately under a hole in the roof; a hook and chain fastened to a stick, to hang an iron kettle on; a deal table; a piece of board on which oatcakes are prepared; a dresser, with some little earthenware; an old press; a pickling tub for mutton; some pieces of mutton hung in the smoke, which winds round them on its way to the roof; a shelf with many cheeses ... The beds were a filthy mattress and a filthy blanket – no sheets; no floor – only the ground trodden hard; a window of four small panes, not one entire.[50]

And yet, as Monsieur Simond looks through the smoke, he is surprised to see books on the shelf propped up among the cheeses. One is the collected sermons of a Glaswegian minister, in Gaelic. Another is a catechism, also in Gaelic. A third is the Bible, in English. This dwelling might be medieval in its living conditions, and the family might live in 'abject poverty' – to use Simond's own description – but the owner is not only bilingual, he and his family are literate. And welcoming to Frenchmen. You have to rethink what 'abject poverty' means when those who experience it do not care for worldly comforts yet pride themselves on their learning, their piety and their hospitality.

THE UPPER CLASSES

Generally speaking, aristocrats and members of the landed gentry who have inherited a country seat prefer to continue to live in it rather than knock it down and start again. So if you are invited to stay with one of them, the chances are that your accommodation will be old – in some cases, medieval. Rest assured, most hosts understand that there is a balance to be struck between antiquity and comfort. Grand old mansions and castles have been modernised, to make them suitable to receive distinguished guests. Some have been substantially extended, with comfortable new wings. The question is: what style does your rich friend prefer? Is he a neoclassical man, admiring the restraint and order of the Ancient Greeks and Romans? Or does he adore the self-indulgence of the Renaissance – so that he now is surrounded by Italianate splendour? Or maybe he is a romantic soul, living in a gothic mansion that evokes the drama of the Middle Ages? It is perhaps fitting in the Age of Excess that, whereas most periods of British architectural history see one new trend emerging, the Regency comes up with three.

Perhaps the most outlandish creation of the era – surpassing even Brighton Pavilion – is Fonthill Abbey in Wiltshire, designed by James Wyatt for the eccentric plantation owner William Beckford, the author of the gothic novel *Vathek*. Vast, imposing and gloomy, the house is largely the product of Beckford's own romantic imagination. The front doors on the west side, which are 35 feet high, open into a baronial hall 68 feet long and 78 feet high. It is like the nave of a gothic cathedral. At the far end you ascend a grand staircase into the Great Octagon, a room 132 feet high, which makes up the centre of the house. But this is only the ground floor of the 276ft-high central tower.[51] It doesn't just dominate the land for miles around: at a time when the word 'skyscraper' is used to refer to the topsails of sailing ships, this is the tallest secular structure in the whole of Great Britain. The wing to the north contains an oratory and the Edward III Gallery, which is lit by stained-glass windows and filled with a huge library. The wing projecting south from the Great Octagon contains St Michael's Gallery, which leads by way of folding *glass* doors to two large drawing rooms, decorated in yellow damask. The east wing houses the Crimson Breakfast Parlour, the Great Dining Room, the Crimson Drawing Room and the Grand Drawing Room. These rooms are huge: the Grand Drawing Room is 30 feet square. Consequently the whole building is freezing cold, even in summer. I'm not sure Mr Beckford himself feels that much at home here. He lives alone in a single room and dines by himself, hardly ever inviting any guests to join him. In 1822 he sells the estate for £300,000 to John Farquhar, the gunpowder manufacturer. It is a reluctant sale but a very lucky one for him, because at three o'clock in the afternoon on 21 December 1825 the central tower cracks and collapses in a storm, taking with it the Great Octagon, the hall and considerable portions of each of the four wings. It is testimony to the size of the building that Mr Farquhar, who is in a distant corner of one of the wings, does not notice when the tower falls.[52]

Whether your host's architect is a neoclassicist like John Soane or an all-rounder like James Wyatt, one thing he will be aware of is the need to incorporate physical comforts. Top of the list in this period are flushing loos. In 1789 relatively few grand houses are equipped with them but from 1800 it is rare that one does *not* have this facility. The earl of Moira has six installed at his gothic mansion, Donington Hall, in 1813, including one adjoining his study and another adjacent to his wife's dressing room.[53] As for bathrooms, a sudden dip in very cold water is considered good for a gentleman's constitution. Thus you might see a marble-lined plunge pool in your host's basement, as at Wimpole Hall, or in an exotic building in the gardens, such as the gothic bathhouse at Corsham Court. If you want a hot bath, most of the time the servants will prepare a moveable bathtub for you. This might take the form of a copper 'slipper bath' with high sides, or a hip bath, which looks like a large coal scuttle in which you sit, bathing your hips. Alternatively, you might try a 'boot bath', which has an opening for your head and chest while the lower part of the bath is covered over, to retain the heat. Some houses have a shower bath, in which you stand in a tub surrounded by a waxed canvas curtain and manually pump water through a pipe that connects the footbath to the shower head. If you want a fully plumbed-in bath in a dedicated bathroom with hot and cold running water, these start to appear around 1800. The one at Colworth House has a bath, a fire, a carpet, a sofa, an armchair, a mahogany cupboard for a chamber pot, an eight-leaf screen behind which to hide your modesty from your servants, and eight gilt-framed paintings for you to admire as you wallow in hot water.[54] How do you beat that? Perhaps the countess of Moira goes one better at Donington Hall. Her bathroom is equipped with a bath, a gilt washbasin and ewer, a rosewood bookstand to allow her to read while in the bath and a copper kettle for her maidservant to supply her with cups of tea while she soaks.[55]

As you may realise, a country house can offer you many luxuries. New buildings after 1790 are regularly equipped with central-heating systems piping hot air to the hall, staircase and reception rooms. Of course each room has its own fireplace in addition to this. Kitchens too are equipped to ever-higher standards – cast-iron ranges are often installed in old buildings as well as in new ones – and the furnishings in reception rooms are chosen and displayed to impress and delight visitors. Printed wallpapers from China adorn the walls of at least one room in every grand house. Fine art is to be found in the reception rooms. Whereas a hundred years ago domestic libraries were almost unheard of, now they are ubiquitous – even if the owner of the house is a semi-literate alcoholic who dropped out of university to gamble away the family fortune.

When it comes to the quality of the furniture in a country house, I only need to say three words to illustrate how it has improved over the last fifty years: Chippendale, Hepplewhite and Sheraton. Back in 1754, Thomas Chippendale published *The Gentleman and Cabinet-Maker's Director*, and the furniture world was made light. Elegance took on a new meaning when applied to dining tables and chairs, sideboards, commodes, pier tables, dressing tables and shaving tables, and his influence can still be seen. While fashionable cabinet-makers are no longer using Mr Chippendale's pattern book in the 1790s, those who have bought furniture designed by him certainly do not feel they need to throw it out. It is simply that George Hepplewhite's *The Cabinet-Maker and Upholsterer's Guide*, first published in 1788, and Thomas Sheraton's *The Cabinet-Maker's and Upholsterer's Drawing Book*, published in four parts from 1791, have taken over. But whoever's chair you end up sitting on at dinner, the chances are high that it will be an example of one of the most elegant designs the nation's finest furniture-makers have ever produced.

To describe all the wonderful things you might see in a gentleman's residence would take far more space than is available here. But it would be wrong not to offer you a glimpse of the sort of bedroom you might sleep in. So follow me into Colworth House in 1816, in Bedfordshire: the home of Mr Lee-Antonie. The huge square marble central hall is dominated by a massive gilt neo-rococo staircase rising to the second floor. Upstairs, apart from Mr Lee-Antonie's own sleeping quarters, there are six bedchambers furnished for high-status guests. Let's say you're going to stay in the Green Bedroom. The bed is a lofty four-poster with green-striped cotton hangings and multiple mattresses. Such is the size of the room that there are eight chairs in here, besides a green 18ft-by-15ft Brussels carpet. The two windows have Venetian blinds as well as green curtains. Around the room the walls are covered in pier glasses – long mirrors in gilt frames – and there is another mirror above the mantelpiece. The washstand and dressing table are both painted; the night table is made of mahogany. It all looks very comfortable, so really your only concern will be warmth. Don't worry on that score either: before you come to bed, the fire will have been lit in here, and when you retire for the night, one of the maidservants will bring a hot warming pan to rub up and down your sheets before you get in.

The best bit about staying in a country house, however, comes the next morning, when you step outside. About 600 parks in Britain have been modelled by one of the three great eighteenth-century landscape designers: William Kent, Lancelot Brown (better known as 'Capability Brown') and Humphry Repton. Although Kent and Brown both die before the start of our period, in 1748 and 1783 respectively, now is the time to see their work, as it has had time to mature, especially when it comes to the trees they planted. Their philosophy is that an English park is a remnant of the Garden of Eden, and the more natural it can be made to appear, the closer it is to the divine intention. Garden buildings are an important addition to the whole layout, so they draw up plans for Greek temples, sculpture galleries, colonnades and follies (fake ruined castles) to make this English Eden perfect. The last of the three, Humphry Repton, is still working in our period. He develops Capability Brown's style of arranging driveways and walkways so that they resolve on buildings in the landscape: you turn a bend and suddenly see the principal house, or a feature such as a temple or a monument. In some gardens – such as Cassiobury House and Woburn Abbey – he creates garden 'rooms' dedicated to a particular nation or theme, for example a Chinese garden, an American garden or a rose garden. To walk through one of his creations is an absolute delight, even in winter, because of the twists and turns of the paths, the surprising revelation of a building here or there, and the romantic dripping ferns, the evergreens and ivy.

As you can imagine, it costs a fortune to maintain a park and garden designed by one of the above-mentioned gentlemen. The earl of Essex spends £10,000 per year on the grounds of Cassiobury House. That is more than the entire contents of Colworth House are worth. Yet aristocrats in this age seem to know no bounds when it comes to spending on their corners of Paradise – and on the lakes, green-houses, follies, temples, orangeries, forcing houses and all the other buildings that go with them. In 1815 Robert Heron reports that he has just built a 60ft-long conservatory adjoining his house, Stubton Hall. He is very pleased with it, noting that 'a conservatory is of rather late invention, and it is probably because Jeffery Wyatt and I had seen so few, that we succeeded so well, our imaginations not being restrained by servile imitation'. Three years later he is eating home-grown peaches and nectarines.[56] In 1824, John Nash builds four conservatories at Buckingham Palace for George IV: after that, everyone wants one.

It has to be said, though, that the greatest excesses of the aristocratic garden are to be found in the menageries. Everyone is desperate to see exotic animals. At Stubton Hall, Sir Robert keeps llamas, alpacas, lemurs, porcupines, armadillos, emus, black swans, whistling ducks, kangaroos and 1,100 goldfish. He even has a chameleon, which is sadly killed by a careless gardener in 1820.[57] Lord Castlereagh keeps lions, ostriches, kangaroos and other rare animals at his country seat, North Cray in Kent.[58] But perhaps the top venue for exotic fauna is the duke of Devonshire's amazing garden at Chiswick House. Quite aside from the colossal yew hedges, the fine cedars and the jaw-dropping flower gardens, he keeps a tame elephant there and invites visitors to ride it.[59]

There you have it. Maybe your friends include the richest men in the country, who keep elephants in their gardens; perhaps they include the poorest, who have to sleep in foetid, flooded cellars or rent out half their bed because they have a broken rib. If you imagine staying with either, you will at some point have to confront this fact: while all periods of history see extremes of rich and poor, it is the differences in standards of living that matter most – from cruel suffering to being blinded by so much gold. Probably no period in British history sees such disparities in this regard as the Regency.

9

What to Eat, Drink and Smoke

All parts of the world are ransacked for an Englishman's table. Turtle are brought alive from the West Indies ... India supplies sauces and curry powder ... hams [are imported] from Portugal and Westphalia; reindeers' tongues from Lapland; caviar from Russia; sausages from Bologna; macaroni from Naples; oil from Florence; olives from France, Italy or Spain; cheese from Parma and Switzerland. Fish come packed up in ice from Scotland for the London market, and the epicures here will not eat any mutton but what is killed in Wales. There is in this very morning's newspaper, a notice from a shopkeeper in the Strand, offering to contract with any person who will send him game regularly from France, Norway or Russia.

Robert Southey (1807)[1]

When at home, you choose what you eat; when you go abroad, you have to be satisfied with what is offered to you. You can say much the same for travelling into the past: the further you go back, the more your appetite is constrained by what is available. In some cases this is because a style of cooking has not been invented or a key ingredient has yet to be discovered. In others it is because a foodstuff is unavailable in a certain region. But most of all it is due to the fact that food is not as plentiful as it is in the modern world. Indeed, if there is one historical topic of overriding importance in our national history, it is that of the increasing abundance of food. In 1700, the population of the whole of England, Wales and Scotland stood at about 6.7 million, constrained by the agricultural limitations of that time. By the end of the Regency period it has doubled. How is this possible, given that there has been no increase in the amount of land? The answer is, of course, the Agricultural Revolution. Without it, there would have been no population growth, no cheap workforce and consequently no Industrial Revolution.

The Agricultural Revolution is made up of several developments in farming practices. First, greater attention is paid to fertilising the land: in particular, the use of sophisticated combinations of crops and their rotation, year by year, so that the land does not need to be left fallow. Second, farmers plant more high-calorie foodstuffs. In 1700 potatoes are only eaten in significant quantities in the north-west of England; by 1830 they are consumed right across the British Isles. Other important changes include the breeding of larger animals, as we saw in chapter 1, and the adoption of winter-feeding practices. Whereas in the past many animals were slaughtered at Martinmas (11 November) and then salted down for the winter, now they can be kept alive all year.[2] This not only increases the supply of fresh meat in the winter months, it also facilitates the breeding of more animals. As a result, there are twice as many cows, pigs and sheep as there were in the late seventeenth century.[3] When you add improvements in the transport network, which allow cheeses to travel long distances and fish to be taken to inland markets daily, you can see that food is more plentiful now than it has ever been.

Having said this, the improved supply does not in itself overcome the seasonal limitations. If you live in London and are wealthy, you can obtain almost anything, as Covent Garden Market has dealers who specialise in supplying out-of-season fruit and vegetables. Richard Rush, for instance, eats imported strawberries in April, and Anne Lister has some in December.[4] But if you are not so wealthy, you will still be bound by the limited availability of fresh food at certain times of year. Hannah Glasse's book, *The Art of Cookery Made Plain and Easy*, provides a list of what you can store through the winter months. She tells you which types of apples keep until May and which are likely to go off before the end of January; which vegetables from the kitchen garden can be used in April, and which need to be kept in the green-house so they last that much longer. Remember that poultry, game and fish are also seasonal, due to migration and breeding patterns. According to Glasse, January is a suitable month to eat 'hen-turkeys, capons, pullets, fowls, chickens, hares, wild fowl, tame rabbits and pigeons'. As regards fish, the first quarter of the year is when you should eat lobster, crab, crayfish, garfish, mackerel, bream, barbel, roach, shad, lamprey, dace and prawns.[5] Bear in mind too that chickens lay eggs much more regularly in summer than in winter. Preparing a dinner therefore requires considerable planning.

Fortunately, there are ways of storing food so that it can be consumed out of season. Pickling fish and vegetables and salting meat are old technologies; likewise the curing of bacon and the smoking of fish. Many people are employed in the potting of seafood and meat, preserving it beneath a seal of butter. In the late eighteenth century, ventilated cupboards known as 'meat-safes' are developed, with a zinc mesh to keep the flies off. At the same time, country-house proprietors build ice houses. These are domed brick-lined chambers, mostly underground, in which slabs of ice, taken in winter from a nearby freshwater lake or pond, are stored between layers of straw until needed in the summer. An even bigger technological breakthrough is the tin can. A Frenchman discovers in the 1790s that by sealing food in a glass jar and then heating it, it can be kept fresh until the glass is opened. In 1810, Bryan Donkin, an entrepreneur from Northumberland, discovers that by using tin-lined metal cans instead of the more fragile glass, and heating them slowly, he can preserve meat for long periods. In 1813 several members of the royal family – including the queen and Prince Regent – taste his tinned beef and approve. Soon afterwards you can buy tinned beef, carrots, soups and stews, all courtesy of Mr Donkin. Unfortunately no one has yet invented the tin opener, so you'll need to use a hammer and chisel to open a can of stew. But if you're hungry enough, that should not put you off.

Cooking practices are changing too. Along with the bar grate and the installation of ranges in gentlemen's kitchens, people start to employ a much wider variety of saucepans and implements. You might not have noticed when looking over William Mortimer's house that he owns a fish kettle, a steamer and a flour dredge. You wouldn't have found those things in a tradesman's kitchen a hundred years ago. Nor would you have found so many saucepans and kettles. As for the upper classes, according to William Verrall, the head cook and proprietor of the White Hart in Lewes, a gentleman should equip his kitchen with several boiling pans, frying pans, a stew-pot, at least ten stewpans of varying sizes, ladles, large spoons, colanders, sieves and measuring cups. He recommends anyone still using wooden ladles, skimmers, cabbage-nets or other 'such nasty things' to throw them away and replace them with clean metal ones; the only wooden implements should be large spoons – and these must be reserved for their dedicated purposes.[6]

As we saw in the last chapter, these days ovens are heated by a fire directly beneath them. A hundred years ago they were warmed by burning dried twigs inside them. The problem was that you couldn't reheat the oven after it began to cool. The ability now to sustain a hot temperature encourages cooks to bake much more. Roasting has also changed due to technology. Many new varieties of spit are available: you'll see smoke-jacks, which turn the meat by the power of updraughts from the fire; spits driven by weights, pulleys and rotors; and turnspits, which are powered by a small dog running inside a drive wheel. Just as novel are bottlejacks and danglespits, which suspend the meat within the chimney itself; and the Dutch oven, which is a semicircular metal enclosure that you put in front of the fire and which reflects the heat back on to the meat turning inside.

If all this talk of roast meat is putting you off, you'll be pleased to hear that a few people are giving up eating animals. They don't actually use the word 'vegetarian' – it won't be coined until the 1840s – but they start to explore the concept. Various eighteenth-century medical texts advise that restricted diets should be adopted for health reasons, and this makes people think more generally about the importance of food. If occasionally limiting your diet can be good for you, why should not a permanent avoidance of strong foods eliminate the risk of various diseases altogether? The principal pros-elytiser in this matter is the physician William Lambe, who gives up meat, cheese, milk and eggs to cure himself of certain recurrent ailments in 1806; thereafter he becomes obsessed with avoiding meat. At the same time, people who are moved by compassion for animals begin to wonder about the morality of killing and eating them. In 1813 the poet Percy Bysshe Shelley publishes his famous pamphlet *A Vindication of Natural Diet*, in which he espouses Dr Lambe's prin-ciples and advocates not eating meat on the grounds of health and animal rights. Even Lord Byron is briefly persuaded to avoid eating meat. In November 1813 he notes in his diary that he rarely eats much but 'when I *do* dine I gorge like an Arab, or a Boa snake, on fish and vegetables, but no meat'.[7] In his case, however, the diet doesn't last.

Middle-Class Meals

According to James Malcolm, writing in 1807, 'tea, coffee, cocoa, rolls, toast and bread' form the breakfasts of middle-class Londoners.[8] Outside London, James Woodforde regularly has tea, toast and butter on the breakfast table of his rectory in Norfolk; so too does Elizabeth Ham at her home on the Dorset–Somerset border. Jane Austen only mentions bread rolls and butter at Chawton.[9] Even when staying at an inn or seaside boarding house you should expect nothing more than a bread roll and butter, plus a hot drink. On his visit to Glasgow in 1814, Hans Caspar Escher is given two breakfasts. The first consists of bread and butter and coffee; the second, of bread and butter and a glass of Madeira. In case you are wondering why two breakfasts are necessary, the reason is that each is followed by a visit to church to hear a two-hour-long sermon. Perhaps make that a large glass of Madeira.[10]

When it comes to dinners and suppers, the task of presenting your family with something new and tasty is becoming easier due to the publication of an ever-growing number of cookery books. We've already encountered Hannah Glasse's *Art of Cookery*, first published in 1747 and still in print in 1830, having been revised and expanded in about twenty new editions along the way. Its success is partly due to its simplicity: Glasse wants to enable every literate servant to cook, with no other training required. It not only brings together more than 300 traditional English recipes but introduces hundreds of new French and Italian dishes, as well as some inspired by Indian, South-East Asian and Middle Eastern culinary traditions. And if *The Art of Cookery* fails to excite your tastebuds, at least fifty other cookbooks come into print for the first time in this period. Despite Dr Johnson's declaration that 'women can spin very well but they cannot make a good book of cookery', about half of all of these are written by women. (None, I hasten to add, is written by Dr Johnson.)

With so many recipes to choose from, what is the most popular dish in Britain? 'It is one of the heaviest charges against John Bull,' writes the epicure Ralph Rylance in 1815, 'that when he intends to fare well, he cannot help crying out "roast beef!"'[11] It is perhaps worth pointing out that, although you may have eaten what passes for roast beef many times in the modern world, you have probably never had the genuine article. To roast a joint properly you need to use a spit, directly exposing the meat to the heat of the flames. Meat cooked in an oven is not roasted but baked, according to the definitions of the time, and is nowhere near as satisfying, according to Rylance.[12]

After roast beef, what next? Boiled beef, stewed beef, beef à la mode, beef collops, beef olives, beef escarlot, beef ragout, fried beefsteaks, stewed beefsteaks, Portugal beef, beef gobbet, beef royal, brisket, beef fricassee ... As you'll see, despite some people turning to vegetarianism, the vast majority of those who can afford it are consuming as much beef as they can. Nor are they ignoring other types of meat. In addition to the usual cow, pig, sheep, deer, rabbit, hare, pheasant, pigeon, duck, goose, turkey and chicken, Hannah Glasse gives recipes for partridge, snipe, woodcock, ortolan, ruff, lark and plover, plus many species of fish and seafood. Methods of cooking include broiling (grilling), boiling, baking, roasting, stewing, casseroling, frying and fricasseeing; but Glasse also suggests some unusual ones, such as hashing and jugging. The 1799 edition of her book includes a recipe for 'barbecued pig' and instructs you how to cook pilau rice. It even tells you how 'to dress mutton the Turkish way', how 'to cook a curry the Indian way' and how to make 'mutton kebabs'.[13]

If you want to explore the most exotic foods available, you will need to pay a visit to one of the Italian food warehouses in London. As you would expect, they stock various sorts of pasta and cheeses, such as Parmesan and Gruyere; but they also sell curry powder and many flavoured vinegars, such as red and white wine vinegar, garlic vinegar, cayenne vinegar and chilli vinegar. In addition they have some true delicacies, such as the wonderfully named fish sauce, 'zoobditty mutch' from the Far East, and various forms of ketchup, including mushroom, oyster and walnut ketchup (but not tomato). They can even provide you with 'tablets of portable soup of various flavours, which dissolve quickly in hot water'.[14]

Very few people in Regency Britain get to taste zoobditty mutch or instant soup. Many, on the other hand, eat calf's head, tripe, calf's heart, chitterlings, giblet soup, cow's hoof soup, roast cod's head, hare's brains, lamb's ears, sheep's tongues, sheep's udders, pig's ears and trotters. Large quantities of what you and I would call offal are consumed by the middle classes with great relish.[15] Hannah Glasse gives recipes for dishes such as 'pigs' feet and ears', baked calf's head, baked sheep's head, a stuffing of pig's brains and sage, and so forth. Martha Lloyd's book of household recipes shows that, while Jane

Austen's family occasionally have chicken curry (following Hannah Glasse's recipe), the great novelist also tucks into 'calves' feet jelly', 'cowheel soup' and 'mock turtle soup' (made from a calf's head).[16]

Sweet dishes are much more in line with modern preferences. Many of these are described as puddings – in fact, 'pudding' is one of the most common words you will come across in a middle-class household. Hannah Glasse gives recipes for orange pudding, lemon pudding, apple pudding, rice pudding, custard pudding, bread-and-butter pudding, almond pudding, chestnut pudding, cheese-curd pudding, apricot pudding, plum pudding and prune pudding. She also offers blanc-mange, trifle, apple dumplings, apple pie, cherry pie, pancakes, apple fritters, orange jelly, lemon cheesecake, almond cheesecake, goose-berry cream, orange cream, pistachio cream, gingerbread, macaroons, biscuits, syllabubs and cakes galore. The most popular cookbook at the end of our period, *The Cook's Oracle* by Dr Kitchiner, will further offer you a range of fruit tarts, millefeuille, baked pears, greengages preserved in syrup, lemon chips and orange chips, seed buns and gingerbread nuts. Travel into Devon and it is fashionable to have clotted cream on your fruit tarts. Turn up at William Verrall's inn in Lewes, Sussex, and you might well be treated to strawberry or pine-apple fritters.[17] True, the cooks at that establishment might first serve you 'calves' brains with rice' and the slightly disturbing 'calves' tails with carrots in brown sauce' but the sweet course will be sensational.

So how is all this food served? If you are eating by yourself at an inn, you'll sit down to a dish of boiled or roasted meat with a few boiled vegetables, over which butter sauce is poured. If dining formally with other people, you will be offered two courses and a dessert but each course will consist of multiple dishes. Normally you will have soup as a starter. When the bowls have been handed around, the tureen will be removed and another dish brought to the table to take its place. For example, you might have a pea soup followed by a first course consisting of a dish of boiled leg of mutton with capers; a dish of skate in oyster sauce; and a platter of ham and roast chicken, with the soup being replaced by a roast turkey. For the second course, you might see a dish with fried slices of rabbit set on one side of the table, and a plate of brawn on the other. Between the two there will be several fruit tarts and minced pies.[18] When everything has been consumed, a dessert of fruit is served.

All this food is expensive, especially the meat. Beef, pork, veal and mutton normally cost around 4d–6d per lb and much more in times of dearth. In 1795 you will see butchers charge 7d per lb for beef and veal, 7½d per lb for mutton and 8d per lb for pork chops.[19] As for fish and fowl, the expense is increased by the fact that certain species are only sold whole. Cod costs about 1s 3d per lb – so the average 36-inch fish weighing 15lbs after gutting will cost just under £1.[20] Prawns cost up to 3s for a hundred. A wild duck costs between 3s and 5s, and a goose about the same.[21] Such high prices mean that the weekly grocery bill for a middle-class family with four children and two servants is hefty, as this example from 1790 shows:

Bread for eight people, at 8d per week each	5s 4d
Butter, 7lbs at 9d per lb	5s 3d
Cheese, 3½lbs at 5d per lb	1s 5½d
Vegetables, herbs, spices, etc.	3s 6d
Meat and fish, 1lb each per day, at 6d per lb	£1 8s 0d
Milk and cream	1s 2d
Eggs	4d
Flour	1s 2d
Small beer, at 14s for a 36-gallon barrel, 12 gallons	4s 8d
Tea	2s 0d
Sugar	3s 0d
Total for the week[22]	£2 15s 10½d

And that is for a family that arranges their household affairs with an emphasis on economy. Quite apart from all the other expenses of the household – rent, firewood and coal, servants' wages, taxes, washing, candles, sewing, new clothes, and luxury items like books, newspapers, wine and spirits – just feeding this family costs more than £145 per year.

Working-Class Food

The poorer members of society face two major challenges in their diet. The first is one of *quantity*: obtaining enough basic carbohydrates, whether in the form of wheat, oats, barley, rye or potatoes; the second is the problem of *nutrition*: finding the essential vitamins, fats, minerals and protein necessary to maintain the good health of the family. Both of these challenges are accentuated by wildly fluctuating prices. Wheat normally costs about £2 a quarter (480lbs) in the late 1780s and early 1790s, which allows a standard bread loaf of 4lbs 5½oz to be bought for 6d.[23] But due to the poor harvests of 1794 and 1795, the price of wheat goes up until your standard loaf costs 9d. And wheat prices keep rising, reaching £6 18s 4d per quarter in Berkshire in 1800.[24] Your old 6d loaf now costs 20d – if you can get one. As a result, the demand for alternatives also rises, so all food prices increase simultaneously. Meat and fish become unaffordable. Unless a family has a garden to grow herbs and vegetables, picks freely available fruit like blackberries, sloes and whortleberries, and maintains their own cow for milk, butter and cheese, their diet will be very restricted indeed.

For breakfast, a labourer in London will normally have bread and butter washed down with tea, although some replace the tea with small beer.[25] In the north of England, breakfast usually consists of 'hasty pudding' and milk or beer. Hasty pudding is a very popular dish made by boiling oats in salted water until thickened, then mixing in a little milk or treacle and placing a knob of butter in the middle. In Scotland, a working man's breakfast may well amount to 1½lbs of porridge but during harvest, when the working day is much longer, he might consume twice as much.[26] However, this may well be his main meal of the day, and the rest of the family cannot expect such generous helpings.

Dining with a poor family in the 1790s is unlikely to be a great gastronomic experience – especially if they have a large number of children. Let's say you are staying with a labourer and his wife and their five children in Barkham, in Berkshire. Each week they buy 7½ gallons of flour at 10d per gallon, plus yeast and salt, which amounts to a total of 6s 7d for their daily bread. They also buy 1lb of bacon, which they boil up with greens and herbs from their garden. As they grow their own potatoes, they serve these in the water left over from boiling the bacon and greens. In addition, they consume 1oz of tea, ¼lb of sugar and ½lb of butter or lard per week. And that's it. No beer. No cheese. No other meat. Of their total earnings of 8s 6d per week, 8s 3d goes on food, most of that being bread. So when the price of wheat trebles in 1800, their life gets much tougher.[27] You might want not to join them at their table in such circumstances. They will have nothing to offer you.

As you visit other parts of Britain, you will find working people everywhere doing their best to create nutritious meals despite the high prices of wheat. In Devon, potatoes are boiled, mashed and mixed with a little flour to make bread.[28] This is eaten for breakfast and, with peas pottage, for supper. As for dinner:

> A large quantity of broth is prepared in the farmhouses, by stewing pickled pork or bacon with cabbage, carrots, turnips, potherbs, onions and leeks, in abundance. When pork or bacon is not to be got by the peasantry, they make use of mutton suet cut very small, and stewed with the garden-stuff above-mentioned.[29]

In the north of England, working-class cookery is even more inventive. Those who can afford to will fry potatoes in bacon fat or stew them with mutton or pork in a meat hash. In some places you will find them roasted and eaten with salt. In Northumberland and Cumberland, an excellent everyday pottage is produced from mutton, onions, oatmeal, barley, water and herbs. Water gruel – made with water, oatmeal, butter and salt – is regularly eaten. Crowdie is a great favourite among miners and is made by pouring boiling water over oatmeal, which is then eaten with milk or butter. Frumenty or barley-milk consists of barley boiled for two hours and then mixed with milk and sugar. And then there is peas-kail, a local variant on peas pottage, made with milk rather than water. Rye bread and barley bread are often eaten in the North. These keep much better than white bread: Cumberland barley bread can be used for four to five weeks in winter, and two to three weeks in summer.[30]

As you travel into Scotland, you come across people eating clap-bread. A dough of oatmeal, water and salt is placed on a board and 'clapped out' until it covers it, then slipped off on to a round piece of flat iron, which is then placed over the fire. The result is an unleavened dry flatbread.[31] This, along with water gruel, peas pottage, potatoes and a little meat, provides the principal sustenance for many people in the Highlands throughout the year. Around the coasts, this diet is supplemented by herring.

If you find yourself in the workhouse, the meals you'll be served will reflect local customs. In the Carlisle workhouse, breakfast consists of hasty pudding, served with milk or beer. Dinner for most of the week is either beef broth and bread, or potatoes with a little milk and butter, plus broth. On Fridays it consists of two slices of boiled beef and soup. Supper is hasty pudding or bread every day except Saturday, when inmates are given bread and cheese. Drink is milk or small beer. Some of the best-fed paupers in the 1790s are those in the Derby workhouse. They only ever get milk pottage for breakfast, and bread and beer for supper, but they are fed meat for dinner every day except Saturday, when they get suet dumplings.[32] A great many agricultural labourers can't afford to eat as well as that in their own homes.

Upper-Class Food

Most upper-class people do not follow the three-meals-a-day routine. They enjoy five opportunities to indulge themselves: at breakfast, luncheon, afternoon tea, dinner and supper. This does not mean that they all eat five times a day: most just take something at three or four of these mealtimes, according to need. As so often in life, the rules and routines that govern the lives of the middle and working classes are matters of choice for the wealthy.

If you are a lady or gentleman going about your day by yourself, your breakfast may be an unceremonious affair – simply hot rolls or toast and butter, with a cup of coffee or tea. Anne Lister, getting up early to catch a 6 a.m. coach, has a crust of bread and a glass of white wine. On another occasion, while staying in Hull, she has 'a couple of cups of coffee and a glass of cold water & cold bread and butter'.[33] Breakfast at a country house will be more elaborate. When Jane Austen's mother visits Stoneleigh Abbey she is given plum cake and pound cake as well as hot and cold rolls and buttered toast.[34] Of course if you are a German prince, you're likely to be served something better still. Hermann Pückler-Muskau walks into the breakfast room of his inn one morning to see a large tea urn in the middle of the table set for him, with both green and black tea leaves in adjacent caddies, and milk in a jug. His place setting is laid with 'three small Wedgwood plates with as many knives and forks and two large cups of beautiful porcelain'. Around it are four dishes: one filled with boiled eggs; one of grilled pig's ears; one of muffins kept warm by a hot-water plate; and the fourth laden with cold ham. There are also plates of dry and buttered toast and rolls of white bread, plus a glass dish of fine butter, cruets of French and English mustard, and salt and pepper. This quite surprises him because he only asked for a cup of tea.[35]

Luncheon is an informal meal most frequently consumed by women. The reason is that it is considered unseemly for ladies to consume a lot of food at dinner, so eating earlier saves them from having to ask for disgracefully large portions later. Otherwise luncheon has much in common with supper, in that it is eaten in the breakfast room, not the dining room. You do not need to dress up; seating is not bound by etiquette; and you will normally help yourself to the food rather than be waited on. Suitable dishes for luncheon include cold cuts of meat, tongue and ham, potted meat, and sandwiches made from slices of chicken, mutton or beef.[36]

Dinner is your main meal of the day, whatever time you take it. Among the rich, it is served late – the later the better – and you will be expected to dress appropriately. You will also need to observe all the formal etiquette associated with the dining room. Women take precedence over men of the same rank, so the mistress of the house always sits at the head of the table and her husband at the foot. Where two women are of the same rank, married women take priority over unmarried ones; if both are married, the elder takes priority. John Trusler, in *The Honours of the Table*, explains what you can expect when dinner is announced at the start of our period:

> The mistress of the house requests the lady first in rank, in company, to show the way to the rest, and walk first into the room where the table is served. She then asks the second in precedence to follow, and after all the ladies are passed, she brings up the rear herself. The master of the house does the same with the gentlemen.[37]

When you enter the dining room in this fashion, everyone sits according to precedence too, with all the ladies at one end of the table in order of seniority and all the gentlemen at the lower end, likewise in order. As the 1790s wear on, however, things start to be done differently. Now gentlemen lead ladies into the dining room by taking their arm and processing in, two by two. Ladies and gentlemen sit next to each other, alternately male and female. Note, however, that you still enter and sit according to precedence. If you want to chat over dinner to a particularly handsome officer or delightful debutante of a lower status than you, you might have to belittle yourself. But whatever you do, don't try to *elevate* your status. It is considered shameful to claim a rank to which you have no right.

Let's say you are invited to a formal dinner for ten people at a London town house similar to that attended by Louis Simond in 1808.[38] Taking your seat, you should find a soup bowl on top of your dinner plate, a fork to the left, a bread roll to the left of the fork, and a knife to the right. Your napkin may be rolled up on the left or laid flat across the empty soup bowl, with the soup spoon on top. Your wine glass might be to the left of your fork or on the right, above your knife; there is no right or wrong position for the glass in this period.[39] At the head of the table, the silver soup tureen holds a turtle soup; the other dishes are still hidden under their silver and china covers. When everyone has eaten their soup, and a large turbot has taken the place of the tureen, all the covers are removed by the servants. You may see a plate of roast beef, with two large dishes of vegetables on either side of it; a plate laden with many rashers of bacon; a dish of several small birds, such as roast ortolans; a large dish of spinach in butter; and a jug of oyster sauce (made with oysters, milk, flour and butter). Each gentleman will carve the nearest meat, helping the lady beside him to the best cuts. For serving the fish, there is a wide-bladed fish knife placed beside the relevant dish. (You will use your normal knife to eat the fish, however; individual fish knives do not yet exist.) Waiters will pour the wine throughout the meal. When you wish to drink, it is necessary to do so in conjunction with someone else, catching their eye and raising your glass as you say their name. Note that it is impolite to do this with the same person more than once in each course.

When you have finished eating, cross your knife and fork in the middle of your plate to indicate to the waiters that you do not wish to eat any more. They will then take it away, clean any crumbs from around your place and serve you a clean plate and knife and fork ready for the next course. This may consist of a meaty ragout as a principal dish, with cream and celery as the corner dishes at the head of the table, and cauliflowers and pastries in the corners at the lower end. More pastries and a dish of macaroni cheese are placed in the middle;

and a platter of venison at the foot. You are certainly not going to go hungry. But if you feel in danger of over-eating, spare a thought for the master and mistress, as it is considered bad manners for them to finish while any of their guests is still at it.

At some formal dinners the second course is followed by a small preliminary dessert. This normally consists of cheese, butter, salad, celery and other nibbles.[40] After that, your place is laid one last time with a small dessert plate, suitable cutlery and a clean wine glass. Several decanters are placed before the master of the house, filled with port, sherry, Madeira, claret or brandy. All of these are passed one by one to the master's left, and thus around the table, with each gentleman filling his own wine glass and that of the lady beside him. The dessert itself consists of another suite of dishes: fresh and stewed fruit, nuts, a large display of cakes and a bowl of oranges. If any other types of hot-house fruit are available, then these will be served as part of the dessert. Pineapples are particularly prized, as they cost two guineas per piece.[41] If you can obtain anything out of season, this too is highly appropriate for a dessert. In summer, ice creams may be served, which are a real sign of wealth as you need to have a good ice house and a freshwater lake to be able to produce enough ice.

Politeness requires the ladies to remain at table for a quarter of an hour after the last person has stopped eating. When the mistress judges the time is right, she announces the fact to the other women present and gets to her feet. All the men should rise as the ladies get up, and the gentleman nearest the door should open it for them. The master then takes his wife's place at the head of the table, the men occupy the seats closest to him, and the circulation of the decanters resumes. At the end of our period, any gentleman who wishes to withdraw may do so at any time after the ladies have left; he is quite at liberty to join them in the withdrawing room too, for tea and coffee.[42] At the start of our period, however, gentlemen are expected to remain with the host – no matter what. Monsieur Simond notes in 1808 that:

> in a corner of the very dining room, there is a certain convenient piece of furniture to be used by anybody who wants it. The operation is performed very deliberately and undisguisedly, as a matter of course, and occasions no interruption of the conversation. I once took the liberty to ask why this convenient article was not placed out of the room, in some adjoining closet, and was answered that in former times,

when good fellowship was more strictly enforced than in these degenerate days, it had been found that men of weak heads or stomachs
took advantage of the opportunity to make their escape shamefully,
before they were quite drunk, and that it was to guard against such
an enormity that this nice expedient had been invented.[43]

Extreme drunkenness and urinating in front of your fellow guests
are not the limits of dining-room outrageousness. There is also glut-
tony. As a leading member of The Sublime Society of Beef Steaks,
the duke of Norfolk has been known to consume fifteen steaks in one
meal.[44] The prince of Wales's accounts record that the 120 members
of his household consume 5,264lbs of meat in one month in 1816 –
more than 22oz per person per day – and of course the prince himself
and his closest friends consume the lion's share.[45] One dinner might
see a choice of two soups followed by a selection of four different
fish and fourteen other dishes as part of the first course, followed by
a second course of twenty-two dishes, including roast quail, roast
chicken, roast peafowl, roast hare, truffles with wine, a pudding made
with fifty crayfish, lobster salad, pineapple jelly, cherry tarts, four joints
of roast meats, four more sweet dishes; and, on a side table,
a haunch of venison, a saddle of mutton, four pullets, a bean-and-
bacon casserole, a pheasant pie, and a selection of cold ham, tongue,
beef and veal. Obviously the prince does not consume all this single-
handedly but this particular menu is for a day when he is *not* entertaining important guests. Supper later that same day consists of
another fourteen dishes. No wonder he weighs more than twenty-two
stone by the time he dies.[46]

Dining Out

If in doubt about where to eat in London, I suggest you consult a
copy of *The Epicure's Almanack* by Ralph Rylance, published in 1815.
It's the nearest thing there is to a Regency *Good Food Guide*. Rylance
lists almost 600 places to eat, advising you on all their respective
specialities. The most common sort is a cook shop or eating house
– the difference between the two being that the cook shop only
provides takeaway food whereas the eating house is where you can
also eat in. In both places you will find joints of meat roasting

on spits: you can select which variety you want and pay for it by weight, if taking it away in a sandwich, or by plate, if eating in. Expect to pay between 1s and 1s 6d if sitting down to eat.

Taverns are more upmarket than eating houses and cater predominantly to the professional classes, but they will rarely charge more than 2s for lunch or supper. Some are very busy: The Cock behind the Royal Exchange in the city serves more than 500 people every day.[47] Some places are enormous, able to seat up to 2,000 people for a grand dinner. For large-scale entertaining, I suggest you talk to the manager of The Crown and Anchor Tavern in the Strand, or The London Tavern in Bishopsgate Street, or The Shakespeare Tavern in Covent Garden.

Then there are the old inns, most of which offer informal meals as well as formal dinners. Many coffee houses also provide light meals, such as soups, broths and sandwiches. At the very end of our period, in the 1820s, the word 'restaurant' – previously used only of establishments in Paris – starts to be applied to top-notch eating houses in London, although it has to be said that the quality of their food is not up to that of their French counterparts.[48] On top of all of these you have the pastry shops and confectioners, and in a few prosperous towns, ice-cream vendors. In Bath, for example, you can pick up ice creams from a shop on Pulteney Bridge. Thomas Farrance, the famous London pastry cook, serves ices as well as sweet and savoury tarts from the Spring Garden Coffee House on Cockspur Street.[49] Late at night, street vendors emerge in the larger towns, selling baked potatoes and pies from coal-heated, tin-furnace stands. For a few brief years there is even an Indian restaurant in London, established by Deen Mahomet, selling authentic curries to those nabobs who have developed a taste for them in India.[50]

Rarely will you find an extensive menu. Almost none of these places lists more than a dozen dishes on its bill of fare and specialist shops may offer only one.[51] Some inns and lodging houses in seaside towns will quote you a price for 'the ordinary', which is the single offering to all guests that day. Most catering establishments in a city lay a list of their prices on each table, or pin up a menu by the door. At Pagliano's in St Martin's Street, London, the chef offers as extensive a menu as you are likely to see in any eating house. For starters there are three soups: broth (4d a bowl), herb soup (4d) and vermicelli soup (6d). For fish, he has boiled skate (6d), boiled halibut (9d), boiled cod

(8d), boiled salt fish (6d) and fried fish (8d). If you stump up another 6d you can order either a plate of beef with turnips for your second course; or beef with radishes, plain roast beef or fried liver. If you are prepared to spend another 8d, you can have an omelette, mutton à la mode or macaroni. A boiled or roast chicken will cost you 1s 6d. Lastly, you can order a salad or a bowl of broccoli for 6d and extra potatoes for 2d. Bread and a half-pint of porter will add 3d to your bill. A whole two-course meal will therefore set you back between 1s 6d and 3s, not including the tip to the waiter.

It is of course possible to spend much more than this. 'The ordinary' at the Albion Tavern on Aldersgate is said to cost three guineas, and dinner at the Clarendon Hotel is three or four guineas, not including wine (which will cost you an extra guinea per bottle). Specially commissioned dinners can cost a lot more. At The Shakespeare Tavern, they cater for the most extravagant tastes. One special dinner there, which involves a 40lb turbot among a total of 108 cooked dishes, costs seven guineas a head. At the Albion, Sir William Curtis spends a mind-boggling £40 *per head* on a single dinner for his guests, which includes a specially selected ham sent over from Westphalia in Germany.[52] Regency people may serve you pig's ears and calves' heads but you have to be impressed by the extravagance of their catering.

Alcohol

How much do people drink in this period? You'd have thought that downing six bottles of claret in one evening would make you a heavy drinker. Even if each bottle contains one *old* pint (about 473ml) as used in England and Wales before the Weights and Measures Act of 1824, six of them contain about forty units of alcohol, which can't be good for you. Yet that amount of wine is what the duke of York regularly drinks without it noticeably affecting him. William Pitt and Richard Sheridan imbibe that much in port, which is half as strong again, every day.[53] However, these gentlemen are hardly representative of the population as a whole. Therefore it is difficult to say how much alcohol the average man or woman drinks. Nevertheless, I am not one to let the difficulty of answering a question put me off, so we will return to it in a short while, when you have first had a glimpse of all the drinks on offer.

To begin with spirits: this is a huge growth period for the Scottish whisky industry, with output trebling between 1800 and 1830. By the 1820s, production has passed five million imperial gallons a year.[54] But this is only what is reported to the excise officers; no one has any idea how much whisky is produced on the quiet. For example, it is common for Highland farmers to exchange grain for whisky, without any money changing hands.[55] Thus even licensed stills may be producing more than they admit. When you enter a Scottish public house, don't expect to sip a small measure neat from a glass. True Scotsmen drink it from tumblers in units of a mutchkin, which is 424ml, or approximately three-quarters of an imperial pint (568ml). Sometimes they mix it with hot water and sugar, sometimes with ale, and sometimes with cold water.[56] But however you take it, remember that the standard measure is seventeen times that of a modern one, or more than half a bottle by our reckoning. I would strongly caution you against asking for a double.

In England and Wales, gin remains the favoured spirit, especially in London where 90 per cent of the nation's legal gin is produced.[57] As for the illegal stuff, the 'moonshine', who knows? Even a clergyman like Mr Woodforde will bend the law a little and busy himself 'bottling two tubs of gin that came by moonshine this morning'.[58] The widespread illicit trade is a response to the trebling of duty between 1794 and 1819. Already people are paying more in duty than they are for the gin itself. The good news is that there is relatively little mark-up on booze in public houses at this time. Thus if you go into a pub and ask for a quarter-pint of gin, it should cost you in the region of 2½d in the 1790s, 6d in the 1810s and 5d after 1825, when the duty is significantly reduced and the size of a pint increased to its imperial measure. Note that some unscrupulous distillers and wholesalers adulterate their gin with water or sulphuric acid, so anything cheaper than these prices is not necessarily good value for money.[59]

What other alcoholic drinks are there? Rum and brandy are imported in large quantities, although they are relatively expensive.[60] Or you might try arrack, imported from Ceylon, which is distilled from the sap of coconut flowers. Then there are the liqueurs, which are generally home-made. Jane Austen's family makes cherry brandy by adding a pint of sugar-sweetened concentrated cherry juice to a pint of brandy; others do the same with apricots.[61] Most types of liqueur are described as 'ratafias': one recipe book from 1826 gives recipes for thirty-four different flavours, so you might choose to have an aniseed, coffee, orange or chocolate liqueur. If you're very brave you might even try one known as *Urine d'éléphant* – euphemistically translated as 'Elephant's milk' – made from rectified spirits and the juice of the Benjamin tree.[62] In addition, cider and perry are fermented to great strength, almost 10 per cent alcohol, and drunk in large quantities in the West Country and the Marches of Wales. And if none of the above catches your fancy, there is always beer.

Beer is the traditional drink of the English and has been since the sixteenth century, when it took over from ale (which is brewed without hops). Generally it is divided into small beer, which is weak – about 2½ per cent alcohol by volume – and strong beer, which is in excess of 6 per cent alcohol.[63] Of the two, it is strong beer that is growing in popularity. Large breweries like Bass, Whitbread, Truman and Barclay Perkins are finding more ways to produce ever-greater quantities at competitive prices; by 1815, Barclay Perkins is making almost 30,000 gallons per day.[64] Small brewers cannot compete, so urban landlords increasingly contract with large breweries to supply their alehouses, inns and taverns. Gradually strong-beer production increases, from 4.4 million barrels nationwide in 1789 to 6.6 million in the late 1820s.[65] Note that you don't have to buy it in a pub – it is sold in bottled form too. Also available in bottles are several foreign beers, including Brunswick mum, from Germany; and white and brown spruce beer, from America.[66] You can also buy bottles of sparkling ale to serve in champagne glasses at mealtimes.[67] All these bottled beers are sealed with a wax-covered cork, so you'll need a corkscrew for your beer as well as your wine.

If you go into a London pub in the 1820s, expect to pay 5½d for a quart of strong beer – which is 2¾d a pint. But if you go into one of the crowded gin palaces that are then springing up in the capital, with long counters and no chairs, you can get 1 fluid ounce of gin (slightly larger than a modern single measure) for 1d. Eight out of ten customers knock that back in less than a minute.[68] What do you do – do you go for the cheap hit or the long, drawn-out pleasure? The amount of alcohol you're getting per penny is about the same. It is the beginning of the battle of the pub *versus* the gin palace. The result is that city landlords invest heavily in their businesses. They build alehouses on street corners with cellars for the storage of barrels and skittle alleys for the entertainment of drinkers, as well as upstairs accommodation for themselves and their families. The most upmarket types have saloons furnished with mahogany and decorated with mirrors, framed prints and even stuffed animals. Newspapers are available for clients to read, and tobacco and pipes are on sale. Unlike a gin palace, in which everything is geared around the rapid exchange of alcohol for cash, the emphasis in a new public house is on comfort, social interaction and encouraging clients to spend more time drinking. But the pub does follow the gin palace in one important respect: it borrows the idea of presenting drinks over a serving counter or, as we know it, a bar.[69] The difference is that, by 1830, the bar in a pub is furnished with hand-pumps. Joseph Bramah – that blessing of a genius who gives us the modern flushing loo – is also the inventor of the beer pump. Few people in history can claim to have done so much for our physical comfort – both in filling ourselves up at one end and in emptying ourselves at the other.

Wine is drunk much less frequently than spirits or beer but is treated with greater reverence than either. This is because it is the preferred drink of the rich and thus a status symbol. Port is the most popular variety: it accounts for more than half of all the wine imported into Britain in the 1820s. Spanish wine comes second, with about 20 per cent of the market, followed by wines from South Africa, Madeira and the Greek Islands. France comes sixth on that list, sending us less than 5 per cent of our needs, even after the end of the war. Rhenish wine, Hungarian Tokay and Malmsey from the Canaries are also imported in quantity.[70] The alcoholic strengths are, on the whole, quite high. According to contemporary hydrometer readings, port is about 23.5 per cent alcohol by volume, sherry almost 19 per cent and Madeira nearly 22 per cent, due to being fortified or 'heightened' with brandy.[71] Claret averages 14.4 per cent and Burgundy a mere 11.8 per cent. Both red and white champagne are imported, with the white version being slightly more alcoholic at 12.8 per cent.[72] If these are not strong enough for you, then you could mix your own punch. George IV's preferred version contains two mandarins, a Seville orange, two lemons, half a pint of syrup, a pint of strong green tea sweetened with sugar, a glass of fine Jamaican rum, a glass of cognac, a glass of arrack, a glass of pineapple syrup and two bottles of white champagne – all strained through fine linen and chilled. Given that the strength of the spirits is about 53 per cent alcohol, that is quite a powerful mix.[73]

In most cases, good-quality wines are bottled, corked and stored on their sides in the modern fashion, following the eighteenth-century discovery that, if kept in this way, they improve with age. Hence, unlike most earlier periods of history, you will find that vintages are identified in cellars and increasingly prized. Expect to pay £1 3s in the 1790s for a dozen bottles of ordinary red wine.[74] In 1798 Mr Woodforde complains that he now has to pay £1 13s for a crate of port – whereas at Oxford University in the 1770s he paid less than £1.[75] Ah, those were the days! But vintage wines are still relatively cheap. If you call in at Priddy's foreign warehouse and vaults in Poland Street, London, in 1795, you can still pick up a crate of 1788 port for £1, a dozen bottles of ten-year-old sherry for £1 5s or a crate of champagne for £3 10s.[76] In fact you have to go some way to find wine that is truly unaffordable. Perhaps the record at this time is set by the duke of Queensberry's executors, who sell a dozen quarts of a very fine Tokay in 1811 for £84.[77] Even so, a crate of the finest wines known to the aristocracy for less than a tradesman's annual salary seems relatively inexpensive when compared with the extraordinary prices paid in the modern world.

Not all wine is of this quality. Thus you could do worse than try some of the many fruit wines that are made in the country. Hannah Glasse's *Art of Cookery* gives recipes for more than a dozen sorts, including raisin, orange, cherry, birch, quince, turnip, raspberry and blackberry wine. Gooseberry and currant wine are the most common 'home wines', and orange wine, made with Seville oranges, is probably the most prized. At Chawton, Jane Austen's family make orange, gooseberry, currant, cowslip and elderberry wines, as well as ginger beer and mead (made with fermented honey).[78] In some places there is quite a trade in such drinks: Matthew Flinders pays 11s for two gallons of orange wine in 1795, which is as much as he pays for port.[79] The high price reflects the high alcohol content. Currant wine is measured at more than 20 per cent alcohol, gooseberry wine not much less, and raisin wine can exceed 25 per cent.[80] If you have enough gooseberries in your garden, all you need is sufficient sugar and clean water – and the patience to wait four months before you can drink the results.

So how much alcohol *do* the good people of Regency Britain consume? Adding all the wine and spirits imported in the 1820s to the total domestic production of spirits and beer, it turns out that, officially, each person over the age of fifteen consumes an average of twenty units of alcohol per week.[81] This is only a little higher than the early-twenty-first-century figure (about eighteen units at the time of writing) and a long way short of the highest drinking levels in the world today (Belarus consumes about thirty-three units of alcohol per person per week). However, these figures only include those drinks reported to the excise men. When you consider the large quantities of beer brewed privately as well as the fruit wines, mead, cider and perry made on farms and in cottages, you realise that a lot of alcohol evades the government inspectors' eyes. If you then add the thousands of barrels of brandy smuggled in by the Kent and Sussex 'free traders', and all the illicitly distilled spirits up and down the country – including the produce of hundreds of unlicensed stills in Scotland – you have to conclude that the Regency consumption of alcohol is nearer that of twenty-first-century Belarus than of modern-day Britain.

Non-Alcoholic Drinks

Beer might be the traditional drink of the English but it is fast acquiring a rival in tea. Indeed, although the value of the brewing industry increases by 50 per cent over the course of our period, the tea business expands by almost 150 per cent.[82] As Richard Rush puts it:

> The use of tea in England is universal. It is the breakfast of the wealthy, as of the poorer classes. On rising from the sumptuous dinner, coffee is first handed [out] but black tea comes afterwards ... Servants in London take it twice a day, sometimes oftener, and [it is] spreading among labouring classes at all hours.[83]

All tea comes from China; production has not yet started in India or Ceylon. There are two main varieties: green tea and black tea, otherwise known as bohea. Green tea is further subdivided into four types (imperial, singlo, hyson and gunpowder tea) and bohea into five (souchong, camho, pekoe, congo and common bohea). Green tea will normally cost you about 8s per lb, with hyson and other rarefied varieties costing 10s or more. Souchong, congo and the finer sorts of bohea normally cost about 5s–6s per lb but common bohea can cost as little as 1s 9d.[84] Given that you can make about 200 cups from a pound of tea, that makes it a far cheaper drink than beer, even when you include the cost of sugar. Thus most working-class families in England drink a lot of bohea. Even the poorest people set aside 3d–10d per week to spend on tea and sugar. But it is not quite the same drink as that consumed in the drawing rooms of the wealthy. As the Revd David Davies points out, in a well-to-do house you might be offered 'fine hyson tea sweetened with refined sugar and softened with cream', while the labouring classes drink 'spring water just coloured with a few leaves of the lowest-priced tea, sweetened with the brownest sugar'.[85] Moreover, those few leaves are often reused. Tea might be rapidly advancing on beer as the national drink in England but Richard Rush's declaration that it is 'universal' does not mean that it is an equaliser.

Coffee is growing in popularity even more rapidly: consumption per head increases by about 600 per cent over the period.[86] What you will have to pay for it depends on whether it comes from the British colonies (notably Jamaica), the East Indies (Java) or Latin America. Prices vary between 2s and 4s per lb at the grocer's, which makes it sound as if it is comparable with tea; however, you will need at least 2oz of coffee to make a pot for eight cups at the strength that most Regency people drink it, and 3oz to suit Continental taste. Thus your 1lb of coffee only makes a maximum of sixty-four cups. As a result, few poor people drink it. Retail establishments tend to water it down too much, so English coffee has a very bad reputation among European visitors. 'I would advise anyone who wants to drink coffee in England to mention beforehand how many cups should be made from half an ounce, otherwise he will get an atrocious mess of brown water,' declares Karl Moritz after a particularly disappointing experience.[87] But things could be worse. Many people who cannot afford real coffee buy cheap alternatives, such as 'Hunt's Economical Breakfast Powder', which is nothing more than roasted rye. Some bulk out the real coffee with ground roast mustard seeds or chicory.[88] Joseph Lackington concocts a substitute coffee by frying wheat. Mr Richard Hall, despite being a gentleman, makes a version by grinding up roast turnips. If you look around, you can find all sorts of dregs being sold as coffee, from roast acorns to powdered horse liver.[89]

Whatever you drink, avoid consuming water, especially in a town or city, for it will have been drawn from a river into which people have thrown all sorts of rubbish and detritus, from excrement to dead dogs. Well water is similarly unsafe. Spring water, while it is the cleanest natural sort, can also be contaminated, as can the rain in industrial areas, so you should boil all your water prior to drinking it. Women and children tend to drink whey and milk. Lemonade and cordials are made but only in private houses. One of the few non-alcoholic drinks you can buy is carbonated soda water, invented by Joseph Priestley in 1767 and manufactured from the 1780s by Jacob Schweppe of Geneva. In 1792, Mr Schweppe relocates his business to London. His success inspires others to follow suit, and by the 1820s there are dozens of soda-water manufacturers up and down the country. Their product is not cheap: it is sold in half-pint bottles for 5d or 6d.[90] And not everyone likes it. In the words of Robert Southey, 'the fixed air ... hisses as it goes down your throat as cutting as a razor, and draws tears as it comes up through the nose as pungent as a pinch of snuff'.[91]

Tobacco and Drugs

As you will know once you've stepped inside a Regency alehouse, the consumption of alcohol and the smoking of tobacco are inseparable. You'll find ½oz packets of pipe tobacco on sale in the taproom, priced at about 1¾d in the 1790s and 2½d in the 1820s.[92] The price increase leads to a slight decline in the levels of smoking over the period but even at its highest, Regency people consume less than a quarter of what their descendants will smoke in the mid-twentieth century.[93] Not that you will notice it, though, because the smoking is concentrated in places like alehouses. There are no cigarettes as yet and lighting a pipe with a tinderbox is a tricky process, so all the smokers resort to somewhere with a fire, and that is invariably an alehouse, inn, tavern, clubhouse or hotel.

While the amount of tobacco consumed in the Regency period does not greatly change, the ways in which people smoke do. You will still find many people using the old-fashioned clay pipes that have been around for two centuries but now manufacturers are starting to experiment with new designs. Brightly coloured creamware pipes are made in the Staffordshire Potteries, often in elaborate snake-like shapes with many coils. Highly decorated earthenware pipes with patterned bowls are produced. Meerschaum pipes are imported from Austria and Turkey, resplendent with large white bowls carved into extremely detailed and lifelike heads. Cherry-stick pipes with long stems are produced domestically and even Turkish hookahs are introduced, which enable the smoke to be cooled as it passes through a water basin. Anne Lister joins a company of men and women in smoking Turkish tobacco through a hookah in 1818.[94] Cigars too make their appearance in England for the first time, brought back by soldiers serving in Spain during the Peninsular War. Lord Byron smokes them in 1814, and later mentions them in his poetry. From the very start, they are high-value items: whereas 1lb of tobacco costs about 4s at a tobacconist in 1828, 1lb of cigars is nearer £1.[95] Hence the production of high-quality cigar-tubes and cigar boxes in which to keep them.

Some people prefer to snort their tobacco in the form of snuff. In case you are unfamiliar with it, this is a powdered form of tobacco that has undergone several processes, including fermentation, scenting with oils and long periods of maturing in storage. It is sold by weight, kept in a snuffbox and then pinched between the thumb and forefinger and sniffed up the nostrils. The cheapest varieties available from a tobacconist will cost you about 5s per lb but the finest, such as Spanish Bran, Macouba, Masulipatam, Frankfort and French Prize, will cost a lot more. Many of the types that you'll see stacked in stoneware jars on the shelves of Messrs Fribourg and Treyer at 34 Haymarket, London, are in excess of 10s per lb, with one or two fetching £3.[96] Men and women buy each other gifts of scented snuff in snuffboxes decorated with their portraits or those of their children. It is an intimate, delicate and refined way of consuming tobacco – the very opposite of having to enter a smoky pub to light a pipe.

The cognoscenti of Regency Britain are familiar with a wide range of other stimulants. Extensive descriptions are published of the purposeful consumption of hashish, henbane, belladonna, datura, digitalis and fly agaric but no one, it seems, is much interested in the recreational use of these drugs here in Britain; they are more a sort of curiosity, like the religious practices of a foreign country.[97] The principal exception to this generalisation is opium. In 1797 *The Times* reports that 'the Turkish custom of taking opium is beginning to prevail in what are called the first circles of London. This dissipation is spreading wide among female fashion.'[98] The amounts of opium imported into Britain amount to an average of 7 tons per year before 1800, rising to 10 tons a year in the 1820s. Almost every Romantic writer of the period tries it out, most famously Samuel Taylor Coleridge and Thomas De Quincey, who both become addicted and write about their experiences. Coleridge pens his most lauded poem, 'Kubla Khan', while high on opium, and De Quincey writes his most famous book about the pleasures and pains of the drug in *The Confessions of an English Opium-Eater*, published in 1822.

Opium reaches far beyond the intellectual set. You can buy it in the form of pills for between 10s and £1 per lb or in its most common form: a tincture of opium in alcohol, called laudanum, at the price of 4d for 100 drops. People use it in all-purpose medicines, such as Godfrey's Cordial and Darby's Carminative. They calm babies with it when they are teething and when they cannot sleep. They reach for it as a painkiller and a relaxant. Women take it to deal with premenstrual tension and the menopause. You might even take it to soothe a cough. Gradually your tolerance to the drug grows and, as you become addicted, so does your dependence. Coleridge ends up taking as many as 8,000 drops of laudanum per day.[99] The fallout is inevitable: physicians and writers soon spend as much time talking about the miseries as the ecstasies brought on by the drug.

The only other stimulant in which people are greatly interested is an artificial one: nitrous oxide. In 1799 Humphry Davy, the scientist who gives this substance the colloquial name 'laughing gas', holds a series of parties to find out more about its effects. He persuades his guests to write down what it feels like to inhale it and publishes the results as an appendix to his scientific work on the gas. Many prominent businessmen and politicians take part. The entrepreneur Josiah Wedgwood feels 'as if I were lighter than the atmosphere, as if I was going to mount to the top of the room'. The surgeon Stephen Hammick is given the silk bag containing the gas and then refuses to give it up, declaring 'Let me breathe it again, it is highly pleasant! It is the strongest stimulant I ever felt!' Robert Southey feels 'a thrill in my teeth' and is 'compelled to exercise my arms and feet'. And Coleridge cannot help but laugh at everyone looking at him, with 'more unmingled pleasure than I have ever before experienced'. But undoubtedly the most poetic description is that given by a paralysed person to whom Mr Davy delivers a dose as part of his experiment: 'I feel like the sound of a harp.'[100]

George IV as Prince Regent, portrayed by Sir Thomas Lawrence in 1816. Charles Greville speaks for many when he declares of the prince that 'a more contemptible, cowardly, selfish, unfeeling dog does not exist'. However, he is one of the greatest of all royal patrons of arts and architecture.

William Pitt addressing the House of Commons in 1793. Note that the clothes of the gentlemen around the chamber are all of the old style—breeches and stockings—before the changes in male dress introduced by Beau Brummell in the 1790s.

Contrast the clothes worn here by George Henckell in this portait of about 1800 with the breeches and stockings in the House of Commons. As a consequence of Brummell's influence on society, men dress in clothes that are cut to fit perfectly, and which look elegant but never bright or gaudy.

At the other end of the social spectrum, here we see a Yorkshire collier in his white suit and heavy boots making his way to work in 1813. Behind him is one of the earliest depictions of a steam locomotive.

The Cloakroom at the Clifton Assembly Rooms in 1818, by Rolina Sharples.
Here the ladies are wearing embroidered muslin dresses and the gentlemen
a variety of breeches, trousers and pantaloons in readiness for a ball.

The daily dress of working-class women in Yorkshire in 1813 has very little in common
with the evening dress of the Bristol ladies above. Note the oatcakes cooking
on a hotplate, separate from the fireplace, in the background.

Ladies wearing muslin dresses driving in a phaeton, as illustrated in *The Gallery of Fashion* in 1794. The growth of owner-driven carriages in the Regency period means it is perfectly acceptable for women to drive themselves about town.

The Bath coach. Travelling on top in this manner is normally about half the price of an inside place but it is often cold and dangerous. You would be well-advised to carry an umbrella – not that it will help you if you topple over on a sharp corner.

Velocipedes become all the rage amongst young gentlemen when they appear in London in 1818. Here, some of them are learning how to balance on two wheels at a velocipede school.

George Shillibeer's omnibus – the world's first 'bus' service – makes its first appearance on the road between Paddington and the City of London in July 1829. The same vehicle does the route four times each day – so there is no danger of three coming along at once.

In 1815, steamships suddenly become common on British waters. They offer comfortable travel and guaranteed sailing times – unlike sailing ships, which are dependent on the wind. Reliability remains an issue, however – hence the need for a mast as well as a funnel.

The world's first regular passenger train service between Liverpool and Manchester starts in 1830. This image depicts the train taking on water at Parkside Station in 1831.

The kitchen of a gentleman's residence, Langton Hall, painted by Mary Ellen Best. A cast-iron range with a roasting spit has been installed in the fireplace, and the cook has the choice of a plethora of utensils.

The dining room of a middle-class family at York, painted by Mary Ellen Best. Although this image dates from 1838, it closely resembles the décor of similar rooms described in Chapter 8 and the layout of a formal dinner table in Chapter 9.

The old system of watchmen or 'charleys' in London is hardly adequate for policing the city. They are given scant respect as a result. Here a couple of young gentlemen are 'getting the best of a charley' on a rowdy night out in 1823. Six years later the Metropolitan Police Force is established and the policing of the city professionalised.

Many forms of corporal punishment remain in force throughout the period. The pillory, shown here at Charing Cross in 1810, is abolished for most crimes in 1816 but remains the standard penalty for perjury until 1830.

This view of the interior of the Drury Lane Theatre, before the fire of 1809, makes it look bright and civilised. But in truth you should reckon on those lights being much dimmer, and the rowdy crowds in the galleries showering the better-off patrons below with discarded orange peel – even during performances of Shakespeare.

People flock to view animal fights as readily as they do plays. Here you see the famous lion, Wallace, doing battle with the dogs, Tinker and Ball, in the Factory Yard, Warwick, as depicted by the cartoonist George Cruikshank, in 1823. People pay up to 3 guineas for the best seats.

10

Cleanliness, Health and Medicine

Every country village has its doctor. I allude to that particular department of the medical world which is neither physician nor surgeon nor
apothecary, although it unites the offices of all three; which is sometimes an old man and sometimes an old woman, but generally an
oracle and always (with reverence be it spoken) a quack ... We have
a quack of the highest and most extended reputation in the person of
Doctor Tubb, inventor and compounder of medicines, bleeder, shaver,
and physicker of man and beast.

Mary Russell Mitford (1826)[1]

In the modern world, we generally take good health for granted – to
the extent that we panic when faced with a fatal illness. Even a virus
that kills 2–3 per cent of those it infects can bring society to its knees.
Regency people are far more attuned to expect the worst, living in the
shadows of smallpox, tuberculosis and other deadly diseases. Sickness
strikes young and old alike even in wealthy families. Among the poor,
we have already seen how the majority of children in some places do
not reach their teenage years. The result is a different attitude to being
ill: whereas we are complacent, they are cautious and apprehensive.
They need reassurance, not just remedies. The best doctors therefore
are those who can give their patients a reliable explanation of what is
wrong with them and, if their case is terminal, estimate realistically
how long they have to live, so they can put their affairs in order. Dr
Henry Halford, physician to both George III and George IV, freely admits
that there are many diseases he cannot cure and that, in such cases, all
he can do is tell his patients honestly what to expect and alleviate their
suffering. But they have such confidence in him as a result that he is
very popular. One lady even remarks that she would rather die under
his care than recover under that of any other physician.[2]

Understanding Health and Infection

The chief problem affecting the health of the population is ignorance. People believe that diseases spread through miasmas and contagion; they have no idea about germs. Miasmas are foetid pools of rotting matter whose effluvia are believed to infect those who smell them. Contagion is simply the idea that illnesses spread through contact between people. Don't be surprised if someone tells you that you can catch a venereal disease from using the same chamber pot as an infected person or drinking out of the same glass.[3] At the same time, people believe all sorts of things are beneficial for their health that are actually harmful. Many of those breathing in coal smoke are convinced that it is good for them.[4] In a similar vein, you will find people who believe that drinking copious amounts of alcohol every day is medicinal. William Pitt can blame his extraordinary port consumption on the fact that his doctor told him at the age of fourteen to drink a bottle a day to cure his inherited gout. He dutifully obliges.

On top of plain ignorance, you have wilful self-deception. Many gluttons know that large quantities of rich food are bad for them but they shut their minds to the likely consequences. You can say the same for those who rely heavily on laudanum. There is in all periods a propensity for people to satisfy their appetites despite the risks to their health, and to lie to themselves about the probable eventual outcomes. Similarly, there is a timeless fear of medical intervention, whereby people refuse to take a medicine because the thought of it repulses them. When Richard Brinsley Sheridan is on the point of dying, he is told he will need an operation. He replies that he has 'already undergone two, and that is enough for one man's lifetime'. Upon being asked what they were, he replies, 'having my hair cut and sitting for my picture'.[5] It proves to be one of his last quips.

'Taking the waters' has been a mainstay of health regimes for the last two hundred years. People do this either by drinking the produce of a mineral-rich spring or immersing themselves in the water, dressed in a yellow canvas bathing gown. Faith in such cures remains strong. Most of the characters in this book visit Bath at some point in their lives. Jane Austen also visits Cheltenham; John Soane takes the waters at Harrogate; and Anne Lister, being based in the north of England, goes to Buxton as well as Harrogate. They try out the spas, one by one, and if their afflictions remain uncured, they move on to the next. In the process they get to meet new people, attend balls, visit libraries and play cards. What's not to like? The water from the Royal Pump Rooms and Bath at Leamington Spa is said to cure you of jaundice, bilious complaints, tuberculosis, paralysis, tumours, distorted vertebrae, suppressed menstruation, piles, ulcers, intestinal worms, dyspepsia, rheumatism, gout and kidney disease.[6] The fact it also has a laxative effect on the body is gently glossed over, but you might want to bear it in mind and avoid drinking more than is absolutely necessary.

Bath itself is declining in popularity in these years. It is not that people are losing faith in its sulphurous waters, it is rather that the sea is taking over as the most fashionable form of water cure. Hence the meteoric rise of Brighton. According to Dr Richard Russell, sea water is far better than spa water because of its 'saltiness ... bitterness ... nitrosity ... [and] unctuosity'. If you're wondering what he means by *unctuosity*, it is explained as 'fatness' or 'viscosity' in his great work on sea water.[7] To be frank, neither drinking sea water nor bathing in it is going to cure you of 'glandular consumptions' as Dr Russell promises. But if you are going to follow medicinal fashions, at least a cold dip won't cause your bowels to loosen involuntarily.

Having said all these things, medical knowledge is advancing faster than ever before. One of the key reasons is the availability of a book entitled *Domestic Medicine, or a Treatise on the Prevention and Cure of Diseases* by the Scottish physician, Dr William Buchan. First published in 1769, it goes through nineteen editions by the time he dies in 1805. In pithy no-nonsense sentences, Dr Buchan informs ordinary people how they might lengthen their lives through personal cleanliness, diet and exercise. He is particularly strong on how to reduce the risk of infection. For instance:

Many diseases are infectious. Every person ought therefore, as far as he can, to avoid all communication with the diseased. The common practice of visiting the sick, though often well meant, has many ill consequences. Far be it from us to discourage any act of charity or benevolence, especially towards those in distress, but we cannot help blaming such as endanger their own or their neighbours' lives by a mistaken friendship or an impertinent curiosity.

The houses of the sick, especially in the country, are generally crowded from morning till night with idle visitors. It is customary in such places for servants and young people to wait upon the sick by turns and even to sit up with them all night. It would be a miracle indeed should such always escape. Experience teaches us the danger of this conduct. People often catch fevers in this way, and communicate them to others, till at length they become epidemic.[8]

At the same time as Dr Buchan is indoctrinating the people with his plain wisdom, surgeons are educating greater numbers of students in the newly founded hospitals and thereby bringing about a revolution in medical education. Medical journals start to be published, including *The Lancet*, which is founded in 1823. Campaigners agitate for higher standards of public health and doctors put a strong emphasis on ventilation in homes and workplaces. Although it would be rash to say that by 1830 the medical profession is fit for purpose, it is undoubtedly more professional than it was at the beginning of our period.

Personal Cleanliness

By 1830 the phrase 'the great unwashed' is in use as a synonym for the working classes.[9] People who use it clearly presume that those of high rank are generally clean whereas the poor are predominantly dirty. But this simple distinction is already long-since out of date. While there are some people who do little or nothing to improve their appearance or their fragrance, the Regency period sees every sector of society make great strides towards higher standards of personal cleanliness.

What brings about this upsurge in washing? One factor is the greater availability of water, which is increasingly piped directly into people's homes. Another is the provision of public baths in the large towns. In Manchester, a cold bath will cost you 6d, a warm one 1s and a steam bath 5s. These developments mainly affect the middle classes but a third factor affects everyone – namely, the proliferation of medical advice. 'The want of cleanliness is a fault that admits of no excuse,' declares Dr Buchan, adding:

Where water can be had for nothing, it is surely in the power of every person to be clean. The continual discharge from our bodies by perspiration renders frequent change of apparel necessary ... When that matter which ought to be carried off by perspiration is either retained in the body or reabsorbed from dirty clothes, it must occasion diseases.[10]

Dr Buchan then goes on to outline the problems arising from a lack of personal cleanliness, including diseases of the skin, lice, fleas, and 'putrid and malignant fevers'. As illnesses among the poor lead to a loss of income, this is a serious matter for them too. It is also crucial that their colleagues and neighbours get the message. As Dr Buchan puts it, 'It is not sufficient that I be clean myself while the want of it in my neighbour affects my health as well as his own. If dirty people cannot be removed as a common nuisance they ought at least to be avoided as infectious.'[11]

It is generally the upper classes that lead the way for the rest of society in matters of personal presentation. As with so many aspects of their appearance, these leaders of society are themselves shown the way by Beau Brummell, who insists that a well-dressed gentleman must be scrupulously clean. He personally sets a very high standard, spending three hours washing and grooming himself every morning, including scrubbing his skin with a pig-bristle 'flesh brush'.[12] If you aren't spotless, Brummell won't look at you, let alone talk to you, no matter who you are. As far as he's concerned, it isn't about avoiding disease or prolonging life: it is about appearing at your best. If you want his advice on how to achieve this, he will tell you: 'no perfumes, but very fine linen, plenty of it, and country washing'.[13]

Ladies have their own advisory manuals. The anonymous authoress of *The Art of Beauty* informs her readers in 1825 that 'bathing ... is an essential part of beauty training, for clearing the skin of its impurities and giving transparency and freshness to the complexion. Whoever neglects it therefore cannot with justice complain of eruptions and other [skin] disorders.'[14] Such books pay special attention to the face, recommending a wide range of products from lavender water and rose water to virgin milk and *eau de veau*. Virgin milk, in case you are wondering, is made by taking a quantity of benzoin (resin) and boiling it in wine until it becomes a rich tincture; adding a few drops of this to a glass of water makes it look like milk. If you then wash your face with it, 'it will, by calling the purple stream of the blood to the external fibres of the epidermis, produce on the cheeks a beautiful rosy colour, and if left on the face to dry, it will render it clear and brilliant'.[15] Unsurprisingly, it's hugely popular. *Eau de veau* is a paste to be spread on the skin in the hope of obtaining similar results. It is made by boiling a calf's foot in river water and adding rice, white bread steeped in milk, butter, egg whites, camphor and alum and then distilling the whole revolting mixture.[16] If I were you, I'd stick to soap, which you can now buy in solid bars, scented with lavender or violets.[17]

When it comes to personal grooming, the implements you need are growing in number and increasing in quality due to the mid-eighteenth-century invention of cast steel. From the 1770s you can buy sharper and more durable scissors, clippers, scrapers, knives, razors and surgical instruments. You can walk into a Regency shop and order a nail-care set with nail scissors (at 3s 6d a pair), a nail file for 1s and a pair of nail clippers or 'nail nippers' (as they are known) for 5s. Yes, the good news is that contemporaries of John White – the man with whom we began this book, who dies from paring his toenails too carelessly with a penknife in 1790 – have the option of using nail clippers instead. And if you find yourself in 1790, you'd be wise to add nail clippers to your shopping list, for at least two other men die that same year in an almost identical manner: Anthony Henley of Bath in cutting his toenails and Mr Le Fevre his fingernails. Five shillings might sound like a lot of money for a simple, small tool but not when you realise it might save your life.[18]

The great innovation in haircare in this period is the introduction of hairbrushes. Surprisingly, although clothes brushes have been around for centuries, those for the hair are first manufactured by William Kent at his factory in Hertfordshire in 1777. Soon the shops are stacked with them. An ordinary one with a lacquered wooden handle should cost you between 2s and 2s 6d. You will also want to consider acquiring a comb made of horn, ivory, steel or silver (which will cost between 6d and 2s), a pair of scissors (3s 6d) and perhaps a set of curling irons for 1s, with which to shape your hair or wig.[19] Gentlemen who wish to shave regularly will need to spend 2s on a good razor and an extra 6d on a razor case. You will also want a leather razor strop on which to hone the edge (1s); a shaving mirror (4s); a shaving brush, made with badger hair (4s 6d); 'shaving cakes', as shaving soap is called (4d each); and a shaving dish (3s 6d). Aftershave has yet to make an appearance but *eau de Cologne* is available for 2s a bottle. Finally, Beau Brummell recommends extracting any remaining hairs with tweezers, which you can add to your dressing kit for 1s 6d.[20] Note that old women who wish to avoid wisps of white hair on their cheeks do not generally shave but use hair-removing lotions, such as Mr Gibson's Curious Compound. How much skin they remove in the process, I dread to think.[21]

Teeth-Cleaning and Dentistry

People are very conscious of the whiteness of their teeth and the smell of their breath, especially women. As the surgeon Francis Spilsbury puts it, 'to the fair sex, nothing is more disagreeable, or gives a greater damp to their vivacity, than carious teeth or foetid breath'.[22] But there are additional reasons for the sensitivity. When you remember that bad smells are believed to convey diseases, you can see that unwholesome breath is alarming on health grounds as well as aesthetic ones, like smelling effluent. Unfortunately, the Regency period is a particularly challenging time in which to maintain dental hygiene. While professional dentists like Thomas Berdmore, dentist to George III, are absolutely clear that sugar causes dental caries, many people are simply in denial. The authoress of *The Art of Beauty* states in 1825 that 'the cause of decay in the teeth is still unknown ... Sugar and sweet things were, at one time, denounced as the common cause of bad teeth and toothache, but this is now believed to be a vulgar error.'[23]

The list of basic implements you need for oral hygiene begins with a toothpick. You can buy a silver one for 1s but I would recommend those made of the quill of a goose feather, which will not damage the enamel. Tongue-scrapers of silver or whalebone are also sold in large quantities, to clear the tongue of fur. Toothbrushes are available from barbers and hairdressers as well as dentists. These are quite cheap, rarely costing as much as 1s and often as little as 2d, after William Addis pioneers their mass-production in the 1780s. Otherwise, you can use a tooth-cloth, a piece of liquorice or a stem of marshmallow. Tooth salves, toothpastes and tooth powders or dentrifices are all available. A recipe for a white toothpowder consists of 6oz chalk, ½oz of cassia powder and 1oz of orris root.[24] Lord Byron prefers a red version made up for him by his dentist, John Waite.[25] Whatever colour you choose, do be careful when applying your toothpowder: some of them work by abrading the enamel and thus do more harm than good.[26]

By the early nineteenth century wealthy people have started going to the dentist for check-ups. Lord Byron regularly makes his way to no. 2 Old Burlington Street, London, where he sits on John Waite's velvet-covered adjustable chair, opens his mouth and dreads what will happen next. On one occasion, in 1814, he reports that Mr Waite has told him that his 'teeth are all right and white but he says that I grind them in my sleep and chip the edges'.[27] In 1827 Prince Hermann Pückler-Muskau visits Samuel Cartwright, George IV's own dentist, at no. 32 Old Burlington Street. It is said that Cartwright makes £10,000 a year from his practice, seeing up to fifty patients a day, being on his feet from 7 a.m. to 7 p.m. You have to apply for an appointment at least a week in advance and await the card that says 'Mr Cartwright will have the pleasure of receiving you' at a certain hour on a specified day. When you turn up, you'll be ushered into a smart waiting room decorated with framed prints on the walls, a bookcase of interesting volumes and a piano, which is just as well as you can be kept waiting for some considerable time. Prince Pückler-Muskau has to be patient for an hour while Mr Cartwright does a check-up for a duchess and her daughters. But it is worth it. He reports that 'Mr Cartwright is the most skilful and scientific man of his profession I ever met with ... He also has a settled price, and not an exorbitant one.'[28]

In all probability you are going to lose some of your teeth, so you will need to consider dentures. At the cheap end of the scale, you can make your own false tooth with white wax, shaping it with a penknife and pressing it into place. According to Francis Spilsbury, the author of *Every Man and Woman Their Own Dentist* (published in 1791), such home-made examples can stay in place for three or four days.[29] If you can afford a professional dentist's services, you will probably opt for teeth carved from walrus ivory, fitted with silk ligatures, each of which will cost you in excess of 10s. Real human teeth – or 'Waterloo teeth' as they are often called – cost £2, including fitting. These are taken from the corpses of hanged felons, recently deceased bodies in the keeping of undertakers, and pauper donors – often teenagers – for whom a guinea represents undreamt-of wealth. (Hence the joke, to be heard in every London pub, 'I might be here but my teeth are at court.'[30]) As you can see, having a whole row replaced with donated teeth is very expensive – often in excess of £30. You can pay even more for a porcelain set made by Nicolas Dubois de Chémant, a maker of dentures who escapes the French Revolution and sets up business in London. But before you rush to book an appointment, remember that even the best dentures have their drawbacks. The plates holding the teeth together are often made of lead, which is poisonous. It is easy for food to be trapped in them, and that gives you the most incredibly bad breath – which will not win you any friends. If you have two rows of false teeth, they will be joined by springs, which have a tendency to project the teeth out of your mouth when eating or speaking. And if you have anyone else's teeth directly implanted into your gums, not only will they fall out within a year but they may also give you the disease that killed their last owner.

This brings us to the important question of how dentists remove teeth. For most people, this is not normally the prerogative of the dentist but a tooth-drawer, of the sort you might meet at a fairground. The old cliché about tying a cord around the tooth and suddenly pulling it is true. Some tooth-drawers loop a thread around the tooth and then burn the patient with a hot coal, causing them to jump and the tooth to come out. Or for a shilling you might ask a blacksmith to apply his pliers. Most surgeons and apothecaries will assist with an old-fashioned 'pelican', which is a tool that levers out a rotten tooth with a fulcrum on the jaw. Up-to-date dentists use a 'tooth key', which clamps on to the tooth and allows them to remove it by turning the key. Injuries are common, however, even when consulting a profes-sional.[31] In 1820 Anne Lister goes to Mr Sunderland to take out her right rearmost bottom tooth. Unfortunately he removes a portion of her jaw in the process. Her gum bleeds and, shortly afterwards, her mouth swells up. So she summons a local woman, who applies six leeches just under her chin. Anne then gargles with vinegar – against doctor's orders – and makes up a toothache medicine for herself, which includes a fair quantity of opium.[32]

That's the thing. In the Regency period, whatever is wrong with you, there is always opium. And when it comes to toothache, it might be your best bet. As Thomas De Quincey, the author of the classic *Confessions of an English Opium-Eater*, admits, 'Most truly I have told the reader, that not any search after pleasure but mere extremity of pain from rheumatic toothache – this and nothing else it was that first drove me into the use of opium.'[33]

The Landscape of Disease

The prospect of visiting any country devoid of modern medical expertise is daunting but it is even more frightening when you don't know what you're up against. Even the diseases with which you are familiar may be different. Like most living things, they evolve. This is one of the reasons why it is common for a disease that kills many people in one century to kill far fewer in the next. Dysentery, for example, which wipes out thousands in the early eighteenth century, is nowhere near as deadly a hundred years later.[34] Smallpox, which is the most feared infection in Regency Britain, used to be considered a children's ailment before 1560. Conversely, a disease might weaken as a result of changes in human behaviour. Plague has not been seen in Britain since the last outbreaks of the 1660s, due principally to improvements in hygiene and building standards. Malaria, which was a major killer prior to the late eighteenth century, has predominantly disappeared from these shores as a result of the draining of marshland in the course of the Agricultural Revolution.[35]

Across England, the annual death rate is dropping from 2.6 per cent of the population every year to 2.3 per cent. In London the decline is even more noticeable: from 5 per cent to 3 per cent. But these proportions are still distressingly high: in modern Britain, the figure is about 1 per cent. And it isn't just the scale of the mortality that is disturbing: it is also its character – who is dying and what is killing them. At the start of our period, one-third of those London fatalities are children under the age of five.[36] As for the adults, one in three is a victim of consumption (or tuberculosis, as we call it today) and one in seven of smallpox. There aren't many silver linings to these dark clouds. All I can say is at least you won't have to worry about cancer. Chances are that you'll die from something else before you notice you have a tumour.

Causes of death in the London area per 100,000 people per year[37]

	1771–80		1801–10	
Childhood diseases	1,682	33.6%	789	27.0%
Consumption	1,121	22.4%	716	24.5%
Fever	621	12.4%	264	9.0%
Smallpox	502	10.0%	204	7.0%
Old age and bedridden	324	6.5%	241	8.3%
Dropsy	225	4.5%	131	4.5%
Asthma and phthisic	85	1.7%	89	3.0%
Accidents	70	1.4%	40	1.4%
Apoplexy and sudden death	55	1.1%	49	1.7%
Measles	48	1.0%	94	3.2%
Childbirth and miscarriage	47	0.9%	32	1.1%
Inflammation	31	0.6%	101	3.5%
Palsy and lethargy	18	0.4%	19	0.7%
Dysentery	17	0.3%	1	0.0%
Pleurisy	5	0.1%	4	0.1%
Other	149	3.0%	146	5.0%

One of the good-news stories of this period is the development of inoculation to counter the spread of smallpox. This disease, which is caused by the *variola* virus, is transferred by person-to-person contact. The first symptoms are a high fever and fatigue about two weeks after infection. Two or three days after that, a rash will appear on your skin. By then your internal organs will already be infected. Over the next few days your fever will worsen, you'll ache all over and you'll start vomiting. You will probably be too weak to stand. The rash will grow into a mass of large pustules covering most of your body. If you survive, these pustules will form scabs and drop off, leaving your skin scarred. This is why people fear this disease so much: walking around a town, you are constantly reminded of its presence by the disfigured faces of those who have recovered. If you catch it, there is no cure. One in three infected people dies from it.

There is hope, however. One ray shines forth from the early eighteenth-century adventuress, Lady Mary Wortley Montagu. She accompanies her husband on an embassy to Constantinople where she observes the local custom of inoculating children by giving them small doses of smallpox in order to encourage their bodies to develop an immunity. Back in England, when a smallpox epidemic threatens her own children, she has them inoculated. After that, many more people follow her example. By 1794 there are two specialist smallpox hospitals in London, at Coldbath Fields and St Pancras, where children are inoculated against the disease. At the same time, country people are starting to realise that they can acquire an immunity to smallpox by catching the less-dangerous cowpox. The most notable experimenter in this field is the Dorset farmer Benjamin Jesty, who deliberately infects his wife and two of their sons with cowpox when a smallpox epidemic threatens their village. All three survive. Finally, in 1798, Dr Edward Jenner publishes his *Inquiry into the causes and effects of the variolae vaccinae*, which is the first scientific treatise to demonstrate the efficacy of the process. It persuades the medical establishment to accept vaccination as the most effective way to combat the spread of this disease. Jenner's *Inquiry* is translated into half a dozen languages by 1801, and in that year he predicts the complete eradication of smallpox. It takes a little longer than he imagines – in fact, it won't be declared extinct across the globe until 1980 – but from the research he conducts in this period, Western society begins to gain mastery of one of its most-feared killers.

A less-positive story is the rise of occupational illnesses and injuries, which will surely put you off the idea of working your way around Britain during the Industrial Revolution. One of the most dangerous activities of all is mining, due to shafts collapsing, boilers blowing up, flooding in the lower levels and explosions from pockets of methane being ignited by unguarded candles. The last risk is partly alleviated by the development from 1813 of a range of non-explosive 'safety lamps' by Dr William Clanny, Humphry Davy and George Stephenson. However, mining is beset by many illnesses too, caused by the dust created by the drills and explosives, the lack of ventilation, and the effluent and bacteria in the water in the mines. Boys and girls start work in this industry at the age of six or seven, and in their early years they are regularly to be seen vomiting at work as their bodies struggle with the dust. By the time they are adults their spines are curved, their legs are bowed, their skin is grimy, sallow and unhealthy, and their eyes appear small, inflamed and intolerant of daylight. Rarely do they live beyond the age of fifty.[38]

In 1829 an enterprising young doctor, Charles Thackrah, decides to undertake a systematic investigation of all the occupational diseases in the Leeds region. He describes the problems of posture, lack of exercise, inhalation of dust, lack of ventilation and other causes of sickness in working men and women. Overall, he reckons that poor working conditions are killing 450 men prematurely every year in Leeds alone. Reading this seminal work – the first treatise on occupational health in Britain – will alert you to the hidden horrors of the Industrial Revolution. If you're offered a job as a glaze-dipper in the Potteries, be warned: dipping ceramic jugs into lead-based glazes leads to chronic lead poisoning. If you're thinking of taking up tailoring, think again. Thackrah finds that tailors have problems with their bowels, stomach and heart, partly because they work sitting cross-legged on their workbenches, with their backs bent forward. He measures their chests and notes that they average just 33 inches – three inches smaller than that of the average artisan in Leeds. Worse conditions are suffered by young boys who are sent up chimneys naked: they develop scrotal cancer. As urban chimneys are becoming smaller and more efficient, so very young boys are required for the work, sometimes as young as six. But the grinding industries are the worst of all. These tend to be concentrated around the cutlery-producing towns of Sheffield and Birmingham. The work is exceptionally dangerous because it generates a lot of dust from the stone and metal and is carried out in poorly ventilated shops, sometimes in cellars, by subcontractors who only get paid for what they produce. They don't take time out for ill-health because they can't afford to stop work. Almost 90 per cent of the fork-grinders of Sheffield die before the age of forty. None lives to fifty.[39]

Factories too have the most horrifying health-and-safety records. Here the problems are accidents from the unguarded machinery, the dangers of contagious diseases spreading through poorly ventilated buildings, and the brutal treatment of boys and girls. The younger you are, the harsher the conditions you can expect. The early life of

Robert Blincoe is typical. Born around 1792, he enters the St Pancras Workhouse as an orphan at the age of four. There he is treated quite well but, after three years, he is sold along with about eighty other seven-year-olds to be indentured servants at Lowdam Mill near Nottingham. This is effectively slavery by another name: the boys and girls have no legal way of leaving their employer until they are twenty-one years of age. They are required to work at the spinning frames for fourteen hours a day, six days a week, in dusty, hot conditions. They are beaten regularly. They are given very little clothing, no soap with which to wash themselves and an inadequate amount of food. Blincoe tries stealing dough balls from the troughs in the factory's pigsties but the pigs get wise to his pilfering and, when they see him coming, eat their dough balls quickly or throw them into the mud. When the punishments cause Blincoe to become incontinent, his food is stopped altogether. A journalist who interviews him records:

> In the faded complexions, and sallow looks of his associates, he could see, as, in a mirror, his own altered condition. Many of his comrades had, by this time, been more or less injured by the machinery. Some had the skin scraped off the knuckles, clean to the bone, by the [flywheels]; others a finger crushed, a joint or two nipped off in the cogs of the spinning-frame wheels. When his time to suffer came, the forefinger of his left hand was caught and, almost before he could cry out, off was the first joint. His lamentations excited no manner of emotion in the spectators, except a coarse joke. He clapped the mangled joint, streaming with blood, to the finger, and ran off … to the surgeon, who, very composedly put the parts together again, and sent him back to the mill. Though the pain was so intense [that] he could scarcely help crying out every minute, he was not allowed to leave the frame.[40]

At the age of ten, Master Blincoe sees one of his young friends from St Pancras suffer a horrific accident. She catches her skirt in the mechanism of a spinning frame and is drawn into the machine. Blincoe hears the bones of her arms and legs snap, and sees her blood 'thrown about like water from a twirled mop'.[41] As you can imagine, it is not only the physical state of children in factories that is deplorable. Mentally they are deeply scarred too.

The Medical World

What should you do when you get ill? If you've just got a bit of a sniffle, you're not going to send for a physician. If it's a persistent problem, you will probably ask for advice from family members or the older women in your parish, who tend to have a wealth of medical wisdom. Such advice is likely to include a mixture of folklore, herbal remedies, medicines obtainable from druggists, and ringing lines from Dr Buchan's *Domestic Medicine*. In every part of the country there are traditional procedures for dealing with ringworm, ruptures, whooping cough, toothache, epilepsy, rheumatism, sties and warts. Indeed, there are almost as many strategies to remove warts as there are warts themselves. In some places they will recommend you try rubbing them with a snail and then killing the poor creature on the nearest thorn bush; in others, putting as many stones as you have warts into a bag and burying it at a crossroads; elsewhere, rubbing your warts with a piece of stolen meat, which you then throw away, and so on.[42] It might sound like madness but there's a certain logic to it: folklore is free whereas physicians are expensive.

Traditional remedies tend to be more effective when they involve herbs that have genuine healing properties. Goosegrass, for example, is used on skin ailments; comfrey is applied to wounds and bruises; and certain crocuses limit the effects of gout. Having said that, just because a herb is considered to have medicinal properties in the modern world doesn't mean it is efficacious in Regency times. Although William Withering publishes *An Account of the Foxglove and some of its Medical Uses* in 1785, observing that the plant is a genuine natural remedy for some heart conditions, most herbals will advise you to use it externally, to aid recovery from wounds, for which it is not beneficial. Worse, a concoction of it is sometimes prescribed to purify the body by emptying it 'both downwards and upwards', as the medical writers delicately put it. The problem is that foxglove is poisonous when ingested. The Revd John Skinner's brother doses himself so heavily with it that he loses his sight, suffers violent spasms and eventually dies.[43]

Despite such dangers, many Regency people feel they can do without doctors. They rely instead on family recipe books and printed guides. Collections of tried and trusted medical recipes are passed down from generation to generation within families. If you don't have a volume approved by your forebears, your best bet is to acquire a published herbal, which will give you details of the various types of plant and their supposed medicinal properties. The most popular is *The English Physician Enlarged with Three Hundred and Sixty-Nine Medicines made of English Herbs* by Nicholas Culpeper, which was first published in 1652 and has been through dozens of editions since. The Mortimer family in Plymouth rely on a 1770 edition of this work, although someone has written in the front, 'it is necessary to have a dispensatory with this book to direct the practitioner what progress to take to make these herbs useful'. You may assume this is good advice as 'Crosby's improved edition' of 1814 contains exactly this additional information.

Given this state of affairs, it will hardly surprise you to hear that charlatans are eager to exploit vulnerable people by selling them medicines of dubious efficacy. You see 'cures' advertised everywhere – in newspapers, on street corners, above shop frontages, on billboards and in books. Robert Southey describes being given a dozen handbills for 'never-failing pills' in the time it takes him to walk the length of Fleet Street.[44] If you buy a 3oz bottle purporting to contain Godfrey's Cordial or Dalby's Carminative for 3d – half of its usual price – you won't have a clue what it actually contains. Many patients who are initially only slightly sick take a concoction of noxious chemicals and then find themselves sinking into a cycle of worsening symptoms and increasingly dangerous and more expensive medicines.

The word most people employ to describe such charlatans is 'quack'. This can be used affectionately of a local personage, as Mary Russell Mitford makes clear in the quotation at the start of this chapter. However, most of the time it is used to reflect the deceptive nature of ignorant medical practitioners. Of course none of them ever refers to *himself* as a quack. Indeed, everything he says and does will be calculated to instil a sense of confidence in you that he is the genuine article. For example, on your first consultation he will ask you to describe your symptoms. In so doing, you will be furnishing him with the means to lure you in. He will follow up by asking you questions that make it sound as if he is sure of his subject. What he is looking for is your trust, not the cause of your suffering: it is much easier to fool you than cure you. He will be *so* sympathetic, all the time increasing the level of your anxiety. The more he convinces you that your ailment is serious, the more he can charge for the supposed cure. If you worsen as a result, that is too bad: he's already got his money. Sadly, the most desperate people are the most easily deceived.

There is a telling story about an eminent physician, who one day happens to meet one of the most famous quacks of all, Richard Rock, on Ludgate Hill. The envious physician asks the so-called 'Dr Rock', the purveyor of Rock's Restorative Viper Drops, how come he is so rich that he can afford a town house, a country house and a fine carriage, despite his lack of medical training, while he himself can hardly manage to keep his London house going. 'Dr Rock' smiles and asks him how many people he thinks have passed them on the street since their conversation began. The physician estimates the number at about a hundred. 'And how many out of those hundred do you think possess common sense?' 'Not many,' the physician admits, 'perhaps just the one.' 'Then,' replies the quack, 'that one comes to you, and I take care of the other ninety-nine.'[45]

So how do you distinguish between a competent practitioner and a charlatan in 1800? One way is to judge the man by his qualifications. This is not as straightforward as it sounds. Officially, in order to give medical advice, he needs to hold a medical degree from a university or a licence from one of six British institutions: the Royal College of Physicians, the London Company of Surgeons (which becomes the Royal College of Surgeons in London in 1800), the Society of Apothecaries, the Royal College of Physicians of Edinburgh, the Royal College of Surgeons of Edinburgh or the Faculty of Physicians and Surgeons of Glasgow. That number of officiating bodies can hardly guarantee consistently high standards. It doesn't help that, if a practitioner has enough well-connected medical friends, he can simply buy a doctorate from a Scottish university by sending references in the post. Even so, only a few hundred men in Britain are qualified by these criteria and most of them are based in London, Edinburgh and Glasgow.[46] They accordingly charge huge fees and considerable travel expenses. How do you choose which one to employ? If you are rich enough, you won't consider the doctor's qualifications so much as a personal recommendation from a trusted friend. If you cannot afford their services, it doesn't matter whether they are qualified or not. You'll have to look elsewhere.

Outside a major city, your best bet will be to make an appointment with a local surgeon-apothecary or physician who has served an apprenticeship. Many such men spend part of their time serving the ailing poor and are paid modest fees by the parish overseer for this public service. As no overseer wants to be seen handing ratepayers' money to a doctor who is locally regarded as incompetent, this is a recommendation in itself. However, their services are often in great demand. Nor are their private fees cheap. If you can't afford them, you will have to choose between consulting a man who calls himself a physician and may well claim to hold a medical licence – but who is really a quack – or visiting a druggist, a retailer of patent medicines who sells 'cures' in bulk in his shop. Which, then, do you choose: the physician who lies about his qualifications or the druggist who admits he has none?

As you can see, the system of medical regulation is desperately in need of reform. The initiative is taken in 1804 by Edward Harrison, a Lincolnshire physician, who carries out a survey that shows in some places 90 per cent of medical practitioners have no medical education or qualifications whatsoever.[47] He recommends that the government should legislate to regulate the training, examination and licensing of physicians, surgeons and apothecaries, and that a separate licensing system be introduced for druggists and midwives. Unfortunately, the whole idea runs up against the Royal College of Physicians and the recently founded Royal College of Surgeons. Both organisations are concerned that these proposals will undermine their influence over their respective professions. This will strike you as extraordinary: professional doctors are trying to *prevent* the raising of professional standards! However, the tide of middle-class opinion is against the colleges, and on 12 July 1815 the Apothecaries' Act finally receives royal assent. This enforces compulsory apprenticeship, training and examination in anatomy, botany, surgery, chemistry and medicine, and requires at least six months' work experience in a hospital prior to the granting of a licence from the Society of Apothecaries and a diploma of Membership of the Royal College of Surgeons. These two pieces of paper are henceforth necessary for anyone to call himself a 'general practitioner'. As a result, this Act marks a great step forward – if only because it establishes a basic standard for the general practitioners who serve the bulk of the population. If you fall ill after 1815, make sure the man you consult holds the licence and diploma. You might still die from his ministrations but, if you do, you will perish for medical reasons, not mercenary ones.

Hospitals and Dispensaries

In London there are seven general hospitals: the two ancient foundations of St Bartholomew's and St Thomas's and a handful of voluntary hospitals, namely the Westminster Hospital, Guy's Hospital, St George's Hospital, the London Hospital and the Middlesex Hospital. The latter are all established in the eighteenth century by groups of wealthy gentlemen who each subscribe a guinea a year and thereby acquire the right to recommend one person to be treated at any time. Therefore if you need to go to hospital, you will first need to get a letter of recommendation from a subscriber. This is not the only limitation. Pregnant women are not welcome in hospitals, nor are children, lunatics, people with fever or anyone with a contagious disease or an incurable condition. The majority of inmates are therefore people who have serious injuries. If you are admitted, you won't be charged a fee but you may have to pay a deposit to cover the expenses of your funeral, in case the worst should happen. And the worst *does* happen quite regularly: about 10 per cent of hospital admissions in the eighteenth century end up with the patient dying. Gradually, however, through better nursing and cleaner facilities, the death rates in hospitals are coming down: they are running at 6 per cent in the early nineteenth century.[48] Towns and cities across the country see the advantages of following the London example. Thirty-one provincial voluntary hospitals have been established by 1800.[49]

Dispensaries are similar institutions to hospitals but without beds for overnight stays. They too are funded by private subscribers who recommend patients to be treated for free. The pioneering institution is the General Dispensary established in Aldersgate Street, London, in 1770. As with hospitals, physicians and surgeons are available for consultation six days each week; they also make home visits when required. Some dispensaries have experienced accoucheurs or man-midwives on their staff too. If you arrive with your letter of recommendation, the apothecary on duty will either decide to treat you immediately himself or will make an appointment for you to see a physician or surgeon. Unlike a hospital, a dispensary will help you with venereal diseases, childbirth and contagious infections such as typhus. It is hardly surprising that the number of dispensaries mushrooms in the late eighteenth century. In the capital, sixteen are operational by 1792, seeing a combined total of 50,000 people annually – twice as many as the hospitals.[50] Outside London, two dozen dispensaries are functioning by 1800, in addition to several that serve as the outpatient wing of a hospital.

Regency philanthropists also establish many specialist hospitals. In London there are dedicated institutions for patients with venereal diseases, lung diseases and ruptures. The first ear dispensary opens in 1816. A more risky establishment is the Institution for the Care and Prevention of Contagious Fevers, which opens its doors in 1802 to look after typhus patients. The neighbours in Gray's Inn Lane are none too happy about this and in 1815 they force the hospital to close and move to the same building as the London Smallpox Hospital.

In 1800 there are no specialist eye hospitals in Britain, despite the great advances made in recent years by brilliant eye-surgeons such as Michael de Wenzel and John Taylor, successively oculists to George III. Using very fine cast-steel surgical instruments, de Wenzel can remove a cataract in just thirty seconds – which is a good thing when he has to cut open your eye with nothing better than laudanum for pain relief.[51] Such treatments remain out of reach to the ordinary man and woman until the Royal Infirmary for Diseases of the Eye opens its doors in London in 1804. As eyesight is so important for everyone who is trying to earn a living, this is an absolute godsend. Eighteen more eye hospitals are founded across Britain in the next twenty years.

Childbirth is dangerous to women of all classes. Three of Jane Austen's brothers lose their wives in this way; even George IV's only daughter, Princess Charlotte, falls victim to maternal mortality. Wealthy ladies can afford their own accoucheurs and surgeons but ordinary women have to rely on midwives. These do not receive any formal training. In difficult cases, they have to call for medical help. As women in childbirth are barred from general hospitals, the establishment of lying-in hospitals saves many lives. These are institutions where women can give birth attended by experienced nurses, midwives, accoucheurs and surgeons. Equally importantly, they are looked after in the dangerous days following the birth, when puerperal fever is a particular risk. There are five such hospitals in London, as well as the Royal Maternity Charity, which provides specialist help for poor married women in their own homes.[52] In the mid-eighteenth century

2.4 per cent of mothers in England die in childbirth or immediately afterwards. In some years in London, that figure is 10 per cent. But as a result of these hospitals, by 1830, in both London and further afield, the numbers are down to just 0.4 per cent. Some general practitioners do even better than this. Mr Waddington of Margate, in Kent, who starts his practice in 1788 and delivers more than 2,000 babies over the course of his long career, sees a maternal mortality rate of less than 0.1 per cent. The medical, nursing and midwifery professions will not improve on these figures for another century.[53]

Lunatic Asylums

In 1790 there are four public institutions caring for the mentally ill in Britain: the Manchester Asylum, the York County Asylum and two places in London: Bethlehem (better known as 'Bedlam') and St Luke's Hospital for Lunatics. Bedlam is the oldest of the four, having looked after the unwell since at least 1403. You would have thought that, with four centuries' experience to draw on, the hospital would have developed a considerable level of expertise in dealing with mental illness. Not a bit of it. Staff still use manacles and chains in 1803, just as they did 400 years earlier. Patients are restrained day and night, often with a metal collar around their necks. They are left scantily clad or completely naked, and kept in freezing conditions in unglazed halls. Members of the public can pay to come in during the day and watch them as they would view animals in a zoo. In fact inmates are treated exactly like animals, for they are given only straw to lie on and are left to foul it in public. Many are beaten like animals too; some die of the injuries inflicted in the course of their 'care'.

Conditions at Bedlam do not improve for the first half of our period. When Edward Wakefield visits in 1814, he notices about ten women in a side room:

Each chained by one arm or leg to the wall, the chain allowing them merely to stand up by the bench fixed to the wall, or to sit down on it. The nakedness of each patient was covered by ... a dressing-gown, with nothing to fasten it with in front; this constitutes the whole covering; the feet even were naked. One female in this side room, thus chained, was an object remarkably striking; she mentioned her maiden and married names, and stated that she had been a teacher of languages … [she] held a coherent conversation with us, and was of course fully sensible of the mental and bodily condition of those wretched beings, who, equally without clothing, were closely chained to the same wall with herself. Unaware of the necessities of nature, some of them, though they contained life, appeared totally inanimate and unconscious of existence.[54]

Thinking back to poor Jane Toulmin, whom we encountered drowning herself in the sea at Branscombe at the start of this book, you can understand that these conditions would not benefit her in the slightest.

Things are not much better at the York County Asylum, founded in 1777. The determined reformer Godfrey Higgins learns of the mistreatment of a patient there in 1814 and pays £20 to be appointed to a position on the board of governors, which enables him to inspect the building. Having been shown around, he notices a door that has not been opened for him, hidden behind that to the kitchen. The keepers pretend not to know where the key is. Only when Mr Higgins seizes a poker from the kitchen fireplace and threatens to break the door down do they produce the key. He describes the women's cells on the other side in a statement to a parliamentary committee the following year:

When the door was opened, I went into the passage, and I found four cells, I think, of about eight feet square, in a very horrid and filthy situation; the straw appeared to be almost saturated with urine and excrement; there was some bedding laid upon the straw in one cell, in the others only loose straw … The walls were daubed with excrement; the airholes, of which there were one in each cell, were partly filled with it.[55]

Abuses are common in these institutions. At York, Higgins uncovers cases of keepers impregnating the women in their care and concealing the deaths of patients.[56] Relatives and friends are still paying for loved ones who have already died. And places here are not cheap. Indeed, the reason why the York keepers conceal the state of their most poorly kept patients is so they can present the institution as a caring place in order to justify their high fees. Matthew Flinders notes in his diary that:

On Tuesday March 3rd [1801] my wife set off with my unfortunate son John for the York Lunatic Asylum and I thank God returned safe on Saturday 7th having lodged him safe in this excellent repository of such unfortunates. We seem every way satisfied that this is the best situation we have been able to procure for him & as to his recovery the event must be left with Providence. The expense, with clothes, I expect will be about £30 per annum.[57]

The alternatives to the lunatic hospitals are the private 'madhouses' that you can find in London and some of the county towns. These are smaller institutions regulated by a 1774 Act that requires them to be licensed. There is no system of inspection, however, so the licence is no guarantee of high standards. The madhouses in London that are run by Dr Warburton are no better than the lunatic hospitals and, in the case of the doctor's three houses at Bethnal Green, arguably worse. At one of them, the White House, a keeper beats a delusional naval officer to death in front of the house surgeon and his assistant; none of the men reports the killing. Conditions still have not improved in 1827 when Anthony Ashley Cooper, 7th earl of Shaftesbury, visits the White House on behalf of a parliamentary committee. He finds that the patients are chained up naked on beds of straw from Saturday afternoon to Monday morning, when they are rinsed of their urine and excrement. No attempt is made to cure them; they are simply kept alive as cash cows while their relatives pay for their keep. From 1809, John Soane pays Dr Warburton two guineas a week – £110 a year – for the care of his servant, Anne Collard, in the White House. He continues paying this sum for the next twenty years in the honest belief that she is being well looked after.[58]

There is, however, another side to mental health in this period and it is much more uplifting. It begins back in 1751 when Dr William Battie grows tired of the lack of care at Bedlam and establishes St Luke's Hospital. He insists that manacles, chains and other restraints should only be used where absolutely necessary. Inmates are given decent bedding and clothing, and they are made to take cold baths regularly – to keep them clean as well as to invigorate them – but are otherwise kept warm. Male keepers are not allowed unsupervised access to female patients. The institution prospers and in 1786 it moves to a magnificent new building in Old Street. When the parliamentary committee enquires into the state of the hospital in 1815, it finds that only five of the 300 patients in St Luke's are chained up, in marked contrast to Bedlam's practice of keeping them all permanently under restraint.

The success of St Luke's inspires other reformers. When a Quaker woman dies in the York County Asylum after a six-week incarceration in 1790, her fellow Friends are deeply distressed. One of them, William Tuke, decides to start a hospital for Quakers along the lines espoused by Dr Battie at St Luke's. This institution, known as the Retreat, opens its doors in 1796. Almost immediately it becomes the example for all others to follow. In 1801 subscribers open a lunatic hospital in Exeter based on the model of the Retreat. Between that date and 1830, about twenty new asylums are established, and in most cases the governors send their keepers to the Retreat for training and guidance. Thus its principles of care and compassion spread across the country. Even the governors of Bedlam realise that reform is inevitable and agree to rebuild and re-staff the hospital. The new Bedlam opens in 1815. Thirteen years later, as a result of legislation promoted by the earl of Shaftesbury, fifteen commissioners in lunacy are appointed to oversee all the mental-health institutions in the London area to ensure that the abuses of the past do not happen again.

The care of mentally ill people is still far from perfect in 1830 but at least society has taken the bold step of trying to do something positive, rather than just contain the problem and exploit those who suffer from it. And if you want a happy ending to this story, I can tell you that when Edward Wakefield revisits the rebuilt Bedlam in 1815, he finds only one of the patients in the hospital chained up. He also makes the acquaintance of Mrs Fenwick, the teacher of languages he had previously seen chained to the wall in a state of semi-nakedness. She is well dressed and keen to hear news of her former employer. As Mr Wakefield bids her good day and leaves, the keeper who accompanies him admits that 'she is an entirely different creature since she has been treated like a human being'.[59]

11

Law and Order

If there be one thing by which the English are peculiarly distinguished from all other people in the world, it is by their passion for exercising authority and enacting laws.

Robert Southey (1807)[1]

Nothing moves as slowly as the law, and the common law of England and Wales seems to be the slowest of all. The threshold for hanging someone guilty of theft was set at 12d in Saxon times – and it is still 12d in the Regency. The medieval penalty for people who refuse to plead in court – crushing them to death slowly under huge weights of stone – isn't abolished until 1774. The law against receiving stolen goods is so ancient it doesn't even take money into consideration: in 1800, you can be arrested and charged for receiving a pilfered pocket handkerchief but not the proceeds of a bank robbery.[2] Although politicians attempt to reform the legal system from the 1790s, it is not until the 1820s that significant progress is made, wiping many old offences off the statute books. Times may change but the law doesn't – except with the most extreme reluctance.

Patterns of crime do alter, however. One of the most striking examples of this is the decline in female criminal activity. A hundred years before the Regency, almost half of all those arrested for breaking the law were women.[3] In our period, the proportion of female offenders is about 20 per cent – roughly the same as in the modern world.[4] The overall percentage of the population arrested every year is also comparable with modern figures (approximately 1 per cent). However, the crimes for which they are arrested are very different. In 1820, almost 90 per cent of those committed for trial at the county assize courts are accused of some form of theft – whether the crime be burglary, larceny, robbery, housebreaking or embezzlement. At the Old Bailey in London, it's even higher: 92 per cent.[5] In the modern world, theft-related crimes collectively account for just under a quarter of all cases.

It might surprise you to hear that very few people are arrested for violent offences in Regency Britain. This is not because society is much more peaceful – you know from chapter 4 that it isn't – but rather that violence is such a common feature of everyday life that it doesn't warrant court action. Punching a man in the face might result in your victim reporting you to a constable but, even if he does, your action will be considered a misdemeanour, not a crime. It will thus be heard by the local magistrates in the county petty sessions or, at worst, the quarter sessions. If you hit your victim so hard that he suffers a life-changing injury, *then* you might find yourself in the assize courts, facing a charge of assault with intent to commit murder, but otherwise you can expect merely to be fined. When a man is allowed to beat his wife, children and servants with impunity, most acts of domestic violence are within the law and thus no arrests can be made.

Policing

It is often said that the London Metropolitan Police Service, established in 1829, is the oldest law-enforcement agency in the world. This is incorrect: the Met. isn't even the oldest police force in London, let alone the world. The Thames River Police is older, being officially established in 1800. Glasgow's police force is founded that same year and Edinburgh's in 1805. However, it is true that there are very few policemen in Britain before 1829. Who then is responsible for arresting all the people committed to trial every year? The short answer is that communities do it themselves. For instance, in 1789 a number of Cornish miners march into the Devon town of Chagford, near the mines where they've been working. They are in an angry mood, feeling they are being treated unfairly by the local people. They are armed with shovels and makeshift weapons and declare they are going to burn the town to the ground. The townsmen have no time to get a message to Devon's deputy lieutenant to call out the militia; instead they themselves come out in force, arrest the would-be arsonists and march them off to be locked up by a local magistrate. As you can see, the lack of a police force does not necessarily imply an absence of law enforcement.

The system whereby communities police themselves dates back to the Middle Ages. In those days, when the 'hue and cry' was raised, all the men within earshot would drop everything and pursue a malefactor. A similar practice still prevails in Regency towns, when someone shouts 'Stop, thief!' and everyone does their best to catch the culprit. In rural areas, people have their own ways of protecting themselves and their property. When Anne Lister hears reports of men attempting to steal her chickens, she drives into Halifax and buys a pistol. She doesn't know how to shoot but that does not stop her waving her gun around in the faces of some men loitering near her house one night, threatening to 'blast their brains out'.[6] Most of her fellow landowners similarly feel they can rely on mantraps and gun-toting gamekeepers to protect their property. They don't need a police force. Nor do they want one. They look across the Channel and observe the role played by the Parisian police in the Terror. Why should they run the risk of a similar organisation in Britain taking sides with the revolutionary spirit to be encountered in many of the larger towns? They have little to gain and everything to lose.

Communities are assisted in their self-policing by the appointment of a constable in each parish. This man is selected from the principal inhabitants and serves for a year in England and Wales, or six months in Scotland. It is his responsibility to arrest anyone he believes might have committed a felony and to bring the suspect before a magistrate. He also undertakes other duties in accordance with the magistrates' instructions: searching premises for stolen goods; conveying vagrants back to their home parishes; collecting local taxes; checking alehouse licences; escorting suspects to prison; and organising the fighting of fires and the repair of highways. In most large towns, where there are several constables, they are supported by watchmen or 'charleys', whose principal role is to watch out for thieves at night. They are mainly old fellows equipped with staves, lanterns and sometimes a rattle or horn to raise the alarm. Unfortunately, they are not very effective. Many make a few extra shillings by agreeing to turn a blind eye when thieves carry out their raids.

Despite the haphazardness of the system, some constables take a very positive approach to investigating crime. The murder of a young Jewish man, Isaac Valentine, in 1811 is a good example. Mr Valentine lives in Plymouth, and is known locally to carry a lot of money about with him. Having been invited on business down to Fowey in Cornwall by a publican called Wyatt, who has moved there from Plymouth, Mr Valentine sets off with a friend. After arriving in Fowey, he disappears. His friend goes to Mr Wyatt's public house where he enquires after Mr Valentine – only to receive the astonishing news that he drowned that evening. Sure enough, Mr Valentine's body is discovered in the estuary a few days later. The pockets of his coat are empty except for Mr Wyatt's letter inviting him to Fowey. The coroner is called, and he summons a surgeon, who ascertains that the dead man's skull has been fractured and his jaw broken. These details are enough in themselves to point the finger of suspicion at Mr Wyatt, especially as he seems to have known that the man drowned before his body was even discovered. But the damning evidence comes from the Fowey constables' thorough investigation. They appeal for witnesses: two sailors come forward to say that, on the evening in question, they were both on a boat in the estuary smoking their pipes when they heard a man on the pier scream out, 'Oh, Mr Wyatt!' and then a splash. In the twilight they saw a figure climb down from the pier and reach into the water. The constables search Mr Wyatt's stables and find a roll of Plymouth banknotes, soaked with salt water, buried in the dung. They contact the issuing banks and establish from the numbers that these notes were indeed issued to Mr Valentine. Mr Wyatt is tried for murder and theft at the county assize court in Launceston and is found guilty on both counts. He is hanged three weeks later.[7]

You cannot always rely on the local constables to investigate a case as thoroughly as this. If you are the victim of a crime, you will normally have to take the lead yourself. However, you will not be on your own. In many places you will find a local Association for the Prosecution of Felons, which will offer a reward for the arrest of persistent offenders. Alternatively, the town authorities might offer a sum for the apprehension of a dangerous criminal. Such financial incentives encourage 'thief-takers' to set up business – not only to earn the rewards on offer but also to gain payments from victims for the recovery of stolen possessions. These men aren't well thought-of; many are considered corrupt, arresting the wrong man simply in order to gain the bounty. But if you have no other help, it is worth drawing on their specialist services. You can also have posters printed advertising your own reward or appealing for witnesses. In the absence of an official police force, no one will be surprised at you taking matters into your own hands.

In London, members of the public who have been the victims of a crime are expected to go to a rotation office, where a magistrate is on duty during the day. The magistrate might give instructions to an official thief-taker, known as a Principal Officer, to make enquiries and see if a suspect can be brought to justice. By 1792 there are nine of these rotation offices. One of the earliest is in Bow Street, near Covent Garden, which gives rise to the nickname by which the Principal Officers are best known, 'Bow Street Runners'. They bring in criminals for identity parades and secure the identification of suspects by having victims sign affidavits that can later be produced in court. They do much to deter criminals by going after armed gangs and highwaymen, and generally creating the impression that law-breakers can – and will – be brought to justice.

Such is the state of policing in 1796, when Patrick Colquhoun publishes *A Treatise on the Police of the Metropolis*. He reckons there are in the region of 115,000 people operating either illegally or immorally in London but no more than 1,000 constables and associates actively trying to control them, and these are all divided between about seventy different jurisdictions.[8] In addition, he points out that no one is doing anything to stop organised crime in the Port of London. Every time a merchant ship sails up the Thames, it is surrounded by a flotilla of small boats waiting to take off some of the goods without the knowledge of the owner or the customs officers. Colquhoun's proposals for a city-wide police force are opposed by the City of London and accordingly dropped. However, with the encouragement of certain international merchants, in 1798 he and another magistrate set up a private marine police force. A total of about fifty constables and supervisors patrol the river in rowing boats, armed with guns and equipped with warrants from the duty magistrate. On the shore, special officers watch the quays. Two years later, the government passes the Marine Police Act making this enterprise official, with eighty-eight officers and watchmen.[9] The success of this venture in combating both the public crime of smuggling and the private one of theft gradually leads to a better understanding of the benefits of policing.

As mentioned above, it is Glasgow that shows the way forward for cities struggling to contain their criminal elements. The Glasgow

Police Act of 1800 enables an official force to be funded by a rate levied across the city. Commissioners are appointed to supervise a Master of Police, and he in turn supervises three sergeants and six police officers, who man a central police station twenty-four hours a day. These full-time officers oversee a total of sixty-eight watchmen, each of whom carries the traditional stave and lantern and wears a uniform that includes a brown overcoat with a number painted on the back. Such is the effectiveness of the Glasgow Police Force that many criminals decide to shift their operations to the Gorbals on the other side of the River Clyde. The solution is obvious – to set up another police force over there – and so the Gorbals Police Act is passed in 1808.[10] By then Edinburgh has already followed Glasgow's example. Slowly people come around to the idea that a modern city needs a strong, well-funded, professional force, capable of maintaining the highest standards. Eventually, in 1829, Sir Robert Peel oversees the passing of the Metropolitan Police Act, whereby a police force is established to serve the whole of London, with powers that extend to the neighbouring counties. Now if you are the victim of a crime in the capital, you will report it at a police station manned by professional policemen who patrol the streets twenty-four hours a day – dressed in blue and unarmed, to reassure property owners that they pose no revolutionary threat.

The Legal System

There are two legal systems in operation in Great Britain: one in England and Wales and another in Scotland. The one that applies in England and Wales is the common law of England, which very roughly means that everyone is bound by the same law, and that what has been allowed in the past is still allowed, and what has been forbidden is still forbidden, unless legislation has been passed that specifically changes either of these things. Scotland, like Continental Europe, follows a different system, based on Roman law, in which the will of the government is the basis of the law. There is insufficient space in this chapter to go through what will happen under both systems and so, for the purposes of describing an experience in court, what follows relates only to England and Wales. If you find yourself arrested in Regency Scotland, you'll need a specialist to help you. Everything said

below about the necessity of obtaining legal counsel applies all the
more when you are dealing with a legal system that is not your own.

There is a helpful guide to the laws of England and Wales available
in the form of Sir William Blackstone's *Commentaries on the Laws of
England*, which is published between 1765 and 1770. It tells you all
you need to know about the law as it applies to people, property and
the state. The only problem is that it extends to four hefty volumes.
Boiling down what Sir William has to say into just a few words, there
are five ways in which you may break the law. First, you can commit
a crime against religion. This is uncommon but you can still be arrested
for sacrilege, as a handful of people are every year. The second form
of crime you can commit is against international law. Again, unless
you're a pirate or planning to murder a foreign ambassador, this is
unlikely to concern you. The third category is those offences against
the king, such as high treason (including coin-clipping) and contempt
of the government. The fourth is crimes against society, such as insur-
rection, riot, acts against the justice system, acts against the nation's
economy, smuggling, damaging public amenities, causing nuisances
and disturbances and so on. The fifth and final category is actions
injurious to private individuals, such as murder, rape, sodomy, theft,
burglary, robbery, arson and forgery.

Obviously you are not the criminal type and the only reason you
might find yourself consulting Blackstone's *Commentaries* in a hurry
is because you have unfortunately become the victim of a crime.
Nevertheless, there is still a chance that someone might accept a bribe
in return for giving evidence against you. False accusations are
common, false testimony even more so. Hence you need to see the
legal process from both sides of the dock. And as the defendant has
so much more to lose than the plaintiff, it is best that you understand
how the court works from the position of the accused.

After a constable has arrested you, he will take you to the house
of a magistrate or a rotation office to be examined. If the magistrate
decides there is no case for you to answer, you will be free to go. If,
however, he thinks there is sufficient basis for a trial, he will either
order you to be bound over to appear at the next meeting of the
quarter sessions (if the crime is a misdemeanour) or to be taken to
prison to await trial. If you go to prison, you will have your ankles
chained together, with one of them attached by a second chain to a
heavy metal ball.[11] In some places, but not all, women are chained as

well as men.[12] You will be responsible for your own upkeep while in prison. And you may be there waiting for several months before the circuit judges visit. Some counties only hold assize courts once a year.

Before your day in court, you will want to arrange for a lawyer or 'special pleader' to represent you. Approximately one-third of defendants have the benefit of a lawyer in the 1790s – most cannot afford the fee – but there is no doubt that you will need a legal expert on your side. Trials are conducted so rapidly that you won't have a chance to get used to the courtroom before the jury has heard enough evidence to convict you. If a witness is lying about your involvement in order to enrich himself, you will need an experienced advocate to tease out the inconsistencies in his or her testimony. What's more, you will not be able to see any of the evidence against you before the trial, which will put you at an additional disadvantage. Although your representative will not be allowed to address the jury directly, he should be able to undermine a witness's false testimony by asking leading questions. By the 1820s the need for defence lawyers has grown so obvious at the Old Bailey that the judge may appoint one to represent you, free of charge, if he believes you genuinely cannot afford legal help.[13]

When the day comes, you will be chained or handcuffed to another prisoner and marched to the court. By then your indictment will already have been read to a grand jury and your accuser's lawyer will have outlined the case against you. No one can speak on your behalf at this point. If the grand jury decides there is no case to answer, you can walk out of court a free man or woman. But don't bank on this happening: seven out of eight times the charge will be deemed a 'true bill' and the trial will go ahead.[14] When you go into the courtroom, you will find yourself facing the judge as well as your prosecutor, his lawyer, your defence lawyer, the clerk and the jury, members of the press and the public. The charges will then be read by the clerk and, shockingly, this may be the first time you have heard them. The jury will be watching you to see how you react. You will then be asked, 'How do you plead?' If you say 'Guilty', there will be no trial. Likewise if you refuse to enter a plea.[15] Instead, the judge will proceed straight to sentencing.

Assuming you plead 'Not Guilty', the trial will begin with the prosecutor outlining his case. After he has done so, he will summon witnesses who are required to swear on the Bible that their testimony is the truth. (You, the defendant, do *not* have to swear such an oath; you are not expected to perjure yourself.) When each witness has spoken, you or your lawyer may question him or her. After all the prosecution witnesses have finished, it's your turn. You or your lawyer will outline your defence and then present your witnesses. Even if you have none, it is still worth calling several people to testify to your good character as they may persuade the judge that he should be lenient in sentencing you, if you are found Guilty. When both parties have presented all their material, the judge will sum up. He is quite at liberty to tell the jury what he thinks they should decide but, in the end, he is legally bound to accept their verdict.

In all probability you'll hear the summing up far sooner than you'd expect. Sometimes a trial at the Old Bailey lasts less than ten minutes. There are exceptions but they are not normally criminal cases. People spend far more time and money arguing about property than a person's life. In 1796, *The Times* reports that a legal case concerning a lead mine in Yorkshire has been rumbling on for ninety-three years.[16] The will of the phenomenally rich William Jennens, who dies in 1798, is the subject of a court battle that is still in progress at the end of our period – in fact it will not be dropped until 1915. Criminal trials only tend to be lengthy when they are political. The treason trial of Thomas Hardy – the founder of the pro-revolutionary London Corresponding Society – is described by James Woodforde as being 'a very long trial indeed' when it concludes with Hardy's acquittal after nine days.[17] The impeachment of Warren Hastings, the ex-governor of Bengal, goes on for seven years, ending with his exoneration in 1795. In your case, politics will not apply. You will probably hear the foreman of the jury give the verdict within half an hour of entering the court-room. Then you will be sentenced. If the penalty is death, you will be allowed a final speech to the court. This is supposed to be for you to demonstrate remorse but is also an opportunity to appeal for mercy. As all death sentences are reviewed by the Crown, it is possible that something you say will persuade the judge to recommend that the king look upon your case mercifully. A good speech at this point can thus save your life.

What are the chances of you being found Guilty? It depends. Seventy-two per cent of all theft cases heard at the Old Bailey result in a Guilty verdict. In contrast, only half of forgery charges do. One of the reasons for the difference is that juries know that judges rarely show any clemency in forgery cases, so they are often reluctant to return a Guilty verdict as this will probably result in the accused being hanged.[18] Other factors include how tired the jury is – they may have been hearing cases all day before yours is presented in court – and the number of death sentences the judge has already handed down that day. As hangings become rarer, so juries become readier to deliver a Guilty verdict. Overall, the proportion of those found Guilty of a felony in England and Wales increases from two-thirds in the 1790s to three-quarters in the 1820s.[19]

Punishment

If you plead Guilty to a felony prior to 1823, the judge has no discretion in sentencing you. If the statute books state that the penalty is death, then you shall be hanged. This leads to some shockingly inappropriate outcomes. In February 1814, three boys are caught breaking a pane of glass in a shoemaker's shop window and stealing a pair of shoes, worth 8s. As it happens, the crime is witnessed by a Bow Street Runner. The boys accordingly plead Guilty. The judge has no choice but to sentence all three of them to death. Two are aged nine and the third only eight. All the judge can do to mitigate the sentence is recommend that the king treat them with mercy on account of their tender years.[20]

If you plead Not Guilty but lose your case, the judge will have much greater flexibility in sentencing you. He might order you to be fined, whipped, transported to Australia or hanged, or given a more unusual punishment, such as being forced to serve in the navy, being hanged in chains, or being hanged and then dissected by surgeons. If he feels so inclined, he may be very lenient – to the point of lessening the charge against you, so that he can justify a reduced sentence. On the other hand, he is equally at liberty to hand down a very tough punishment indeed. His purpose in doing so will be not only to punish you but also to deter other would-be criminals. As Lord Halifax famously said at the end of the seventeenth century, 'men are not hanged for stealing horses but that horses may not be stolen'.[21] Most Regency people would agree – especially those who own horses.

PRISON

If you are tried at the county assizes and found Guilty, there is a two-thirds chance that you will be imprisoned.[22] Fewer people are committed to gaol in London but, even there, almost one-third spend time behind bars. The good news is that most prison sentences are relatively short. Of those handed down in the assize courts, 94 per cent are for less than a year. The bad news is that the conditions in which prisoners are held are very poor. They're not as awful as they were in the days before John Howard's report but there is nothing lenient about a prison sentence, even in the 1820s.

There are four types of prison in Britain: gaols (also known as prisons); penitentiaries, which are like gaols but specifically for those serving long terms or awaiting transportation to Australia; bridewells, otherwise known as 'houses of correction'; and debtors' prisons.

Gaols are the oldest and most common variety. They range greatly in size, from a small room above the town gate capable of holding two or three men, to obsolete medieval castles incarcerating a hundred or more, and huge complexes like Newgate with about 700 inmates. The new National Penitentiary at Millbank is even larger. This vast fortress-like structure, which opens in 1816, is designed to hold 1,000 prisoners. Some prisons are relatively clean. Some have bedding. Some even sell beer. But almost all are detestable. There is no glass in the windows, only iron bars. A large number have day rooms in which all the prisoners are held together during daylight hours and underground dungeons in which they are forced to sleep at night. Food is bread and nothing else. Water is only provided as and when the gaolers see fit. And those are just the start of the horrors.

On entering a prison, you will be told to pay 'garnish'. This means you have to strip and hand over your clothes to the longer-serving prisoners or pay a fine to them, normally between 2s and 5s. This is why so many prisoners are dressed in their underclothes when they appear in court: they couldn't pay their garnish. In most of the smaller prisons and even a few of the larger ones, there is no segregation of the sexes. At the county prison in Gloucester Castle, John Howard remarks that 'there is no separation of the women ... The licentious intercourse of the sexes is shocking to decency and humanity. Many children have been born in this gaol.'[23] But generally it is the appalling living conditions that destroy the soul. In Oxford Castle, Howard notes there is 'no infirmary, no bath, no straw [for bedding]; the prisoners lie in their clothes on mats. The men's dungeon swarms with vermin ...' Smallpox and 'gaol-fever' (typhus) frequently kill a large proportion of the inmates. By the end of our period, although many prisons are cleaner than they were, a significant number are woefully overcrowded as arrest rates quadruple between 1805 and 1829.[24] Stafford Gaol is meant to hold up to 170 prisoners but it is occupied by 297 in 1818. The new state-of-the-art Gloucester County Gaol, which opens in 1791, has space for 137 inmates but in 1820 it has 215. And these places are schools of vice in themselves: fifty-five of the prisoners chained up in Gloucester are not yet seventeen.[25]

Bridewells are like prisons but are intended for the reformation of lesser offenders. You will find them in almost every major town in England and Wales. The idea is that prisoners should redeem themselves through hard labour: hence the alterative name, 'house of correction'. As the terms of incarceration are short, there is a reduced risk of young offenders learning from old crooks. In Wisbech Bridewell, in Cambridgeshire, there are eleven 11ft-square rooms on each of the two floors, plus a 42ft-long workroom, a chapel, a hospital room and gaoler's apartment. A total of 271 people come and go over the course of a year. The majority are committed to the house for vagrancy, assault, misdemeanours or siring a bastard; the others are mostly deserters or runaway apprentices.[26] No one measures reoffending rates but there is a fair chance these inmates will redeem themselves. However, Wisbech is a well-equipped and well-organised institution. Most are not. Many are overcrowded. Men and women are kept in irons from the time of their arrival, just as they are in prisons. They have to work in irons, go to the communal privy in irons, and sleep in their irons. If there is a chapel, they even have to attend religious services while attached to their ball and chain.[27] Needless to say, women are every bit as much the victims of sexual exploitation in these institutions as they are in gaols. In some places they are treated as prostitutes by the male prisoners, who control the keys to their cells.[28]

Since the Middle Ages it has been lawful for a merchant to apply to a court to detain a customer who doesn't pay his bills on time. Gradually the law expands until anyone can have a debtor incarcerated. It now happens with distressing frequency. When John Howard carries out his survey in the 1770s, he records 2,437 people locked up for debt – more than half the entire prison population of England and Wales.[29] The total is about the same fifty years later.[30] Most are kept in gaols but a substantial minority live in a debtors' prison. The most famous such institutions are in London: the Marshalsea in Southwark; the King's Bench Prison, also in Southwark; and the Fleet Prison in Clerkenwell.

You can get an impression of what a debtors' prison is like by visiting the one in St Thomas's, Exeter. On arrival you will be escorted by a bailiff through the gatehouse and across the yard to an old building containing a total of fourteen rooms. Like every debtors' prison, these are divided into those on the 'keeper's side', which are for gentlemen and better-off tradesmen, and those on 'the common side', which are for everyone else. Neither side is fit for purpose. By 1808 the building is in a terrible state, with sagging floors that creak as you walk across them, falling ceilings, and chimneys on the point of collapse. Normally there are about thirty-six prisoners within its walls but families often join their menfolk in debtors' prisons. In 1809, there are fifty-four male prisoners and six female ones but the men are accompanied by a total of forty-four wives and 169 children. That's 273 people in fourteen rooms.[31] And the behaviour is hardly appropriate for young children. One lawyer describes a debtors' prison in 1812 as 'an incessant continuance of riot and disorder, indecent language, reviling blasphemy, gaming, drunkenness and sexual debauchery, and almost every species of vice to which human nature is prone'.[32]

A debtor has not broken any laws: he simply has debts that he cannot pay, which happens to most of us at some point in our lives. Nevertheless, debtors are often treated with greater severity than felons. A thief who is sentenced to three years in prison knows when he will be released, if he survives. A debtor does not. In addition to his original debt, he has to pay fees to his gaolers. At St Thomas's these include 13s 4d on entry, then 3s per week for a bed, or 1s 3d if you share a bed with another prisoner, plus 1s per week for bedding. These sums increase your indebtedness, week after week, making it harder for you to obtain your freedom. All the time you're stuck inside you can't work, so you are unable to earn anything to reduce your debts. In theory, if you come into some money, you can appeal to the magistrates to request that your creditor release you but, extraordinarily, your creditor doesn't have to agree. In this way someone who has put you behind bars for debt can keep you there for years. In 1793 *The Times* reports that a man has now spent fifteen years imprisoned at Newgate for a debt that originally amounted to £2 5s. At St Thomas's, John Howard notes that one old woman has spent forty-three years behind bars there – for what was once a modest debt.[33]

The first step towards reforming this system is taken in 1808. An Act of Parliament is passed which states that, if the original debt is less than £20, the debtor has to be released after he or she has spent a year in gaol. Conditions thereafter improve slowly. Several debtors' prisons are rebuilt, including the Marshalsea in 1811 and St Thomas's in 1818. Fees in such prisons are abolished in 1813. Nevertheless, you will doubtless think that the government of such a rich country could do more. Let's face it, it could simply end the imprisonment of debtors. But still people are locked up. John Dickens finds himself committed to the Marshalsea in 1824 for his inability to pay £40 to a baker. It splits apart his family and deprives his son Charles of a happy home at the age of twelve. Imprisonment for civil debt will not be abolished in England and Wales until 1869 and not in Scotland until 1880.

CORPORAL PUNISHMENT

You would have thought that punishments like the ducking stool, the pillory and the whipping post would be things of the past. However, corporal punishment is alive and kicking in Regency Britain. And while it is true that some forms are in decline, new ones are being devised. In 1817 the treadmill is invented at Brixton Prison. It consists of a cylinder about 6 feet in diameter with steps all around it, forming an everlasting staircase on which groups of men and women have to climb for between eight and ten hours every day, thereby powering a mill. The fear it instils in prisoners at Brixton means it is seen as a great success by the authorities. Soon afterwards it is introduced in other prisons as a form of hard labour.

The ducking stool is frequently confused in modern minds with the swimming of witches (the superstition that a woman can be revealed as a witch by seeing whether she floats or sinks). This is incorrect: it has nothing to do with witches or any other superstitious belief. It is a form of cucking stool – a seat of shame – which simply has the refinement of 'ducking' or dipping the occupant into a stretch of water. Its purpose is to humiliate scolds and women who are deemed to be bad-tempered or foul-mouthed. There are two basic forms. One is a wooden armchair on a long pole that pivots on a cart: the woman is tied into the seat and wheeled through the town, prior to being taken to a river or millpond, where she is ducked in the water up to her chin. The other form is an iron-framed seat in which the woman sits as she is craned over the water and lowered in. You will still find examples of one sort or the other on display in Chesterfield, Cambridge, Sandwich, Banbury and Ipswich, among other places. Those at Derby, Manchester and Liverpool have been used as recently as the 1770s; those at Skipton and Leicester were only made in 1768. If you want to see one in action, go to these places or to Scarborough in 1795, Plymouth in 1808 and Leominster in 1809. The Leominster ducking stool is wheeled out for one last time as a cucking stool in 1817, when Sarah Leeke is paraded around the town in it by order of the magistrates (but is not ducked). In 1822, in the Devon hamlet of Doccombe, it is said that 'the lord of the manor is obliged to keep a cucking stool for the punishment of scolding women' – and he still does. Perhaps someone should tell the lord in question that he is out of step with public opinion? You just try. The lord of the manor is the dean and chapter of Canterbury Cathedral.[34]

Once upon a time every town had to have its pillory, for the punishment of perjurers, fraudulent bakers, brewers and butchers, and people found guilty of spreading false rumours. The condemned man stands with his head bowed and clasped by two blocks of wood, with his hands fastened immovably on either side. You can still see examples in many old market towns. Rye in Kent uses its pillory for the last time in 1813, to punish a publican for helping a French general to escape; Manchester's very tall example, on top of a pedestal, is in use until 1816.[35] However, the place you will most frequently see them employed is London. Among the dozens of men pilloried in the capital is William Whittingstall, who is sentenced in May 1814 to a year in Newgate and 'to be placed twice in and upon the pillory in Bishopsgate Street, near Sun Street ... for the space of one hour each time'.[36] His crime is attempting to burn down the house in which he lives – to claim on the insurance – thereby endangering the lives of the four families who live in the same building and all those living in houses nearby. Whittingstall lives in Sun Street; this pillory is therefore near his neighbours' houses. He can expect to be 'greeted by a large mob with a discharge of small shot, such as rotten eggs, filth and dirt from the streets ... followed up by dead cats, rats, etcetera ... collected in the vicinity ... by the boys in the morning'.[37] In some cases, they throw stones. In 1816 the pillory is abolished by an Act of Parliament for all crimes except perjury. It is only used a handful of times after this. Peter James Bossy has the distinction of being the last man to be pilloried, on 24 June 1830.

If you are appalled by the ducking of women and the pillorying of perjurers, you will be horrified by the whipping of men and women. It is particularly vicious when applied by order of a court martial. Prince Edward, duke of Kent, sentences a man to no fewer than 900 lashes, the most brutal sentence of this sort ever handed down.[38] As Robert Southey explains, when a soldier is sentenced to be treated in this manner:

> A surgeon stands by to feel his pulse during the execution, and [to] determine how long the flogging can be continued without killing him. When human nature can sustain no more, he is remanded to prison. His wound – for, from the shoulders to the loins, it leaves him one wound – is dressed, and as soon as it is sufficiently healed to be laid open again in the same manner, he is brought out to undergo the remainder of his sentence.[39]

Whipping is by no means restricted to soldiers. Three per cent of all sentences at the county assizes involve public or private whipping. At the Old Bailey, whipping is used even more regularly, in 9 per cent of Guilty verdicts. Thousands of people are flogged, mostly for shoplifting or petty theft. They include the very old, the very young, and women as well as men. In April 1799 Catherine Squires is caught stealing a tablecloth and a brass candlestick from a nobleman's house. When asked if she has anything to say in her defence, she simply replies, 'I beg mercy of the court, for I am almost dead with poverty and starving.' She is sentenced to be whipped in public even though she is seventy-five years of age. Eighty-year-old Martha

Burgess is sentenced to be whipped for taking a pair of stockings worth 2s from a washing line in 1813. At the other extreme, in May 1822, John Vaughan and John Sheen are caught stealing a hammer, a pair of compasses and two pieces of tin, together worth 18d. They are both whipped in public. Vaughan is aged eight, Sheen just seven.[40]

TRANSPORTATION

Transportation is the second-most-common sentence in this period, after imprisonment. Thirty per cent of all felons sentenced at the Old Bailey and 21 per cent of those at the assizes are sent to Botany Bay, better known to you as New South Wales. Alternatively, from 1812, they are sent to Van Diemen's Land (Tasmania) or, from 1824, to Norfolk Island in the South Pacific. That equates to roughly 60,000 men, women and children by 1830. Among the youngest are William Appleton, aged nine, who is transported in 1802 for stealing thirty-seven pennies and forty-seven halfpennies from a milkman's cart, and John Gable, aged eight, who breaks into a shop one evening in 1806 with a ten-year-old boy and steals a few pairs of stockings, worth about 21s. Technically they could be hanged for these crimes, so transportation for seven years is seen as a merciful sentence. Transportation for *fourteen* years is the penalty handed down to seventy-five-year-old William Stevens in 1829 for pickpocketing a handkerchief, worth 4s. When William Cook, aged eighty-three, is found guilty of the same crime in 1825, he is transported for life.[41]

Most people who are transported are guilty of theft. Fraud, perjury, kidnapping, forgery, threatening behaviour, manslaughter and violent assault can also earn you a one-way ticket to Botany Bay. One man is transported for an acid attack on a married woman walking along a London street with her husband and son in 1814.[42] Most bigamists find themselves sent into penal exile and, in some cases, you can see why. You have to feel sorry for Rachel Parsons. She works hard as a servant and saves up nearly £20 over the first ten years of her employment. Then along comes John Harwood, twenty-seven, who sweeps her off her feet and marries her on 2 October 1820. Her brother and mother are in the throng celebrating the happy day. But three weeks later, she discovers that he is already married. He immediately walks out on her, taking her cash. Her family catch him, however, and after a brief trial, he arrives in Botany Bay in July 1822.[43]

Transportation is a very tough sentence. Not only are you removed from your friends, family and all the support networks that you take for granted but you are also forced to eke out a living in a barren country about which you know nothing. There is no European colony in Australia prior to the arrival of the first prison fleet in 1788, so there is no infrastructure to help you in the early days. Everyone is hungry. Theft is common. Many men are hanged or banished from the community in the first months after arrival. On top of that, there is the difficulty of getting there. The second fleet sets out in January 1790 and arrives at the end of June, having lost 273 of the 1,038 convicts on board. Some die due to shipwreck; others because they cannot cope with being chained up, waist-deep in sea water, for five months. Nearly 200 people die during the voyage of the third fleet too.

Even before you set foot on a ship bound for Australia, you will have to endure a period of incarceration on a hulk. This is a prison ship converted from a permanently moored redundant warship, which has had its masts and guns removed and its gun ports barred with 2-inch-thick iron grilles. Conditions in such vessels are unspeakable. Imagine the experience of a boy like William Appleton, the nine-year-old mentioned above, arrested for taking a purse from a milk-man's cart. He is despatched under guard to the River Thames. Chained convicts row him across to a hulk at full tide. After they've hauled him up on to the deck, he is issued with a canvas jacket and clothes, plus a single blanket. His ankles are chained together with iron fetters, which he'll have to wear day and night. Then he is sent below, into the foetid air where hundreds of men are confined, and is allocated a lice-infested hammock or, more probably (given his age), a place on the floor.[44] Such is the violence below deck that the guards simply do not go down there after dark. The next few months are a series of adversities: hard labour in the dockyard, bullying, hunger, cold, disease, darkness and despair. Then William is trans-ferred to the *Calcutta* with 292 other convicts, still in his chains, and spends the next eight months at sea. He survives, however, and lands in Port Philip on 4 October 1803, 12,000 miles away from his family. All for stealing 5s ½d.[45]

THE DEATH PENALTY

On the morning of Tuesday 21 March 1815, Eliza Fenning, a twenty-year-old servant, lights the fire in the basement kitchen of Mr Robert Turner's house in Chancery Lane, London. She sets about cooking dinner for Mr Turner, his wife and his father. She has been in service since the age of fourteen but has only been with this family since late January. She knows Mrs Turner does not like her, as she thinks Eliza is a hussy, having once caught her showing herself off to the young men in the house in a semi-dressed state. Nevertheless, today Eliza makes dumplings and a beefsteak pie. These are to be served with a sauce made by Mrs Turner herself. The Turners sit down to dinner at 3 p.m. Very shortly after tasting the food, all three of them fall ill. An apprentice working for the family comes into the kitchen and helps himself to a piece of dumpling and lots of the sauce; he also falls ill. Eliza too suffers the same symptoms. The other housemaid in the building does not eat with the family and is not affected. So alarming is the illness that Mr Turner sends for his surgeon, who arrives at 8.45 p.m. He tells Mr Turner their symptoms are like those following the ingestion of arsenic. Fortunately, all five of them make a full recovery. However, Mr Turner wants to know what has caused this sudden affliction. It has to be something to do with the food they ate and, because his surgeon mentioned arsenic, he becomes convinced this is indeed the cause. After all, he keeps arsenic in the kitchen, in an unlocked drawer, for poisoning rats (as many people do). It is marked 'Arsenic – deadly poison'. Eliza knows about it because the paper for lighting the fire is kept in the same drawer and she lights it every day. And she can read and write. Mr Turner decides she must be the guilty party.

Before he goes to a magistrate, he conducts his own investigation. He asks his surgeon to take a sample from the pan used to cook the dumplings. These noticeably went black and did not rise, unlike Eliza's normal white fluffy dumplings. The surgeon obtains half a teaspoon of white powder after subjecting the pan to a series of scientific processes of his own devising. He tells Mr Turner that this white powder looks like arsenic. Mr Turner accordingly decides that, although Eliza too fell ill, she must have been trying to kill all three of them. He has her arrested on four charges: attempting to murder the Turner family; administering poison; trying to poison Mr Turner in particular; and trying to poison Mrs Turner.[46]

On 5 April 1815, Eliza enters the dock at the Old Bailey. She is terrified. She does not have a lawyer – she can't afford one. She pleads Not Guilty. She hears the surgeon's evidence and Mr Turner's. When she is questioned herself, she cannot explain how arsenic could have entered their food. She grows most distraught and repeatedly protests her innocence. She pleads with the judge, saying, 'My lord, I am truly innocent of all the charges, as God is my witness; I am innocent, indeed I am; I liked my place, I was very comfortable.' Four witnesses appear in court to attest to her good character. Despite this, the twelve members of the jury find her Guilty. The judge sentences her to death. He does not recommend clemency. When asked if she wishes to say anything further, Eliza is unable to speak. A witness later says 'she was carried from the bar convulsed in agony and uttering frightful screams'.[47] Although the case is referred to the Home Secretary, he does not wish to intervene, and accordingly recommends that the sentence be carried out.

On the day of her execution, 26 July 1815, a huge crowd gathers outside Newgate. Many ordinary Londoners do not believe she is guilty. When her distraught parents come to see her for the last time, Eliza assures them that she is innocent. When she is asked by the chaplain if she has anything to say to him, she replies, 'before the Just and Almighty God, and by the faith of the Holy Sacrament I have taken, I am innocent of the offence with which I am charged'. Even on the gallows – dressed in white, with the noose around her neck and her hands tied together before her – she repeatedly calls out that she is innocent. The hangman ties a handkerchief over her eyes. He attaches her noose to the gallows, and then there is long pause before he moves the lever to open the trapdoor.

You cannot watch people die like this and not feel pity. The trial is a farce. Eliza is traumatised by the accusations against her. She has no legal advisor to pick apart the flimsy case of the prosecution. The judge fails to ask the obvious questions, such as why she too fell ill. The surgeon's professional opinion – that the substance he isolated was arsenic – rests on his assumption that arsenic was the cause of the poisoning. Moreover, his opinion isn't independent; it is wholly constructed to support his client's accusation. What about the ingredients Mrs Turner used for the sauce? If the house arsenic supply was genuinely the cause of the poisoning, anyone in the building could have added it to the food. No one explores these lines of enquiry. What's more, none of the Turners dies from this poisoning. Yet they bring no fewer than four specific charges against Eliza, demonstrating that they have taken professional legal advice and want to see her condemned. Mrs Turner is, no doubt, delighted by the outcome. It is deplorable that the law supports the Turners in every way, even though the defendant has so much more to lose. You can see that all the new investigative work that is so useful in catching suspects is only used on behalf of the moneyed middle and upper classes. No one puts that level of detection and analysis into defending a working-class girl. And once you realise that, it is not just pity that you feel at her dying, it is outrage.

In the 1790s, 671 individuals are sentenced to death at the Old Bailey. In the 1820s, more than twice as many – 1,673 – hear the fatal words 'hanged by the neck until you are dead'. This is despite the 1823 Act removing many capital offences from the statute books. As a proportion, however, there is no increase: both figures represent about 11–12 per cent of Guilty verdicts. The same proportion receives the death penalty in the assize courts. Fortunately, the numbers actually hanged decreases because the government increasingly shows mercy. In 1805, approximately a quarter of those sentenced to death are hanged; twenty years later, only one in twenty is actually executed.[48]

As you can see, the death penalty is itself dying. The old Tyburn Tree is no longer used for London hangings: condemned men and women are now executed at Newgate on a specially constructed gallows that employs the short-drop method. After the trapdoor opens, the condemned person falls about 18 inches. Prisoners are no longer launched into eternity by having the cart they are standing on driven away, so that they swing like a pendulum as they die. They no longer have to travel to a place of execution in an open wagon, as they had to when Tyburn was still used. Nor do they have to ride to the gallows sitting on their coffins, which is the rule in Gloucester until 1792.[49] At Newgate they only have to walk from the condemned prisoners' yard to the front of the building. But the cruelty of the law – or, rather, the law of cruelty – has plenty of last hurrahs. These include the gibbeting of criminals. If you see an iron frame suspended from a gallows swinging in the breeze containing the skeletal remains of a body, this is someone who has been executed and gibbeted close to the scene of his crime. The idea is that the unburied corpse, denied a last resting place in consecrated ground, should be a deterrent. Travelling in Cheshire, Robert Southey notices 'two bodies swinging from a gibbet by the roadside; they had robbed and murdered a post-boy, and, according to the barbarous and indecent custom of England, were hanged up upon the spot till their bones should fall asunder'.[50] If you sail up the Thames you can still see sailors' and pirates' bodies gibbeted in the water. Anne Lister is quite shocked in 1821 when she sees, at the river's edge, 'three gibbets standing at a little distance from each other, the first showing remains of one man, the others remains of two men each. They were Malays executed perhaps eight or ten years ago for murdering their captain.'[51]

12

Entertainment

Mr Salomon most respectfully acquaints the nobility and gentry that the last of his subscription concerts will be on Tuesday next, 23rd inst. Part I: ... New Grand Septetto ... for principal violin, vielo, violoncello, clarinet, bassoon, corno and double bass [by] Luigi van Beethoven.

The first reference to Beethoven in *The Times*, 22 April 1801

The world is your oyster, as Shakespeare says. If I may be permitted to broaden the metaphor to the world *and time*, Regency Britain is the pearl at its heart. There is simply so much to do. People of all classes now read out of curiosity as well as necessity. Those with money go to theatres and the opera. They visit ancient castles and museums. They ride with the hunt or sit quietly fishing for trout. On a summer's evening they might relax at the Vauxhall pleasure gardens, listening to music and chatting with friends; on a winter's afternoon they might watch a boxing match or go ice-skating before listening to a concert and then gambling away the rest of the night in a London club. Those of a more studious disposition can pore over their printed editions of ancient texts or their collections of coins, medals, fossils or geological specimens, while their wives and daughters sew ever-more-intricate designs into their samplers. Visual displays are not simply restricted to pictures and sculptures but also include projected images. And those in search of the picturesque can go on a hiking tour of the Highlands of Scotland or visit an art gallery and see the beauty of the natural world displayed in oils. Regency Britain can provide you with every form of entertainment that the modern world has to offer – as long as it does not require electricity, a combustion engine or wings.

Competitive Sports

Just as the fine arts have their stars in the famous painters, writers and composers of the day, so the sporting world has its heroes too. But their reputations have dwindled over time. Are you familiar with Mad Jack Mytton? Or George Osbaldeston? Probably not. If anyone remembers them in the modern world, it is as eccentrics. Yet each in his way epitomises the Regency gentleman-sportsman.

John Mytton – known to his friends as 'Jack' – is a force of nature. A heavy drinker (four to six bottles of port per day, beginning in the morning, while shaving), his achievements are not reckoned in records or times so much as the spirit with which he lives. If tracking ducks across a frozen pond in winter requires him to strip naked to do it, that is what he will do. If someone bets that he cannot drive a cart across the county on a moonless night in a certain time, he will do it. His ordinary sporting achievements include winning many trophies and gold cups as a racehorse owner but these are eclipsed by his undoubted prowess as a rider. How many men would attempt to jump a 6ft fence when following the hunt with one arm in a sling, having broken it on the previous hunt? How many huntsmen, when coming to the River Severn in hot pursuit of a fox that can swim, would plunge in with their horse, shouting, 'Let all who call themselves sportsmen follow me!' Not many. In fact, very few do on that occasion. Often when riding he attempts to jump a ridiculously wide canal or river and gets a soaking. It isn't about the achievement or the failure; and as for the supposed eccentricity, that is merely our impression. It is all about the combination of determination and imagination on the spur of the moment, which together make sport so compelling. Yes, it is eccentric to allow a pair of foxes out of a box at an inn and let them run wild around the drawing room, smashing all the glasses and crockery. The sport lies in catching them again.[1]

George Osbaldeston similarly dedicates himself to sporting success – no, *excess* – from an early age. He is simply obsessed by winning. He bowls and bats for the All-England cricket team and scores centuries for the MCC and Sussex. In real tennis, he takes on first the French champion and then the Italian, defeating them both without a racquet, using only his gloved hand. With a gun he is a demon, often killing 100 per cent of the birds released at 21 yards, and 75 per cent when doubling the distance. In fox hunting he is the master of no fewer than eight hunts and regularly spends six days a week in the saddle. Although his mother persuades him to stand for Parliament in 1812, Osbaldeston decides that government 'is a great bore'. As he puts it in his autobiography, 'I was so entirely engrossed with hunting, shooting and athletic feats that I could not turn my thoughts to politics.'[2] Arguably his finest sporting moment is riding 200 miles in 8 hours 42 minutes at Newmarket, as mentioned in chapter 7. But his whole life is a succession of bets. If you see a man driving a chariot at breakneck speed around a London square, sending up clouds of dust as if it's the Circus Maximus, the chances are you're watching Squire Osbaldeston in pursuit of a wager.

As the careers of the above gentlemen suggest, you cannot be a sportsman and not ride. Hence horse racing – 'the sport of kings' – takes pride of place among all the competitive sports. The wealthy and well-connected flock to Newmarket, Ascot and Epsom Downs to bet and then to celebrate or drown their sorrows in good company. Many others attend the races for the sheer spectacle. Almost all events are flat races – and thus demonstrations of the fastest speeds attainable on land. No animal these days can quite match the legendary Flying Childers, which in the early eighteenth century could sustain 34mph for more than four miles, carrying a jockey of 128lbs, but some Regency racehorses are able to go just as fast over the shorter race distances of about 1¼ miles that are now in favour.[3]

As a result of this popularity, many racing institutions are founded in the eighteenth century. The Jockey Club comes into being around 1750; by the 1790s it is the governing body for the sport. Tattersalls starts auctioning racehorses in the 1770s. All five classics of the English flat-racing season date from around this time: the St Leger, run at Doncaster, dates from 1776; the Oaks and the Derby, both run at Epsom, from 1779 and 1780; and the 2,000 Guineas and the 1,000 Guineas, both run at Newmarket, from 1809 and 1814 respectively. The Ascot Gold Cup starts in 1807; the Cheltenham Gold Cup in 1819; and dozens of provincial races are run for prizes of gold cups or large purses up and down the land.

All horse races are run under strict rules, so that jockeys have to wear their owners' colours and must weigh in after every race. The 'judge' sits in a covered coach directly opposite the winning post. Another white post 100 yards away is where the bettors assemble. The bookmakers stand on wooden crates, holding pocket-books and pencils. Among the waving arms and upturned faces you can see lords and ladies, servants, tradesmen and shopkeepers all betting equally, without rank, as the great god of Chance gives preference to no man or woman over any other. When the cry goes up, 'The horses have started!', everyone scampers to the winning post and jostles for a position along the ropes there, or climbs on to the roofs of the stage-coaches parked alongside the finishing straight.[4] And as the leading riders cross the line, there are the usual shouts and cries of jubilation and the wordless expressions of shocked defeat. All in all, it is an event not to be missed, from the ostentatious displays of the rich in all their finery to the sideshows and fairground atmosphere of the booths away from the finish line.

The second most-cherished sport of the age is boxing. Fashionable young gentlemen – collectively known as 'the Fancy' – attend the London schools of famous pugilists such as Daniel Mendoza and John Jackson. It is just as popular at the other end of the social spectrum. As Robert Southey puts it, 'a boxing-match settles all disputes among the lower classes, and when it is over they shake hands, and are friends'.[5] Although a gentleman would never fight publicly for a prize, etiquette dictates that he should not shrink from going several rounds with a man of a lower class, if he is challenged. Mad Jack Mytton once breaks off hunting when a Welsh miner gets in his way. Mytton dismounts angrily and challenges the fellow to a fight. The miner warns him, 'You'll find me a tough 'un' and rolls up his sleeves. Twenty rounds later, having beaten the miner to his knees, Mytton gives him 10s for being such a good sport and rides off.[6]

Organised boxing matches are actually illegal but magistrates do nothing to stop them. The time and venue are discreetly circulated in coffee houses, public houses, barbers' shops and among the Fancy. The rules are those laid down by the eighteenth-century prizefighter Jack Broughton. You may not strike your opponent before coming up to the 'scratch' mark in the centre of the 'stage'; if you fail to 'come up to scratch' within thirty seconds, you are beaten. You may not hit a man anywhere below the waist, nor may you hold him by any part of the leg or his breeches. You may not hit him when he is down – and being on his knees counts as 'down'. Otherwise you may hit him, hold him in a headlock, elbow him, grab him around the waist, fling him to the ground and even pull his hair. There is no obligation to wear 'mufflers' or boxing gloves: these are generally only used for sparring. Each round lasts until a man is down. Broughton's rules state that the only reasons for ending the fight are when a fighter fails to come 'up to scratch' within thirty seconds or when a team throws in the towel. Hence some fights go on for more than twenty rounds. In 1825 one carries on for 276 rounds and sees the participants pummel each other for four and a half hours.[7]

If you want to see a bare-knuckled fight, make it a classic contest. One of the greatest is said to be the match at Hornchurch in April 1795 between the two masters: John Jackson and the all-England champion, Daniel Mendoza. Jackson wins in the twentieth round by grabbing Mendoza's hair and repeatedly punching him in the face. Alternatively, try to catch the match on Hungerford Common in December 1821 between Bill Neate, 'the Bristol bull', and Tom Hickman, 'the Gas Man'. William Hazlitt travels down in a coach to watch it. His words describing the end of the fight give you a flavour of what to expect:

Neate just then made a tremendous lunge at [Hickman] and hit him full in the face. It was doubtful whether he would fall backwards or forwards; he hung suspended for about a second or two, and then fell back, throwing his hands in the air, and with his face lifted up to the sky. I never saw anything more terrific than his aspect just before he fell. All traces of life, of natural expression, were gone from him. His face was like a human skull, a death's head, spouting blood. The eyes were filled with blood, the nose streamed with blood, the mouth gaped blood. He was not like an actual man but like a preternatural, spectral appearance, or like one of the figures in Dante's *Inferno*. Yet he fought on after this for several rounds, still striking the first desperate blow, and Neate standing on the defensive, and using the same cautious guard to the last, as if he had still all his work to do; and it was not till [Hickman] was so stunned in the seventeenth or eighteenth round, that his senses forsook him, and he could not come to time, that the battle was declared over. Ye who despise the Fancy, do something to show as much pluck, or as much self-possession as this, before you assume a superiority which you have never given a single proof of by any one action in the whole course of your lives![8]

Faced with that challenge from Mr Hazlitt, you might opt instead to head to the nearest cricket ground. You will see the game played in many English villages, for it is common for gentlemen to wager a few guineas on a match between teams composed of their respective tenants. More formally, there are dozens of established clubs, especially in the south of the country, several of which employ professional players. Great pride is placed on the inter-county matches: Sussex, Surrey, Kent, Hampshire, Middlesex and London all vie for the reputation of the best, although there is no championship as yet. Most choose their home grounds at this time too. The Marylebone Cricket Club sets up its camp at the ground established by Thomas Lord in west London in 1787. This is also where the first Eton and Harrow cricket match is played in 1805. Mr Lord moves his ground in 1811 and again in 1813, when he finally brings Lord's Cricket Ground (as it becomes known) to its permanent site in St John's Wood.

If you are tempted to play yourself, you will find much that is familiar. Gentlemen play in whites, the leg-before-wicket rule is widely accepted, the pitch has acquired its traditional 22-yard length and the wicket is made of three stumps, not two as it used to be. The rule limiting the width of a bat to 4¼ inches is universal: no longer can you turn up with a bat wider than the wicket. However, there are many differences too. There are only four balls per over, not six; the wicket is lower and narrower; and the bowling is normally underarm, never overarm. Most annoyingly, there is no wide rule before 1811. It is only introduced due to the bad sportsmanship of George Osbaldeston, who, in that year, orders his bowler to bowl repeatedly wide to a player with whom he has a bet. On that note, I'm afraid to say that the interests of gambling often take priority over the quality of the match. Many poorer players are open to being bribed. The man against whom Osbaldeston has the wides bowled, Lord Frederick Beauclerk, later president of the MCC, is reputed to make 600 guineas a year by bribing scorers, even though he is a clergyman. Much more wholesome is the idea of a women's cricket match, such as the one played at Ball's Pond Road, Newington, in October 1811. Eleven ladies from Hampshire take on eleven from Surrey for a prize of 500 guineas. The Hampshire women win – and, as far as anyone knows, they do so without cheating.[9]

Pedestrianism is another sport driven by gambling. How fast can you walk 100 miles? Can you run 10 miles in less than an hour? Robert Barclay Allardice – better known as Captain Barclay – is the most celebrated pedestrian of the age. At the age of seventeen he wins 100 guineas for walking six miles in under an hour. In 1801, aged twenty-two, he wins 5,000 guineas by walking 90 miles in 21 hours 30 minutes.[10] One particularly celebrated match takes place in 1807 against a famous runner called Abraham Wood, to see who can cover the greatest amount of ground in twenty-four hours. Wood is the clear favourite but, come the day, he is in agony after six hours and has to retire. Captain Barclay, who has kept up a brisk 6mph to that point, carries on for another hour to make sure he wins the 600-guinea prize.[11] And his most famous feat still lies ahead of him: the long-standing challenge of walking 1,000 miles in 1,000 hours by doing just one mile every hour. That's a gambler's dream: the prolonged anticipation, the see-sawing of the odds, and the spectacle of seeing a man go without sleep for more than forty minutes at a time for six weeks. But on 12 July 1809 Captain Barclay crosses the line, triumphant.

Captain Barclay's achievements inspire hundreds of other people to attempt extraordinary walks. Huge amounts of money are staked on them completing or not completing their challenges. Frequently those who have bet against them try to make their tasks more difficult by dampening the course to make it muddy, being rowdy at the pub where they are trying to sleep, bribing them to give up and, on one occasion, starting a riot so the competitor is arrested by the magistrates. Nevertheless, some men overcome these obstacles. Josiah Eaton, a baker from Northamptonshire, is the most notable walker to follow in Barclay's footsteps. In 1815 he completes an extended 'Barclay Match', covering 1,100 miles in as many hours, at one mile every hour. He then goes on to walk 2,000 half-miles in 2,000 half-hours the following year and, in 1818, he attempts 4,032 quarter-miles in 4,032 quarter-hours. This means he cannot sleep for more than ten minutes at a time, for six weeks. Amazingly, on 30 June, he completes this incredible feat.[12]

If running is more your thing, you will be disappointed to hear that there are no athletics clubs in the Regency period. There are races galore but they are all of an amateur nature and mostly put on for gambling purposes. A typical example is the foot race reported in *The Times* on 13 October 1806 between two gentlemen over three miles. After a description of the course and the victor's winning margin, the article concludes with the words 'the match was for 100 guineas'. As there are no stopwatches, there are no recognised performance records. However, there *are* watches with second hands and, as a result, there are some noteworthy achievements over set distances. Most impressively, on 10 October 1796, a runner from Oxford called Weller runs a mile along the Banbury road in 3 minutes 58 seconds, thereby winning himself three guineas.[13] You can't argue about the distance covered and, although an eighteenth-century spring-driven watch is not the most precise instrument, it is not likely to be more than a second or so out over such a short space of time. Even if the judges exaggerate slightly, just getting *close* to a four-minute mile in leather shoes on ordinary roads is a phenomenal achievement. Nor is Weller the only one.[14] In 1813, Walter Thom publishes *Pedestrianism*, in which he records that the Scottish runner John Todd has done a mile in 4 minutes 10 seconds – a time that is anything but *pedestrian*. Over longer distances, the fastest young men run 10 miles in 52–3 minutes.[15] Interestingly, it is in these years that upper-class men start to compete in person, rather than be represented by their servants. Even members of the aristocracy join in. Thom describes a race over a mile on 6 July 1804 between Lord Frederic Bentinck and the Hon. Edward Harbord, which Mr Harbord wins in just over five minutes. The match is for 100 guineas.[16]

Women's running events are occasionally arranged for betting purposes but are almost never timed. The majority take place at village fairs for the traditional prize of a fine linen smock. Working-class girls and women run wearing only the skimpiest clothing – either a half-shirt and drawers or a short cloth covering only their private parts. It is not unknown for women to run completely naked.[17] Either way, such exhibitions excite a lot of interest as it is practically the only opportunity people have of seeing large numbers of scantily clad women. If it weren't for the competitors' enthusiasm for such races, you'd have to conclude that women's running is as closely intertwined with sex as men's is with gambling.

'Football,' declares one writer in 1801, 'was formerly much in vogue among the common people of England, though of late years it seems to have fallen into disrepute and is but little practised.'[18] This is hardly surprising: it is a particularly rough game. In Yorkshire the toecaps of the players' shoes are 'heavily shod with iron; frequently death has been known to ensue from the severity of the blows inflicted thereby'.[19]

Yet the game proves increasingly popular at the major English public schools. This is ironic: the sport of 'the common people of England' is kept alive by the upper-class boys at elite educational establishments. The explanation, I suspect, lies in the equalising character of the sport. Football doesn't cost anything, so it does not matter whether you are a duke's son or a commoner: you have an equal chance of winning. Football also offers boys the opportunity to display the above-mentioned 'combination of determination and imagination on the spur of the moment', which is so important in the crucible of boarding-school life. As it happens, schoolboys are the ideal people to develop the game, for they are not afraid to experiment with the rules. Westminster School develops one form of football, Winchester College another and Rugby School a third, and so on. In case you're wondering about the Rugby version, it is a myth that William Webb Ellis creates Rugby Football by picking up the ball and running with it in a match in the latter half of 1823. Running with the ball won't be tolerated at Rugby for another twenty years.[20] Nevertheless, the story illustrates how versatile these schoolboy games are. Football and rugby as we know them are both developed in the early nineteenth century through a constant process of trial and error.

The other competitive sports are very much a regional matter. Golf is well established in Scotland, with courses maintained at St Andrews, Musselburgh and many other places. You won't find it played south of the border, however. Wrestling is still popular in its traditional heartlands – the north of England and the West Country. Tennis remains a niche activity due to the small number of real-tennis courts in Britain. Perhaps the one other sport that deserves to be singled out for your attention is rowing. By 1800 Eton College and Westminster School both have rowing clubs on the Thames. Famously, in 1829 Oxford and Cambridge compete against one another at Henley in the first University Boat Race. The individual colleges also compete against each other in their respective towns. Just picture the scene at an Oxford regatta: there you are, relaxing beside the Isis with a glass of wine, watching two teams of young men flying through the water in an eight-oared cutter, each rower stripped to his shirt sleeves. The waves gently splash against the grassy bank as groups of students and young ladies nearby shout encouragement.[21] That, you have to agree, is quite the antidote to a boxing match.

Blood Sports

Although Parliament comes close to banning cockfighting in 1802, blood sports are still fashionable at both ends of the social spectrum. In 1817, a number of British noblemen accompany Grand Duke Nicholas of Russia – the future Tsar Nicholas I – on a visit to the Cockpit Royal in Birdcage Walk, London.[22] I'd have thought that once you've seen one killer cockerel launch himself at another – wings flapping in feathery anger, with steel spurs attached to his legs – you'd have seen them all. Apparently not. The grand duke stays to watch five fights over the course of ninety minutes and is greatly 'amused', despite the heat, the smell, the tobacco smoke and the rowdiness of the proceedings. The upper classes also frequent dog fights. The Westminster dog pit is a two-storey wooden structure that encloses a 12ft-square fighting arena. Terriers are set upon each other, with their owners urging encouragement. Often you'll see a hundred gentlemen staring down from the gallery, yelling at the bloody show. Again, it is a mixture of appalling spectacle and high-stakes gambling. Rather disturbingly, the private London gambling club, Crockford's, has a dog pit in its basement.[23] It is a powerful contrast: the chandelier-lit card tables above ground and the candlelit bloody barbarity below.

In a country town you will regularly see terriers set upon a chained-up bull. The bull tosses the dogs with its horns, and men stand by with sticks to catch them and break their fall. The attempt to outlaw the practice on the grounds of cruelty in 1802 meets with the opposition of men such as George Canning, the future prime minister, who declares that bull baiting 'inspires courage and produces a nobleness of sentiment and elevation of mind'.[24] Robert Southey, who is an expert on Spanish culture, points out that that might be true if those doing the baiting were to expose themselves to danger, as in a Spanish bullfight, but they don't. Instead all they do is fasten the bull to a ring and then:

> the amusement is to see him toss the dogs, and the dogs lacerate his nostrils, till they are weary of torturing him, and then he is led to the slaughter-house to be butchered ... The bear and the badger are baited with the same barbarity; and if the rabble can get nothing else, they will divert themselves by worrying cats to death.[25]

One evening in 1827, Prince Hermann Pückler-Muskau is taken to an old barn in the London suburbs to witness the exploits of a famous terrier called Billy. He can see the moon through gaps in the roof. Lanterns hang down from the beams and there is a wooden-walled dog pit in the centre, with a gallery and ladder for the better-off, who pay 3s for the privilege of climbing up and taking a seat. This is what Prince Hermann does, as those sitting around him bet large sums on the outcome of the fight. The challenge, they tell him, is whether Billy can kill 100 rats in ten minutes. A man with a massive, bulging sack enters the small arena and loosens the top. Out into the candle-light spring the rats, darting this way and that. The official timekeeper looks at his watch and gives the signal. Billy rushes in and 'sets about his murderous work with incredible fury'. As soon as a rat lies lifeless, the rat man picks it up and flings it back into the sack. All 100 are despatched in 9 minutes 15 seconds. After a short break, Billy is brought back to fight a badger. This he does with the same savagery, ripping off both of its ears early in the proceedings.[26]

At least shooting has the merit of trying to cause as little suffering as possible to the animal. Country parsons and professional men join the landed gentry in the annual slaughter of pheasants, partridges, woodcocks, ducks, pigeons, hares and rabbits. Aristocratic estates vie with each other as to which establishment offers the best sport, encouraging the wealthy to kill thousands of birds over the space of four or five days. Shooting clubs similarly promote the mass slaughter of our feathered friends, especially in summer. If you are invited to join members of one of the London pigeon clubs, such as the Kent Road Club or the Red House Club, you will find yourself having a champagne breakfast at midday in a large garden, with a double-barrelled shotgun at the ready. Eight pigeon houses stand 21 yards from the shooting point. When you shout 'Pull', someone tugs one of the strings opening a door and a bird flies up. If you kill it before it can fly out of the grounds, it is fetched by the club spaniel and you have a score. Each member might shout 'Pull' up to a hundred times every afternoon. Men like George Osbaldeston and Captain Ross, his rival for the title of the best shot in Britain, almost never miss.[27]

The other blood sport you will need to enjoy – or endure – in order to fit in with country society is hunting with hounds. There are three principal types of quarry: deer, hares and foxes (otter hunts are very rare at this time). It is not a cheap sport. By law you have to have an annual income of £100 to hunt. You'll also require the appropriate clothes, a horse specially bred to jump and a subscription: maintaining a pack of eighty hounds can cost more than £1,000 a year. But everyone can watch for free, and spectators can ride along with the hunt if they wish, even if they are not subscribers. As for the sporting skills, it enables gentlemen to demonstrate their energy, drive and horsemanship. In the words of the biographer of Thomas Assheton Smith, one of the foremost huntsmen in England, 'the manly amusement of fox hunting is the best corrective to those habits of luxury and those concomitants of wealth which would otherwise render our aristocracy effeminate and degenerate'.[28] Moreover, it is the only sport in which upper-class men participate that does not primarily exist to facilitate gambling. Women, I should add, almost never take part. Although they are not expressly forbidden from hunting, it is considered indecorous for ladies of quality to ride astride a horse, so they ride side-saddle, which prevents them from jumping over hedges, walls and ditches. As a result, hunting with hounds is a sort of rural gentlemen's club – which is why men like Jack Mytton, George Osbaldeston and Thomas Assheton Smith dedicate so much of their lives and fortunes to it.

Indoor Games

After hearing so much about gambling you're probably wondering which games you need to practise in order to make a splash – socially, if not financially. In a word, faro should be top of your list. This is a card game in which a set of clubs is fixed to a board and then players, known as 'punters', make their bets by placing tokens on the chosen card. The banker then draws the cards that determine whether the punters win or lose: a winning card and a losing one each time. If a punter has bet on a six and the banker draws a six as a winning card, he or she receives his stake back and as much again from the bank. If the losing card is a six, he loses his stake to the bank. The only skill lies in the various ways of cheating. Many of these are deployed to great effect by those lovely ladies who manage private faro banks in the West End. Punters can easily lose track of how the cards are being twisted against them when they are half-drunk, being flirted with and entirely happy.

Among the other card games, the devilishly complicated quadrille is going out of fashion, played only by older people after 1790. The rather stiff Lady Catherine de Bourgh – Jane Austen's character in *Pride and Prejudice* – plays it at her grand house, Rosings, as does the Revd James Woodforde at his rectory.[29] Gradually it is giving way to cassino, picquet, loo and 'vingt-un'. Woodforde also likes to play commerce and cribbage. The most important card game, however, is whist.[30] This has its great authority in Edmond Hoyle's book *A Short Treatise on the Game of Whist*, which enables everyone to be confident of the rules.[31] It is also a sociable game as you can play it in pairs. Hazard is a dice game, very popular in the London clubs; I should warn you, playing it is an easy way to lose a large fortune very quickly. The other amusement that is causing a stir in the 1790s is 'E. O.', which stands for 'Even and Odd'. This is based around a wheel that is like a roulette wheel except that the compartments into which the ivory ball might fall are marked 'E', 'O' or are left blank, for the bank. Given that the bank's section is up to one-eighth of the entire circum-ference of the wheel, you might prefer to look for games of 'roly poly' or roulette with numbers, in which the bank's share is just the zero.[32]

Those who wish to eliminate chance altogether will go straight for chess, 'the game of kings'. In the past this has been dominated by French and Italian players but after the French Revolution the centre of the chess world shifts to London. In 1792, the greatest player of the age, François-André Philidor, is forced to flee France and settle in England. He is already famous here for playing three simultaneous games of chess blindfold against the three best players in England and winning all three. Now he joins Parsloe's Chess Club as their master and raises the standard of the English game. When he dies in 1795, he is followed by a string of excellent players who establish clubs and play matches by correspondence with their counterparts in Paris and Edinburgh. They include William Lewis, the pre-eminent English chess player of the early nineteenth century. In addition to these masters, many middle-class people play. It is one of the very few games requiring skill that men and women can play against each other on an equal footing. If you join in a game, watch out for the shapes of the pieces: they are much more like one another than modern ones, so it is hard for us to tell them apart. The famous Staunton pattern with which we are familiar won't be created until 1849.

Displays

Just as in the modern world, some of the most compelling spectacles of the Regency period are organised shows. Given our fascination with the moving image, I particularly recommend two innovations, which point the way to the entertainments of the future. One is the London Diorama, created in 1822 by two Frenchmen, Charles Bouton and Louis Daguerre. It consists of a series of scenes that appear to move, due to the clever effects of front and back lighting and painting on glass. One panorama shows you a hamlet in an Alpine valley and, as you watch, you can see a stream flowing down from a mountain, with the water actually in motion. The clouds drift across the sky and the sun comes out, brightening the peaks. Gradually, for fifteen minutes, you can watch the progress of a whole afternoon over this valley, the sheep moving to better grazing areas, the light fading and the moon and stars coming out.[33] The other must-see is a phantas-magoria. The original is the creation of Paul de Philipsthal, which you can see at the Lyceum Theatre in the Strand from 5 October 1801. In the darkened theatre he uses magic lanterns to project images of unearthly figures on to walls and clouds of smoke, creating the illu-sions of ghosts. As the shows prove so popular, so his fame grows and he tours the country, employing multiple magic lanterns in order to create images of figures moving or dissolving into the landscape. The Frenchwoman Madame Tussaud joins him on his travels, bringing her collection of waxworks to show wherever de Philipsthal is demon-strating his eerie moving images.

Fairs used to be centres of trade; now they exist almost wholly for the sake of entertainment. Along with the usual stalls supplying food and drink there are acrobats and tightrope walkers, boxing matches, wrestling contests, Punch and Judy shows, exhibitions of animals and freaks. Anne Lister makes a special trip into Halifax in 1819 to see a 7ft 5 inch giant and a 6ft 5 inch giantess who are on show, along with a dwarf from Strasbourg. In 1827 Prince Hermann also sees 'the famous German dwarf and his three dwarf children' along with 'the living skeleton' and 'the fattest girl on Earth'. Unfortunately, the living skeleton has done quite well since coming to England and, having put on a bit of weight, is now in danger of losing his job.[34]

The larger urban fairs attract the most unusual demonstrations. You will come across dozens of pigs that can spell and dogs that can count. 'Toby the Sapient Pig', which shares the stage with a mermaid at Tetbury in 1823, can spell words by picking up a card for each letter. He can also do basic maths and tell the points of the compass – if you believe the handbills pasted up around the town. The mermaid doesn't do much; she just sits in a tub and combs her hair, looking at all the admirers who have paid 1d to see her. More interesting is the Terrible Turk – a life-size chess-playing machine – that is on show in London in 1818–20. Almost everyone who plays it loses. The secret, in case you want to know, is that William Lewis, the English grand master, is hidden inside the fez-topped mechanical figure.[35]

Although the start of our period is too late to witness the first balloon flights in Britain, which take place in 1784, displays of aeronautical endeavour continue to be popular throughout the period. Nathaniel Wheaton sees a launch in north London in 1824. He waits amid a crowd of 'hawkers of cakes and small beer, blind fiddlers, music-grinders, showmen, and squalling brats, scolding drabs, and swearing coachmen'. There are faces at all the windows in the houses facing the launch; the roofs too are lined with men and women. When the balloon starts to rise, he records that 'it was an object quite worth looking at, especially when it was considered that it bore two human beings, voyagers through the trackless air'.[36] Even larger crowds gather to watch parachute displays. Part of the reason for their huge popularity is that parachutes are a French speciality and thus rare in England, due to the war. Those who watch André-Jacques Garnerin leap out of a balloon 8,000 feet above London, in September 1802, are amazed. They are even more impressed in December 1818 when he returns to England to repeat the performance and his seventeen-year-old niece, Elisa, jumps with him.[37]

Houses of Ill-Repute

It goes without saying that I would not presume any readers of this book would dream of taking advantage of a visit to the Regency period to call on ladies of the night. However, I would not be doing my duty in guiding you around the past if I were to turn a blind eye to its immoral shadows and moral dangers. This is especially the case as the sex trade affects a huge number of men and women. In 1796 magistrates estimate the number of prostitutes in London to be about

50,000; by 1807 that figure has increased to 70,000.[38] This means that approximately one in five females between the ages of fifteen and sixty-five in the capital is selling sex.[39] As Christian Goede observes, not even Paris has so many prostitutes. His explanation is that married middle-class women in France regularly have affairs, so prostitutes are superfluous to requirements. Married middle-class women in England, on the other hand, rarely take lovers. So Englishmen whose sexual appetites extend beyond their own bedrooms have no option but to keep a mistress or pay a prostitute.[40] As a bed in a cheap brothel is obtainable for as little as 2s for the night, and a hasty liaison in a dark alley is even cheaper, there is a flourishing trade in female flesh.

The guidebook to the expensive end of the London sex industry is *Harris's List of Covent-Garden Ladies*, published annually from 1757 to 1795. In its pages you will find descriptions of the most attractive and seductive women working in the West End. It lists their addresses, ages and prices. It also describes their virtues in the most flowery language. Thus you may read in the 1793 edition about Mrs Godfrey, at no. 6 Newman Street, who:

> Has every requisite to make an agreeable bedfellow. Every nerve during the preludes to enjoyment seems trembling alive to all the refined sensations, and every part about the frame is blessed with that corresponding aptness that cannot fail of producing the most desirable effects. Neither has the too-frequent use of the most bewitching spot rendered it the least callous to the joys of love; she still feels all that torrent of rapture [that] the mutual dissolution of two souls in liquid bliss can possibly afford; [she] meets the oncoming moment with uncommon ecstasy, and asks the speedy return ... Her price is £1 1s although 10s 6d will do.[41]

Rather more expensive is Miss Bedford, who lives and works at no. 4 Mortimer Street:

> This languishing fair one, when in bed with a gentleman of her own loving disposition, is amorous to distraction. Her feelings at the *critical* moment are so excessively tender that she generally occasions her *blind* visitor to shed tears ere he quits her *covered* apartment. Her panting orbs, her pouting lips, delicate shape, love-sparkling eyes (which are dark), regular set of teeth, together with a tempting leg and foot,

compose the principal attractions of this goddess of pleasure ... This offspring of delight is indebted to eighteen summers for the attainment of such charms as the reader may, for the compliment of five guineas, be in full possession of.[42]

Reading between the lines, every imaginable sexual preference is catered for somewhere in London. Those looking for a certain form of entertainment need look no further than big-breasted Betsy Miles of Clerkenwell: 'Backwards and forwards are all equal to her, posteriors not excepted, nay indeed, by her own account, she has most pleasure in the latter ... Entrance at the front door tolerably reasonable but nothing less than £2 for the back way.'[43] Likewise you are left in no doubt as to the special services offered by Miss Halsbury at no. 14 Goode Street: 'A great linguist ... her tongue [is] attuned to more airs than one; but she never admits either of her mouths to be played with for less than two guineas.'[44] If pain is your predilection, then Theresa Berkeley's whipping parlour is the place to go – for her birch rods, leather straps and a 'hook and pulley attached to the ceiling by which she [can] draw up a man by the hands'.[45]

The vast majority of working girls are not able to charge anything like the rates quoted in *Harris's List*. Many more allow themselves to be taken advantage of outside a pub for a pint of porter and a shilling. There is no book advertising their charms. They make their services known by leaning out of the windows of brothels or walking the streets and propositioning men in a state of intoxication. For all the talk of 'the mutual dissolution of two souls in liquid bliss', the reality is that very few women would opt for prostitution as an occupation, if they had a choice, because it leaves them so vulnerable. This is especially true of the very young, who are regularly sold as virgins. Mary Mathews keeps a brothel in Brighton where she specialises in offering sex with girls of fourteen and under; one of them is only eleven.[46] Prostitutes are vulnerable to diseases too: it is only a matter of time before they contract gonorrhoea or syphilis; after that, their looks quickly fade and their teeth fall out. Some men use condoms made of pigs' bladders, and a few upmarket establishments employ uniformed footmen to offer condoms tied up with ribbons to clients, to minimise the spread of disease.[47] However, most women have no choice but to run the risk. It is yet another occupational hazard – to add to that of pregnancy and the violence of drunk clients. The discovery of the head of a prostitute floating in a well in Brighton in 1794 is a stark reminder that a business seen by some as 'entertainment' is a matter of life and death for others.[48]

Reading

In his memoirs, published in 1791, the bookseller James Lackington reflects that:

> Four times the number of books are sold now than were sold twenty years since. The poorer sort of farmers, and even the poorer sort of country people in general, who before that period spent their evenings in relating stories of witches, ghosts and hobgoblins etc., now shorten the winter nights by hearing their sons and daughters read tales [and] romances. On entering their houses you may see *Tom Jones*, *Roderick Random* and other entertaining books up on their bacon racks. If John goes to town with a load of hay, he is charged to be sure not to forget *Peregrine Pickle's Adventures*, and when Dolly is sent to market to sell her eggs, she is commissioned to purchase *The History of Pamela Andrews*. In short, all ranks and degrees now read.[49]

Lackington's observation is supported by his own prosperity: he starts with nothing and ends up as the proprietor of one of the largest bookshops in London. He is right too to note how the lower classes have started to read for pleasure. Part of the reason for this is a House of Lords legal decision in 1774 that sets the limit of copyright protection at twenty-eight years. As a result, many classic works become available in cheap editions. However, the rise in reading is not purely driven by novels. If you remember the parlour in William Mortimer's house in Plymouth, there is a mahogany bookcase in one corner containing thirty-six volumes. Not one of these is a novel. The sole literary work among them is John Milton's *Paradise Lost*. Twenty-one volumes are theological.[50] Among the fourteen others are William Buchan's *Domestic Medicine*; Jean-Antoine Chaptal's three-volume *Elements of Chemistry*; a history of the British navy in three volumes; and Oliver Goldsmith's three-volume *History of England from the earliest Times to the Death of George II*. Such are the tastes of a dyer working near a naval dockyard who, together with his brother, is probably the first generation of his family to own any books other than the Bible.[51]

Bookshops are now regularly to be found in most market towns. In London the principal two are Lackington's 'Temple of the Muses' in Finsbury Square and Payne & Foss in Pall Mall. Major booksellers not only have their volumes on display, they also print and distribute catalogues: Lackington's runs to more than a thousand pages.[52] Prices vary considerably. You'll have to pay 18s for the three-volume set of Jane Austen's *Pride and Prejudice* when it first comes out in 1813, and 21s for her *Emma* two years later. Some literary works cost much more than this. The first two cantos of Lord Byron's epic poem *Childe Harold's Pilgrimage* will set you back a whopping 50s in their quarto edition in 1812.[53] Second-hand books are considerably cheaper. Of all William Mortimer's volumes, the highest value placed on any of them is 12s for the three volumes of Goldsmith's *History*. His copy of *Paradise Lost* is worth only 2s.

Many families cannot afford even a couple of shillings for a book. If you are lucky enough to live in Manchester, Bristol, Ipswich or Norwich you can use the public libraries in these places but otherwise there is scant provision for ordinary people to read for free. Hence circulating libraries and subscription libraries come into being from the mid-eighteenth century. In return for a modest subscription (normally between 4s and 7s 6d per quarter), readers can borrow one or two books at a time. The greater your subscription, the more books you can borrow and the newer and better-quality those books may be. The difference between the two types of library is that circulating libraries lend out large numbers of novels in order to make a profit for their proprietors. Subscription libraries are higher-minded; they do not normally lend popular novels but books on history, antiquity, exploration, literature and, in some cases, technology and the manu-facturing arts. Both sorts flourish: there are eight private libraries in Bath in the 1790s and fourteen in 1830. Across the whole of England there are 390 by 1800.[54] Tradesmen like William Mortimer might not own any novels but that does not mean they do not read them.

With so many books available, what should you actually read? It is a difficult choice: English literature is going through one of its richest periods ever. Following the publication of *Lyrical Ballads* by William Wordsworth and Samuel Taylor Coleridge in 1798, the flame of Romantic poetry burns with an extraordinary light. All the Romantic poets produce their finest work in this period – including Wordsworth and Coleridge, Sir Walter Scott, Robert Southey, Lord Byron, Percy Bysshe Shelley and John Keats. So too do those individual writers of idiosyncratic genius, William Blake, John Clare and Robbie Burns. To repeat lines from their works would be patronising to readers; you know all the best ones already. Suffice to say that they are read in great numbers, and Byron in particular is a major celebrity. Hundreds of women write fan letters to him, all emboldened by his work to pour out their passionate feelings for him and his poetry.[55] As he says shortly after the publication of the first two cantos of his *Childe Harold's Pilgrimage*, in 1812, 'I woke up one morning and found I was famous.'[56] This is despite an absolutely stinging review of his first book, *Hours of Idleness*, just four years earlier:

> Far from hearing with any degree of surprise that very poor verses were written by a youth from his leaving school to his leaving college, inclusive, we really believe this to be the most common of all occurrences; that it happens in the life of nine men in ten who are educated in England; and that the tenth man writes better verse than Lord Byron.[57]

Apart from Romantic poetry, the public are avid readers of the established classics of English literature. Foremost among these are the plays of Shakespeare, whose reputation is higher in this period than ever before. When Karl Moritz comes to Stratford-upon-Avon on his walking tour, he writes, 'In this place was born possibly the greatest genius that nature has produced.'[58] This is quite something, coming from a native of eighteenth-century Germany. If you ask a librarian at a subscription library which other works are regarded as classics, he will probably suggest John Bunyan's *Pilgrim's Progress*; the poetry of Milton and Alexander Pope; the novels of Daniel Defoe, Samuel Richardson, Henry Fielding, Laurence Sterne and Tobias Smollett; and a few large-scale historical works, especially Edward Gibbon's *Decline and Fall of the Roman Empire* and David Hume's *History of England*. He may also mention general writers like Samuel Johnson and Oliver Goldsmith. Louis Simond would add that 'the English are very fond of biography and posthumous letters of illustrious persons'.[59] True, we love to delve into other people's private lives. Nor can anyone deny the enthusiasm with which ladies and gentlemen subscribe to monthly and quarterly periodicals. Among the most popular are *The Edinburgh Review*, *The Quarterly Review*, *The London Magazine*, *The Ladies' Magazine*, *The Entertaining Magazine* and *Blackwood's Magazine*, all of which have circulations of 10,000 or more.

Despite the undeniable popularity of the foregoing publications, nothing quite rivals the demand for contemporary novels. Romantic stories frequently sell out on the day of publication. They appeal to most people who can afford them, men as well as women. The Prince Regent is a great fan of Jane Austen's works, as is Sir Walter Scott. In 1826 Scott writes in his diary, 'read again and for the third time at least Miss Austen's very finely written novel of *Pride and Prejudice*. That young lady had a talent for describing the involvements and feelings and characters of ordinary life which is to me the most wonderful I ever met with.'[60] Horror fiction is almost as popular. The success of Horace Walpole's *The Castle of Otranto: a Gothic Story*, first published in 1764, paves the way for William Beckford's *Vathek*, Ann Radcliffe's *The Mysteries of Udolpho* and many other 'gothic' visions of medievalism and fear entwined. While the novel may be derided as immoral, sensational and intellectually weak by some gentlemen, its capacity to affect people's hearts and excite their imaginations shows it has developed to the point of being the most compelling form of contemporary literature available, excepting perhaps only Byron's poetry.

One literary phenomenon worth dwelling on in this respect is historical fiction. Its existence as a genre is almost entirely due to Sir Walter Scott. It is not that he invents it – many earlier novels are set in 'olden times' – but that he is the first writer to persuade society that a creative approach to understanding the past may actually be more meaningful than an objective, wholly accurate one. He begins his novel-writing career quietly, with *Waverley*, which is published anonymously in 1814 in an edition of 1,000 copies. It does not remain quiet for long. Its impact, and that of its successors, is immense. Print runs increase – to editions of 10,000 copies – and prices go up to 1½ guineas. So remarkable is Scott's success that many people find themselves wondering at the reason. After all, everyone knows a historical novel is at least partly invention and thus at least partly a literary trick. Why do so many respectable readers allow themselves to be fooled? The historian Thomas Macaulay struggles with this question in his memorable review of Henry Hallam's *Constitutional History of England* in 1828. First, he succinctly outlines the issue:

> To make the past present, to bring the distant near – to place us in the society of a great man, or on the eminence which overlooks the field of a mighty battle … to call up our ancestors before us with all their peculiarities of language, manners and garb, to show us over their houses, to seat us at their tables, to rummage their old-fashioned wardrobes, to explain the uses of their ponderous furniture – these parts of the duty which properly belongs to the historian have been appropriated by the historical novelist …

And then Macaulay suggests an explanation:

> Sir Walter Scott gives us a novel, Mr Hallam a critical and argumentative history. Both are occupied with the same matter. But the former looks at it with the eye of a sculptor. His intention is to give an express and lively image of its external form. The latter is an anatomist. His task is to dissect the subject to its inmost recesses, and to lay bare before us all the springs of motion, and all the causes of decay.[61]

Although Macaulay's analogy is both clear and striking, it does not explain why a novelist is able to steal such a large proportion of the history market from historians. The fact is that there is much more to Scott's success than 'an express and lively image'. He illustrates the Middle Ages and the sixteenth, seventeenth and eighteenth centuries with all their respective disturbing social features: poverty, male power, anti-Semitism, the harshness of the law and the abuses of justice. In so doing, he seems to be suggesting there has been progress in the intervening years and that society is much better off in the present day than it was in the days of yore. However, at the same time, his novels are set in periods into which the freedom-loving soul can escape. His characters are not hemmed in by standardisation and centralisation. Nor are they dominated by the commercial imperative; they know nothing of mills and smoke-belching chimneys. As a result, a contrary suggestion also runs through his work: that the past was a *better* world than the present. By directly juxtaposing the present and the past, historical writing becomes a moral act – far more so than when simply analysing the past and judging the dead by their own standards. Moreover, in posing serious questions about liberty, social progress, equality and individuality within romantic, historical settings, Scott creates a more powerful form of historical literature than anyone since Shakespeare. Later historical writers are in his debt for demonstrating that, while we should all aim to be accurate, it is better to write approximations of the past that have profound meaning than exact accounts of it that have none.

Books are not only valuable for the written word; some are finely illustrated too. In fact the improvement in the production of published images over these years is quite astonishing. In the 1790s most illustrations are woodcuts, or engravings on copper plates. Both have their limitations. The woodcuts tend to look cumbersome. Engravings on copper are much more detailed but, as copper is a soft medium, they wear out quickly and constantly need re-engraving. The result is that high-quality illustrated books are expensive. Nevertheless, craftsmen are improving their techniques all the time. You will certainly be impressed by Thomas Bewick's boxwood engravings in his *History of British Birds*, published in two volumes in 1797 and 1804. Many topographical books incorporating copper mezzotints are also very fine. But as the technological limits are lifted, so the quality of book illustration improves. First comes lithography – printing from a chemically treated limestone plate – and then, from 1820, engraving on steel. This is transformational. The fine detail, subtlety of tone and lighting effects are dazzling. By 1830 a small army of highly skilled engravers is reproducing the fine drawings and paintings of landscape artists such as J. M. W. Turner and specialist illustrators like J. P. Neale and W. H. Bartlett in the plate sections of architectural, antiquarian and travel books. Between them, they start to circulate a visual record of the country's principal landmarks, creating icons of them – in many cases for the first time.

Museums and Galleries

When Napoleon's troops march into Egypt in 1798, they trigger a wave of interest in everything Egyptian. It proves to be much more than a fleeting fashion, especially after they find the Rosetta Stone, with its trilingual inscription in hieroglyphs, demotic Egyptian and Ancient Greek. Egypt remains a mystery for educated Europeans who have grown up with texts from classical Rome and Greece but who cannot read hieroglyphs. People realise the Rosetta Stone is the key to understanding thousands of years of culture. In 1801, the French hand it over to the British and the following year it arrives in London. The fashionable world goes Egypt-crazy. Ladies start to wear crocodile ornaments and Egyptian-style dresses. Gentlemen have sphinxes and pyramids cast in the plasterwork mouldings of their houses. Their furniture and ornaments are similarly decorated with Egyptian motifs. Even shop signs are repainted with Egyptian-looking letters.[62] Meanwhile, scholars in England and France vie with each other to be the first to translate hieroglyphs. Little by little the ancient symbols reveal their secrets until finally, in 1824, Jean-François Champollion makes the breakthrough – and Egyptomania starts all over again.

You would have thought all this excitement about an ancient culture would make people conscious of the value of their public museums. In some respects, it does; it raises awareness of both of them: the British Museum in London and the Ashmolean Museum in Oxford. It may also encourage the spirit of public ownership that leads to the foundation of new institutions, including the Hunterian Museum in Glasgow, established in 1807, and the Fitzwilliam Museum in Cambridge, which opens in 1816, as well as several private museums in London, such as The Egyptian Hall in Piccadilly, built in 1812. However, the fact that there are only two public museums in Britain at the start of our period shows you that people think very differently from us about the care of antiquities. Most rural people have not heard of a museum, let alone been inside one. As for the private museums in London, such as the East India Company's collections or the exhibition at the Royal College of Surgeons, only those connected with them know they exist. Members of the public can pay to look around the Tower of London, as they have been able to for more than a hundred years, but that doesn't have any exhibits except its own collections. You won't find any fashionable hieroglyphs or mummies in there.

The British Museum in Great Russell Street is a must-see attraction for most visitors to the capital. However, gaining access is not easy. First you must write requesting a ticket, giving your name, address, occupation and the time and date you wish to visit. Every evening all the applications are presented to the Principal Librarian, who decides whom to admit – the criterion being whether he thinks you are a 'studious and curious person' or not. If he thinks you are, then he directs the gatekeeper to issue a ticket. This allows you to walk through the gate, across the courtyard and into the entrance hall. There you will be directed to wait until all ten people allocated to your time slot have arrived. Half of you will be led by one officer through the museum and half by another. These tours, I hasten to add, go at breakneck speed; and the guides don't tell you anything about the objects. There are labels but you won't have time to read them, as your group has to stay together and you are not allowed to dawdle. In 1808, after the opening of a new sculpture gallery, the growing number of applications forces the trustees to raise the maximum number of people admitted at any given time to fifteen and dispense with the need for a ticket. But still visitors are marched through the departments without stopping. It is absurd. It seems as if the museum prides itself on how many objects it can prevent people from seeing. Only in 1810 do the trustees relax the rules and allow anyone who is suitably dressed to wander through the galleries at his or her pleasure. Thereafter you may do this on Mondays, Wednesdays and Fridays between the hours of 10 a.m. and 4 p.m. As a result, visitor figures go up, reaching 33,074 in 1815. I suspect the Principal Librarian is most disappointed.[63]

There is far more to the British Museum besides Egyptian antiquities. The building itself is splendid, having previously been the duke of Montagu's town mansion. Its aristocratic chambers are decorated with *trompe l'oeil* ceilings painted by the leading French decorators of the 1680s. When you reach the top of the grand staircase, two enormous stuffed giraffes are there to greet you, standing guard beside the door.[64] The exhibits themselves are based around Sir Hans Sloane's huge personal museum of ethnographic artefacts, exotic flora and fauna, coins and medals, books and antiquities. Thousands of medieval manuscripts have been added to this core collection, as well as Ancient Greek vases, objects brought back by explorers and countless botanical specimens. Every year the museum receives more items by donation or purchase: Charles Townley's magnificent collection of classical sculptures arrives in 1805, Lord Elgin's selection of figures from the Parthenon in 1816, and George III's huge library in 1823. Anyone who has anything wonderful to give to the nation donates it to the British Museum, and everyone who comes to London makes an effort to see it. Louis Simond notes that many of the stuffed birds and animals are in a state of decay but he is very excited to see the Rosetta Stone, artefacts from Pompeii and Herculaneum, tribal ornaments from the Pacific, and one of the originals of Magna Carta.[65] Prince Hermann

Pückler-Muskau admires the giraffes, the Portland Vase and a bust of Hippocrates but is disappointed to see that the Elgin Marbles are kept in a shed.[66]

There are no public art galleries in Britain in 1800. The first one is the Dulwich Picture Gallery, which opens in 1814. Prior to that, the only opportunities you'll have as a member of the public to view fine art are the Royal Academy's annual Summer Exhibition in Somerset House and the temporary exhibitions arranged at the British Institution on Pall Mall, which is founded in 1805. The good news is that, as the country is awash with highly accomplished artists, you will find many famous names represented in both places. Sir Joshua Reynolds, president of the Royal Academy, still rules the roost at the start of our period. His rivals and successors in the portrait business include Richard Cosway, George Romney, Thomas Lawrence, William Beechey, Thomas Phillips and George Hayter. If you are interested in landscape painting, this is the age of Constable, Turner, George Morland and Joseph Wright of Derby. Among the grand history painters of the age are Benjamin Haydon, James Northcote, Benjamin West and Angelica Kauffman. George Stubbs and Edwin Landseer specialise in painting animals; Mary Moser, flowers.

This explosion of interest in painting culminates in the establishment of the National Gallery. The impetus comes from two directions. One is yet another unexpected consequence of the French Revolution. After the execution of the French king and queen in 1793, the French royal art collection is appropriated for the people and displayed at the Louvre. Thus France – governed by middle-class revolutionaries, whom the British establishment despises – has a national gallery, whereas Britain does not. That doesn't seem quite right. Second, connoisseurs like Sir George Beaumont believe that British artists must have access to the greatest masterpieces of the Italian Renaissance if they are to reach new artistic heights. Hence national pride and artistic aspirations come together in a single demand for there to be a publicly owned, permanently accessible art collection in London. It finally comes to fruition in 1823, when the banker John Julius Angerstein dies, leaving a collection of thirty-eight masterpieces by Titian, Claude, Poussin, Raphael, Rembrandt, Rubens, Velázquez and Van Dyck as well as a house conveniently situated on Pall Mall. Sir George Beaumont persuades the government to buy the paintings for £57,000 and use them as the basis of a national collection to be exhibited in

Angerstein's house. Sir George adds sixteen Old Masters from his own collection. On 10 May 1824 the National Gallery opens to the public. Admittance costs 1s.

Dancing

Dances are some one of the most class-conscious activities there are in Regency Britain. Obviously hostesses arranging private balls pay careful attention to their guest lists, but assembly-room dances are almost as exclusive. You must be a subscriber in order to gain admittance or be introduced by someone who is. Subscribers who receive tickets to invite ladies to join them are not permitted to ask a female who is not of suitable rank. A season's subscription to the dress balls held every Monday at the Upper Assembly Rooms in Bath will cost you 26s. Each gentleman subscriber receives two tickets to give to ladies. The Upper Assembly Rooms also holds fancy balls on Thursdays for cotillions (four couples dancing in a square formation); a subscription to this is 14s per season, but gentlemen may only invite one lady. Everyone must also pay 6d on admission to cover the cost of tea.[67]

Formal dances are subject to a number of rules, which you will see pinned up at all the assembly rooms. They are mostly matters of common sense. Gentlemen who wish to dance with a lady should not crowd her and may not wear boots unless they are officers in uniform. You mustn't complain if your intended partner chooses to dance first with someone else. Don't dance more than two numbers in a row with the same partner. And when the advertised hour for the end of the dance comes around, the entertainment ends exactly as the hour strikes, even if a dance is still in progress.

If all that formality fills you with dread, wait until you see Almack's Assembly Rooms in King Street, London. That's if you can get in. It is famous for its exclusivity, which is maintained with steadfast severity by seven aristocratic patronesses. Captain Gronow writes, 'one can hardly conceive of the importance attached to getting admission to Almack's, the seventh heaven of the fashionable world'. Prince Hermann Pückler-Muskau notes that 'intrigues are set on foot months beforehand and the lady patronesses flattered in the meanest and most servile manner to secure so important an advantage, for those who have never been seen at Almack's are regarded as utterly unfashionable'.[68] Absolutely no banker or industrialist is admitted. If you forget your ticket, you will not be allowed in. No one may enter after 11 p.m.: even the duke of Wellington is turned away for arriving late. If a gentleman walks in wearing trousers rather than breeches, the patronesses turn him around and march him out again; the duke of Wellington is barred entry for this transgression too. To be a member costs 10 guineas a year – if they will have you – and each ball costs a further 10s admittance. Once inside, you'll probably be disappointed. The music is generally sprightly, the candelabra are dazzling and there are many well-dressed young women hoping to attract the attentions of the most eligible young aristocrats, while balding poets and grizzled army officers – friends of the ageing patronesses – look on. But the rooms themselves are sparsely decorated and the food is unappetising. The only dances until about 1815 are country dances and cotillions. After that, revellers may dance the quadrille and even the scandalous waltz. But don't get your hopes up. As Prince Hermann observes, 'God knows, nowhere do people jump about more awkwardly; and a man who waltzes in time is a real curiosity.'[69]

The Theatre

By law, theatres have to hold a royal patent in order to put on plays. That means there are only three official venues in London – the Theatre Royal in Drury Lane, the Covent Garden Theatre and the Theatre Royal, Haymarket – and the last of these is limited to the summer months. But as you might have noticed, there are many more theatres in the city besides these three. The King's Theatre in the Haymarket operates legally as an opera house. About a dozen other theatres around the capital in the 1790s are run by impresarios who hold 'burletta licences', which permit them to put on shows that include music. As these places are unable to stage the best plays, they have to make up for it with entertaining tunes, better-painted sets, surprising lighting effects and sheer variety. You might enjoy a programme consisting of five or more of the following acts: a musical production, a short tragedy, a comedy, a ballet, a rope-walking demonstration, a pantomime, a display of balancing tricks, a masquerade, the feats of a strong man and an operetta. At the Amphitheatre near Westminster Bridge, Philip Astley combines plays with horse-riding displays. At Sadler's Wells you can see slapstick comedy from 'Joey the clown', otherwise known as Joseph Grimaldi, by far the most loved pantomime actor in London. Whether you are looking for traditional acting, a combination of music and drama or a variety performance, London, as always, has something for everyone.

Outside the capital, the demand for high-quality theatre is also high. Prospective proprietors accordingly obtain patents to establish provincial theatres. By 1800 you will come across a 'Theatre Royal' in almost every substantial town in Britain, from Aberdeen in Scotland to Truro in Cornwall. Magistrates can also authorise premises to be used as temporary playhouses. These provincial performances can be of a very high standard. Drury Lane and Covent Garden both close in the summer, during which time their star actors and actresses tour the provinces. If you are in Liverpool or Leeds and want to catch a performance by a major star, you will be able to do so in the summer months. Just look out for the theatre bills around town advertising what's on.

What can you expect if you visit the Theatre Royal in Drury Lane in 1800? Even before you're inside you'll be struck by the vastness of the structure – more than 120 feet high and 300 feet long. As you make your way to the entrance, pushing through the crowds, you'll be accosted by women selling oranges, the traditional snack of the theatre-goer. Having resisted their entreaties, you'll head to the cashier's desk in the foyer to pay for your seats. Prices are the same as they have been for the last century: 5s for a seat in a box; 3s for the benches in the pit; 2s for the circle; and 1s for the gallery. Presuming that you're going for a box or the pit, you'll come next to a large chandelier-lit saloon where you may buy tea, coffee or fruit. Then you'll go into the theatre itself. I guarantee you will be awestruck by its cavernous appearance. It seats 3,611 people. Although a candelabra is fixed to each of the many metal columns supporting the four raised tiers of seating, they all seem like so many pinpricks of light in the vast darkness. Unless you are in one of the boxes very close to the stage, you will not be able to see the actors' expressions. You will barely hear their voices. You'll also notice that many seats are still empty. Gentlemen often reserve places in the boxes and then don't turn up, because they don't have to pay until they arrive. The benches and the gallery are also sparsely occupied because people often wait until the end of the third act when they can gain admittance at 'second price', which is normally half the full price. Not all of the incomers are there for the show: many are prostitutes hoping to meet men with money to spend. Consequently the second half is more disturbed than the first. Those in the circle and the gallery who want to annoy the better-off people in the pit idly flick their orange peel down on them.[70] Many buy food and drink throughout the performance from a bar area at the back of the pit. Considering programmes at Drury Lane consist of a satirical prologue, followed by a five-act play and then a one-act farce to finish – so they may well go on for five hours or more – the need for sustenance is quite understandable. Nevertheless, it is not an ideal venue for hearing and seeing the best performances. It is not a complete disaster that the massive building burns to the ground on 24 February 1809, as Sheridan watches, warming himself at his 'fireside'.

When Drury Lane goes up in smoke, the nearby Covent Garden Theatre is also a building site, having burnt down on 19 September the previous year. But the foundation stone for a new theatre has already been laid by the prince of Wales, thanks to Robert Smirke's astonishingly rapid production of designs. The new building is a magnificent structure, from its elegant portico and the grand staircase inside to its well-proportioned saloons and horseshoe-shaped auditorium.[71] Everyone expects the opening night to be a triumph: John Kemble and Mrs Siddons are playing opposite one another in *Macbeth*. What could possibly go wrong? But during the performance, riots break out over the prices. Box seats have increased from 6s to 7s and those in the pit from 3s 6d to 4s. Worse, a tier of seating that used to be public now consists of private boxes. The proprietors try to explain that this is necessary to recoup the £150,000 they have spent on the new building. The audience is unpersuaded. They suspect this is an attempt to move the theatre upmarket and exclude ordinary Londoners. The 'Old Price Riots' continue every night for more than two months, with customers not buying tickets before the second-price stage of the evening, then coming in and disrupting the performances. On the sixty-seventh day, the actor-manager John Kemble finally gives in and restores the old prices.

What plays should you see? The three London patent theatres all regard Shakespeare as their bread and butter. Therefore, for a new play, they want something that Shakespeare might have written. The problem is that new works by the Bard are rather hard to come by.

William Henry Ireland does his best to re-create a lost play in *Vortigern and Rowena* but, sadly, Ireland is no Shakespeare. Although *Vortigern* is accepted by Sheridan for production at Drury Lane in April 1796, the audience can't stand it. It is stopped in the fifth act. Many other neo-Shakespearian histories are also derided. So what should a theatre manager do? One popular solution is to put on gothic horror stories and supernatural melodramas with dazzling lighting effects. Hence plays like Matthew Lewis's *The Castle Spectre*, first performed in 1797, take the place of Shakespeare at Drury Lane. Another option is to revive an old play, such as one of Sheridan's hits from the 1770s – especially *The Rivals* or *School for Scandal* – or a tried-and-trusted work by an earlier eighteenth-century writer like Henry Fielding, Oliver Goldsmith or David Garrick. There are some notable new plays, such as the works of Elizabeth Inchbald, Hannah Cowley, Richard Cumberland, Thomas Dibdin, John O'Keefe, George Colman and Thomas Morton, all of whom have great success writing comedies for the London stage. Nevertheless, the standout performances that you will want to see are those of the leading actors and actresses playing Shakespeare.

Among the male stars, John Kemble and Edmund Kean have to take top billing as the best tragic actors since David Garrick's retirement in 1776. Kemble is a lean, tall, serious and authoritative man. He makes his Drury Lane debut as Hamlet at the age of twenty-six and thereafter gradually builds himself a reputation as the second-greatest Shakespearian actor of the age – second only to his sister, Sarah. Often the two play opposite each other in *Macbeth* or *Hamlet*, to great acclaim. When he takes over the management of the Drury Lane theatre in 1788, his vision is to make it the pre-eminent venue for Shakespeare in the nation, with him playing most of the lead roles himself. Thus you will want to see him in *Coriolanus* in 1789, *Macbeth* in 1794 and *King Lear* in 1795. His attention to detail captivates people. The critic Leigh Hunt remarks, 'He never pulls out his handkerchief without a design upon the audience.'[72] After the failure of *Vortigern*, in which he reluctantly plays the lead role, Kemble moves to Covent Garden. Here you will want to see his *Hamlet* in 1803. Unfortunately in later years ill-health, heavy drinking and dependence on opiates take their toll. Then he suffers the financial calamity of the fire that destroys the Covent Garden Theatre, in which he is a shareholder. He recovers but his role in *Macbeth* when the new theatre opens is overshadowed by the Old Price Riots. After that he loses his drive. He returns for one last well-reviewed stint as Coriolanus, his favourite role, in 1814, and gives his last performance on 23 June 1817.[73]

By the time Kemble takes his final bow, his successor as the hottest ticket in town is equally famous and, arguably, already past his best. Edmund Kean is the unwanted son of an actress who supplements her income with prostitution, and an alcoholic father who commits suicide when Edmund is six. His teenage years are hardly any happier than his childhood, as he struggles to make his mark as a leading man in provincial theatre companies. It does not help that he is short whereas tragic actors are expected to be tall and imposing, like John Kemble. Temperamental, passionate and selfish, Kean is exceedingly volatile. Any setback results in an outburst – followed by self-recrimination, womanising and heavy drinking. However, his explosive performances, driven by an internal psychological drama of his own, start to make a mark on audiences. The turning point comes in November 1813 in the rather unlikely surroundings of a theatre in Teignmouth, in Devon, where Kean is playing Octavian in Richard Cumberland's *The Mountaineers*. He is spotted by Dr Drury, the retired headmaster of Harrow School, and is brought to the attention of the management of the Theatre Royal, Drury Lane. After his personal tragedy worsens with the death of his four-year-old son the following month, Kean travels to London, to play Shylock in *The Merchant of Venice*. He makes his debut on 26 January 1814 – and no one who sees it ever forgets it. Self-loathing, inner fury and a deep grief combine to make Kean the ultimate Shylock. A month later, he plays Richard III – and masters that part, displaying both rage and fear. Then he takes on the challenge of playing Othello. Then Hamlet. And Macbeth. Thus he proves himself the quintessential romantic leading actor. If you go to the theatre in 1814, yes, do go to Covent Garden to see Kemble playing Coriolanus for the last time. But then head to Drury Lane to see Kean in *anything*. William Hazlitt writes, 'We wish we had never seen Mr Kean. He has destroyed the Kemble religion and it is the religion in which we were brought up.'[74] Sadly, the rest is all a downhill slide into alcoholism, debauchery, venereal disease, erratic performances and unsatisfied audiences. Kean remains a star attraction throughout the period but a more reliable leading actor is the public-school-educated William Charles Macready. If you go to the theatre in the 1820s you are probably better off booking one of his shows – there's a risk that Kean will be too drunk to turn up.[75]

In looking for two leading ladies to recommend, the choice is similarly easy. One of them is simply the greatest female tragic actress of the age – and quite possibly of any age – Mrs Siddons, known to all as the muse of tragedy. The other is her counterpart, the muse of comedy, Dorothy Jordan, whose life ironically is even more tinged by tragedy than Mrs Siddons'.

Dorothy has a difficult start in life, one of the nine children of an actress and an Irish gentleman who abandons her and prohibits the family from using his name. At the age of eighteen she joins the theatrical company of Richard Daly, who habitually takes advantage of his actresses. She becomes pregnant by him but then escapes his embraces. For the next three years she works for a theatre company in York until she is spotted and brought to London to perform under Sheridan's management at Drury Lane. She specialises in breeches roles – those in which she dresses as a man – and traditional female Shakespearian parts, such as Rosalind in *As You Like It* and Viola in *Twelfth Night*. Her style is natural and spontaneous, avoiding the rehearsed rhythms of the traditionally trained actress. Thus she catches the eye of William, duke of Clarence, the king's third son. In 1790 she leaves her lover Richard Ford, with whom she has lived for the last five years (and with whom she has two children), and goes to live with the duke. As the years pass, she has another ten children with him and is accepted as his common-law wife, even hosting his dinner parties. Then comes the fateful day, 2 October 1811, when the duke summons her and coldly terminates their twenty-one-year relationship, so that he can clear his debts by marrying a rich bride. To add insult to injury, he insists that Dorothy give up the stage. If she doesn't, he will remove their daughters from her. She means to comply but she has no other way of making any money. When in 1813 one of her sons-in-law racks up massive debts, she feels an obligation to do what she can to help. Thus she goes on tour through England and acts for another season at Drury Lane, winning new admirers and the plaudits of old ones. The duke carries out his threat. She loses her allowance and her daughters. Facing financial ruin, Dorothy does what Beau Brummell and so many others in her position have done before: she goes to France. Like Brummell, she does not return. The muse of comedy dies alone in a boarding house at Saint-Cloud, near Paris, on 5 July 1816. Two days later, Sheridan – the man who made her famous – also dies. He too is penniless at the end: the bailiffs are ransacking his house as he expires. Both are buried on 13 July – she at the age of sixty-one in Saint-Cloud, he at sixty-four in Westminster Abbey. That day, an era comes to an end.

This brings us to the greatest stage actress of them all, Sarah Kemble, the sister of John Kemble. At eighteen she marries an aspiring actor, William Siddons, who unfortunately never proceeds past the 'aspiring' phase. In marked contrast, Sarah's career as 'Mrs Siddons' goes from strength to strength. She learns her profession through touring the provincial theatres: Liverpool, Manchester, York, Birmingham, Bath and Bristol. Like her brother, her speciality is tragedy. When they act opposite one another, sparks fly. They match each other in theatrical authority – and, if either of them has the upper hand, she does. She even plays Hamlet to his Laertes. She makes her debut at Drury Lane in 1782, when she is approaching twenty-seven and the mother of three children. Within a year she is a household name; within ten she is an icon. She grows stronger and more magnificent as an actress as the years pass. People in the audience scream or experience fainting fits; others are overcome with tears. She plays her roles with such conviction that people speak about her being *merciless*. For women who feel trapped by society, she represents their breaking free from convention. For men, she conjures up all the human powers they fear and yet cannot control. Her performance as Constance in Shakespeare's *King John* is described as 'maternal tenderness, desperate and ferocious as a hunted tigress in defence of her young'. But it is as Lady Macbeth that she rules the theatrical world. Critics declare her performance to be definitive. Artists attempt to capture her terrifying glory as the ruthless, ambitious and manipulative yet loving queen. William Hazlitt writes of her:

> it seemed almost as if a being of a superior order had dropped from a higher sphere to awe the world with the majesty of her appearance. Power was seated on her brow, passion emanated from her breast as from a shrine; she was tragedy personified ... she glided on and off the stage like an apparition. To have seen her in that character was an event in every one's life, not to be forgotten.[76]

Louis Simond also sees Mrs Siddons play Lady Macbeth and describes her acting like 'a merciless tigress, thirsting for blood and carnage'.[77] Thus, if you need a recommendation, go and see her. See her as Hermione in *The Winter's Tale* or as Queen Katherine in *Henry VIII* or as Constance in *King John*. Even watch her play Hamlet. But most of all, see her as Lady Macbeth. It is in this role that she gives her farewell performance at Covent Garden Theatre on 29 June 1812. So intense is the experience for everyone present that, after the sleep-walking scene, they cannot bear the play to continue. They want that to be the end, the defining moment of a wonderful night and an unbelievable career. The audience does not stop applauding. So they bring the curtain down. When it rises again, Mrs Siddons is alone on the stage, seated in white satin. She stands, steps forward and gives her valedictory speech. At the end, she bows and walks offstage, leaving behind a legend.[78]

Operas and Concerts

Music is to be heard everywhere in Regency Britain: at every ball and in every suite of assembly rooms, in churches and in the streets. Nathaniel Wheaton notes that when he is in London, 'our street is enlivened every evening with serenades, and while I am writing, clarionets, French horns and the reed of Pan are performing a concert under my window'.[79] The patent theatres put on as many concerts as they do plays. The burletta houses all employ dozens of musicians and composers because they constantly require new music for pantomimes and masquerades. There are several venues in London dedicated to the performance of music of the highest quality, most notably the Hanover Square Rooms. Opera at the King's Theatre is big business. Every summer's night at the Vauxhall and Ranelagh pleasure gardens there are musical productions. Instrument-makers abound in the capital, including the finest piano-makers in the world. For instance, Beethoven plays a six-octave piano made by John Broadwood & Sons; he doesn't let anyone else *touch* it – let alone play it – not even to clean it. He calls it 'an altar' upon which he places 'the choicest offerings of my mind'.[80] Newspapers are filled with advertisements offering singing lessons and musical tuition. Hundreds of books on music and musicians are published – from instruction manuals to scores and biographical dictionaries. All around the country there are local madrigal societies and glee clubs promoting amateur singing. Dozens of musical festivals are held in towns around Britain, showcasing the finest professional musicianship of the day. In the villages and fields there are folk-music traditions that are centuries old. There is even a Royal Society of Musicians to help distressed performers and their families. Music is pouring out of every corner of society; it is in the very breath of the nation.

In addition to all this public music, a great many performances take place in private. Gentlemen often hold concerts in their country houses for their neighbours. A significant number of ladies keep practising their 'accomplishments' long after they have married, especially if their singing and playing are appreciated by their husbands or are joys shared with their children. Jane Austen practises the piano daily before breakfast and, in the evenings, sometimes sings old songs while accompanying herself on the piano.[81] Some gentlewomen have music libraries of more than a hundred volumes of manuscript scores and printed editions, often featuring the latest pieces by the most fashionable composers.[82] Friends frequently come together to perform string quartets in private: one group in Leicester starts in 1788 and is still going strong in 1830, albeit with some changes of line-up.[83]

The best classical music, however, is of foreign origin. Although there are dozens of composers in Britain, none can rival the likes of Mozart and Beethoven. Nor are there any of the standing of the many composers who visit England in these years. Joseph Haydn, Muzio Clementi and Jan Dussek all live in London in the 1790s. Luigi Cherubini comes at the invitation of the Philharmonic Society in 1815; Fernando Sor does likewise two years later, to play a concert of Spanish guitar music. Several more composers arrive in the 1820s. Louis Spohr, a virtuoso violinist as well as a composer, tours in 1820 with his wife, Dorette, herself a virtuoso harpist. He makes a dashing impression, playing with great passion in a red waistcoat – even continuing to play a concert while a rioting mob outside in the street smashes the windows of the house next door.[84] Gioacchino Rossini comes for a season at the King's Theatre in 1823–4. He has a wonderful time but does not make himself popular with George IV. Having been commanded to go and see the king at Brighton, he is insufficiently deferential when he gets there, twirling his hat on his finger in the king's presence.[85] Carl Maria von Weber arrives in 1826 at the invitation of Sir George Smart to conduct the premiere of his opera *Oberon* at Covent Garden. Three years later, the twenty-year-old Felix Mendelssohn comes for a season of concerts. He plays the piano in the British premiere of Beethoven's 'Emperor' concerto and conducts the premiere of his own first symphony on 11 May 1829.[86] The British may not produce any first-rate composers in the Regency period but we are not 'unmusical', as some people claim.[87]

With this international context in mind, the years of the Regency and the two previous decades – covering between them the careers of Haydn, Mozart and Beethoven – are simply the richest in the history of music. There is no point trying to guide you around all the many venues, composers, soloists and types of music you might hear, from the recital of old works by Handel to the performance of new ones by Mendelssohn. Instead I will mention just a couple of areas of interest: female opera singers and orchestral concerts of the music of Haydn and Beethoven. As you will see, if you are a music lover, you will find plenty to amuse you, and some things that will bring you to tears.

THE DIVAS

The word 'diva' is not yet in use but if you want to see several ladies who fit that description, Regency London is the place to come. One you must see – or, rather, hear – is Elizabeth Billington, the English-born daughter of German parents and the mainstay of the English operatic stage for many years. She has an incredibly powerful soprano voice. She also has a tempestuous love life, having affairs not only with the prince of Wales but also his brother the duke of Sussex, the duke of Rutland, the infamous theatre manager Richard Daly and many other men. But she survives all that and makes a reputation for herself as a great singer at Covent Garden in the 1780s. She also sings at all the major festivals up and down the country and by 1790 is a household name. In 1793 she makes a prolonged visit to Italy and becomes an international celebrity. When she returns in 1801, her fame precedes her. The managers of both Drury Lane and Covent Garden beg her to appear at their respective theatres. They eventually agree that she will sing at each venue alternately, for a salary of 3,000 guineas. She continues to perform serious operatic roles until her farewell performances in 1806, when she takes part in the first Mozart opera to be staged in London, *La Clemenza di Tito*. After that she only performs occasionally, and finally retires in 1811.[88]

Mrs Billington's chief rival, prior to her departure for Italy, is the German soprano Gertrud Elisabeth Mara. Madame Mara is fifteen years older than Mrs Billington and no great beauty. Her international standing is due entirely to her intensive training and her astonishing voice: she is capable of sustaining an E in altissimo. She amazes people with her ability to sing a great many notes in extraordinarily quick succession. Her life is full of drama. Mozart recalls her and her alcoholic husband having a fight onstage in front of the prince-elector of Bavaria, which ends up with the conductor getting involved and eventually the whole orchestra.[89] In England the rivalry between her and Mrs Billington is operatic in itself. Each woman regards the role of Mandane in Thomas Arne's opera *Artaxerxes* as her own. Each of them has extra arias written for her, so her version is better than the other diva's. The tension subsides when Mrs Billington travels to Italy but on her return in 1801 the press stokes up anticipation of them resuming the battle of the sopranos. A year later, and after some complications in her love life (involving taking two men half her age as her lovers), Madame Mara decides to return to the Continent. On her last night onstage in England, 3 June 1802, she and Elizabeth Billington come together to sing a duet. Now *that's* a performance worth hearing. Looking back on Madame Mara's career in 1824, the author of the *Dictionary of Musicians* declares: 'We place Madame Mara at the very summit of her profession because, in majesty and simplicity, in grace, tenderness, and pathos, in the loftiest attributes of art, in the elements of the great style, she far transcended all her competitors in the list of fame.'[90]

Another lady you must hear is the lovely half-English, half-Italian soprano Anna Selina Storace, better known to everyone as Nancy. She is the same age as Mrs Billington but spends much of the 1780s in Italy and Vienna, where she performs roles created for her by Mozart, Salieri and Vicente Martín y Soler. Mozart becomes a personal friend and writes the part of Susanna in *The Marriage of Figaro* for her. When Nancy plays the role in Vienna, she 'enchants eye, ear and soul'.[91] After enduring a brief, unhappy marriage to an abusive husband, she returns to Britain in 1787 and becomes the highest-paid singer at Drury Lane, as well as performing at provincial music festivals in the summer months and the annual Handel festival in Westminster Abbey. In 1796 she meets the leading British male singer John Braham and lives with him as his common-law wife for twenty years. She retires from the stage in 1808.

In 1804 the internationally celebrated Italian star Giuseppina Grassini arrives in London and becomes the leading lady at the King's Theatre. Her voice is lower in pitch, described as 'a contralto of uncommon sweetness'.[92] At thirty-one, she is eight years younger than Mrs Billington and stunningly beautiful: she was previously one of Napoleon's mistresses. Once again the papers see potential for rivalry. However, the highly regarded composer at the King's Theatre, Peter von Winter, will have none of it and bravely composes *Il Ratto di Proserpina* to star both women. He even writes a duet for them. It is fantastic: the combination of their voices is the talk of London. Signorina Grassini continues to thrill audiences until her return to Paris in 1806. Incidentally, many years later, she makes a conquest of the duke of Wellington too – completing a sort of amatory double-first – and her love life becomes an even bigger talking point on both sides of the Channel.

As Grassini is packing her bags and preparing to head back to Paris, the formidable Italian opera singer Angelica Catalani is in Paris packing hers and preparing to come to London. She is twenty-six. Mrs Billington, who is fifteen years older, promptly retires from singing opera. It is as well she does, because Madame Catalani doesn't like rivals. She doesn't like anyone who might draw any of the applause away from her. She has incredible vocal power and range; critics are surprised at how she can project with such volume and yet retain such agility in her voice. Her first season's contract guarantees her a basic salary of £2,000 plus benefits. In 1807 that goes up to 5,000 guineas – but she *trebles* that with fees for other appearances, earning a total of £16,700 for the year. She even charges £200 for singing the national anthem.[93] Unlike her predecessors, there is no gossip of affairs or evidence of a lover. Nevertheless, by May 1811 the press is turning against her. An article in *The Examiner* explains the situation succinctly:

Madame Catalani's ... powers are nearly confined to a wonderful voice and rapid execution, which, unrestrained by musical knowledge, have run wild and indulged in every extravagance that false taste could adopt. From her ambition to outshine others, she prefers the works of those servile composers who, depending for their existence on her smiles or frowns, are ready in all respects to conform to her will, by keeping the rest of the performers in the background, and rendering the accompaniments of the orchestra too insignificant to share with her the admiration of the audience.[94]

Madame Catalani leaves England in 1813 to take control of the Italian Opera in Paris. Before she goes, however, she and Mrs Billington both attend the debut of a nineteen-year-old singer called Catherine 'Kitty' Stephens at the Covent Garden Theatre. Miss Stephens is playing Mandane in Thomas Arne's *Artaxerxes*. She is triumphant. The new generation has arrived.

There's one final singer I want to introduce you to: Lucia Vestris, otherwise known as Madame Vestris, who makes her debut aged eighteen in 1815. She has a moderately successful career onstage until, in 1820, she plays Don Giovanni – her first 'breeches role' – and reveals her legs. They are sensational! Like Byron, she becomes famous over-night. People might not be able to recognise facial expressions in the vast auditoria but no one can miss such shapely limbs. One reviewer describes them as being 'of such a symmetry ... that the mere sight of them is enough for the art lover'.[95] The mixture of her alluring acting, charming singing and physical perfection is compelling. It does not harm her box-office power that she becomes the subject of gossip everywhere, supposedly taking lovers from every nation in Europe. If she plays a breeches role, receipts for the night can go up by as much as £300.[96] No other woman's *voice* can rival Miss Stephens's as the star attraction of the 1820s opera scene – that cannot be denied – but Madame Vestris's legs can.

HAYDN AND BEETHOVEN

The names of the great composers are so revered in the modern world that sometimes it is difficult to remember they are living in these years – and that you can visit them. In November 1790, Johann Peter Salomon, the virtuoso violinist and impresario, does just that. He goes to Vienna, knocks on Joseph Haydn's door and declares, 'I am Salomon from London and I have come to fetch you.'[97] The astounded composer then listens as Salomon offers him a substantial amount of money to leave his unloving wife and come to England to compose six symphonies and direct their first performances. Haydn says yes. He enjoys his eighteen months in London. His concerts, which start on 6 March 1791, take place in the Hanover Square Rooms. They are all a great success – so much so that, after eighteen months back in Vienna, he agrees to do it all again. In 1794 he returns to spend another year and a half in England, writing and performing new works, including six more symphonies. Thus Haydn's twelve London symphonies, his Sinfonia Concertante and six quartets come to be written and premiered in England.

Despite Salomon continuing with his Hanover Square concerts for a few years, orchestral music in London after Haydn's visit starts to dwindle in quality. Salomon tries to draw Beethoven to London, sure that such a visit would reinvigorate the orchestral music scene here. But Beethoven declines every invitation. In 1801, Salomon obtains the manuscript of Beethoven's Septet and announces its forthcoming performance in *The Times*. The paper prints the composer's name as *Luigi* van Beethoven; it is perhaps an inauspicious start. Indeed, although the Septet is a success, orchestral music is soon back in the doldrums. Salomon does not put on any more concerts. No other impresarios step forward to take his place. Within ten years of Haydn's London symphonies being written, no one is playing them in England.

Twelve years later, concert music in London is at a very low ebb. You will find nothing to excite you at the Hanover Square Rooms. No leading composers have come here since Haydn. Criticisms of Madame Catalani and the lack of diversity in the opera world could equally be applied to the orchestral music scene. Concerned by this, five gentlemen meet to discuss the matter on 24 January 1813. They decide to call together a number of leading musicians and businessmen to be the core subscribers of a society to perform new music and revive lost masterpieces. As a result, on 6 February, the thirty founding members of the Philharmonic Society of London meet for the first time. Sir George Smart is among them, so too is Salomon. They agree to arrange and fund a concert series in the Argyll Rooms, in Regent Street. Impressively, the first concert is held just a month later, on 8 March. From the start, Beethoven, Mozart and Haydn dominate the programme.[98] And as Mozart and Haydn are both dead by then, Beethoven is the only one of the three who might come here in person. People start to talk about inviting him to Britain again.

The Philharmonic Society's concerts prove a great success. They are held once a month between February and June each year. Each one showcases at least one work by Haydn, Mozart and Beethoven and two or three by other composers. Some of these are men who have fallen out of fashion, such as Johann Sebastian Bach and Christoph Gluck. Others are simply less well-known composers: Salieri, Pleyel, Dussek and Cimarosa. Priority is given to works that only exist in manuscript or have never been performed in England. In 1815 the composer Luigi Cherubini comes to London to direct the first performance of a symphony commissioned by the Society. Members hope this will be an incentive for Beethoven to do the same. On Monday 15 April 1816, the Society stages the British premiere of Beethoven's Fifth Symphony, which increases the level of expectation.

In 1817 the Society writes to Beethoven again, offering him 300 guineas for two symphonies if he will come to London to direct them in person. Still he declines. More and more of his music is being played here; it is increasingly apparent that his compositions are loved in England more than those of any other living composer. Over the next five years you can hear Beethoven's works performed at every single concert arranged by the Philharmonic Society – especially his Septet, his overtures and his first seven symphonies, with the very popular Fifth Symphony being repeated several times. In 1822 the Society writes yet again to Beethoven, asking for just one new manuscript symphony. They have no great hope of success but, as it turns out, Beethoven happens to be short of cash. He accepts. The Society enthusiastically writes back, with no idea of what they have just commissioned, expressing the hope that he will come and direct the first performance in person. There are delays, and more delays. Still Beethoven does not come. However, on 27 April 1824, the manuscript of his Ninth Symphony, dedicated to the Philharmonic Society of London, is placed in the hands of the Society's agent in Vienna.[99]

As things turn out, Austrian politics intervene, and the first performance takes place in Vienna, not London, on 7 May 1824. A few weeks later the members of the Philharmonic Society read the ecstatic reviews in the Viennese music press. Beethoven is referred to as 'the musical Shakespeare' and praised for 'revealing the divinity in humanity'.[100] So the best the Society can do is to produce the *British* premiere. But it does not matter. If there is one concert in Regency Britain that you should attend, it is the performance of Beethoven's Ninth Symphony on Monday 21 March 1825, in the Argyll Rooms on Regent Street. You probably don't need me to explain why. Beethoven's symphonies are to the early nineteenth century what Shakespeare's plays are to the late sixteenth, or the gothic cathedrals of Europe are to the Middle Ages. They are artworks that encapsulate the essence of their own time yet escape the circumstances of their creation to become timeless evocations of the human spirit. And the Ninth Symphony is, by popular consent, the greatest of them all. The English music press in 1825 sneers at its length and its supposed imperfections. It is true there are faults with the first performance, which is sung in Italian, not German, due to a conviction in London that Italian is the language of song. But if you have any doubt, go along to the second performance on 26 April 1830 in the King's Theatre. What you will hear on both occasions is the culmination of a process that has taken Beethoven not two years but *thirty*. He has been planning a great musical statement to the world based on the lyrics of the 'Ode to Joy' by Friedrich Schiller since 1792. The end result is a drawing together and rationalisation of all the contradictions and complexities of the age. It is like the French Revolution and all that happens in its wake in one piece of music. It faces the inequality of society with no self-deception. It rips away the pomposity and snobbishness of the old aristocracy. It understands what makes poverty bearable – that ecstasy can be experienced even by those suffering the most miserable of existences – and that the freedom to feel such joy is all that humanity really needs to keep going. It holds the hand of the sick and the poor, the young and the old, the unjustly wronged and the oppressed, and it offers hope to all. For its essential message is simply that we are all brothers and sisters under the starry sky of eternity. 'You millions, I embrace you,' run the lyrics. 'This kiss is for all the world.' If you join me there for that concert in 1825, you will no doubt be filled, like me, with admiration. You know what that music will come to mean to people down the ages. We are not one set of brothers and sisters in our own time – different from our parents, who are another;

and from our Regency forebears, who are yet another. Rather we are all human, one humanity, one flesh and one blood, under that same eternal starry sky.

Beethoven's kiss is for all the world, yes – and for all time too.

Envoi

Our ancestors are very good kind of folks but they are the last people
I should choose to have a visiting acquaintance with.

Richard Brinsley Sheridan[1]

In the introduction to the first book in this series, *The Time Traveller's
Guide to Medieval England*, I wrote that 'in order to understand your
own century, you need to have come to terms with at least two others'.
Those words have been quoted back to me many times since 2008
– much to my delight because they succinctly sum up my original
purpose in writing these *Guides*. By directly juxtaposing our daily lives
with those of our ancestors, we may get a better impression of the
quality and significance of what it means to be alive now as well as
then. We can see the many advantages that we take for granted but
which our forebears were denied, as well as those things that they
enjoyed but which we do not. Some people might claim this is anachronistic because it mixes up the values of the present and the past.
However, this is no more of an issue in a *Time Traveller's Guide* than
it is in any other history book: all historical writing is anachronistic
to a certain degree because everything we say and appreciate about
the past is filtered through the experiences of our own lives. To talk
about pain in the Middle Ages or the Renaissance requires us to know
what pain is. If we refer to hate, fear, starvation or enslavement, again
our understanding of these things is based on our personal knowledge
of what it means to be despised, feel afraid, go hungry or be denied
freedom. If you haven't experienced them, you need to imagine them,
based on what you do know. Thus the contemporary world of the
historian intrudes on every historical understanding. But this does not
stop us writing about other centuries; indeed, it helps us do so. The
soul of history does not lie in separating the past and the present and

examining the former in isolation, as if it were the fossil record of an extinct species, but in connecting the two and discovering they are equally full of life.

An important lesson follows on from this. Academic historians are constantly reminding us that we should judge historical individuals according to the values and standards that they themselves recognised. Obviously if you want to know why a historical figure did something, or why someone reacted in the way he did, yes, you need that contemporary understanding. But in a *Time Traveller's Guide* I find myself constantly questioning this narrow view – that we should only judge people by their own values – by exposing those values themselves to judgement. And in this particular volume the results are perhaps more striking than in any of the others. If you *only* judge an eighteenth-century man by the values he and his contemporaries shared, you will wind up with a form of history that has no relevance to the modern public, who do not share those eighteenth-century values. For example, consider the slavers and colonialists whose names and statues adorn so many public buildings in Britain today. According to the values of the time, they were the great and the good, and, according to the traditional academic approach, we have no right to condemn them. However, they certainly do not count as 'good' any more. The academic approach to the past is increasingly out of step with the modern world in insisting that we should judge such characters by their own standards despite their cruel exploitation of their fellow human beings. Similarly, if we do not condemn the eighteenth-century disregard of female education, we are tacit supporters of the oppression that marred the lives of women like Mary Wollstonecraft and Elizabeth Ham. While it is interesting *historically* to know how individuals in the eighteenth and nineteenth centuries were seen by their contemporaries, it is more important *socially* to see how millions of people – the ordinary as well as the rich – lived, loved, dreamed and suffered. It is all very well making finely balanced academic points about contemporary values but if we neglect the impact on people's lives, we are not presenting the full picture. What's more, we are failing in our public responsibilities as historians, through inadequately explaining to people how their ancestors lived and died. And if we fail in that, we fail altogether.

I cannot say farewell to this fascinating period of British history without reflecting on a couple of the things that have surprised me about it. The first of these is how much we owe to the French Revolution. Many developments experienced in Britain were due, indirectly or directly, to events on the other side of the Channel. Calls for political and social reform and the fear of a bloody revolution on these shores were predictable consequences. More surprising is the fact that the French uprising also influenced fashion, culinary traditions, chess playing, women's liberation and even the foundation of the National Gallery. One particularly interesting consequence was its effect on people's awareness of social change. Prior to 1789, most commentators were only conscious of the most obvious political and religious developments; afterwards, many realised that all the old values and certainties were up in the air. In describing England between 1760 and 1803, Robert Southey wrote:

> Perhaps no kingdom ever experienced so great a change in so short a course of years without some violent state convulsion as England has done during the present reign ... a metropolis doubled in extent; taxes quintupled; the value of money depreciated as rapidly as if new mines had been discovered; canals cut from one end of the island to the other; travelling made so expeditious that the internal communication is tenfold what it was; the invention of the steam-engine, almost as great an epoch as the invention of printing; the manufacturing system carried to its utmost point; the spirit of commerce extended to everything; an empire lost in America, and another gained in the East; these would be parts of the picture. The alteration extends to the minutest things, even to the dress and manners of every rank of society.[2]

The feeling that life was not just different but changing faster than ever before is one that has subsequently become common. Rightly or wrongly, most people since the French Revolution have believed that their generation has seen more change than any other.

As a consequence of the developments of the period, society strikes me as being recognisably modern by 1830. In saying this, I am fully aware that people lacked many features of life that we associate with modernity, such as aeroplanes, space travel, electric utensils, the Internet, telephones and so forth. In addition, the country was still dominated by the nobility and landed gentry, and women and people of colour suffered hugely from male and white prejudices. Nevertheless, it strikes me as being modern because almost every present-day social concern was being discussed, including these prejudices. The drive to the standardisation of everything from burial registers to screw threads was a clear trend by 1830. People were deeply concerned with over-population and social inequality. Reformers were increasingly deter-mined to do something about living conditions. Few cared about prisons before John Howard but his prison-reform work is ongoing even today. The lack of opportunities for females, which came to be a key concern for many women in the 1790s, was even more in people's minds by 1830. Anne Lister and the ladies of Llangollen show that sensibilities about living as a lesbian couple were in circulation. Transvestitism and gender-identity issues were beginning to be notice-able, as was the question of whether it was morally right to hang men for homosexual acts. Animal rights were on the agenda. Race relations too were a topic of discussion – not only with regard to slavery but also with respect to independent black citizens. Professionals were taking over from amateurs in almost every aspect of life – from medicine and sport to teaching and the civil service. People were also beginning to be aware of the destruction of the natural beauty of the land, commenting on the factories and pollution and lamenting the loss of the countryside and open spaces. Whatever your current social concerns, you could have found like-minded people in the Regency period, energised by the same themes in very similar debates.

Another surprise for me in writing this book follows on from this – namely, the continuity between the Regency and the modern world. For a start, a great deal of Regency culture is still current. Music before 1700 is normally classed 'early music' but not the productions of Mozart, Haydn and Beethoven. Modern architects frequently imitate the designs of John Nash and his contemporaries but rarely do they reproduce earlier forms. Men still wear trousers, not breeches. Many old houses are decorated in a Regency style but few are presented as they were before the late eighteenth century. I myself wrote this book sitting on an eighteenth-century chair at a Regency library table with a grandfather clock made in 1808 chiming away in the back-ground; very few people have anything from an earlier period in daily use. Almost every thinking person has at least one favourite Regency writer, whether it be Jane Austen, Lord Byron or someone else – and, even if not, they have decided views on those Regency writers they *don't* like. But on top of all these things, it is interesting that we engage with their attitudes far more than we do with those of any earlier generation. We feel justified in judging men and women from this time. We condemn slave owners and applaud men like William Wilberforce for fighting against enslavement. We condemn cruel husbands (especially when they were princes of the royal blood) and praise women like Hannah More and Elizabeth Fry for their roles in correcting what we see as injustices. These people's positive and negative influences extend far beyond their own time and we judge them accordingly, as if the society to which they contributed was ours – for the very good reason that it was.

What surprised me most, however, was realising that this sense of continuity is not all one-way. You would have thought it would be: after all, how could Regency people have known anything about us? But the works of forward-thinking intellectuals like Godwin, Wollstonecraft and Mr and Mrs Shelley indicate a confident belief that one day things would be different, and that we, their descendants, would benefit. Likewise, when Beethoven had his chorus sing 'You millions, I embrace you', he was not just referring to his contemporaries but to the millions yet to be born. It is comparable with our awareness of those who will come after us, to whom we are referring when we acknowledge that we are doing irreparable damage to the world of a hundred years' time with our carbon emissions, greenhouse gases, urban sprawl, plastic waste and mineral extraction. Although the writing of novels and non-fiction works that actually predict the future are a late-nineteenth- and early-twentieth-century development, the people of the Regency were already thinking of the generations yet to come. Many of those who took the time to write diaries also demonstrated a mindfulness of the future – by casting their respective stones into the pools of time so that their thoughts might ripple out to us, to let us know what it was like to be alive in the early nineteenth century. I am thinking here of modest people like Elizabeth Ham, Robert Blincoe and Karl Moritz; middle-class clerics like James Woodforde, John Skinner and Thomas Puddicombe; foreign visitors such as Louis Simond, Richard Rush and Nathaniel Wheaton; and the nobility and gentry like Prince Hermann Pückler-Muskau, Lord Byron and Anne Lister. They speak to us collectively and whisper to us intimately, and we listen.

Of course, the truth of the matter is that they are the real time travellers. Thousands of sincere voices reach us from the past. They are your real guides. We hear their words as if they are gathered around us now – generation after generation talking to us, wanting their thoughts and feelings to live on in our minds and our hearts. Perhaps you too will join them one day, leaving a whispered testimony to your descendants in the twenty-fifth or thirtieth century, becoming another voice in the almighty chorus of humanity. I recommend you do so. The more we communicate with our fellow men and women across the centuries, the more we enrich each other's lives.

Notes

Full details of publication are given on first citation. The following abbreviations are used:

FRCISLT   *First Report of the Commissioners for Inquiring into the State of Large Towns and Populous Districts* (1844)

SRCISLT   *Second Report of the Commissioners for Inquiring into the State of Large Towns and Populous Districts* (1845)

OBPO   *Old Bailey Proceedings Online*

ODNB   *The Oxford Dictionary of National Biography*

OED   *The Oxford English Dictionary*

All places of publication are London unless otherwise stated.

1 The Landscape

1. Quoted in Lady Saba Holland, *A Memoir of the Reverend Sydney Smith by his daughter, Lady Holland* (2 vols, 1855), i, p. 262. • **2.** For the visibility of a single candle flame from a distance of 2.6 km, see https://arxiv.org/abs/1507.06270, downloaded 20 April 2020. However, several lighthouse lanterns were lit with banks of 24 candles in the eighteenth century, and that was considered sufficient for them to be seen by passing shipping. The Lizard lighthouses were lit by coal fires until 1811, after which they were modernised with Argand oil lamps. The Eddystone lighthouse (Smeaton's Tower) was lit by two dozen candles from 1759; https://www.trinityhouse.co.uk/lighthouses-and-lightvessels/eddystone-lighthouse, downloaded 20 April 2020. • **3.** Prince Hermann Pückler-Muskau (trans. Sarah Austin, ed. E. M. Butler), *A Regency Visitor: the English Tour of Prince Pückler-Muskau described in his Letters 1826–1828* (1957), p. 159. • **4.** Rose Collis, *The New Encyclopaedia of Brighton* (2010), p. 241. This states that the pier is 13 feet wide. Pigot & Co., *Royal National and Commercial Directory and Topography of* the Counties of Kent, Surrey and Sussex (1839), p. 223, states it is more than 1,100 feet long and about 30 feet wide. • **5.** Sue Berry, Georgian Brighton (Chichester, 2005), p. 110. • **6.** Pückler-Muskau, Regency Visitor, p. 159; Berry, Georgian Brighton, p. 27. • **7.** John Feltham, Guide to all the Watering and Sea-Bathing Places (1815), p. 120. • **8.** Todd Gray, Margery Rowe (eds), Travels in Georgian Devon (4 vols, Tiverton, 1997), ii, pp. 139 (Sidmouth), 173 (Dawlish). • **9.** Karl Philipp Moritz, Journeys of a German in England (paperback edn, 1983), p. 176. • **10.** These figures relate to England, but as the table of populations in the main text shows, Scotland experienced a similar urbanisation. For the English statistic, see C. M. Law, 'The Growth of the Urban Population of England and Wales, 1801–1901', Transactions of the Institute of British Geographers, 41 (1967), pp. 125–43 at p. 130 (table 5). • **11.** Pigot & Co., London & Provincial New Commercial Directory of Bedfordshire, Berkshire, Buckinghamshire, Cambridgeshire, Cornwall, Devon, Dorset, Gloucestershire, Hampshire, Herefordshire, Huntingdonshire, Monmouthshire, Norfolk, Northamptonshire, Oxfordshire, Somerset, Suffolk, Wiltshire and South Wales (1830), p. 350 • **12.** The figures in this table were drawn from the Accounts and Papers Relating to Population, in Five Volumes, 5: Comparative Account of the Population of Great Britain in the years 1801, 1811, 1821 and 1831 (1831), from the sections dealing with the town returns (not the composite values given on p. 13). The reason for this is that past writers have skewed the figures for their own purposes. For example, the 1801 census gives the population of Sheffield as 31,314. However, the town then lay in a much larger ancient parish, which included a number of other hamlets, and the whole parish had a total population of 45,755. Thus many historians give this latter figure. The University of Portsmouth project, A Vision through Time, takes the modern boundaries of the city and applies them to past data, so residents of Sheffield can see how many people were living in 1801 in the area that we *now* know as Sheffield: that total is 60,095. Obviously, had you arrived in Sheffield in 1801, you would have found only half that number resident in the town. Much the same can be said for the largest provincial town, Manchester. John Rickman, in his analysis, put the population at 90,399, having added various undefined suburbs. Joyce Ellis, 'Regional and County Centres 1700–1840' in Peter Clark (ed.), The Cambridge Urban History of Britain, volume 2: 1540–1840 (Cambridge, 2000), similarly added undefined suburbs to Manchester in her table of the largest provincial towns c. 1700–1841 on p. 679: it appears as having a population of 95,000. In that same table, Liverpool is raised to a population of 82,000 whereas Edinburgh is lowered to 81,000. Likewise, Sheffield's population is given as '45,000' even though the figure of 45,755 given in the census is clearly that of the parish, not of the town, and even a cursory glance at a contemporary map reveals extensive fields between the outlying hamlets and the town itself. Similar problems with town boundaries have made the population figures given in many other reference works unreliable. The frequently cited lists compiled by W. G. Hoskins, 'The Ranking of Provincial Towns 1334–1861', in his *Local History in England* (1959), pp. 176–8, are affected by issues of over-exclusion as well as over-inclusion. Hoskins does not include Gateshead in his figures for Newcastle, even though they are as closely connected as London and Southwark. With regard to Stoke-on-Trent, Hoskins gives this 'town' a population of 16,414 – but there was no such town of that name in 1801. The six settlements that went to make up Stoke-on-Trent in later years were still separate, and none of them individually had a population of more than 7,000; hence, Stoke does not appear in my list. In putting together these totals, the following suburbs have been included with their main town: the figure for Manchester includes Salford; Edinburgh includes Leith; Liverpool includes Toxteth Park; Birmingham includes Ashton & Edgbaston; Bristol includes Clifton & Stapleton; Plymouth includes Devonport & Stonehouse; Newcastle-on-Tyne includes Gateshead; Portsmouth includes Portsea; Hull includes Sculcoates; Aberdeen includes Old Machar; Sunderland includes Monkwearmouth and Bishopwearmouth; Bolton includes Tonge with Haulgh; Rochdale includes Castleton & Spotland; and Tynemouth includes North Shields. • **13.** Trevor Fawcett, *Paving, Lighting, Cleansing: Street Improvement and Maintenance in Eighteenth-Century Bath* (Bath, reprinted May 2000), n.p. • **14.** Alison Campsye, 'When Glasgow's gas lamps went out for the last time', *The Scotsman* (22 September 2017). • **15.** The large towns with gas companies established prior to 1830 include Bath (1818); Birmingham (1825); Bolton (1820); Brighton (1818); Bristol (1823); Bury (1826); Canterbury (1822); Coventry (1821); Derby (1820); Dover (1822); Dudley (1821); Edinburgh (1818); Exeter (1816); Glasgow (1818); Gloucester (1820); Halifax (1822); Ipswich (1821); Leeds (1818); Leicester (1821); Lincoln (1828); Liverpool (1818); London (1812); Macclesfield (1826); Manchester (1824); Norwich (1820); Nottingham (1818); Oldham (1825); Oxford (1818); Portsmouth/ Portsea (1821); Preston (before 1821); Reading (1819); Rochdale (1824); Sheffield (1818); Shrewsbury (1820); Wakefield (1822); Warrington (1822); Wigan (1822); Wolverhampton (1820); Worcester (1818); York (1823). The dates refer to the Act of Parliament setting up the gas companies in each case except Preston, whose gas company was supplying gas by 1821 even though there is no record of an Act. • **16.** *Second Report of the Commissioners for Inquiring into the State of Large Towns and Populous Districts* [hereafter *SRCISLT*] (1845), appendix, part ii, p. 7. • **17.** *SRCISLT*, appendix, part ii, pp. 15–16. For the higher density, see I. C. Taylor, 'The court and cellar dwelling: the eighteenth-century origin of the Liverpool slum', *Transactions of the*

Historic Society of Lancashire and Cheshire, vol. 122, for the year 1970 (1971), pp. 67–90 at p. 72. • **18.** Taylor, 'Court and cellar dwelling', p. 76. • **19.** The population-density figures for Crosbie Street in Taylor, 'Court and cellar dwelling' p. 85 – of 1,700 per acre in 1789-90 and 2,860 per acre by the mid-nineteenth century – are somewhat misleading. They are based on an assessment that a sample of 130 houses occupies a total area of less than 20,000 square feet, which is less than half an acre. This does not allow anything for roads, courts, latrines or alleys. The measurements on the to-scale map reproduced in his article indicate that the 130 houses in question, including the courts and facilities, occupied an area 274ft long by 145ft wide. Checking the size of the streets on *Gage's Trigonometrical Plan of Liverpool* (1836) reveals that Crosbie Street measured about 30ft wide and Blundell Street on the other side of the block measured about 36ft. Taking the average at 33ft and adding this to the width of the block means that these 130 houses occupied an area of 274ft x 178ft = 48,772 square feet, which is considerable more than the 'less than 20,000 square feet' figure he came up with, even without adding any allowance for the intersecting roads. The correct number of houses per acre in this area would appear to be 116. Using this figure in conjunction with the average occupancy figures he gives – of 6.7 people in 1789-90 and 11.27 people in 1851 – results in population density figures in the Crosbie Street sample of 777 per acre in 1789-90 and 1,307 per acre in 1851. • **20.** *SRCISLT*, appendix, part ii, p. 85. • **21.** Nathaniel S. Wheaton, *A Journal of a residence for some months in London; Including Excursions through Various Parts of England; and a Short Tour in France and Scotland* (Hartford, 1830), p. 31. • **22.** Robert Southey, *Letters from England by Don Manuel Alvarez Espriella* (3 vols, 1807), ii, p. 122. • **23.** Louis Simond, *Journal of a Tour and Residence in Great Britain During the Years 1810 and 1811 by a French Traveller* (2 vols, Edinburgh, 1815), i, p. 242. • **24.** W. O. Henderson, *Industrial Britain under the Regency: the diaries of Escher, Bodmer, May and de Gallois, 1814–18* (1968), p. 36. • **25.** *SRCISLT*, p. 41. • **26.** *SRCISLT*, appendix, part i, p. 18. • **27.** Southey, *Letters from England*, ii, pp. 71–2. • **28.** Edmund Newell, 'Atmospheric Pollution and the British Copper Industry, 1690–1920', *Technology and Culture*, 38, 3 (1997), pp. 655–89. • **29.** Leslie Tomory, 'The environmental history of the early British gas industry', *Environmental History*, 17, 1 (January 2012), pp. 29–54 at pp. 35–7. • **30.** R. J. White, *From Waterloo to Peterloo* (1973), p. 11. • **31.** Todd Gray (ed.), *East Devon: The Traveller's Tales* (Exeter, 2000), pp. 63–4, quoting George Lipscomb, *Journey into Cornwall through the counties of Southampton, Wilts, Dorset, Somerset & Devon* (1799), pp. 140–51. • **32.** Pigot & Co., *London & Provincial New Commercial Directory of Bedfordshire ... and South Wales* (1830), p. 177. • **33.** Patrick Colquhoun worked on the basis that there were 861 towns in England, 78 in Wales and 244 in Scotland. This includes some very small places, referred to as 'towns' – usually on account of having a market. See Patrick Colquhoun, *A Treatise on the Wealth, Power and Resources of the British Empire in Every Quarter of the World* (1814), p. 20. • **34.** Simond, *Journal*, i, pp. 11 (Falmouth), 197 (Salisbury), 237 (Llangollen), 239 (Chester), 261 (Carlisle). • **35.** Wheaton, *Journal*, p. 32 (Wolverhampton), 71 (Ware), 103 (Stamford). • **36.** Stephen Broadberry, Bruce M. S. Campbell, Alexander Klein, Mark Overton, Bas van Leeuwen, *British Economic Growth, 1270–1870* (Cambridge, 2015), p. 109. • **37.** Broadberry et al., *British Economic Growth*, p. 97. • **38.** J. R. Wordie, 'The Chronology of English enclosure, 1500–1914', *Economic History Review*, 36, 4 (1983), pp. 483–505 at p. 502. • **39.** Roy Porter, *The Penguin Social History of Britain: English Society in the Eighteenth Century* (2001), p. 209. • **40.** Quoted in A. F. Scott, *Every One a Witness: the Georgian Age* (1970), p. 213. • **41.** Pückler-Muskau, *Regency Visitor*, p. 54. • **42.** Simond, *Journal*, i, pp. 201 (Stourhead), 210 (Wales). • **43.** Moritz, *Journeys*, p. 118. • **44.** Broadberry et al., *British Economic Growth*, p. 106. • **45.** James Ramsay (ed. Alexander Allardyce), *Scotland and Scotsmen in the Eighteenth Century* (2 vols, 1888), ii, p. 519. • **46.** Daniel Guy Brown, 'The Highland Clearances and the Politics of Memory', PhD thesis, University of Wisconsin-Milwaukee (2014), pp. 13–16, 194.

2 London

1. James Boswell, *The Life of Samuel Johnson* (2 vols, 1791), ii, p. 160. • **2.** https://www.bl.uk/collection-items/broadside-albion-mills-on-fire, downloaded 2 October 2018. • **3.** Moritz, *Journeys*, p. 26. • **4.** John Mazzinghi, *The History of the Antiquity and Present State of London, Westminster and the Borough of Southwark* (1793), pp. 278–82. The 1785 edition, entitled *The New and Universal Guide through the Cities of London and Westminster* ... (pp. 186–8), recorded a very similar list, differing with regard to the statistics. The number of houses in the 1792 and 1793 editions is the same: 37,360 in the city of London; 26,804 in the city of Westminster; 76,814 in the suburbs in Middlesex and Surrey; and 10,714 in Southwark. • **5.** M. Dorothy George, *London Life in the Eighteenth Century* (1964), p. 110, quoting Archenholz, *A Picture of England* (1797), p. 131. • **6.** Jerry White, *London in the Eighteenth Century: a Great and Monstrous Thing* (2012), pp. 62–3; George, *London Life*, p. 109. • **7.** George, *London Life*, pp. 100–1, 113 (pigs). • **8.** Moritz, *Journeys*, p. 33. • **9.** Colin Stephen Smith, 'The Market Place and the Market's Place in London, *c.* 1660–1840', PhD thesis, UCL (1999), p. 29. • **10.** Mazzinghi, *State of London* (1793 edn), pp. 212, 214, lists 34 markets on 32 sites. For the sake of simplicity, his gross figure of 34 has simply been reproduced in the main text. • **11.** The statistics on food consumption in 1791 come from Mazzinghi, *State of London* (1793 edn), pp. 142–6. I doubt the accuracy of the figure given for spirits. • **12.** George, *London Life*, p. 52 (quoting *Commons Journals*). • **13.** As described in Wheaton, *Journal*, pp. 218–19. • **14.** Venetia Murray, *High Society: a Social History of the Regency Period, 1788–1830* (1998), p. 103. • **15.** Moritz, *Journeys*, p. 42. • **16.** Moritz, *Journeys*, pp. 45–6. • **17.** C. A. G. Goede, *A Stranger in England* (3 vols, 1807), vol. i, p. 21. • **18.** Simond, *Journal*, i, pp. 37–8. • **19.** Mike Rendell, *The Journal of a Georgian Gentleman: the Life and Times of Richard Hall, 1729–1801* (2011), p. 14. • **20.** Goede, *Stranger in England*, p. 24. • **21.** Southey, *Letters from England*, iii, p. 180. • **22.** https://www.home.barclays/news/2017/08/from-the-archives–barclay-perkins-brewery.html, downloaded 26 September 2018. • **23.** Southey, *Letters from England*, i, p. 140. • **24.** Goede, *Stranger in England*, p. 42. • **25.** Goede, *Stranger in England*, pp. 24–6. • **26.** White, *London in the Eighteenth Century*, p. 73. • **27.** William Hone, *The Table Book*, vol. 1 (1827), column 121. • **28.** The quotation is from Pückler-Muskau, *Regency Visitor*, p. 238. • **29.** Pückler-Muskau, *Regency Visitor*, p. 239. • **30.** Richard Rush, *A Residence at the Court of London* (1833), pp. xi–xii; Anne Lister (ed. Helena Whitbread), *The Secret Diaries of Anne Lister, 1791–1840* (paperback edn, 2010), p. 237. • **31.** Pückler-Muskau, *Regency Visitor*, pp. 38–9. • **32.** Simond, *Journal*, i, p. 176. • **33.** George, *London Life*, pp. 345–6. • **34.** George, *London Life*, pp. 111–12. • **35.** Edwin Chadwick, *Report … on an inquiry into the Sanitary Condition of the Labouring Population of Great Britain* (1842), p. 45. • **36.** Edwin Chadwick, *A Supplementary Report of the Results of a Special Inquiry into the Practice of Interment in Towns* (1843), p. 15. • **37.** Wheaton, *Journal*, pp. 156–7. • **38.** Wheaton, *Journal*, p. 43. • **39.** From 1805 the apothecary's shop of Lardner & Co. in Piccadilly was illuminated with hydrogen gas every evening, after which several other apothecaries did likewise. From 1810 the interior of Rudolph Ackermann's famous print shop in the Strand was lit by gas too. Opinions on the date of the latter differ. The year 1808 is given in some sources but Kathryn A. Morrison, *English Shops and Shopping* (2004), p. 37, states 1810.

3 The People

1. John Quincy Adams, diary entry for 8 November 1816. See Margaret Miner, Hugh Rawson (eds), *The Oxford Dictionary of American Quotations* (2nd edn, Oxford, 2006), p. 447. • **2.** Figures for England for 1791 are from E. A. Wrigley and R. S. Schofield, *English Population History, 1538–1871* (Cambridge, 1981), p. 529. Those for 1801–31 are from *Comparative Account of the Population*

... (1831), p. 6, subtracting the total for Wales from the 'England and Wales' figures. • **3.** The phrase is attributed to an unnamed earlier French princess in Jean-Jacques Rousseau's *Confessions* (1765), more than twenty years before the French Revolution. • **4.** Thomas Robert Malthus (ed. Donald Winch), *An Essay on the Principle of Population* (Cambridge, 1992), p. 14. • **5.** B. R. Mitchell, *British Historical Statistics* (1988), p. 474. • **6.** Quoted in Patrick Colquhoun, *A Treatise on the Wealth, Power and Resources of the British Empire in Every Quarter of the World* (1814), p. 20. • **7.** Southey, *Letters from England*, iii, pp. 286–7. • **8.** E. A. Wrigley, R. S. Davies, J. E. Oeppen and R. S. Schofield, *English Population from Family Reconstitution 1580–1837* (Cambridge, 1997), p. 615. • **9.** Wrigley et al., *English Population from Family Reconstitution*, p. 615. All the quinquennial data they report have the proportion of over-60s in excess of 7% except the years 1826–66. • **10.** The 1801 and 1831 figures are from Wrigley et al., *English Population from Family Reconstitution*, p. 615; the 2011 ones are from http://www.ons.gov.uk/ons/rel/census/2011-census/ population-and-household-estimates-for-the-united-kingdom/rft-table-1-census-2011.xls, downloaded 12 November 2018. • **11.** Wrigley et al., *English Population from Family Reconstitution*, p. 614. • **12.** *First Report of the Commissioners for Inquiring into the State of Large Towns and Populous Districts* [hereafter *FRCISLT*] (2 vols, 1844), i, p. 126; *SRCISLT*, appendix, part ii, p. 55. • **13.** *SRCISLT*, appendix, part ii, pp. 49 (Ashton), 55 (Preston). • **14.** A. Meredith John, 'Plantation Slave Mortality in Trinidad', *Population Studies*, 42 (1988), pp. 161–82 at p. 172. • **15.** *Comparative Account of the Population*, pp. 16–17. These figures are based on a study of Essex in the years 1813–30. • **16.** John, 'Slave Mortality', p. 172. • **17.** *SRCISLT*, appendix, part ii, p. 55. • **18.** Elizabeth Ham (ed. Eric Gillett), *Elizabeth Ham by Herself* (1945), p. 61. • **19.** Peter Quennell (ed.), *Byron: a self-portrait: letters and diaries 1798 to 1824* (2 vols, 1950), i, p. 206. • **20.** See her gravestone in the graveyard of St Nicholas, Brighton. • **21.** Juliet Gardiner, Neil Weborn (eds), *The History Today Companion to British History* (1995), p. 639. • **22.** Pückler-Muskau, *Regency Visitor*, pp. 88–9. • **23.** Colquhoun, *Treatise*, p. 124. • **24.** Charles C. F. Greville (ed. Henry Reeve), *The Greville Memoirs* (8 vols, Cambridge, 1888), i, p. 159; Robert Heron, *Notes by Sir Robert Heron, baronet* (2nd edn, 1851), p. 185. • **25.** Colquhoun, *Treatise*, p. 124. • **26.** David Cannadine, 'The Landowner as Millionaire: the finances of the dukes of Devonshire: c. 1800–1926', *Agricultural History Review*, 25, 2 (1977), pp. 77–97 at p. 77; Murray, *High Society*, p. 235; J. Steven Watson, *The Reign of George III 1760–1815* (Oxford, 1960), p. 335. • **27.** Murray, *High Society*, p. 85. • **28.** His estates at the time of his death in 1842 generated about £50,000, which suggests their value was about £1.25 million. He also owned consols (shares) worth £1.25 million; personal possessions amounted to another £1 million; and his silverware and jewels another

£1 million. See William Carr (revised by K. D. Reynolds), 'Vane, William Harry, first duke of Cleveland (1766–1842), aristocrat', *The Oxford Dictionary of National Biography* [hereafter *ODNB*] (2004). • **29.** Rush, *Residence*, p. 51. • **30.** Rush, *Residence*, p. 211. • **31.** *The Times* (20 July 1798), p. 2. • **32.** R. J. White, *Life in Regency England* (1963), p. 53. • **33.** Murray, *High Society*, p. 22. • **34.** James Woodforde (ed. John Beresford), *The Diary of a Country Parson 1758–1802* (paperback edn, Norwich, 1999), p. 410. • **35.** *ODNB* has £600,000; *The History of Parliament* states that he was rumoured to be worth £1 million. See http://www.historyofparliamentonline.org/volume/1790-1820/member/whitbread-samuel-ii-1764-1815, downloaded 20 February 2019. • **36.** Colquhoun, *Treatise*, p. 124, estimates that the 3,500 highest-ranking officers in the state's employment earnt about £980 per year, and the 18,000 officials who worked under them about £300. • **37.** J. F. Payne, rev. Roy Porter, 'Lettsom, John Coakley (1744–1815), physician and philanthropist', *ODNB*. • **38.** Simond, *Journal*, p. 181. • **39.** William Cobbett (ed. Asa Briggs), *Rural Rides* (2 vols, 1967), i, pp. 266–8. • **40.** *Elizabeth Ham by Herself*, p. 13. • **41.** Using Colquhoun's figures, just over a million families in the British Isles fell into the above-mentioned status groups. But the whole population, including Ireland, amounted to 3.5 million families in 1811, of which 2,461,366 families may be termed working class. • **42.** James Woodforde paid his servants' annual wages on 6 January 1790: 'to my man, Ben Leggatt, £10; to my man, Bretingham Scurl, £8; to my boy, John Dalliday, £2 2s' (Woodforde, *Diary*, pp. 245–6. • **43.** William Daniel and Richard Ayton, *A Voyage Around the Coast of Britain* (8 vols, 1814–25; Folio Society edn, 2008), pp. 43–4. • **44.** P. A. B. Raffle, W. R. Lee, R. I. McCallum and R. Murray, *Hunter's Diseases of Occupations* (6th edn, reprinted 1991), p. 132. • **45.** David Davies, *The Case of Labourers in Husbandry Stated and Considered* (1795), pp. 136–7. • **46.** Broadberry et al., *British Economic Growth*, p. 329. • **47.** John Skinner (ed. Howard and Peter Combs), *Journal of a Somerset Rector 1803–1834* (Oxford, 1971), p. 76. • **48.** Colquhoun, *Treatise*, p. 124; John Wade, *A Treatise on the Police and Crimes of the Metropolis* (1829), p. 144. • **49.** Davies, *Case of Labourers*, pp. 136–7. • **50.** Porter, *English Society*, p. 94; J. D. Marshall, *The Old Poor Law 1795–1834* (1968), p. 26. • **51.** Sir Frederick Eden, *The State of the Poor* (3 vols, 1797), ii, pp. 184–5. • **52.** Porter, *English Society*, p. 131. • **53.** 54 George III cap. 101. • **54.** *SRCISLT*, appendix, part ii, pp. 71–2. • **55.** Lister, *Diaries*, p. 176. • **56.** Scott (ed.), *Every One a Witness*, p. 181, quoting Arthur Young, *A Six-month tour through the north of England* (1770). The wages were stated to be 12s and 7s 6d respectively. • **57.** Simond, *Journal*, i, p. 14. • **58.** Woodforde, *Diary*, pp. 245–6, 315, 369. • **59.** Simond, *Journal*, i, p. 276; Henderson (ed.), *Industrial Britain*, p. 39. • **60.** Porter, *English Society*, p. 87. • **61.** Woodforde, *Diary*, p. 314. • **62.** Nicola Phillips, *The Profligate Son or a True Story of Family*

Conflict, Fashionable Vice, and Financial Ruin in Regency England (2013; paperback edn, Oxford, 2015), p. 72. • **63.** Thomas Moore, *Life, Letters and Journals of Lord Byron, complete in one volume* (1838), p. 547. • **64.** Cindy McCreery, 'Fischer [*married name* Norris], Catherine Maria [*known as* Kitty Fisher]' (1741?–1767), *ODNB*. • **65.** Martin J. Levy, 'Robinson [*née* Darby], Mary [*Perdita*] (1756/1758?–1800)', *ODNB*. • **66.** K. D. Reynolds, 'Wilson [*née* Dubouchet], Harriette (1786–1845)', *ODNB*. • **67.** Joan Perkin, 'Beauclerk [*née* Mellon; *other married name* Coutts], Harriot, duchess of St Albans (1777?–1837)', *ODNB*.

4 Character

1. Percy Bysshe Shelley (ed. Mary Shelley), 'England in 1819', *The Poetical Works of Percy Bysshe Shelley* (3 vols, 1847), ii, p. 412. • **2.** Rush, *Residence*, p. 196. • **3.** Southey, *Letters from England*, i, pp. 177–9. • **4.** Marquis de Condorcet, *Outlines of an Historical View of the Progress of the Human Mind* (1795), p. 316. • **5.** Condorcet, *Historical View*, p. 317. • **6.** Condorcet, *Historical View*, p. 355. • **7.** Alexander Pope, *An Essay on Man. In Epistles to a Friend* (1733–4), epistle 1, last lines. • **8.** John Trusler, *The London Adviser and Guide* (2nd edn, 1790), pp. 213–15. • **9.** Goede, *Stranger in England*, i, p. 68. • **10.** Henderson, *Industrial Britain*, p. 39. • **11.** Callum G. Brown, *The Death of Christian Britain* (2nd edn, 2009), p. 22. • **12.** Quoted in Murray, *High Society*, p. 16. • **13.** White, *Waterloo to Peterloo*, p. 126. • **14.** The last two cases appear in the table for female executions 1735–99 on the website http://www.capitalpunishmentuk.org, downloaded 12 February 2019. • **15.** *Fifth Report of the Society for the Improvement of Prison Discipline* (1823), p. 13. • **16.** *Memoirs of the Life of Sir Samuel Romilly edited by his sons* (3 vols, 2nd edn, 1841), i, p. 169. • **17.** Hansard, 9 February 1810. • **18.** Lister, *Diaries*, p. 192. • **19.** A. Dyce (ed.), *Recollections of the Table Talk of Samuel Rogers* (1856), p. 1. • **20.** Gray (ed.), *East Devon*, p. 112. • **21.** Southey, *Letters from England*, i, p. 168. See the same page for sheep being covered in their own blood. • **22.** Wheaton, *Journal*, pp. 285–6. • **23.** Jeremy Bentham, *An Introduction to the Principles of Morals and Legislation* (1789), cccviii–cccix. • **24.** I am indebted to Greg Roberts's website, http://www.wickedwilliam.com/tag/the-strand/, downloaded 13 February 2019, for these details about Chunee. The detail about the 152 shots comes from the Museum of London's description of its print of the 'The Destruction of the Elephant destroyed at Exeter 'Change' (1826), https://www.museumoflondonprints.com/image/141316/william-belch-the-destruction-of-the-elephant-detroyed-at-exeter-change-1826, downloaded 28 April 2019. • **25.** *The Times* (10 March 1826), p. 4. • **26.** Manuel Eisner, 'Long-term Historical Trends in Violent

Crime', *Crime and Justice*, 30 (2003), pp. 83–142 at pp. 96, 99. • **27.** See for example *The Trial of Major Campbell for the Murder of Captain Boyd in a Duel on the 23rd of June 1807* (1808). • **28.** *The British Critic*, vols 17–18 (1822), pp. 380–1; J. G. Millingen, *The History of Duelling* (2 vols, 1841), ii, p. 84. • **29.** Details of the process have been taken from Phillips, *Profligate Son*, pp. 73–4; *The British Critic*, vols 17–18 (1822), pp. 380–5. The latter includes the statement that Gilchrist's statistics are underestimates of the true figure. • **30.** *The British Critic*, vols 17–18 (1822), p. 384. • **31.** John Ashton, *Old Times: a picture of social life at the end of the eighteenth century* (1885), pp. 275–6; *The Gentleman's and London Magazine for July 1789*, p. 388. • **32.** Ashton, *Old Times*, p. 276. • **33.** Millingen, *Duelling*, p. 275. • **34.** Other prime ministers have fought duels but not when in office. The earl of Shelburne fought a duel in 1780, two years before becoming prime minister; and George Canning became prime minister in 1827, eighteen years after his duel with Lord Castlereagh (see text). • **35.** John Gore (ed.), *Creevey . . . from the Creevey Papers and Creevey's Life and Times* (revised edn, 1948), p. 145. • **36.** Letter dated 6 September 1813 in Peter Quennell (ed.), *Byron: a Self-Portrait. Letters and Diaries 1798 to 1824* (2 vols, 1950), i, p. 173. • **37.** Lord Byron, from 'Detached Thoughts', quoted in Jane Stabler, *Byron, Poetics and History* (Cambridge, 2002), pp. 127–8. • **38.** Murray, *High Society*, p. 163, quoting John Timbs, *Club Life of London* (2 vols, 1866), i, p. 85. • **39.** G. S. Street, 'The Betting Book at Brooks's', *North American Review*, 173 (1901), pp. 44–55. • **40.** Street, 'Betting Book', p. 50; L. G. Mitchell, *Charles James Fox* (Oxford, 1992), p. 96. • **41.** John Ashton, *Social England under the Regency* (new edn, 1899), pp. 404–5. • **42.** Woodforde, *Diary*, pp. 332–3. • **43.** Ashton, *Social England*, p. 25. • **44.** Ashton, *Old Times*, p. 298; Jan Bondeson, *The Two-Headed Boy, and Other Medical Marvels* (paperback edn, 2004), p. 264. • **45.** Murray, *High Society*, p. 55. • **46.** Boswell, *Life of Samuel Johnson*, ii, p. 302. • **47.** Faramerz Dabhoiwala, *The Origins of Sex: a History of the First Sexual Revolution* (2012), p. 120. • **48.** Dabhoiwala, *Origins of Sex*, pp. 120–1. • **49.** Dabhoiwala, *Origins of Sex*, p. 344. • **50.** Originally attributed to 'Pego Borewell' in its 1763 printing; quoted in Declan Kavanagh, *Effeminate Years: Literature, Politics and Aesthetics in Mid-Eighteenth-Century Britain* (2017), p. 54; Dabhoiwala, *Origins of Sex*, p. 117. • **51.** Dabhoiwala, *Origins of Sex*, p. 344 and plate opposite p. 337; see also *The Most Ancient and Most Puissant Order of the Beggar's Benison and Merryland, Anstruther* (1892). • **52.** Dabhoiwala, *Origins of Sex*, pp. 120–1. • **53.** Chadwick, *Sanitary Condition*, pp. 125–6. • **54.** Peter Laslett, *The World We Have Lost* (2nd edn, reprinted with corrections, 1979), p. 142. • **55.** *SRCISLT*, appendix, part ii, p. 56. • **56.** White, *London*, p. 350. • **57.** Quoted in Scott (ed.), *Every One a Witness*, p. 71. • **58.** Dan Houston, 'The Literacy Myth? Illiteracy in Scotland 1630–1760', *Past & Present*, 96 (1982), pp. 81–102; Michael Lynch (ed.), *The Oxford Companion to Scottish History* (Oxford, 2001), p. 563. •

59. *SRCISLT*, appendix, part ii, p. 68. On p. 70 it is noted that seven times as much money is spent here on alcohol as on education. • 60. *SRCISLT*, appendix, part ii, pp. 70–1. • 61. Southey, *Letters from England*, ii, pp. 116–18. • 62. Skinner, *Journal*, p. 101. • 63. Skinner, *Journal*, p. 286. A six-monthly bill was £113. • 64. Sir John Bowring, *Autobiographical Recollections of Sir John Bowring, with a brief memoir by L. B. Bowring* (1877), pp. 44–50. • 65. Porter, *English Society*, p. 166; *SRCISLT*, appendix, part ii, pp. 85–6. • 66. James Lackington, *Memoirs of the First Forty-Five Years of the Life of James Lackington … in Forty-Six Letters to a Friend* (new edn, 1792), p. 63. • 67. The National Archives, London: IR 1/38 fol. 68. These payments are all for January 1800. • 68. M. G. Brock and M. C. Curthoys (eds), *The History of the University of Oxford, vol. 6: Nineteenth-Century Oxford, Part 1* (Oxford, 1997), p. 18. • 69. *Royal Kalendar* (1835), p. 290. • 70. Fiona MacCarthy, *Byron Life and Legend* (2002), pp. 64–5. • 71. Quoted in Roy and Lesley Adkins, *Jane Austen's England* (2013), p. 64. • 72. Barbara Taylor, 'Wollstonecraft, Mary (1759–1797)', *ODNB*. • 73. Feltham, *Watering Places* (1815 edn), p. 123. • 74. *Elizabeth Ham by Herself*, pp. 39–40. • 75. Lister, *Diaries*, p. 97. • 76. James Edward Austen-Leigh, *A Memoir of Jane Austen* (1871), p. 83. • 77. *A Short Account of George Bidder the celebrated Mental Calculator, with a Variety of the Most Difficult Questions Proposed to him at the Various Towns in the Kingdom and his surprising Rapid Answers!* (4th edn, Exeter, 1820), pp. 7–8. • 78. *Brief Remarks on English Manners* (1816), p. 17. • 79. Sydney Smith, 'A review of Adam Seybert's Statistical Annals of the United States of America', *Edinburgh Review*, 33 (January 1820), pp. 69–80. • 80. George, *London Life*, p. 118. • 81. Woodforde, *Diary*, pp. 357, 372, 373. • 82. White, *Waterloo to Peterloo*, p. 84. • 83. *SRCISLT*, appendix, part ii, p. 85. • 84. George, *London Life*, p. 124. • 85. George, *London Life*, p. 118. • 86. Pückler-Muskau, *Regency Visitor*, pp. 166, 168. • 87. A. D. Harvey, 'Prosecutions for sodomy in England at the beginning of the nineteenth century', *The Historical Journal*, 21, 4 (1978), pp. 939–48 at p. 947. • 88. *Old Bailey Proceedings Online* (https://www.oldbaileyon-line.org, version 8.0) [hereafter *OBPO*]: December 1810, trial of Thomas White, John Newball and Hepburn (t18101205-1). • 89. Rictor Norton (ed.), 'Newspaper Reports, 1823', *Homosexuality in Nineteenth-Century England: A Sourcebook*, 29 December 2014; expanded 19 August 2016; http://rictornorton.co.uk/eighteen/1823news.htm, downloaded 12 March 2019. • 90. Lister, *Diaries*, pp. 6, 61, 76–7. • 91. Lister, *Diaries*, p. 5. • 92. Lister, *Diaries*, p. 5. • 93. Norton (ed.), 'Newspaper Reports, 1792–1793', *Homosexuality in Eighteenth-Century England*, 3 October 2014, updated 1 November 2018; http://rictor-norton.co.uk/eighteen/1792news.htm, downloaded 12 March 2019. • 94. Ashton, *Social England*, pp. 25–6. • 95. Lister, *Diaries*, p. 141. • 96. Woodforde, *Diary*, p. 100; *The Female Soldier; Or, The Surprising Life and Adventures of Hannah Snell* (1750). • 97. Sydney Brandon, 'Barry, James (c. 1799–1865), army medical

officer and transvestite', *ODNB*. • **98.** George, *London Life*, p. 140. • **99.** Skinner, *Journal*, p. 89. • **100.** Myles Birkett Foster, *The History of the Philharmonic Society of London 1813–1912* (1912), p. 7. • **101.** For example, John Anthony, the man in charge of the Chinese community in London, became a British citizen by Act of Parliament in 1800. • **102.** Marc Horne, 'Extraordinary tale of first Chinese Scotsman', *The Times* (16 February 2018), quoting the research of Barclay Price. • **103.** Quoted in George, *London Life*, p. 137. • **104.** Moritz, *Journeys*, p. 105. • **105.** Victor Gray and Melanie Aspey, 'Rothschild, Nathan Mayer (1777–1836)', *ODNB*. • **106.** Quoted in George, *London Life*, p. 137. • **107.** Quoted in Adkins, *Jane Austen's England*, p. 8. Another smock wedding in Grimsby in 1815 is described in Ashton, *Social England*, p. 390. • **108.** E. P. Thompson, *Customs in Common* (1991; paperback edn, 1993), p. 442. • **109.** Bridget Hill, 'Macaulay [*née* Sawbridge; *other married name* Graham], Catharine, 1731–1791)', *ODNB*, quoting *Monthly Review*, 29 (1763), p. 373. • **110.** Hill, 'Macaulay …, Catharine', *ODNB*, quoting C. Macaulay, *Letters on Education* (1790), p. 47. • **111.** Anne Lister is described disrespectfully as a 'bluestocking'. See Lister, *Diaries*, p. 134. • **112.** *Elizabeth Ham by Herself*, p. 27. • **113.** Dabhoiwala, *Origins of Sex*, p. 125. • **114.** Dabhoiwala, *Origins of Sex*, p. 353. • **115.** Ashton, *Old Times*, pp. 316–17. • **116.** Woodforde, *Diary*, pp. 301, 354. • **117.** James Sharpe, *Instruments of Darkness* (paperback edn, Philadelphia, 1997), p. 282. • **118.** Moritz, *Journeys*, p. 70. • **119.** Lord Byron, *Don Juan*, 'canto the tenth', lines 14–16. • **120.** Pückler-Muskau, *Regency Visitor*, p. 330. • **121.** Pückler-Muskau, *Regency Visitor*, pp. 119–20. • **122.** *The Spectator* (9 May 1835), p. 3; *Recollections of the Table-talk of Samuel Rogers* (2nd edn, 1856), pp. 215–16; Murray, *High Society*, p. 37. • **123.** Lister, *Diaries*, p. 253; Southey, *Letters from England*, i, p. 186. • **124.** Most of the quotations in this section come from *The Oxford Dictionary of Quotations* (2nd edn, reprinted with revisions, 1966), and *Sheridiana; or Anecdotes of the Life of Richard Brinsley Sheridan* (1826). The last one is found on p. 216 of the latter work.

5 Practicalities

1. Pückler-Muskau, *Regency Visitor*, p. 61. • **2.** This is a figure for 1844, as reported in the *SRCISLT*, appendix, part ii, p. 5. • **3.** C. Edward Skeen, '"The Year without a Summer": a historical view', *Journal of the Early Republic*, 1, 1 (1981), pp. 51–67 at p. 58. • **4.** Murray, *High Society*, p. 85; for the overnight temperatures, see Heron, *Notes*, p. 70. • **5.** 'I no longer wonder why these people talk so much of the weather; they live in the most inconstant of all climates …' Southey, *Letters from England*, iii, pp. 67–8. • **6.** Gordon Manley,

'Central England temperatures: monthly means 1659–1973', *Quarterly Journal of the Royal Meteorological Society*, 100 (1974), pp. 389–405. • **7.** Ashton, *Old Times*, p. 4. • **8.** Woodforde, *Diary*, pp. 300–1. • **9.** Matthew Flinders (Martyn Beardsley and Nicholas Bennett, eds), *Grateful to Providence: the Diary and Accounts of Matthew Flinders, Surgeon, Apothecary and Man-Midwife, 1775–1802*, Lincoln Record Society (2 vols, 2007–9), ii, p. 149. • **10.** Woodforde, *Diary*, pp. 319–21. • **11.** Woodforde, *Diary*, p. 307. • **12.** Lister, *Diaries*, p. 43. • **13.** Smith, 'Marketplace', p. 102. • **14.** Lackington, *Memoirs*, p. 111. • **15.** George, *London Life*, p. 206. • **16.** Southey, *Letters from England*, i, p. 166. • **17.** Skinner, *Journal*, p. 160. • **18.** Susan Palmer, *At Home with the Soanes: Upstairs, Downstairs in 19th Century London* (1997; paperback edn, 2015), p. 78. • **19.** Gilbert White, *Natural History of Selborne* (1st edn 1789; 1841 edn), pp. 232–3, states that 6lbs of common animal fat may be obtained for 2s, which will be sufficient to coat 1lb of 30-inch rushes, containing about 1,600 peeled stems and costing another 1s. Each stem will last between half an hour and an hour. • **20.** Quoted in Ashton, *Old Times*, p. 297. • **21.** *The Times* (23 November 1831), p. 3; John Strachan, *Advertising and Satirical Culture in the Romantic Period* (Cambridge, 2007), pp. 31–4. • **22.** Lackington, *Memoirs*, p. 173. • **23.** *Annual Register ... for the year 1783* (1785), p. 200. • **24.** Rudolph Ackermann, *Microcosm of London* (3 vols, 1808–10), ii, p. 41. • **25.** Nicholas Daly, 'Fire on Stage', *Interdisciplinary Studies in the Long Nineteenth Century*, 25 (2017); https://19.bbk.ac.uk/article/id/1796/, downloaded 19 June 2019. • **26.** These figures are drawn from *SRCISLT*, appendix, p. 56. • **27.** Pigot & Co., *London & Provincial New Commercial Directory of Bedfordshire ... and South Wales* (1830), p. 215. • **28.** Mitchell, *British Historical Statistics*, p. 690. • **29.** *SRCISLT*, p. 34. • **30.** Heron, *Notes*, appendix, p. 76. • **31.** Jeremy Black, *The English Press 1621–1861* (2001), p. 90. • **32.** *The Sunday Times* was originally published in 1821 as *The New Observer*. • **33.** Black, *English Press*, p. 90. • **34.** Southey, *Letters from England*, iii, pp. 25. • **35.** A. C. Price, *Leeds and its neighbourhood* (Oxford, 1909), pp. 282–4; Black, *English Press*, pp. 90, 111. • **36.** Wheaton, *Journal*, p. 268. • **37.** Palmer, *At Home with the Soanes*, p. 103; Lister, *Diaries*, p. 30. • **38.** Lister, *Diaries*, p. 63. • **39.** White, *Waterloo to Peterloo*, pp. 1–2. • **40.** Wheaton, *Journal*, p. 120. • **41.** Flinders, *Grateful*, ii, pp. 157, 195. • **42.** Mazzinghi, *State of London* (1793 ed.), p. 234. • **43.** In understanding all these rates I have depended on the Post Office website, http://www.gbps.org.uk/information/rates/inland/local-posts.php, downloaded 1 July 2019. • **44.** Lister, *Diaries*, p. 181. • **45.** Johnson, *Western Isles*, p. 380. • **46.** Lister, *Diaries*, p. 145. • **47.** Ashton, *Social England*, p. 5; Simond, *Journal*, p. 21; Wheaton, *Journal*, p. 216. • **48.** *Brief Remarks on English Manners* (1816), p. 22;

Pückler-Muskau, *Regency Visitor*, p. 188. • **49.** Wheaton, *Journal*, p. 201. • **50.** Hall, *Georgian Gentleman*, p. 192; Southey, *Letters from England*, p. 242. • **51.** Ashton, *Old Times*, pp. 62, 237–42. • **52.** For the case of a man being sentenced to transportation for owning a fake note – along with £33 in genuine notes and a lot of gold coins – see *OBPO*: April 1804, trial of Henry Foss (t18040411-51), downloaded 4 September 2019. • **53.** Simond, *Journal*, i, p. 10. • **54.** Trusler, *London Adviser* (1790 edn), p. 31. • **55.** Kathryn A. Morrison, *English Shops and Shopping: an Architectural History* (2003), p. 111. • **56.** Morrison, *English Shops*, pp. 38, 95. • **57.** This overview is largely taken from John Jeffrey-Cook, 'William Pitt and his Taxes', *British Tax Review*, 4 (2010), pp. 376–91. • **58.** Daniel Ricardo, *The Principles of Political Economy* (1817) Ch. 8. • **59.** Woodforde, *Diary*, p. 404. • **60.** Flinders, *Grateful*, ii, pp. 218, 230. • **61.** Sydney Smith, 'Review of Seybert's Annals of the United States', *The Edinburgh Review*, 33 (January 1820), pp. 77–8.

6 What to Wear

1. *The Times* (19 January 1790), pp. 2–3. • **2.** Murray, *High Society*, pp. 94–7. • **3.** Murray, *High Society*, p. 34. Gronow's words have been rendered in the present tense to fit the flow of the narrative. • **4.** Although the *OED* does not record a reference to the tape measure before 1873, it was in general use by 1818. See Lucy Johnson, *19th-century Fashion in Detail* (revised edn, 2016), p. 8. Plate One of Hogarth's *Rake's Progress* (*c.* 1735) shows the tailor measuring the heir with a strip of parchment; this does not appear to have any regular markings along its length. • **5.** Wheaton, *Journal*, p. 202. • **6.** Woodforde, *Diary*, pp. 335, 338; Moritz, *Journeys*, p. 158. • **7.** Alun Withey, *Technology, Self-Fashioning and Politeness in Eighteenth-Century Britain: Refined Bodies* (2016), p. 98. • **8.** Wheaton, *Journal*, pp. 39, 218, 232; Withey, *Technology*, pp. 98–102. • **9.** These figures are from the probate inventory of William Mortimer (1773–1823), my great-great-great-great-great-uncle. The original document is in my possession. A transcript is available from the National Archives – National Register of Archives 41004, http://www.national-archives.gov.uk/nra/lists/GB-800819-Mortimer.htm, downloaded 2 April 2020. It should be noted that the prices for second-hand clothes in a shop in London given in Sir Frederick Eden, *The State of the Poor* (3 vols, 1797), i, pp. 557–8, are substantially more than these sums. • **10.** Rush, *Residence*, p. 20. • **11.** Wheaton, *Journal*, p. 194. • **12.** White, *Life*, p. 38. • **13.** *Elizabeth Ham by Herself*, p. 27. • **14.** *The Mirror of the Graces; or, the English Lady's Costume* (1811), p. 90. • **15.** Ashton, *Old Times*, p. 77. • **16.** C. Willett Cunningham and Phyllis Cunningham, *The History of Underclothes* (1951),

p. 114; Palmer, *At Home with the Soanes*, p. 50; Lister, *Diaries*, pp. 36, 45, 170.
• **17.** Lister, *Diaries*, p. 36 • **18.** See *The Art of Beauty* (1825), pp. 194–5, for a vivid description. • **19.** *Mirror of Graces*, p. 202. • **20.** Davies, *Case of Labourers*, p. 136. • **21.** Southey, *Letters from England*, iii, p. 70. • **22.** Wheaton, *Journal*, p. 282; Pückler-Muskau, *Regency Visitor*, pp. 166, 168. • **23.** Simond, *Journal*, i, p. 264. • **24.** Henderson (ed.), *Industrial Britain*, p. 39. • **25.** The main source for these comments on Welsh clothing in the Regency period is the contemporary manuscript in the National Library of Wales, http://hdl.handle.net/10107/1238283, downloaded 28 August 2019. • **26.** *OBPO*, October 1822, trial of Ann Parkins (t18221023-52). • **27.** Caroline Davidson, *A Woman's Work is Never Done: a History of Housework in the British Isles, 1650–1950* (1982), p. 152. • **28.** Woodforde, *Diary*, pp. 37 n. 102, 387. • **29.** Davidson, *A Woman's Work is Never Done*, p. 156.

7 Travelling

1. Simond, *Journal*, i, p. 185. • **2.** Lister, *Diaries*, pp. 193, 212. • **3.** Simond, *Journal*, pp. 5, 11; Gray (ed.), *East Devon*, pp. 114, 134. • **4.** Southey, *Letters from England*, i, p. 356. • **5.** Woodforde, *Diary*, p. 335. • **6.** John Jervis, revised by William Kitchiner, *The Traveller's Oracle* (2nd edn, 2 vols, 1827), i, p. 125. • **7.** Christine S. Hallas, 'Metcalf, John [*called* Blind Jack of Knaresborough] (1717–1810)', *ODNB*. • **8.** Murray, *High Society*, p. 278. • **9.** For example, Richard Rush describes a macadamised highway as being 'like a floor'. See Rush, *Residence*, pp. 17, 19. • **10.** Lister, *Diaries*, p. 212; Rush, *Residence*, p. 18. • **11.** For example, at Bridgwater in Somerset in 1798; Chepstow in 1816; Bigsweir in 1827; Coalport in 1818; Mythe in 1826; Southwark in 1819; and Windsor in 1826. • **12.** Lister, *Diaries*, p. 33. • **13.** Charles Stewart Drewry, *A Memoir on Suspension Bridges* (1832), p. 32. • **14.** Woodforde, *Diary*, p. 346. • **15.** Hallas, 'Metcalf, John', *ODNB*. • **16.** George, *London Life*, p. 355. • **17.** Southey, *Letters from England*, i, p. 29. • **18.** Moritz, *Journeys*, p. 114. • **19.** For example, at the age of thirty-two, the Revd John Skinner rode from Camerton to Sherborne (29 miles) in September in four hours. See Skinner, *Journal*, p. 15. • **20.** The distance of 267 miles is taken from *Lewis's Topographical Dictionary* (7th edn, 4 vols, 1849), ii, p. 210. • **21.** Lister, *Diaries*, pp. 204, 269. • **22.** Jervis, rev. Kitchiner, *Traveller's Oracle*, ii, p. 22. • **23.** Murray, *High Society*, p. 81. • **24.** Jervis, rev. Kitchiner, *Traveller's Oracle*, ii, p. 15. • **25.** Jervis, rev. Kitchiner, *Traveller's Oracle*, ii, p. 59. • **26.** Lister, *Diaries*, pp. 183–4. • **27.** This is now in the Tyrwhitt-Drake Museum of Carriages, Maidstone. See https://www.thecarriagefoundation.org.uk/item/travelling-chariot, downloaded 1 November 2019. • **28.** Woodforde, *Diary*, p. 290; Simond, *Journal*, p. 17; Lister,

Diaries, p. 224. • **29.** Quoted in Clark (ed.), *Cambridge Urban History of Britain*, *volume 2*, p. 681. • **30.** 'The life of a post horse is truly wretched …' See Southey, *Letters from England*, i, p. 33. • **31.** Mazzinghi, *State of London* (1793 edn), p. 256. • **32.** Southey, *Letters from England*, i, pp. 16–17. • **33.** A 24-seater regularly does the journey between Greenwich and London in the 1790s. See Ashton, *Old Times*, p. 159. • **34.** Southey, *Letters from England*, i, pp. 32–3. • **35.** Southey, *Letters from England*, ii, pp. 53–5. • **36.** Pückler-Muskau, *Regency Visitor*, p. 135. • **37.** Moritz, *Journeys*, p. 105. • **38.** Moritz, *Journeys*, p. 178. • **39.** Harriette Wilson, *The Memoirs of Harriette Wilson* (2 vols, 1909), ii, p. 431. • **40.** Rush, *Residence*, p. 17. • **41.** Murray, *High Society*, p. 283. • **42.** Details have been taken from Charles G. Harper, *The Brighton Road, the Classic Highway to the South* (1892; 3rd edn, 1922), pp. 18–41; Collis, *New Encyclopedia of Brighton*, p. 80. • **43.** White, *Life*, p. 11; Porter, *English Society*, pp. 192–3. • **44.** Harper, *Brighton Road*, p. 41. • **45.** Ashton, *Old Times*, pp. 163, 164; Simond, *Journal*, i, pp. 3, 130. • **46.** Harper, *Brighton Road*, p. 30. • **47.** Roger Street, 'Johnson, Denis (1759/60–1833)', *ODNB*. • **48.** Lister, *Diaries*, p. 131. • **49.** Pückler-Muskau, *Regency Visitor*, pp. 290–1. • **50.** Simond, *Journal*, p. 291. • **51.** This figure is from https://www.parliament.uk/about/living-heritage/transformingsociety/transportcomms/canalsrivers/overview/canal-acts/, downloaded 7 November 2019. • **52.** Mitchell, *British Historical Statistics*, p. 535. • **53.** From a poster dated 1811 on display in the National Maritime Museum Cornwall, in Falmouth, printed by 'Harris, printer, Falmouth'. • **54.** Basil Greenhill and Ann Giffard, *Travelling by Sea in the Nineteenth Century* (1972), p. 8. • **55.** Ashton, *Old Times*, pp. 9, 81–2, 90–1, 98, 100–7. • **56.** Henderson (ed.), *Industrial Britain*, p. 39; Greenhill and Giffard, *Travelling by Sea*, p. 36; Mitchell, *British Historical Statistics*, p. 535. • **57.** Lister, *Diaries*, pp. 236–40. • **58.** Greenhill and Giffard, *Travelling by Sea*, p. 39. • **59.** Wheaton, *Journal*, p. 393. • **60.** Daniel and Ayton, *Voyage*, pp. 52–3; Greenhill and Giffard, *Travelling by Sea*, p. 38.

8 *Where to Stay*

1. Goede, *Stranger in England*, i, p. 56. • **2.** 'Immediately upon our landing we were surrounded by boys proffering cards of the different inns by which they were employed to look out for strangers, and contesting who should carry our luggage' (Southey, *Letters from England*, ii, pp. 114–15). • **3.** Southey, *Letters from England*, i, pp. 6–7. • **4.** Jervis, rev. Kitchiner, *Traveller's Oracle*, i, p. 114. • **5.** Woodforde, *Diary*, pp. 184–6. • **6.** Southey, *Letters from England*, ii, pp. 78–80. • **7.** Southey, *Letters from England*, i, p. 23; ii, p. 135. • **8.** Murray, *High Society*, p. 284 (fires, newspapers); Southey, *Letters from England*, i,

p. 19 (prints); p. 24 (sofas, china and plate); ii, pp. 114–15 (slippers). • **9.** Trusler, *London Adviser* (1790 edn), pp. 171–2. • **10.** Woodforde, *Diary*, pp. 184–6, 190–1. • **11.** Walter Scott (ed. W. E. K. Anderson), *The Journal of Sir Walter Scott* (Oxford, 1972), p. 245. • **12.** Simond, *Journal*, i, p. 15. • **13.** Ashton (ed.), *Old Times*, pp. 161–2. • **14.** Robert Dymond, 'Old Inns and Taverns of Exeter' in F. J. Snell (ed.), *Memorials of Old Devonshire* (1904), pp. 63–76 at pp. 74–5. • **15.** White, *London*, p. 142, quoting William Henry Quarrell and Margaret Mare (eds), *London in 1710, from the travels of Zacharias Conrad von Uffenbach* (1934), p. 12. That the German Hotel was well known in 1769 is demonstrated by Michael Parys, describing himself as the keeper of the German Hotel in giving evidence at the Old Bailey that year, when he was robbed by a German guest. See *OBPO*, trial of Jacob Snarbo, September 1769 (t17690906-21). • **16.** J. G. Robertson, 'Sophie von la Roche's visit to England in 1786', *The Modern Language Review*, 27, 2 (1932), pp. 196–203 at p. 199; Kirsty Carpenter, *Refugees of the French Revolution: Émigrés in London 1789–1802* (1999), p. 53. • **17.** Janet Ing Freeman (ed.), *The Epicure's Almanack* (2013 edn), pp. 170–1; *Holden's Directory* (1802 edn); *OBPO* (searching on the word 'hotel'). • **18.** 'The Tsar, on arriving in London in 1814, insisted on staying not at St James's Palace, which had been put at his disposal, but at the Pulteney Hotel where his sister (Princess Ekaterina Pavlovna, Duchess of Oldenburg) had chosen to establish herself, the place being hired at the enormous cost of 210 guineas a week.' https://wellcomecollection.org/works/ktkpd4bf, downloaded 20 November 2019; Freeman (ed.), *Epicure's Almanack*, p. 169. • **19.** Pückler-Muskau, *Regency Visitor*, p. 40. • **20.** Trusler, *London Adviser* (1790 edn), pp. 171–2. • **21.** http://www.nationalarchives.gov.uk/nra/lists/GB-800819-Mortimer.htm. • **22.** Simond, *Journal*, i, p. 50. • **23.** Southey, *Letters from England*, i, p. 155. • **24.** Depicted and described in Palmer, *At Home with the Soanes*, p. 22. • **25.** Palmer, *At Home with the Soanes*, pp. 26–7. • **26.** Freeman (ed.), *Epicure's Almanack*, pp. 231–3. • **27.** Mark Girouard, *Life in the English Country House* (1978), p. 265. • **28.** See Lister, *Diaries*, p. 36, for her use of toilet paper. Toilet paper was not made commercially before 1857. • **29.** Trussler, *London Adviser* (1790 edn), pp. 1–3; Rush, *Residence*, p. 55. • **30.** This figure is actually for the year 1842 but it may be considered indicative of the situation at the end of our period. See *FRCISLT*, i, p. 67; *SRCISLT*, appendix, part ii, p. 24. • **31.** George, *London Life*, p. 100; *SRCISLT*, appendix, part ii, p. 37. • **32.** *FRCISLT*, i, p. 113. • **33.** This is taken from the inventory given in George, *London Life*, p. 101. • **34.** Quoted in George, *London Life*, p. 96. • **35.** *SRCISLT*, appendix, part ii, p. 38. • **36.** Quoted in George, *London Life*, p. 95. • **37.** Eighty-four beds were shared by four people, twenty-eight by five, and seventeen by between six and eight people. See *SRCISLT*, appendix, part ii, p. 24. • **38.** *FRCISLT*, i, p. 68. • **39.** *SRCISLT*, appendix, part ii, p. 15. • **40.** *SRCISLT*, appendix, part ii, p. 38. • **41.** *SRCISLT*, appendix, part ii, p. 22. • **42.** *SRCISLT*, appendix, part ii, p. 26. • **43.** Austen-Leigh, *Jane Austen* (1871 edn), pp. 32–3. • **44.** Austen-Leigh, *Jane Austen* (1871 edn), p. 85. • **45.** *FRCISLT*, i, pp. 122–3. • **46.** Charles Vancouver, *General View of the Agriculture of the County of Devon* (1808), p. 365. • **47.** The cobwebs reference is informed by the description of a very similar room in Chadwick, *Sanitary Condition*, p. 270. • **48.** Chadwick, *Sanitary Condition*, p. 23; Trevor Griffiths and Graeme Morton, *A History of Everyday Life in Scotland, 1800 to 1900* (2010), p. 66; Simond, *Journal*, i, p. 263. • **49.** Wheaton, *Journal*, p. 479. • **50.** Simond, *Journal*, i, pp. 303–4. • **51.** *A New Guide to Fonthill Abbey, Wiltshire* (1822), pp. 21–4. • **52.** Caroline Dakers (ed.), *Fonthill Recovered: a Cultural History* (2018), pp. 94, 103. • **53.** Girouard, *Country House*, p. 265. • **54.** James Collett-White (ed.), *Inventories of Bedfordshire Country Houses 1714–1830*, Bedfordshire Historical Record Society, 74 (1995), p. 65. • **55.** Girouard, *Country House*, p. 265. • **56.** Heron, *Notes*, pp. 41, 95. • **57.** White, *Waterloo to Peterloo*, p. 43; Heron, *Notes*, pp. 55, 116–17, 130, 139, 155, 157, 180. • **58.** Rush, *Residence*, pp. 308–9. • **59.** Pückler-Muskau, *Regency Visitor*, p. 45.

9 *What to Eat, Drink and Smoke*

1. Southey, *Letters from England*, i, p. 169. • **2.** Jennifer Stead, 'Georgian Britain', in Peter Brears, Maggie Black, Gill Corbishley, Jane Renfrew and Jennifer Stead, *A Taste of History* (1993), p. 233. • **3.** Broadberry et al., *British Economic Growth*, pp. 106, 109. • **4.** Smith, 'Marketplace', p. 133; Rush, *Residence*, p. 174; Lister, *Diaries*, p. 85. • **5.** Hannah Glasse, *The Art of Cookery Made Plain and Easy* (new edn, 1799), pp. 378, 381. • **6.** William Verrall, *A Complete System of Cookery* (1st edn, 1759), pp. xvii–xix. • **7.** Quennell (ed.), *Byron*, i, p. 227. • **8.** James Peller Malcolm, *Anecdotes of the Manners and Customs of London ... with a Review of the State of Society in 1807* (2nd edn, 2 vols, 1810), i, p. 416. • **9.** Woodforde, *Diary*, p. 283; Moritz, *Journeys*, p. 27; *Elizabeth Ham by Herself*, p. 39; Peggy Hickman, *A Jane Austen Household Book* (1977), p. 20. • **10.** Henderson (ed.), *Industrial Britain*, p. 43. • **11.** Freeman (ed.), *Epicure's Almanack*, p. 135. • **12.** Freeman (ed.), *Epicure's Almanack*, p. xlviii. • **13.** Glasse, *Art of Cookery*, pp. 55 (Turkish), 76 (barbecued pig), 119–21 (kebabs, curry, pilau). • **14.** Freeman (ed.), *Epicure's Almanack*, p. 235. Curry powder is regularly mentioned in William Kitchiner, *The Cook's Oracle* (1827 edn). For

Parmesan and Gruyere, see Trusler, *London Adviser* (1790 edn), p. 35. • **15.** See for example: Woodforde, *Diary*, pp. 270, 271, 279, 286, 330, 356, 389. • **16.** Hickman, *Household Book*, pp. 43, 53–4, 57. • **17.** Gray, *East Devon*, p. 64; Stead, 'Georgian Britain', p. 257. • **18.** Woodforde, *Diary*, p. 245. • **19.** Woodforde, *Diary*, p. 397 (February 1801); Ashton, *Old Times*, 153 (1795); Flinders, *Grateful to Providence*, ii, p. 224 (19¼lbs pork for 12s 4d); Trusler, *London Adviser* (1790 edn), pp. 28–9 (beef 4d–5d per lb; veal 6d; mutton 4½d–5½d; pork chops 7d or 8d per lb). • **20.** Wheaton, *Journal*, p. 120, states the price is 5s per lb. Trusler, *London Adviser* (1790 edn), has a more reasonable 1s to 1s 3d when in season. • **21.** Trusler, *London Adviser* (1790 edn), pp. 30, 33. • **22.** These sums are taken from the 'estimates of housekeeping' in Trusler, *London Adviser* (1790 edn), p. 181. Note that the 12 gallons from a 14s barrel of small beer therein was calculated at 1s 6d. This seems wrong. A beer barrel was 36 gallons. • **23.** The Weights and Measures Act of 1824 established the quarter as eight bushels, each bushel being eight gallons, and each gallon eight pints. However, the corn trade continued to use the Winchester bushel and quarter until 1835. This weighed 480lbs – 97% of the imperial bushel and quarter (496lbs). Even in 1835 the practice of using non-standard measures did not entirely cease. In April 1921, George Lane-Fox, MP for Barkston Ash (North Yorkshire), said in the House of Commons: 'A quarter of wheat in different parts of the country may be 480lbs, 496lbs, 500lbs, 504lbs or 588lbs. A quarter of rye or oats has even a greater variation.' • **24.** Mitchell (ed.), *British Historical Statistics*, p. 755. • **25.** Malcolm, *Anecdotes*, ii, p. 414. • **26.** Sir John Sinclair, *Analysis of the Statistical Accounts of Scotland* (1831), p. 139. • **27.** Davies, *Case of Labourers*, p. 8. • **28.** Eden, *State of the Poor*, i, p. 206. • **29.** Vancouver, *Agriculture of the County of Devon*, p. 149. • **30.** Eden, *State of the Poor*, ii, p. 510. • **31.** Eden, *State of the Poor*, ii, p. 512; Southey, *Letters from England*, ii, pp. 136–7. • **32.** Eden, *State of the Poor*, ii, pp. 56, 120, 458. • **33.** Lister, *Diaries*, pp. 86, 236. • **34.** Hickman, *Household Book*, p. 20. • **35.** Pückler-Muskau, *Regency Visitor*, p. 114. • **36.** Kitchiner, *Cook's Oracle*, pp. 112, 135, 147, 151, 368–9, 375, 377. • **37.** John Trusler, *The Honours of the Table* (2nd edn, 1791), p. 5. • **38.** Simond, *Journal*, p. 44. This paragraph and the following one are also informed by Pückler-Muskau, *Regency Visitor*, pp. 61–3; Trusler, *Honours*, pp. 4–8; Hickman, *Household Book*, p. 23. The dinner here described by Louis Simond for 'ten or twelve people' in 1808 has been treated as exemplary, as it is similar to the 'very genteel dinner' served by Mr and Mrs John Custance to James Woodforde and eight others at Weston House in August 1794. See Woodforde, *Diary*, p. 309. • **39.** Hickman, *Household Book*, p. 23, quoting Mrs Frazer, *The Practice of Cooking* (1800); Palmer, *At Home with the Soanes*, p. 61. • **40.**

Pückler-Muskau, *Regency Visitor*, p. 62. • **41.** Colin Fisher, *The A to Z of the Royal Crescent: Polite and Impolite Life in Eighteenth Century Bath* (2016), p. 62. • **42.** Pückler-Muskau, *Regency Visitor*, p. 63. • **43.** Simond, *Journal*, p. 49. • **44.** Murray, *High Society*, p. 167. • **45.** Murray, *High Society*, p. 184. • **46.** Murray, *High Society*, pp. 184–5. • **47.** John Feltham, *The Picture of London* (1809), p. 360. • **48.** The *OED* has the following quotation from P. G. Patmore, *Rejected Articles* (1826), p. 250: 'The Haymarket contains half a dozen French houses, which however seem to have been established, more with a view to remind them of what a French Restaurant is not, than what it is.' • **49.** Fisher, *Royal Crescent*, p. 101; Freeman (ed.), *Epicure's Almanack*, p. 92. • **50.** Freeman (ed.), *Epicure's Almanack*, p. xlix. • **51.** Goede, *Stranger in England*, i, p. 57. • **52.** Murray, *High Society*, pp. 172–3. • **53.** Pückler-Muskau, *Regency Visitor*, p. 149 (duke of York); Murray, *High Society*, p. 198 (Pitt, Sheridan). According to Samuel Morewood, *A Philosophical and Statistical History of the Inventions and Customs of Ancient and Modern Nations in the Manufacture and Use of Inebriating Liquors with the Present Practice of Distillation in all its varieties, together with an Extensive Illustration of the Consumption and Effects of Opium and other Stimulants used in the East as Substitutes for Wine and Spirits* (Dublin, 1838), p. 682, claret at this time averages 14.4% and port 23.5%. Six old pints of claret is 473ml x 6 x 14.4% = 408ml of alcohol. • **54.** Mitchell, *British Historical Statistics*, p. 408. • **55.** *Reports from Committees of the House of Commons*, vol. xi (1803), p. 421. • **56.** Wheaton, *Journal*, pp. 484–5; Anthony Cooke, *A History of Drinking: the Scottish pub since 1700* (Edinburgh, 2015), p. 46. • **57.** George, *London Life*, p. 52. • **58.** Woodforde, *Diary*, pp. 303, 316. • **59.** P. Colquhoun, *Observations and Facts Relative to Public Houses in the City of London* (1794), p. 4 (1790s prices); *OBPO*, refs: t18110403-73 (20s per gallon, 1811); t18130217-2 (10s per gallon, 1813); t18160110 (10s per gallon, 1816); t18250407-55 (8s per gallon, 1825); Morewood, *Philosophical and Statistical History*, p. 730 (duties); Murray, *High Society*, p. 795 (acid). • **60.** Prices rise and fall with the duty imposed but for an idea of comparative price, in 1800, when a gallon of gin costs about 7s 8d, a gallon of good rum will set you back 16s and a gallon of brandy 21s. See Woodforde, *Diary*, p. 392. • **61.** Hickman, *Household Book*, p. 99. • **62.** William Scott, *The House Book or Family Chronicle of Useful Knowledge and Cottage Physician* (1826), pp. 329–32. • **63.** Frank Clark estimates strong beer as 8–10% and small beer at 3% in 'A Most Wholesome Liquor: A Study of Beer and Brewing in 18th-Century England and Her Colonies', Colonial Williamsburg Foundation Library Research Report Series, no. 364 (Williamsburg, 2000), p. 21. Ian S. Hornsey, *A History of Beer and Brewing* (2003), p. 436, puts porter at 6.6% alcohol by volume, based on eighteenth-century hydrometer readings. Early nineteenth-century hydrometer readings in Morewood, *Philosophical and Statistical History*, p. 682, put stout at 6.8%

and ale at 8.9%. It is perhaps worth noting that the porter-like beer found in 1977 in the wreck of *The Sydney Cove* off Preservation Island, Tasmania, which sank in 1798, had an alcohol content of about 6%. • **64.** Peter Mathias, *The Brewing Industry in England 1700–1830* (1959), p. 25. • **65.** Mitchell, *British Historical Statistics*, p. 405. • **66.** See the advertisement on p. 4 of *The Times* for 4 August 1818. • **67.** Simond, *Journal*, p. 46. • **68.** Jessica Warner, 'Gin in Regency England', *History Today*, 61, 3 (March 2011). • **69.** There is a description from 1833 of the ideal situation of a bar, to assist the 'barwoman' in her work, in J. C. Loudon, *Encyclopaedia of Farm, Cottage and Villa* (1836), quoted in Peter Haydon, *The English Pub: a History* (1994), pp. 201–2. • **70.** G. B. Wilson, *Alcohol and the Nation* (1940), table 12; Morewood, *Philosophical and Statistical History*, pp. 717–21. • **71.** Simond, *Journal*, i, p. 46. • **72.** Morewood, *Philosophical and Statistical History*, p. 682. • **73.** Eliza Acton, *Modern Cookery* (revised ed., 1863), p. 582. • **74.** Flinders, *Grateful to Providence*, ii, p. 151; Woodforde, *Diary*, p. 349. • **75.** Woodforde, *Diary*, p. 370. • **76.** Ashton, *Old Times*, p. 155. • **77.** Ashton, *Regency*, p. 405. • **78.** Hickman, *Household Book*, p. 96. • **79.** Flinders, *Grateful to Providence*, ii, p. 152. • **80.** Morewood, *Philosophical and Statistical History*, p. 682. • **81.** According to Morewood, *Philosophical and Statistical History*, p. 728, between 1820 and 1829 Great Britain imports a yearly average of 5.8 million imperial gallons of wine and 4.1 million gallons of spirits. (Although Morewood specifies this figure as being for the whole UK, he means Great Britain, as he deals separately with Ireland.) These totals are in addition to the domestic production of 8.7 million gallons of spirits (Mitchell, *British Historical Statistics*, p. 408). Then we have to factor in 223 million gallons of strong beer and 54 million gallons of table beer brewed every year (Mitchell, *British Historical Statistics*, p. 405). For the sake of establishing per capita alcohol-consumption figures, the strong beer has been assumed to be 6% alcohol by volume and the small beer 2.5%. As the spirits are very strong – proof is 57% alcohol by volume, and contemporary hydrometer readings for most hard drinks are 51.6–53.7% alcohol (Morewood, *Philosophical and Statistical History*, p. 682) – this adds up to a total intake of more than 100 million litres of pure alcohol every year. The population of Great Britain in this decade averages 9.3 million people over the age of fifteen, which means that official sources alone suggest the average person drinks about 10.75 litres of pure alcohol per year, or 1,075 units per year, which is 20.7 units per week. • **82.** In the late 1780s Britain imports about £1.7 million of tea and re-exports roughly one-third of it, but by the late 1820s it is shipping in well over £3 million and re-exporting only about 1%. See Mitchell, *British Historical Statistics*, pp. 463–4, 472. • **83.** Rush, *Residence*, p. 141. • **84.** Prices are from Flinders, *Grateful to Providence*, ii, pp. 24, 25, 69, 149, 152, 226. • **85.** Davies, *The Case of Labourers*, p. 39. • **86.**

Mitchell, *British Historical Statistics*, p. 709. This increase took place in two short bursts, 1808–13 and 1825–30, with reduced import duties being the key factor in both cases. The duty on colonial coffee prior to 1807 had been 2s 2d per lb; in that year it was reduced to 7d. In 1819 it was raised again to 1s per lb on colonial coffee, 1s 6d on British Indian and 2s 6d on foreign. These were all halved in 1825. • **87.** Moritz, *Journeys*, p. 35. • **88.** S. D. Smith, 'Accounting for Taste: British coffee consumption in historical perspective', *Journal of Interdisciplinary History*, 27 (1996), pp. 183–214 at p. 208; Scott, *House Book*, p. 591. • **89.** Scott, *House Book*, p. 110; Hall, *Georgian Gentleman*, p. 221; Lackington, *Memoirs*, p. 197. Smith, 'Accounting for Taste', p. 208. • **90.** In 1822 James Cross was indicted at the Old Bailey for stealing 36 bottles containing 18 pints of soda water, from the manufacturer, which a chemist bought in good faith for 13s 6d wholesale. This is 4½d per bottle. Presuming a profit of about ½d–1½d on the bottle, each was sold to the public for 5d–6d. See *OBPO*, ref: t18220911-283. • **91.** Southey, *Letters from England*, i, p. 171. • **92.** A publican selling 800 quarts and 80 pints of gin per week may expect also to sell 16 half-ounce packets of tobacco. See Colquhoun, *Public Houses*, p. 4. • **93.** Mitchell, *British Historical Statistics*, pp.709–11, states that the per capita tobacco consumption was between 0.75 and 1.32lbs. According to Barbara Forey, Jan Hamling, John Hamling, Alison Thornton and Peter Lee, 'International Smoking Statistics: a collection of worldwide historical data. United Kingdom' [an updated version of Chapter 27 of *International Smoking Statistics* (2nd edn, 2002)] (http://www.pnlee.co.uk/Downloads/ISS/ISS-UnitedKingdom_160317.pdf, downloaded 10 January 2020), p. 21, per capita consumption of tobacco reached peaks of 8.7g adult over 15 in 1945 and 1946 and 8.5g in 1960 and 1961. The first of these results from about 120,000 tonnes of tobacco being consumed, the latter from consumption exceeding 125,000 tonnes. The population in 1946 was 48,988,000 (according to the Office for National Statistics) and in the 1961 census was 52,807,000, which imply tobacco consumption levels of 5.4lbs and 5.2lbs per person per year respectively (irrespective of age). • **94.** Lister, *Diaries*, p. 55. • **95.** Christies sale catalogue, 'The Fine Art of Smoking' (23 May 2006), lots 818–40; Lister, *Diaries*, p. 55; Ashton, *Regency*, p. 391; Byron, *Journals*, i, p. 245. For the price of cigars, see the 1828 case of James Mott, *OBPO*, ref: t18281204-271. • **96.** George Evans, *The Old Snuff House of Fribourg and Treyer, 1720–1920* (privately printed, n.d.), pp. 11–15. • **97.** Morewood, *Philosophical and Statistical History*, pp. 118–29. • **98.** *The Times* (10 February 1797). • **99.** Morewood, *Philosophical and Statistical History*, p. 130. • **100.** Humphry Davy, *Researches Chemical and Philosophical Chiefly Concerning Nitrous Oxide or Dephlogisticated Nitrous Air and its Respiration* (1800), pp. 496, 508–9, 517–19, 522.

10 Cleanliness, Health and Medicine

1. Mary Russell Mitford, *Our Village* (5 vols, 1824–32), ii (3rd edn, 1826), p. 179. • **2.** William Munk, *The Life of Sir Henry Halford bart.* (1895), p. 265. • **3.** Lister, *Diaries*, p. 310. • **4.** Hall, *Georgian Gentleman*, p. 209. • **5.** Quennell (ed.), *Byron*, ii, p. 613. • **6.** Feltham, *Guide to all the Watering and Sea-Bathing Places*, p. 330. • **7.** Richard Russell, *A dissertation concerning the use of sea water in diseases of the glands* (Oxford, 1753), pp. ix–x. • **8.** William Buchan, *Domestic Medicine, or a Treatise on the Prevention and Cure of Diseases* (11th edn, 1790), p. 106. • **9.** It first appears in Edward Bulwer-Lytton, *Paul Clifford* (1830), dedicatory epistle, note 7. However, I suspect it was already in general use by this time, as the specific context in that book seems to be a comment on certain critics who drew attention to his own standards of cleanliness and whom he thus derides as 'the Great Unwashed', putting them down socially. See also *Fraser's Magazine for Town and Country*, 5, 1 (June 1830), pp. 531–2. • **10.** Buchan, *Domestic Medicine*, p. 100. • **11.** Buchan, *Domestic Medicine*, p. 101. • **12.** Katherine Ashenburg, *Clean: an Unsanitised History of Washing* (2011), p. 156. • **13.** Quoted in Drs C. Willett and Phyllis Cunnington, *The History of Underclothes* (1951), p. 98. • **14.** *The Art of Beauty* (1825), pp. 157–8. • **15.** *The Art of Beauty*, p. 197. • **16.** *The Ladies' Pocket Magazine for 1829*, part one, p. 138. • **17.** Palmer, *At Home with the Soanes*, pp. 22, 46. • **18.** Withey, *Technology*, pp. 75–6. For the price, see also *OBPO*, t18301209-1, t18290910-305. • **19.** *OBPO*, t18290910-305. • **20.** *OBPO*, t18290910-305 and t18301209-1. • **21.** Withey, *Technology*, p. 78. • **22.** Withey, *Technology*, p. 80; Francis Spilsbury, *Every Man and Woman Their Own Dentist* (1791), preface. • **23.** *The Art of Beauty*, pp. 297–9. • **24.** *The Mirror of the Graces, or the English Lady's Costume ... by a Lady of Distinction* (1830), p. 211. • **25.** Quennell (ed.), *Byron*, i, p. 338. • **26.** Richard Barnett, *The Smile Stealers* (2017), p. 94. • **27.** Quennell (ed.), *Byron*, i, p. 246; ii, pp. 373, 537. • **28.** Pückler-Muskau, *Regency Visitor*, p. 184. • **29.** Spilsbury, *Dentist*, p. 55. • **30.** Barnett, *Smile Stealers*, pp. 88–99. • **31.** Barnett, *Smile Stealers*, pp. 94, 106. • **32.** Lister, *Diaries*, pp. 143–4, 148. • **33.** *The Works of Thomas De Quincey* (4th edn, 16 vols, Edinburgh, 1878), i, p. 4. • **34.** J. R. McCulloch, *Descriptive and Statistical Account of the British Empire* (4th edn, 2 vols, 1854), ii, p. 613. The average (mean) annual number of deaths from dysentery in 1660–79 was more than 800 per 100,000 of the population in the London area; by 1801–10 the death rate among Londoners was 1 in 100,000. • **35.** 'The abracadabra ... of ague ... has almost wholly disappeared within the last generation.' Southey, *Letters from England*, ii, p. 282. • **36.** McCulloch, *Descriptive and Statistical Account*, ii, p. 613. Porter notes that children's death rates were very high in the 18th century: 20% in the first year of life, 33% dead by the age of five (Porter, *Society*, p. 13). According to George, *London Life*, p. 39, burials under five in London were 74.5% of all children baptised in 1730–49 but this declined to 41.3% in 1790–1809. Her explanation is better wages and greater abundance of food at affordable prices. • **37.** McCulloch, *Descriptive and Statistical Account*, ii, p. 613. • **38.** Charles Turner Thackrah, *The Effects of the Principal Arts, Trades and Professions and of Civic States and Habits of Living on Health and Longevity with a Particular Reference to the Trades and Manufactures of Leeds* (1831), pp. 27–8. • **39.** Arnold J. Knight, 'Grinders' Asthma', *North of England Medical and Surgical Journal* (August 1830), quoted in J. S. Waterhouse, 'Contributions Towards the Pathology of Grinders' Disease of the Lungs', *Provincial Medical Journal*, no. 155 (September 1843), p. 299. • **40.** John Brown, *A Memoir of Robert Blincoe, an Orphan Boy, Sent from the Workhouse at St Pancras* (Manchester, 1832), p. 25. • **41.** Brown, *Robert Blincoe*, p. 26. • **42.** William Henderson, *Notes on the folk-lore of Northern England and the Borders* (new edn, 1879), pp. 138–9. Southey also mentions the stolen meat and the bag at the crossroads, although he says peas instead of stones, and you only have to throw it over your shoulder, not bury it. See Southey, *Letters from England*, ii, p. 282. For much more on wart treatments, see Gabrielle Hayfield, *Memory, Wisdom and Healing* (Stroud, 1999), chapter 6. • **43.** Skinner, *Journal*, p. 45. • **44.** Southey, *Letters from England*, i, p. 77. • **45.** Eric Jameson, *The Natural History of Quackery* (1961), p. 11. • **46.** In 1819 there were 82 Fellows of the Royal College of Physicians and about 200 licentiates, over half of whom were based in London. The Royal College of Physicians of Edinburgh had a similar number of Fellows and a handful of licentiates. See *The Royal Kalendar ... for the year 1819*, pp. 282–6, 360. • **47.** Irvine Loudon, 'Medical Practitioners 1750–1850 and the Period of Medical Reform in Britain', in Andrew Wear (ed.), *Medicine in Society* (Cambridge, 1992), pp. 219–48 at p. 232. • **48.** George, *London Life*, p. 62. • **49.** Lindsay Granshaw, 'The rise of the modern hospital in Britain', in Wear (ed.), *Medicine in Society*, pp. 197–218. • **50.** Irvine S. L. Loudon, 'The Origins and Growth of the Dispensary Movement in England', *Bulletin of the History of Medicine*, 55, no. 3 (1981), pp. 322–42; John McGowan, *A New Civic Order: The Contribution of the City of Edinburgh Police, 1805–1812* (Musselburgh, 2013), p. 9. The Edinburgh Hospital saw only 2,000 patients per year in 1800 – compared to 15,000 dealt with by the Dispensary. • **51.** Ayesha Hussain and Anna Maerker, 'Eye Surgery in the Georgian Age', https://georgianpapers.com/2016/11/29/eye-surgery-georgian-age/, downloaded 29 January 2020. • **52.** Lisa Forman Cody, 'Living and Dying in Georgian London's Lying-in Hospitals', *Bulletin of the History of Medicine*, 78, 2 (2004), pp. 309–48. • **53.** Irvine Loudon, 'Deaths in Childbed from the Eighteenth Century to 1935', *Medical History*, 30 (1986), pp. 1–41, especially with regard to tables 2 and 3. The figure of 10% in the 1750s is from Cody,

'Living and Dying', p. 314. • **54.** *Report together with the Minutes of Evidence . . . from the Committee Appointed to Consider of Provision being Made for the Better Regulation of Madhouses in England* (1815), pp. 45–6. • **55.** *Report . . . for the Better Regulation of Madhouses*, p. 12. • **56.** *Report . . . for the Better Regulation of Madhouses*, pp. 18–20. • **57.** Flinders, *Grateful to Providence*, p. 227. • **58.** Palmer, *At Home with the Soanes*, pp. 17–18. • **59.** *Report . . . for the Better Regulation of Madhouses*, p. 49.

11 Law and Order

1. Southey, *Letters from England*, iii, p. 189. • **2.** P. Colquhoun, *A Treatise on the Police of the Metropolis* (7th edn, 1806), pp. 8–9. • **3.** *OBPO*, https://www.oldbaileyonline.org/static/Gender.jsp#gendercrime, downloaded 4 February 2020. • **4.** The figures for the Assizes are drawn from J. Marshall, *Statistics of the British Empire* (1837), pp. 34–7. There are some inconsistencies in the totals on p. 35 but, correcting these in line with the data on pp. 36–7, it would appear that, out of the total of 261,565 people arrested and charged at the assizes between 1805 and 1829 (including the 'no bill' answers from the grand jury), 48,691 were female (19%). At the Old Bailey, over the whole period 1789–1830, 22 per cent of offenders were women and girls (*OBPO*). • **5.** *OBPO* records 48,368 cases tried between 1789 and 1830. The breakdown of types of offence are as follows: breaking the peace (riot, assault, libel, threatening behaviour, vagabondage): 246 (0.51%); damage to property (incl. arson): 56 (0.12%); deception (incl. perjury, forgery, fraud): 912 (1.89%); killing (incl. manslaughter, murder, infanticide, petty treason): 491 (1.02%); miscellaneous (incl. conspiracy, kidnapping, piracy, returning from transportation): 522 (1.08%); royal offences (i.e. coining, sedition, sacrilege, tax and treason): 1,107 (2.29%); sexual offences (i.e. bigamy, rape, sexual assault, sodomy): 402 (0.83%); theft (incl. larceny, burglary, pickpocketing, shoplifting, receiving stolen goods): 42,962 (88.82%); violent theft (robbery, highway robbery): 1,670 (3.45%). Note that these figures are for cases, which may include more than one defendant. • **6.** Lister, *Diaries*, pp. 9, 12, 67. • **7.** Henry Francis Whitfield, *Plymouth and Devonport in times of war and peace* (Plymouth, 1900), pp. 283–4. • **8.** J. L. Lyman, 'The Metropolitan Police Act of 1829: An Analysis of Certain Events Influencing the Passage and Character of the Metropolitan Police Act in England', *The Journal of Criminal Law, Criminology, and Police Science*, 55, 1 (1964), pp. 141–54 at pp. 144–5. • **9.** Details on the origins of the Thames River Police have been taken from http://www.thamespolicemuseum.org.uk/history.html, downloaded 9 February

2020. • **10.** Information about Glasgow Police Force has been drawn from http://www.policemuseum.org.uk/glasgow-police-history/pre-1800/, downloaded 6 February 2020. • **11.** Howard, *State of the Prisons*, pp. 13–14; *Report from the Committee on the Prisons within the City of London and Borough of Southwark: 1. Newgate* (1818), pp. 76–7. • **12.** For example, at Abingdon. See Howard, *State of the Prisons*, pp. 340–1. • **13.** Much of this section dealing with process is drawn from https://www.londonlives.org/static/CriminalTrial.jsp, downloaded 13 February 2020. • **14.** This proportion is an approximation based on the figures taken from Marshall, *Statistics*, pp. 34–5. • **15.** The law changed in 1826. After that date, a refusal to plead was not considered an admission of guilt. • **16.** *The Times* (12 April 1796). • **17.** Woodforde, *Diary*, p. 315. Woodforde states this even though he thought it only lasted seven days. • **18.** Porter, *English Society*, p. 135. • **19.** Guilty verdicts rose from 70% before 1810 to 78% in the 1820s at the assizes, and from 67% in the 1790s to 76% in the 1820s at the Old Bailey. See Marshall, *Statistics*, pp. 34–5; OBPO. • **20.** OBPO, t18140216-22. • **21.** Southey, *Letters from England*, i, p. 253, repeats this quotation and declares it 'as unphilosophical as it is unsympathetic' but his view was very probably in the minority. • **22.** According to Marshall, *Statistics*, pp. 34–5, 63.7% of all those found Guilty at the assizes in England and Wales in the years 1805–29 were sentenced to a term of imprisonment. • **23.** Howard, *State of the Prisons*, p. 363. • **24.** Marshall, *Statistics*, pp. 34–5. • **25.** *Returns from all the Gaols, Houses of Correction and Penitentiaries in England, Wales and Scotland* (1821), pp. 22–3 (Gloucester), 42–3 (Stafford). • **26.** *Returns from all the Gaols*, pp. 10–11. • **27.** *Returns from all the Gaols*, p. 351. • **28.** For example, at Kingston-upon-Thames Bridewell 'there is a door from the men's court into that of the women's and one of the men keeps the key, and can let any of the prisoners into the women's apartments'. See Howard, *State of the Prisons*, p. 278. • **29.** Howard, *State of the Prisons*, p. 17. • **30.** The number of debtors in prison in 1826 was 2,861 – 1,700 of them being in London. See https://media.nationalarchives.gov.uk/index.php/the-real-little-dorrit-charles-dickens-and-the-debtors-prison/, downloaded 16 February 2020. • **31.** Gary Calland, *A History of the Devon County Prison for Debtors in St Thomas* (Exeter, 1999), pp. 25, 35. • **32.** Quoted in Phillips, *Profligate Son*, p. 113. • **33.** Ashton, *Old Times*, p. 266; Howard, *State of the Prisons*, p. 384. • **34.** Mark S. O'Shaughnessy, 'On Certain Obsolete Modes of Inflicting Punishment, with Some Account of the Ancient Court to Which They Belonged', *Transactions of the Kilkenny Archaeological Society*, i, 2 (1853), pp. 254–64 at p. 257; William Andrews, *Old-Time Punishments* (1890), pp. 1–34; Daniel and Samuel Lysons, *Magna Britannia: volume 6: Devonshire, a General and Parochial History of the County* (1822), p. 357. • **35.** Andrews, *Old-Time*

Punishments, pp. 65–89 at pp. 79–80. • **36.** *OBPO*, t18140525-101. • **37.** Andrews, *Old-Time Punishments*, p. 85. • **38.** Murray, *High Society*, p. 18. • **39.** Southey, *Letters from England*, i, pp. 109–10. • **40.** *OBPO*, t17990403-29 (Catherine Squires), t18131201-63 (Martha Burgess), t18220522-144 (John Vaughan and John Sheen). • **41.** *OBPO*, t18060416-3 (William Kennovan, John Gable, Joseph Parker); t18020602-12 (William Appleton); t18290910-80 (William Stevens); t18250407-121 (William Cook). • **42.** *OBPO*, t18141026-141. • **43.** *OBPO*, t18201206-156; The National Archives: HO 11/4, p. 149. • **44.** Phillips, *Profligate Son*, pp. 196–7. • **45.** The National Archives: HO 11/1, p. 342. • **46.** The details from this case are predominantly from *OBPO*, t18150405-18, with supplementary details from G. T. Crook, *The Complete Newgate Calendar* (5 vols, 1926), v, pp. 159–64. • **47.** Crook, *Newgate Calendar*, v, p. 162. • **48.** Marshall, *Statistics*, pp. 34–7. • **49.** Phillips, *Profligate Son*, p. 191. • **50.** Southey, *Letters from England*, ii, p. 101. • **51.** Lister, *Diaries*, p. 237.

12 Entertainment

1. Nimrod, *Memoirs of the Life of John Mytton Esquire of Halston, Shropshire* (2nd edn, 1837), esp. pp. 177–92. • **2.** E. D. Cuming, *Squire Osbaldeston: his autobiography* (1926), pp. 26–7. • **3.** See *The New Sporting Magazine*, 18, 105 (January 1840), pp. 374–5. • **4.** Pückler-Muskau, *Regency Visitor*, p. 57. • **5.** Southey, *Letters from England*, iii, pp. 280–2. • **6.** Nimrod, *Life of John Mytton*, p. 16. • **7.** Ken Sheard, 'Boxing in the Western civilising process', in Eric Dunning, Dominic Malcolm and Ivan Waddington (eds), *Figurational studies of the development of modern sports* (2004), pp. 15–30 at pp. 17–18. • **8.** *Literary Remains of the Late William Hazlitt, with a Notice of his Life by his Son* (2 vols, 1836), pp. 218–19. • **9.** Ashton, *Regency*, p. 49. • **10.** Leslie Stephen, revised by Dennis Brailsford, 'Allardice, Robert Barclay [*known as* Captain Barclay]', *ODNB*. • **11.** *The Times* (16 October 1807), p. 3. • **12.** Davy Crockett, '1,000-milers, Part Two – the Barclay Match', published 9 March 2019, available at http://ultrarunninghistory.com/1000-milers-part-2/, downloaded 27 February 2020. • **13.** John Bryant, *3:59.4: The Quest to Break the Four-Minute Mile* (2004), p. 17. • **14.** The four-minute mile was allegedly achieved twice before 1790. See Thor Gotaas, *Running: a Global History* (2012), p. 78. • **15.** Walter Thom, *Pedestrianism* (1813), p. 73, gives the example of Mr Haselden of Milton, who ran 10 miles along the Canterbury road in August 1809 in 53 minutes 'with considerable ease'. Gotaas, *Running*, p. 79, mentions the case of Pinwire, an early-eighteenth-century runner, who did 10 miles in 52 minutes 3 seconds. • **16.** Thom, *Pedestrianism*, pp. 78–9. • **17.** Peter Radford, 'Women as athletes in Early Modern Britain', *Early Modern Women*, 10, 2 (2016), pp. 42–64, esp. pp. 52–4. • **18.** Quoted in Morris Marples, *A History of Football* (1954), p. 96. • **19.** Quoted in Marples, *Football*, p. 96. • **20.** Marples, *Football*, p. 117. • **21.** Wheaton, *Journal*, pp. 255–6. • **22.** Ashton, *Regency*, p. 400. • **23.** E. Beresford Chancellor, *Life in Regency and Early Victorian Times* (1926), p. 89. • **24.** Quoted in Claire Cock-Starkey, *The Georgian Art of Gambling* (2013), p. 85. • **25.** Southey, *Letters from England*, iii, pp. 191–2. • **26.** Pückler-Muskau, *Regency Visitor*, pp. 282–3. • **27.** Pückler-Muskau, *Regency Visitor*, p. 322; Cuming (ed.), *Squire Osbaldeston*, p. 185. • **28.** Sir John E. Eardley-Wilmot, *Reminiscences of Thomas Assheton-Smith* (1860), p. 2; White, *Waterloo to Peterloo*, p. 41. For the cost of a pack of eighty hounds see Pückler-Muskau, *Regency Visitor*, p. 292. • **29.** Woodforde, *Diary*, pp. 246–8, 250, 295. • **30.** Southey, *Letters from England*, iii, pp. 75–82. • **31.** Cock-Starkey, *Georgian Art of Gambling*, p. 27. • **32.** Ashton, *Old Times*, p. 173, quoting from *The Times* for 25 June 1794. • **33.** Wheaton, *Journal*, pp. 151–2. • **34.** Lister, *Diaries*, p. 106; Pückler-Muskau, *Regency Visitor*, p. 238. • **35.** Thomas Seccombe, revised by Julian Lock, 'Lewis, William', *ODNB*. • **36.** Wheaton, *Journal*, pp. 271–3. • **37.** Monck Mason, *Aeronautica* (1838), p. 232; *Encyclopaedia Britannica* (1911 edn), xx, p. 751; *The Times* (17 December 1818), p. 2. • **38.** Goede, *Stranger in England*, i, pp. 117–18; White, *London*, p. 347. • **39.** Roughly 5% of the population is sixty-five or over in this period. In London the proportion under fifteen is slightly lower than the national average, about 30%. Thus about 65% of the city's female population is between the ages of fifteen and sixty-four. More women live in London than men, by a proportion of about one-tenth. The population of the metropolis in 1807 is about one million, so it is home to approximately 340,000 adult women. Seventy thousand is slightly more than one-fifth of this number. It should be noted that this extraordinary proportion has been questioned by some historians – for instance, White, *London*, p. 347 – but the increase in the magistrates' estimates is a constant proportion of the population and was not uninformed. • **40.** Goede, *Stranger*, i, pp. 117, 120. • **41.** Hallie Rubenhold, *Harris's List of Covent-Garden Ladies* (2005), pp. 98–9. • **42.** Rubenhold, *Harris's List*, pp. 102–4. • **43.** Rubenhold, *Harris's List*, pp. 154–5. • **44.** Rubenhold, *Harris's List*, pp. 156–7. • **45.** Emily Brand, *The Georgian Bawdyhouse* (2012), p. 17. • **46.** Brand, *Bawdyhouse*, p. 19. • **47.** Brand, *Bawdyhouse*, p. 38. • **48.** Collis, *New Encyclopaedia of Brighton*, p. 254. • **49.** Lackington, *Memoirs*, pp. 386–7. • **50.** The religious volumes mentioned in his inventory are: six volumes of *The Evangelical Magazine*; four volumes of *The Baptist Magazine*; four volumes of John Tillotson's *Sermons on Several Subjects and Occasions*; three volumes of Laurence Howell's *A Complete History of the Holy Bible*; Lindley Murray's *The Power of Religion on the Mind*; John Evans's *A Sketch of the Denominations of the Christian World*; 'Westlake on Baptisms'; and one other unnamed religious volume. Besides these and the other volumes named in the text, there were 'four sundry volumes'. • **51.** William Mortimer's older brother, John Mortimer (1768–1825), was literate and also owned books, some of which survive with his inscriptions in the front. Their father, John Mortimer (1733–1797), was a mariner and was rarely at home in Combeinteignhead; it is possible he owned books, as he was at least signature-literate, but there is no indication that he did. The family Bible was started by the younger John Mortimer. William and John's grandfather, William Mortimore of Combeinteignhead (d. 1780), was illiterate. • **52.** Rush, *Residence*, pp. 110–11. • **53.** MacCarthy, *Byron*, p. 159. • **54.** Porter, *English Society*, p. 235. For Bath, see Fisher, *Royal Crescent*, p. 45; *Pigot's Directory* (1830), p. 688. • **55.** MacCarthy, *Byron*, pp. 162–3. • **56.** Moore, *Life, Letters and Journals of Lord Byron*, p. 159. • **57.** *Edinburgh Review* (January 1808), pp. 285–6. • **58.** Moritz, *Journeys*, pp. 144–5. • **59.** Simond, *Journal*, i, p. 187. • **60.** Southey, *Letters from England*, iii, pp. 40–1; Scott (ed. Anderson), *Journal*, p. 114. • **61.** [Thomas Babington Macaulay], 'Art. VI: *The Constitutional History of England, from the Accession of Henry VII to the Death of George II*. By Henry Hallam', *Edinburgh Review*, xlviii (1828), pp. 97–8. • **62.** Southey, *Letters from England*, iii, p. 275. • **63.** *London Encyclopaedia*, p. 92; Simond, *Journal*, i, pp. 83–5; Ashton, *Regency*, p. 233. • **64.** Pückler-Muskau, *Regency Visitor*, p. 53, states there were two giraffes there; prints from the 1830s depict three. • **65.** Simond, *Journal*, i, pp. 83–4. • **66.** Pückler-Muskau, *Regency Visitor*, p. 53. • **67.** Feltham, *Guide to all the Watering and Sea-Bathing Places*, pp. 41, 45. • **68.** Pückler-Muskau, *Regency Visitor*, p. 165. • **69.** Ashton, *Regency*, pp. 383–4; Pückler-Muskau, *Regency Visitor*, pp. 165, 199. • **70.** Southey, *Letters from England*, i, pp. 187–94, gives a description of sitting in the pit in 1807. • **71.** Ackermann, *Microcosm*, iii, p. 263. • **72.** Quoted in Peter Thomson, 'Kemble, John Philip', *ODNB*. • **73.** Thomson, 'Kemble, John Philip', *ODNB*. • **74.** Quoted in Peter Thomson, 'Kean, Edmund', *ODNB*. • **75.** Thomson, 'Kean, Edmund', *ODNB*; William Foulkes, 'Macready, William Charles', *ODNB*. • **76.** Quoted in Robert Shaughnessy, 'Siddons [*née* Kemble], Sarah', *ODNB*. • **77.** Simond, *Journal*, i, p. 135. • **78.** The facts about Mrs Siddons's life and career are largely drawn from Shaughnessy, 'Siddons [*née* Kemble], Sarah', *ODNB*. • **79.** Wheaton, *Journal*, p. 48. • **80.** Arthur Loesser, *Men, women and pianos, a social history* (1954, new edn, 1990), p. 148. • **81.** Austen-Leigh, *Memoir*, p.

83. • **82.** Leena Asha Rana, 'Music and elite identity in the English country house, c. 1790–1840', PhD thesis, University of Southampton (2012), p. 15. • **83.** Nicholas Temperley, 'Domestic Music in England 1800–1860', *Proceedings of the Royal Musical Association, 85th Session* (1958–9), pp. 31–47 at p. 35. • **84.** Myles Birkett Foster, *The History of the Philharmonic Society of London, 1813–1912* (1912), p. 43. • **85.** *The Musical Times and Singing Class Circular*, 41, 683 (1900), pp. 18–22 at p. 19. • **86.** Foster, *Philharmonic Society*, p. 93. • **87.** 'Music is as little the amusement of the people as dancing. Never was a nation so unmusical.' See Southey, *Letters from England*, iii, p. 190. • **88.** Ashton, *Old Times*, p. 205; Rachel E. Cowgill, 'Billington [*née* Weichsel], Elizabeth', *ODNB*. • **89.** Michael Burden, 'Mara, née Schmelling, Gertrud Elisabeth', *ODNB*. • **90.** *Dictionary of Musicians* (2nd edn, 2 vols, 1827), ii, p. 106. • **91.** Joseph Knight, revised by Jane Girdham, 'Storace, Ann Selina [Nancy]', *ODNB*. • **92.** *Dictionary of Musicians*, i, p. 293. • **93.** George Grove, *A Dictionary of Music and Musicians* (4 vols, 1900), i, p. 321. • **94.** Christopher Raeburn, 'Mozart's Operas in England', *The Musical Times*, 97, 1355 (1956), p. 16, quoting *The Examiner*, 19 May 1811. • **95.** Murray, *High Society*, p. 223. • **96.** Jacky Bratton, 'Vestris [*née* Bartolozzi; *other married name* Mathews], Lucia Elizabeth', *ODNB*. • **97.** Marion M. Scott, 'Haydn in England', *The Musical Quarterly*, 18, 2 (1932), pp. 260–73 at p. 260. • **98.** Foster, *Philharmonic Society*, pp. 4–8. • **99.** David Benjamin Levy, *Beethoven: the Ninth Symphony* (revised edn, 2005), p. 122. • **100.** Levy, *Ninth Symphony*, pp. 133–5.

Envoi

1. Richard Brinsley Sheridan, *The Rivals*, Act iv, Scene 1. • **2.** Southey, *Letters from England*, iii, pp. 73–4.

Illustrations

Brighton seafront, 1825 (The Stapleton Collection/Bridgeman Images).

New Lanark Mills, *c*.1815 (The Print Collector/Alamy Stock Photo).

Cotton mill in Union Street, Manchester (Chronicle/Alamy Stock Photo).

The Old and New London Bridges, engraving by E. W. Cooke (Look and Learn/Peter Jackson Collection/Bridgeman Images).

Regent Street, 1828 (Lebrecht Music & Arts/Alamy Stock Photo).

St James's Park, early nineteenth century (Bridgeman Images).

Suspension bridge over the Menai Straits (Pictorial Press Ltd/Alamy Stock Photo).

Duelling in Hyde Park, 1825 (Florilegius/Alamy Stock Photo).

Smithfield Market (Tatu/Alamy Stock Photo).

Old Fish Market, Newcastle (© Tyne & Wear Archives & Museums/Bridgeman Images).

Calico factory, Manchester, 1834 (The Granger Collection/Alamy Stock Photo).

Greengrocer's shop, London, 1819 (Heritage Image Partnership Ltd/Alamy Stock Photo).

James Lackington's 'Temple of the Muses' (Heritage Image Partnership Ltd/Alamy Stock Photo).

Messrs Harding, Howell & Co., Pall Mall (Pictorial Press Ltd/Alamy Stock Photo).

Prince Hermann Pückler-Muskau (INTERFOTO/Alamy Stock Photo).

Lord Byron, portrait by Richard Westall, 1813 (World History Archive/Alamy Stock Photo).

Anne Lister (The Picture Art Collection/Alamy Stock Photo).

The Chevalier d'Eon (The Picture Art Collection/Alamy Stock Photo).

George IV as Prince Regent, portrait by Sir Thomas Lawrence, 1816 (Peter Horree/Alamy Stock Photo).

William Pitt addresses the House of Commons, 1793 (Granger Historical Picture Archive/Alamy Stock Photo).

George Henckell, *c*.1800 (Bridgeman Art Library).

'The Pitman', from *The Costume of Yorkshire*, Leeds, 1813 (Photo 12/Alamy Stock Photo).

Clifton Assembly Rooms during a ball, by Rolina Sharples, 1818 (Granger Historical Picture Archive/Alamy Stock Photo).

Working-class home in Yorkshire, 1813 (Walker Art Library/Alamy Stock Photo).

Ladies driving a phaeton, from *The Gallery of Fashion*, 1794 (Art Collection 2/Alamy Stock Photo).

Johnson's Pedestrian Hobbyhorse Riding School, 1819 (Bridgeman Images).

George Shillibeer's omnibus, London, 1829 (Heritage Image Partnership Ltd/Alamy Stock Photo).

Views of steamship (Bridgeman Images).

Train on the Liverpool–Manchester line taking on water at Parkside Station, 1831 (Niday Picture Library/Alamy Stock Photo).

Kitchen at Langton Hall, painted by Mary Ellen Best (Artmedia/Alamy Stock Photo).

Dining room of middle-class family, York, painted by Mary Ellen Best (Artmedia/Alamy Stock Photo).

'Getting the best of a charley' (Chronicle/Alamy Stock Photo).

Pillory at Charing Cross, 1810 (Granger Historical Picture Archive/Alamy Stock Photo).

Interior of Drury Lane Theatre (Historic Images/Alamy Stock Photo).

Animal fight in Factory Yard, Warwick, cartoon by George Cruikshank, 1823 (© British Library Board. All Rights Reserved/Bridgeman Images).

Index

Abolition of Slavery Bill (1833) 101
actors and actresses 64–5, 85–7, 110, 112, 118, 133, 223, 347–55, 360, 390; *see also* theatre
Adam, Robert 36, 38
Adams, John Quincy 56
Addington, Henry 68
Addis, William 281
Adolphus, duke of Cambridge, Prince 113
Admiralty 143, 178, 202, 214
adultery 3, 65, 114, 165
Adventure, sinking of (1789) 218, 219
Age of Excess 3–4, 243
age, structure of English society and 58–9
agriculture/farming 1, 29–33, 41, 60, 63, 75, 76–8, 90, 95, 123, 152, 237–8, 249–50, 258, 266, 270, 338; agricultural labourers 78, 79–80, 152, 240, 259; Agricultural Revolution 249–50, 284; breeding of larger animals 29–30, 250; cattle farming 28, 29–31, 33, 40–42, 102, 103, 182, 241, 250, 257; communal farming 30, 31; Corn Laws and 94–6; crop rotation and fertilisation, new systems of 30, 250; Dartmoor, attempts to farm on 29; enclosure and 30–2; farmhouses 31, 32, 77, 237–8; harvests 57, 81, 95, 257; Highland Clearances 32–3; husbandmen 76–7; incomes from 76–7; sheep farming 30–4, 41, 75, 76, 98, 182, 250, 254, 334, 379; social status of farmers 61, 77–8; winter-feeding practices, adoption of 250; yeomen 76, 77
alcohol 265–70; consumption levels 3, 41, 169, 194, 265, 268–70, 276, 322; *see also individual alcoholic drink*
Aldridge, Ira 133
ale 222, 266, 267, 390
Alexander I, Tsar 225, 226
Aliens Act (1793) 126
Allardice, Robert Barclay ('Captain Barclay') 326–7
Alvanley, Lord 146–7
Amelia, Princess 64
America 24, 29, 57, 104, 267, 367; British attitudes towards Americans 125–6; intercontinental news, speed of 161; suspension bridges in 200; travel between England and 9, 215
American War of Independence (1775–83) 63, 127, 171
Amiens, Peace of (1802) 127
Ampère, André-Marie 142
anarchism 97
Andersonian Institute, Glasgow 121
Angerstein, John Julius 73, 346–7
Anglican Church 17, 63, 72, 81, 92, 122, 134
animals: baiting and fighting 2, 103, 330, 331; eating 148, 252, 254; fairs and performing 334–5; farming *see* agriculture; hunting 331–2; markets and 40–1, 102–3; menageries/exotic 104, 247–8; slaughter of

102, 250; treatment of 101–4, 252, 368; working 101–2
anti-Semitism 92, 96, 134–6, 342
Antoinette, Marie 57
Apothecaries' Act (1815) 292
Appleton, William 315, 316
apprenticeship 74, 76, 99, 119–20, 123, 134, 153, 292, 310, 317
Arabic 121
arcades, shopping 40, 50, 170
architects/architecture 4, 12, 13, 16, 20, 21, 24, 27, 36, 38, 43, 48, 50–2, 66–7, 75, 90, 155, 188, 211, 230–1, 237, 243–5, 247, 343, 368; *see also* houses
arc lamp 143
Arfwedson, Johan 141
Argand lamp 154–5, 219, 371
aristocracy 2, 15, 32, 36, 51, 52, 67–9, 71, 87, 96–7, 113, 120, 127, 133, 149, 186, 221, 243, 247, 269, 328, 331, 332, 345, 347, 348, 363
Arkwright, Richard, junior 73
Arkwright, Richard, senior 73
British Army 62, 69, 70, 88, 95, 106, 112, 120, 131
Arne, Thomas: *Artaxerxes* 358, 360
arrack 266
Art of Beauty, The (Anon.) 190, 279, 281
art/painting 3, 5, 43, 51, 63, 67, 85, 127, 146, 148, 150, 223, 227, 231, 232, 234, 245, 321, 343, 346–7; galleries/exhibitions 4, 67, 321, 345, 346–7, 367; royal collection 67, 346
Ashmolean Museum, Oxford 344
Ashton-under-Lyne 59, 115, 116, 117
assembly rooms 10, 15, 17, 20, 21, 23–4, 27, 93, 110, 185, 193, 347, 355
assets, ownership of 56–7
Association for the Prosecution of Felons 302
Astley, Philip 348–9
astronomy 63, 121, 141–2
atheism 92
athletics 327–8
Atlantic, expansion of trade across 21
Augustus, duke of Sussex, Prince 112–13
Austen, Jane xi, 2, 7, 69, 89, 123, 138, 238–40, 253, 254–5, 259, 266, 269, 276, 294, 341, 356, 368; Chawton Cottage, life at 238–9, 240, 253, 269; *Emma* 77, 339; *Northanger Abbey* 138, 147, 174; *Persuasion* 5; *Pride and Prejudice* 124, 333, 339, 341; Prince Regent reads 124, 341; *Sense and Sensibility* 71
Austen, Revd George 124
Austen-Leigh, James Edward: *A Memoir of Jane Austen* xi
Australia, transportation to 100, 168, 308, 309, 315–16
Avogadro, Amedeo 141
Axminster, Devon 27–8
Ayton, Richard 78–9